Digital Watermarking in Cloud Environments for Copyright Protection

Ashwani Kumar
School of Computer Science, Engineering, and Technology, Bennett University, Greater Noida, India

Auzuir Ripardo de Alexandria
Instituto Federal de Educação, Ciência e Tecnologia do Ceará (IFCE), Brazil

Satya Prakash Yadav
Department of Computer Science and Engineering, Madan Mohan Malaviya University of Technology, Gorakhpur, India

Antonino Galletta
University of Messina, Italy

IGI Global
Scientific Publishing
Publishing Tomorrow's Research Today

Vice President of Editorial — Melissa Wagner
Director of Acquisitions — Mikaela Felty
Director of Book Development — Jocelynn Hessler
Production Manager — Mike Brehm
Cover Design — Jose Rosado

Published in the United States of America by
IGI Global Scientific Publishing
701 East Chocolate Avenue
Hershey, PA, 17033, USA
Tel: 717-533-8845
Fax: 717-533-7115
Website: https://www.igi-global.com E-mail: cust@igi-global.com

Library of Congress Cataloging-in-Publication Data

Names: Kumar, Ashwani, 1986- editor | Ripardo de Alexandria, Auzuir, 1970- editor | Yadav, Satya Prakash editor | Galletta, Antonino, 1989- editor
Title: Digital watermarking in cloud environments for copyright protection / edited by Ashwani Kumar, Auzuir Ripardo de Alexandria, Satya Prakash Yadav, Antonino Galletta.
Description: Hershey, PA : IGI Global Scientific Publishing, [2026] | Includes bibliographical references and index. | Summary: "This book discusses digital image watermarking, its classifications, and its applications in securing digital content. It explains how watermarking techniques can safeguard sensitive data during transmission and storage"-- Provided by publisher.
Identifiers: LCCN 2025030196 (print) | LCCN 2025030197 (ebook) | ISBN 9798337337852 hardcover | ISBN 9798337337869 paperback | ISBN 9798337337876 ebook
Subjects: LCSH: Digital watermarking | Cloud computing | Copyright and electronic data processing
Classification: LCC TA1636 .D55 2026 (print) | LCC TA1636 (ebook)
LC record available at https://lccn.loc.gov/2025030196
LC ebook record available at https://lccn.loc.gov/2025030197

British Cataloguing in Publication Data
A Cataloguing in Publication record for this book is available from the British Library.

Table of Contents

Detailed Table of Contents

The backbone of current digital content creation and distribution is cloud technology, which concomitantly raises emerging and complicated issues for copyright enforcement. Albeit the cloud allows scalable and global access to media, documents, creative assets, it also opens up the risk of unauthorized copying and redistribution of such content because of mis-configuration, loose control and the inherent openness of distributed systems. This chapter considers the cloud content lifecycle (namely ingestion, storage, delivery, and consumption) and provides analysis of the main threats that may compromise the intellectual property. Based on real-world case studies and examination of contemporary threats, the chapter presents the inadequacy of traditional Digital Right Management (DRM) in the cloud age and argues for the utilization of digital watermarking as an adjunct to provide forensic-grade rights enforcement, content tracking and tracing.

Saving and securing digital assets in the cloud environment is a great concern due to the rapid growth of multimedia data and cloud computing. Digital watermark provides a powerful solution by identifying inaccurate brands in the digital content to verify and detect tampering. However, the use of watermarks in the cloud system introduces unique security risks, such as privacy violations, unauthorized access, and vulnerability to advanced attacks. This chapter presents a concentrated review of modern cloud-based watermark techniques, analyzing the trade-off between safety,

the same time, the digital assets will be easily accessible, copied, and modified. The classical static-pattern-based traditional watermarking is sometimes insufficient to cope with dynamic threats and variant user demands. A for cloud data Adaptive watermarking algorithms use online data analysis, user behavior profiling, and adaptable embedding techniques to dynamically adjust watermark parameters such as the strength, the embedding domain and the location according to different user profiles and usage patterns on the cloud. We leverage the technique of machine learning and context-aware policies for detecting watermark strength and adapting imperceptibility and robustness in order to achieve reinforcement against various attacks (e.g., collusion, forgery, and removal).

In this chapter, the problem of content authentication in cloud computing is addressed, and a Blockchain-Enhanced Watermarking (BEW) system is proposed. With digital assets now stored in the cloud, access and sharing become even more challenging. With content no longer sitting on a server on your premises, how do you ensure that it has come from a trusted source and that it hasn't been altered? Conventional watermark methods safeguard ownership but have an insufficient ability to trace back, are impossible to prevent distortion, and lack an encryptable digital proof for the data in open networks. The BEW utilizes resilient digital watermarking techniques, along with permissioned blockchain, to maintain an indelible, decentralized record of watermark data.

decryption. Additionally, we analyze the computational trade-offs of integrating quantum-safe algorithms into watermarking pipelines—in terms of embedding transparency, capacity, computational cost, and resilience against attacks.

In this chapter, we present the performance of a composite watermarking algorithm that utilizes DCT, DWT, and SVD, building upon previously existing systems for robust digital image watermarking. The proposed DCT-DWT-SVD-based hybrid method uses the energy compaction, resolution in the multi-scale domain, and stability properties of SVD to enhance the imperceptibility and robustness of the embedded watermark. In this work, the watermark insertion process operates in two steps: first, by extracting the DWT of the cover image and then applying the DCT transform to the obtained sub-bands and modifying the singular values using SVD. Comprehensive experiments are conducted on various image corruptions, including noise, cropping, compression, and geometric transformations. We then employ PSNR, NC, and SSIM to quantify the trade-offs and performance of the compared models. Experimental results demonstrate that the hybrid DCT-DWT-SVD outperforms traditional single-transform methods and dual-transform methods in terms of robustness and perceptual quality.

Digital watermarking has emerged as a major method for protecting multimedia content through copyright protection, authentication, and tamper detection. While conventional watermarking methods are useful, they often struggle to strike a balance between impermeability, robustness, and capacity, particularly in the face of signal processing attacks. As smart algorithms and data-driven methods have evolved, watermarking systems have become more adaptive and secure. The latest algorithms make it easier to embed watermarks in various media types and to enhance resistance to compression, noise, and rotation or scaling using powerful computational tools. This chapter provides an overview of digital watermarking, focusing on classical and computational models, upcoming challenges, and prominent applications. Secondly, it discusses upcoming directions aiming at developing cross-domain, secure and privacy-compliant watermarking solutions to meet the requirements of an evolving digital and smart world.

Cloud computing, or remote resource environments, has revolutionized digital service delivery by enabling flexible, on-demand access to computing power. It allows local systems to execute tasks beyond their native capacities, leveraging models like IaaS, PaaS, and SaaS, each offering varied levels of control and abstraction. Most online services today—such as on-demand access, measured billing, and broad network connectivity—are cloud-based. However, challenges like data storage, transmission, exposure risks, and watermarking persist. The chapter highlights encryption, cryptography, GDPR, and HIPAA for improved security and concludes with applications in e-learning, streaming, and watermark detection using WaaS and real-time embeddings

Dynamic watermarking is a paramount tool for protecting intellectual property and sensitive data in multi-tenant SaaS (Software-as-a-Service) environments. In this paper, we present a new dynamic watermarking model designed for multi-tenant SaaS applications where various clients share resources and infrastructure. Compared to static watermarking, dynamic watermarking enables the application of individual, tenant-related watermarks at runtime without compromising performance or user

Since the storage and delivery services are migrating to the cloud which is expected to reach over $678.8 billion by 2027, the cloud-computing industry has emerged with intricate legal issues of enforcing copyright. In this chapter focal point is the issues of infringement in the cloud systems whereby it gives an insight to the liability of the providers in the light of the U.S. Copyright Act as well as the recent court ruling and preceding global regulations. It talks about the influence of cloud models such as SaaS, PaaS and IaaS on the distribution and reproduction of copyrighted materials. It also examines the existing weaknesses of the laws available to deal with cross-border platforms particularly with regards to intermediary liability and DMCA safe harbor provisions. Difficulties in enforcement are illustrated in Dropbox, Google drive, and Mega case studies. The chapter ends with the observations that there are gaps in the law and need to create new policies and technologies such as better DRM and content recognition that will enhance the protection of copyright in the cloud.

Preface

INTRODUCTION

The exponential increase in digital content generation has dramatically reshaped the global media and technology landscape. Content today is no longer stored in isolated systems but flows freely through vast, scalable cloud infrastructures. While this transformation empowers creators and consumers alike, it also invites complex copyright risks. As media is uploaded, shared, and modified across the cloud, identifying ownership and ensuring authenticity have become increasingly difficult.

Digital watermarking, once a niche technique, has now emerged as a central pillar in content security. It embeds ownership or tracking information imperceptibly into digital assets—images, audio, video, documents—making it possible to trace and verify content throughout its lifecycle. However, traditional watermarking techniques struggle in distributed systems where threats are ever-evolving, and performance constraints are critical. This book addresses these shortcomings and proposes modern watermarking frameworks tailored for cloud infrastructures.

By weaving together cloud computing, cryptography, artificial intelligence, blockchain, and even quantum-safe approaches, this volume provides a rich, interdisciplinary perspective. The chapters presented here not only explore watermarking algorithms and security models but also grapple with legal frameworks, performance metrics, and ethical considerations. The result is a roadmap for securing digital content in a volatile and fast-paced technological world.

In the wake of rapid digital transformation, cloud computing has revolutionized the way we create, distribute, and store multimedia content. While this evolution has brought unprecedented convenience and scalability, it has also exposed content creators, researchers, and developers to heightened threats to intellectual property and copyright integrity. The dynamic and distributed nature of cloud environments renders traditional Digital Rights Management (DRM) strategies increasingly inadequate, necessitating a reimagining of content protection methodologies—enter digital watermarking.

This edited research volume, *Digital Watermarking in Cloud Environments for Copyright Protection*, brings together global experts, academics, and technologists to explore the multifaceted dimensions of watermarking in contemporary digital ecosystems. From foundational principles to highly technical models incorporating blockchain, artificial intelligence, and quantum resistance, this book presents a comprehensive overview of current advancements, pressing challenges, and promising futures in watermarking for cloud-based environments.

Our goal in compiling this collection is twofold: to provide a foundational resource for students, researchers, and technologists entering this field, and to offer in-depth, state-of-the-art insights for experienced professionals looking to fortify digital copyright mechanisms. By bringing diverse voices and multidisciplinary perspectives into one cohesive volume, we aim to stimulate innovation and provide a knowledge base that bridges the gaps between theory, practice, and policy in digital copyright protection.

CHAPTER OVERVIEW

Chapter 1 outlines the vulnerabilities in cloud-based content distribution and highlights the limitations of DRM while proposing watermarking as a critical solution.

Chapter 2 explores security challenges specific to watermarking in cloud environments and evaluates emerging techniques to mitigate these threats.

Chapter 3 investigates the potential of integrating blockchain technology into digital watermarking to ensure decentralized and tamper-proof copyright enforcement.

Chapter 4 provides a technical primer on transformer-based Large Language Models (LLMs), their architecture, and their implications in digital systems.

Chapter 5 discusses AI and ML approaches for adaptive watermarking, emphasizing intelligent systems for improving robustness and imperceptibility.

Chapter 6 delves into security analysis, detailing various attack vectors against watermarking systems and the countermeasures to address them.

Chapter 7 introduces adaptive watermarking algorithms designed for multi-user cloud settings, addressing personalization and real-time adaptability.

Chapter 8 presents Blockchain-Enhanced Watermarking systems that fuse blockchain's integrity with watermarking's traceability for authentication.

Chapter 9 focuses on real-time watermarking in cloud-edge infrastructures, balancing latency, performance, and copyright protection.

Chapter 10 explores quantum-resistant watermarking strategies to safeguard content in the face of future quantum computing threats.

Chapter 11 evaluates the performance of hybrid watermarking algorithms (DCT-DWT-SVD) and their superiority over traditional methods.

Chapter 12 revisits the intersection of AI, ML, and watermarking, discussing methodologies, current challenges, and anticipated future trends.

Chapter 13 provides a foundational overview of cloud computing, covering service models, security risks, and applications tied to watermarking.

Chapter 14 introduces dynamic watermarking for SaaS applications in multi-tenant environments, focusing on runtime watermark generation.

Chapter 15 offers an analytical review of cloud computing fundamentals and applications, serving as a context-setting chapter.

Chapter 16 examines the legal and enforcement challenges of copyright protection in cloud environments and proposes regulatory and technological remedies.

CONCLUSION

As the digital ecosystem continues to expand into the cloud, and soon into quantum and edge domains, safeguarding intellectual property becomes not just a technical necessity but a moral imperative. This book has illustrated the evolution of watermarking systems from static, single-use tools into adaptive, resilient technologies that can survive the scrutiny of modern attack models and complex cloud infrastructures.

Throughout these chapters, contributors have demonstrated that watermarking is not a singular solution but a versatile framework capable of evolving with the needs of our interconnected society. From real-time protection in edge environments to multi-tenant SaaS models, and from blockchain-based traceability to quantum resistance, digital watermarking has matured into a robust instrument for copyright protection.

We believe the insights contained in this volume will inspire future research, influence practical implementations, and inform policy decisions around digital content security. It is our hope that this book will serve as both a cornerstone and a catalyst for continued innovation in watermarking technologies and copyright defense in cloud environments.

Ashwani Kumar
School of Computer Science, Engineering, and Technology, Bennett University, Greater Noida, India

Auzuir Ripardo de Alexandria
Instituto Federal de Educação, Ciência e Tecnologia do Ceará (IFCE), Brazil

Satya Prakash Yadav
Department of Computer Science and Engineering, Madan Mohan Malaviya University of Technology, Gorakhpur, India

Antonino Galletta
University of Messina, Italy

Chapter 1
Cloud-Based Content Distribution and Copyright Vulnerabilities

Srinivas Chippagiri
https://orcid.org/0009-0004-9456-3951
Independent Researcher, USA

ABSTRACT

The backbone of current digital content creation and distribution is cloud technology, which concomitantly raises emerging and complicated issues for copyright enforcement. Albeit the cloud allows scalable and global access to media, documents, creative assets, it also opens up the risk of unauthorized copying and redistribution of such content because of mis-configuration, loose control and the inherent openness of distributed systems. This chapter considers the cloud content lifecycle (namely ingestion, storage, delivery, and consumption) and provides analysis of the main threats that may compromise the intellectual property. Based on real-world case studies and examination of contemporary threats, the chapter presents the inadequacy of traditional Digital Right Management (DRM) in the cloud age and argues for the utilization of digital watermarking as an adjunct to provide forensic-grade rights enforcement, content tracking and tracing.

1. INTRODUCTION

The digital medium has shaped a new paradigm for content creation, distribution, and consumption. With the popularization of cloud services, a great change has arisen from physical, centralized model into decentralized and virtualized environment were distributed over places, devices, and networks. This shift has disrupted

DOI: 10.4018/979-8-3373-3785-2.ch001

sectors competing through the distribution of digital content, such as media and entertainment, publishing, education, software and enterprise knowledge management. But as these innovations have enabled the reach, efficiency, and personalization of the Web to date, they have also created new issues of trust and arbitrariness in our online content ownership and usage rights - and their enforcement.

At the heart of this revolution is on-demand, cloud-based content distribution, which allows users to search for and use digital content whenever they need it, where they need it. This paradigm utilizes cloud services (e.g., Infrastructure as a Service (IaaS), Platform as a Service (PaaS), and Software as a Service (SaaS)) to provide content through geographically dispersed data centers, content delivery networks (CDNs), and platform application programming interfaces (APIs).

The characteristics of cloud that provide excellent values – like data replication, auto-scaling, and global access – also undermine the traditional control or copyright enforcement mechanisms. Content 'After the Internet' Content (once the province of physical objects and distribution centers) now moves through the interconnected components of systems, frequently unbeknownst to the author or without the manifest consent of the creator (Tu et al., 2020).

Older methods of copyright protection — watermarking, licensing contracts, and takedown requests –were devised for more static and jurisdictionally-specific media systems. They do not well adapt to such dynamic transformation operations, edge node caches, adaptive stream slicing, or user generated content workflows used in the cloud.

One of the key challenges in this domain is the lack of control on the content visibility and lifecycle. This results in content being copied/stitched/transformed across services and regions in cloud platforms, with limited granular accounting and centralized control. A video uploaded for private viewing could be accidentally leaked through incorrect storage permissions or even accessed from areas that don't respect copyright.

As equally urgent is the threat of unauthorized access and dissemination. Weak authentication, credential leaks, and open APIs can be used by attackers or unauthorized personnel to get hold of high-value material. After obtaining this content, it can be downloaded, saved or further shared by more casual or criminal methods like P2P networks, unindexed sites, and messaging applications. Yet even premium level content - including corporate training videos, research papers and proprietary product documentation - can be leaked to the public domain, if they are not adequately secured. These leaks, in most cases, are not the product of complex technical breaks but of elementary slip ups, like shared logins, weak encryption, or not checking who has access to it.

In the face of these challenges, content providers and platform builders are exploring a set of technical and policy approaches. In this manner, digital watermarking may invisibly track content from distribution. Dynamic watermarking are systems where each distributed copy includes a session-unique identifying mark, that can be used to trace the source of leaked copies to an individual user. Likewise, Digital Rights Management (DRM) technologies govern licensing restrictions by regulating consumption, playback, or distribution of content. Cloud native DRM systems, tightly coupled with content management workflows, can apply fine-grained controls according to user ID, device type, geography or consumption history. Nevertheless, the current trend, illustrated in Figure 1, indicates that still other technologies are under investigation to improve the capabilities of today.

Figure 1. Emerging technology testing

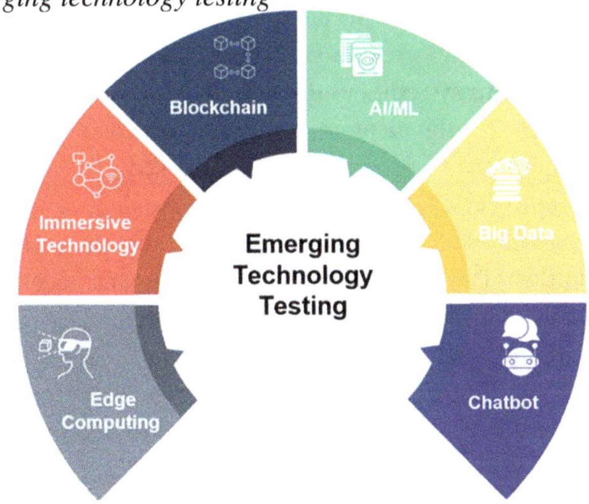

This figure 1 also reflected in the world of testing in emerging tech with six key focus areas which will drive digital transformation in the surface for future shape. Blockchain is leading this revolution by providing secure and transparent transactions in industries. AI/ML (Artificial Intelligence & Machine Learning) are empowering intelligent decision-making, automation and transformative solutions. Big Data is instrumental in generating insights and making data-driven decisions (Tu et al., 2021).

In this regard, this chapter provides an in-depth analysis of the technical, legal and operational issues around copyright protection in cloud, content scenarios. It starts from the history of content delivery direction and migration towards cloud-native and hybrid architecture. It reflects on the consequences of this evolution, most notably the weaknesses it has introduced, regarding exposure, unauthorized access and legal enforcement.

The goal of this chapter is to provide technologists, researchers, legal practitioners and artists the knowledge and tools they need in order to make informed choices in this rapidly moving digital environment by combining technical detail, regulatory overview and real-world use cases.

1.1 Literature Review

It is challenging for administrators and cloud providers to implement potential solutions that consumers need due to the various sorts of threats. This is since different types of assaults provide different kinds of hazards, and the relative importance of these risks differs according to the security requirements of other cloud service users. As a result, to fulfil critical security criteria as service providers, security administrators will assess and execute security measures. It is practically hard to set up a completely secure system, but there is room for improvement in terms of security. Accountability, authentication, and privacy protection are some of the security concerns that must be identified and addressed (Tu., 2021). Full faith in cloud computing to protect data is uneasy for many business and research associations. Cloud and traditional IT systems are also vulnerable to security breaches. Cloud security, like that of any other computing environment, necessitates sufficient protection. It follows that the data and network are secure, can detect anomalies instantly, and can monitor unforeseen occurrences (Tu, S. 2020).

The idea behind cloud computing is to make computer resources available whenever needed. This frees up customers from the responsibility of managing their own specialized infrastructure while yet providing them with access to the processing power and data storage they require. Cloud computing has many advantages, such as being cost-effective, scalable, faster, more efficient, and having better performance and security (Waqas, M. 2020). Concerning cloud computing security, Nafea, R.A. performed research in 2021.

1.2 Background of the Study

Over the past decade, security has consistently emerged as a prominent challenge in the cloud landscape, as highlighted in a series of cloud state reports published by Flexera (Luxner, 2023). Key security issues include data security, confidentiality, and integrity (Bennasar, H 2021). Industry experts have highlighted (Shackleford, D 2022) cloud platform misconfiguration, sensitive data leakage, insecure interfaces/APIs, and unauthorized access as the primary cloud attack vectors. The latter raises a significant question of who bears the responsibility for configuring and safeguarding cloud resources? In traditional settings, organizations assume full responsibility for securing on-premises systems. According to this model, cloud customers must ensure that they uphold security, governance, and compliance measures "in the cloud", while the CSPs are accountable for the security "of the cloud" (physical and infrastructure security) (CloudPassage 2020).

Moreover, various reports and guidelines published by organizations and agencies such as ENISA, the European Union Agency for Cybersecurity (Lopez Velásquez, 2023), and the US National Institute of Standards and Technology (NIST) emphasize that cloud security is a shared responsibility between the involved parties (cloud actors). The NIST Cloud Computing Reference Architecture (Pereira F, 2022) outlines the five main cloud actors, comprising (1) the cloud consumer—a person or an entity that uses cloud services or resources from a cloud provider; (2) the cloud provider—an entity that provides cloud services or resources to cloud consumers; (3) the cloud auditor—the entity that conducts independent assessments of the cloud services or resources, such as security, performance, and compliance; (4) the cloud broker—the entity that intermediates between cloud consumers and cloud providers; and (5) the cloud carrier—the entity that transports data between cloud consumers and cloud providers, such as by providing network connectivity or bandwidth. While we acknowledge the significance of all cloud actors, comprehending their responsibilities and developing policies and procedures for their respective aspects of cloud security, this study particularly emphasizes the responsibilities of cloud consumers (Shackleford, 2022).

Table 1. Framework & method comparison

Aspect	**Chauhan & Shiaeles (Network 2023)(cloud security frameworks)**	**Cotfas & Rekeraho (Appl. Sci. 2023) (SIEMbased monitoring)**	**Symmetry 2023 Study(Symmetry 151981)**
Primary Focus	Comprehensive review of cloud-security frameworks (COBIT5, NIST, ISO, CSA, AWS, Azure) (MDPI)	Proposes and evaluates a SIEM-driven threat monitoring system in public cloud (Azure/AWS)	Investigates symmetric patterns in theoretical/ security contexts (e.g., symmetry in encryption protocols)
Key Frameworks/ Tools Analyzed	COBIT 5, NIST, ISO/ IEC, CSA STAR, AWS Well Architected Model	Microsoft Defender for Cloud, WAF, SIEM/ Sentinel setup	Symmetry-based algorithms/models; specific cryptographic or structural symmetry schemes
Methodology	Comparative evaluation: scope, strengths, limitations, implementation steps	Practical implementation: deploy, monitor, automate response, evaluate compliance	Theoretical modeling and simulation of symmetry properties within a chosen domain

continued on following page

Table 1. Continued

Aspect	Chauhan & Shiaeles (Network 2023)(cloud security frameworks)	Cotfas & Rekeraho (Appl. Sci. 2023) (SIEMbased monitoring)	Symmetry 2023 Study(Symmetry 151981)
Pros	Structured, wide-scope analysis aiding framework selection	Demonstrates real-world feasibility; focuses on automation and compliance	Offers foundational insights; deep theoretical rigor
Cons / Limitations	Lacks practical deployment case studies or real-world data	Limited to a single CSP setup; scalability unclear	May lack applied or empirical validation

Table 1 highlights the distinct focus and contributions of each study. Chauhan and Shiaeles present a comprehensive survey of various cloud security frameworks, evaluating them based on structure, implementation scope, and strategic applicability—making their work particularly valuable for high-level planning and policy formulation. On the other hand, Cotfas and Rekeraho adopt a more hands-on approach by demonstrating the real-world deployment of SIEM and WAF tools in cloud environments (Lopez Velásquez et al., 2023), emphasizing their integration for real-time threat monitoring and compliance enforcement. In contrast, the study published in Symmetry takes a theoretical angle, exploring the role of symmetry in cryptographic models and structural patterns. Unlike the other two, it does not directly address cloud-specific implementations but instead contributes foundational insights into the mathematical principles that may underpin future security frameworks (Waqas et al., 2020).

Table 2. Depth & outcome summary

Dimension	Chauhan & Shiaeles	Cotfas & Rekeraho	Symmetry 151981 Study
Security Issues Covered	Broad threat taxonomy; attack vectors; risk impacts (MDPI)	Cloud misconfigurations, API risks; shared-responsibility gaps	Vulnerabilities in symmetrical models or formal symmetry leaks
Implementation Guidance	Framework application steps; required tools listed	SIEM architecture; Sentinel/ WAF deployment; real-time monitoring	Algorithmic design guidelines, parameter analysis
Evaluation Results	Qualitative strengths/ limits; no empirical scoring framework	Quantitative demonstration: continuous detection, compliance checks	Theoretical performance bounds or symmetry properties validation
Target Audience	Decision-makers, security architects, policy planners	Cloud admins, DevSecOps, compliance teams	Cryptographers, theoreticians, security researchers
Novel Contribution	First unified comparison across major frameworks	Enterprise-level SIEM deployment blueprint in public cloud	Novel exploration of symmetry's role in security models

The insights from Table 2 reveal key distinctions in the scope, implementation approach, and evaluation methods across the three studies. The first study by Chauhan & Shiaeles adopts a broad analytical perspective, offering a high-level comparison of major cloud security frameworks, making it suitable for architecture teams and policy planners (CloudPassage, 2020). In contrast, the second study by Cotfas & Rekeraho focuses on operational tooling, presenting a practical deployment of SIEM-based monitoring systems in a real-world cloud environment, thereby catering to cloud administrators and DevSecOps teams (Lopez Velásquez et al., 2023). The third study, published in Symmetry, delves into the theoretical realm by examining symmetry-based algorithms and models, which appeals primarily to academic researchers and cryptography experts. This range of focus and methodology highlights how each work serves a different segment of the cloud security and copyright protection ecosystem (Shackleford, 2022).

2. EVOLUTION OF CLOUD-BASED CONTENT DISTRIBUTION

The distribution of digital content has been dramatically transformed over the past two decades from static physical media and client-server systems to dynamic, decentralized cloud-computing environments. The changes were driven by the requirements of managing the growing number of multimedia contents in both scalable, flexible and cost-effective way.

2.1 Traditional Distribution Models

Before, the content used to be placed in centralized servers, or in hosting appropriate for the owner/service provider of content occupation in traditional architectures for the distribution of content. Content Delivery Networks (CDNs) such as Akamai and Limelight Networks were some of the early approaches which aimed to alleviate bandwidth constraint and latency by replicating contents to a number of loads balancing servers at geographically distributed edge nodes. However, these solutions were not very scalable and had significant infrastructure overhead.

Moreover, older model content protection was based on static licensing models, simple encryption mechanisms, and simple authentication protocols. Rights enforcement was primarily local and jurisdictionally bounded, meaning that legal action and IP defense were practical only within well-defined legal territories. As digital content consumption began to surge—with the rise of MP3s, DVDs, and peer-to-peer file sharing—these models quickly became insufficient in preventing unauthorized copying and redistribution (Fund, Hosseini, & Panwar, 2016).

2.2 Emergence of Cloud Content Ecosystems

Cloud computing catalyzed a paradigm shift in content distribution by virtualizing resources and introducing scalable delivery mechanisms. Infrastructure-as-a-Service (IaaS), Platform-as-a-Service (PaaS), and Software-as-a-Service (SaaS) offerings allowed content providers to outsource storage, compute, and delivery infrastructure to public and hybrid cloud platforms such as Amazon Web Services (AWS), Microsoft Azure, and Google Cloud Platform (GCP).

Modern cloud-native applications leverage microservices, containerization, and content replication across availability zones to ensure resilience and low-latency access. Real-time encoding, adaptive bitrate streaming, and edge computing further optimize user experience. In this environment, content is not only delivered faster but also transformed on the fly—resized, compressed, or reformatted to match device-specific constraints—complicating efforts to preserve the originality and traceability of copyrighted material (Software Engineering Institute, 2019).

2.3 Implications for Copyright Protection

The separations and obliviating of infrastructure that are fundamental in cloud environments raise serious challenges to copyright enforcement. First, multi-tenancy ensures that the same physical hardware is used to serve multiple customers and isolating the data ownership or forensic investigation from larger tenant is difficult. Second, auto-scaling and replications across regions may lead to unauthorized copies of content being stored and accessed from regions that were not intended legal jurisdiction to access that content.

Furthermore, 'safe harbor' rules such as those in the Digital Millennium Copyright Act (DMCA) protect cloud providers from liability, as long as they have acted based on take down requests in good faith (Wikipedia contributors, 2024b). Despite being tailored to traditional hosting platforms, this model has not adapted well to highly automated cloud environments.

As the content ecosystems in the cloud becomes more sophisticated, the barriers between storage, processing, and delivery start to tumble. How content is algorithmically transformed and then distributed has to matter for rights management, not just access. Moreover, digital watermarking and automatic license verification mechanisms have emerged as important solutions to fill in these gaps (Padhi, Tiwari, & Ali, 2025), although the traffic-king effectiveness of these measures is often voided by AI adversaries that can detect and remove embedded markers (Xue et al., 2024).

3. CORE COPYRIGHT CHALLENGES IN CLOUD DISTRIBUTION

The introduction of cloud computing is changing the ways that digital content is both delivered to and consumed by users, as well as how it is monetized. However, as IP rights holders deploy software on distributed architectures and IP is delivered, CDN-style to cache nodes at the network edge, the protective barriers furnished by the infrastructure and by physical ownership give way to abstractions within abstraction, layers of multi-tenancy, and cloaked federated control.

They are technical, they are legal, and they are behavioral. From unauthorized access to identity misuse, API abuse, jurisdictional unknowns and a constantly evolving landscape of licensing models. This portion explores one of the most significant of these issues, spanning four related dimensions: control decay, security voids, legal enforcement intricacy, and policy enforcement incoherency.

3.1 Loss of Content Control in Abstracted Environments

The core tenant of cloud distribution is abstraction— resources are virtualized, abstracted from hardware, and operated through orchestration layers (Kubernetes, Terraform, or the service-specific control plane such as AWS CloudFormation). This abstract level enables such things as quick provisioning, redundant, and scalable services but it comes at the price of limited visibility into the data itself.

In a cloud-based content delivery workflow, traditional cloud content delivery materials like media, research datasets, or binaries are not statically located. Instead, they are:

- Replicated across zones for fault tolerance
- Cached on edge servers via CDNs
- Indexed and queried through distributed object storage
- Temporarily processed in containers or serverless functions

This architectural dynamism erodes the creator's ability to pinpoint where content resides or how it's being used at any given moment. A graphic uploaded to a cloud-based design tool, for example, could be written to an S3-compatible storage layer in one region, processed by a Lambda function in another, and then rendered by a CDN edge node in a third part of the world.

Without centralized enforcement of policy, watermarking and audit chaining across these elements, risk of uncontrolled duplication or content drift is substantial (Padhi et al., 2025).

3.2 Unauthorized Access and Distribution

Unauthorized access, typically due to misconfigured permissions, leaked tokens, or identity spoofing, still ranks amongst the most observed vectors for content leakage. In contrast to classic infrastructures where perimeters (such as firewalls or VPNs) offer demarcated security, cloud infrastructures enforce access control in the form of fine-grained Identity and Access Management (IAM) policies that are required to be carefully conceived and maintained (Chauhan & Shiaeles, 2023).

Several environments take the shape of flat permissions models such as the overly privileged admin. Common missteps include:

- Assigning global read/write permissions to internal storage buckets
- Failing to rotate access tokens used in CI/CD systems
- Using environment variables or plaintext secrets in container images
- Allowing overly permissive API scopes (e.g., content read granted to all users)

A case study from 2023 demonstrated how an educational cloud platform leaked thousands of licensed textbooks due to insecure pre-signed URLs that were shared publicly. The URLs, which included embedded tokens, allowed full document to download without authentication—bypassing licensing checks entirely.

Cloud-native threats also include side-channel attacks, such as exploiting shared CPU caches (e.g., Meltdown/Spectre), container escape vulnerabilities (CVE-2019-5736), and cross-tenant timing analysis. Each can be used to infer or extract content in multi-tenant hosting setups (Software Engineering Institute, 2019).

3.3 Legal and Jurisdictional Challenges in Multi-Region Cloud

The distributed nature of the cloud makes it extremely difficult to establish legal jurisdiction over content storage and usage. For example:

- A video recorded in Canada might be uploaded to a cloud platform hosted in Ireland, then served to viewers in Singapore.
- Data sovereignty laws in Germany may require content to be stored within national borders, but replication policies in the underlying cloud infrastructure may copy data to the Netherlands for redundancy.

These situations raise significant legal ambiguity around enforcement. Which country's laws apply in the event of unauthorized use? Who is responsible—the uploader, the platform, or the cloud provider? (Fund et al., 2016)

3.4 Evolving Licensing Models and Enforcement Complexity

Traditional licensing—tied to physical distribution or device-based access—is being replaced by dynamic, real-time licensing enforced by digital contracts and API-mediated controls. These licenses may be conditional upon:

- Region (geo-fencing)
- Device or platform (e.g., iOS-only licenses)
- Time (e.g., 48-hour rental windows)
- User identity (verified accounts, MFA)

In cloud-native platforms, these licensing rules must be encoded and enforced by DRM systems or logic-based policy engines. Yet, enforcement is often fragmented:

- Microservices managing identity, content transformation, and delivery may operate in isolation.
- Third-party plugins and browser extensions may bypass frontend restrictions.
- Licensing metadata may be stripped during transcoding or re-uploaded without enforcement hooks.

3.5 AI-Driven Exploitation of Content Vulnerabilities

The emergence of AI tools has added a new layer of complexity. Not only can AI models detect and extract content from cloud services more efficiently, but generative AI systems can now replicate copyrighted works without directly copying them—raising challenges around derivative rights.

For example:

- Language models trained on proprietary eBooks can output summaries or paraphrased versions.
- Image generators trained on copyrighted art can produce visually similar styles.
- AI-powered bots can automatically detect and exploit weak DRM implementations to download, repackage, and redistribute media content at scale.

3.6 Recommendations for Remediation

To counter these threats, organizations distributing content via the cloud should consider the following measures:

1. **Unified Access Governance**: Implement centralized IAM with scoped roles, time-based access, and contextual access policies (e.g., location, device fingerprint).
2. **Zero Trust Security**: Move toward identity-centric security models where all access is continuously verified and monitored.
3. **Hybrid License Enforcement Gateways**: Deploy API gateways that evaluate license compliance in real time before content is served.
4. **Watermark Integration with Licensing APIs**: Dynamically embed license IDs, session tokens, or user hashes into content using watermarking at delivery time.

4. VULNERABILITY ASSESSMENT IN HYBRID CLOUD ENVIRONMENTS

Hybrid cloud architecture combining on-premises, private cloud, and public cloud infrastructure—offer organizations the agility to optimize workloads for performance, compliance, or cost. In digital content distribution systems, hybrid clouds are increasingly favored for their flexibility, especially in media, education, publishing, and enterprise document management.

Figure 2. Areas of hybrid cloud vulnerability assessment.

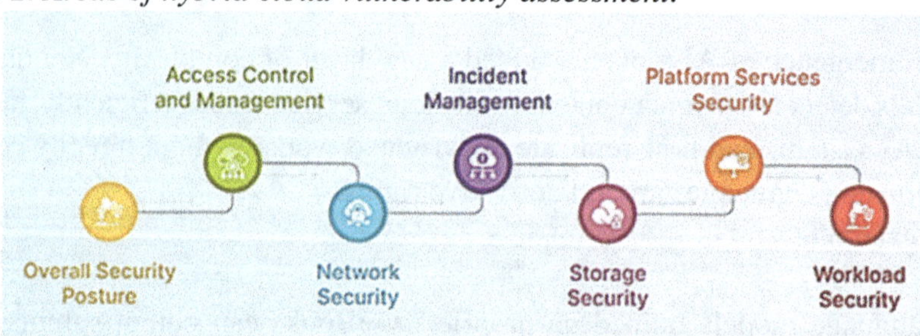

This figure 2 provides a depiction of the principal dimensions for a hybrid cloud vulnerability assessment. This starts with defining an organizing security principle, which offers a general approach to understanding baseline security. Access control and management are considered as an important step where only authorized users are allowed access at the right level of access for managing documents.

The security of platform services thus emphasizes the fact that the underlying platform that supports applications and services must also be secure. Finally, workload security is the security of applications and workloads that operate in the hybrid cloud (Cotfas & Rekeraho, 2023). These interconnected domains together define a holistic approach to securing hybrid cloud environments against vulnerabilities and threats (Nafea & Almaiah, 2021).

4.1 Common Threat Vectors in Hybrid Cloud Architectures

Hybrid environments involve a mix of systems under varied administrative control—some fully owned, others provisioned through third-party vendors. This diversity leads to an explosion in attack surfaces and weak points. Vulnerabilities often arise at key integration points between components such as:

- API endpoints for data and metadata exchange
- Storage services replicating content across environments
- Identity federation systems
- Content transformation and delivery subsystems

Key threat vectors include:

a. Misconfigured Storage Resources

Cloud-based object storage systems like AWS S3, Azure Blob Storage and Google Cloud Storage are popular for storing copyrighted content like eBooks, PDFs, images and video streams. Misconfigured buckets are (like accidentally setting public-read permissions) a constant problem. Attackers are continuously scanning for open buckets with automated tools and have found useful assets with no authentication wall.

b. IAM Misconfigurations

Poorly defined roles, unnecessary privileges, or orphaned accounts can allow unauthorized access. A frequent issue in hybrid environments is **privilege creep**, where users gain excessive access over time, especially during mergers or cloud migrations. Access policies must be harmonized across platforms—a non-trivial task when dealing with native IAM systems like AWS IAM, Azure RBAC, and local Active Directory.

c. Insecure API Design

APIs are often exposed to allow frontend applications, partners, and plugins to retrieve or manipulate content. Common mistakes include:

- Lack of token expiration
- Insecure transport (e.g., HTTP instead of HTTPS)
- Missing rate-limiting
- Insufficient access scoping

d. Lack of Network Segmentation

Hybrid environments may improperly segment private resources from public services. If a public-facing container or API can communicate with backend databases or internal file stores, attackers could pivot and extract content after initial compromise.

e. Weak Encryption and Key Management

Even when content is encrypted at rest and in transit, poorly managed keys or hardcoded secrets render encryption moot. Developers sometimes embed cloud storage access keys in mobile apps or configuration files, which can be reverse engineered to unlock media libraries.

4.2 Data Exfiltration and Leak Scenarios

The distributed nature of hybrid cloud makes it difficult to track the flow of data and enforce consistency in content protections. Common exfiltration scenarios include:

a. Edge Cache Exploitation

Content Delivery Networks (CDNs) are often used to cache high-demand content closer to users. However, improper cache invalidation policies can leave stale, unlicensed, or deprecated versions accessible long after access should have been revoked. Attackers can use tools like wget or cURL to download cached assets.

b. Backup Exposure

Many organizations back up their hybrid infrastructure using snapshots, versioning systems, or cross-region replication. If backup containers are exposed (e.g., via NFS shares or cloud console misconfigurations), sensitive content may be leaked without detection. Old backups often retain watermarks or metadata that can compromise forensic integrity.

c. Side-Channel and Metadata Attacks

Attackers may extract information not from the content itself but from side channels such as:

- Timestamps (to infer update activity)
- File sizes (to predict content type)
- Access patterns (to identify premium assets)

4.3 Public vs. Private Cloud Vulnerabilities

Hybrid deployments inherit the risks of both cloud types and introduce new ones at their integration points.

Public Cloud Vulnerabilities:

- Dependence on vendor-side logging and compliance (e.g., GDPR logging by AWS/GCP)
- Shared tenancy and the risk of side-channel attacks
- Misuse of public cloud APIs (e.g., overexposed REST endpoints)
- Human error in I-a-C (Infrastructure-as-Code) templates

Private Cloud Vulnerabilities:

- Outdated patching routines
- Manual configuration drift
- Lack of central visibility
- Local privilege escalation vulnerabilities (e.g., hypervisor exploits)

4.4 Detection and Monitoring Techniques

Proactive detection and continuous validation are critical to mitigating these threats. Best practices include:

a. Cloud Security Posture Management (CSPM)

Tools like Prisma Cloud, Wiz, and Microsoft Defender for Cloud assess configuration drift, alert on insecure deployments, and enforce policies across multi-cloud systems (CloudPassage, 2020).

b. Data Loss Prevention (DLP)

Modern DLP solutions use regex patterns, fingerprinting, and NLP to identify and block content exfiltration at the endpoint, network, or API layer. For example, outbound traffic containing large blocks of structured text matching licensed material can be flagged.

c. Access and Session Monitoring

Cloud Access Security Brokers (CASBs) can log sessions, enforce step-up authentication for sensitive content access, and analyze behavioral anomalies.

4.5 Mitigation Strategies

Mitigation in hybrid cloud involves both proactive design and reactive response strategies:

- **Zero Trust Enforcement**: Assume no user, device, or service is trusted by default. Every request must be authenticated, authorized, and logged.
- **Federated Identity Management**: Use identity providers that issue consistent claims across private and public cloud resources.
- **Policy-as-Code**: Implement Open Policy Agent (OPA) or HashiCorp Sentinel to enforce cross-platform access and licensing rules.
- **Immutable Infrastructure**: Use container immutability and ephemeral environments to reduce state drift and prevent persistent unauthorized modifications.

4.6 Case Insight: Enterprise eLearning Platform Breach

In 2022, a hybrid cloud-based eLearning platform suffered a breach where over 100,000 protected training videos were downloaded and reposted to unauthorized platforms. Investigation revealed:

- Open S3 buckets in the backup region (unmonitored due to limited SOC scope)
- Lack of dynamic watermarking during content export
- No throttling on API requests, allowing mass scraping
- Static credentials embedded in the mobile app

Post-incident reforms included:

- CSPM deployment across all zones
- Integration of session-aware forensic watermarking
- Redesign of export flows using time-bound URLs and single-use tokens

In conclusion, while hybrid cloud architectures offer unparalleled operational benefits, they demand a high degree of architectural discipline, continuous validation, and technical sophistication to mitigate copyright-specific threats (Nafea & Almaiah, 2021).

5. ROLE OF DIGITAL WATERMARKING AND DRM

In an era where cloud-native ecosystems underpin most of the global digital content distribution, protecting intellectual property has grown increasingly complex. Traditional perimeter-based security and post-distribution legal enforcement are no longer sufficient (Padhi et al., 2025). Two complementary technologies—Digital Watermarking and Digital Rights Management (DRM)—now form the backbone of proactive content protection strategies. Each plays a distinct yet synergistic role in securing digital assets in environments where content can be instantly replicated, transformed, and accessed from nearly anywhere (Fund et al., 2016).

Figure 3. Combined use of DRM and watermarking

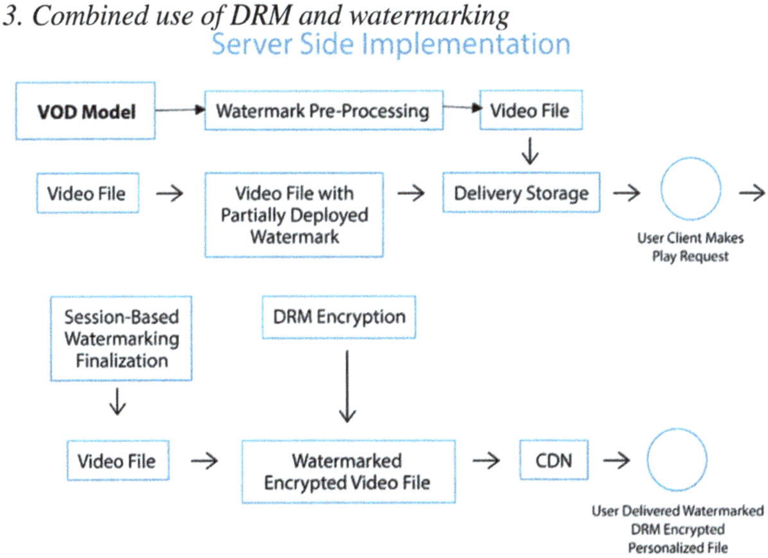

Digital watermarking enables content owners to establish traceable fingerprints within their digital media, ensuring authenticity, ownership verification, and leak source attribution also the Combined use of DRM and Watermarking was shown in figure 3. Figure 3 depicts the server-side realization of Combined Use of DRM and Watermarking in a Video on Demand (VOD) Model.

5.1 Invisible and Robust Watermarks: Enhancing Content Traceability

At its core, digital watermarking is a process of embedding imperceptible information into a digital asset—be it an image, audio file, video, or even structured data—such that this embedded information (the watermark) can later be retrieved to establish source identity, validate licensing, or detect tampering. Importantly, this process must not interfere with user experience.

There are multiple ways to embed such watermarks:

- **Spatial domain watermarking** involves direct modification of content data such as image pixels or audio amplitudes. This approach is simple and computationally inexpensive but tends to be vulnerable to basic editing operations like resizing or re-encoding (Alquwayzani et al., 2024).
- **Frequency domain watermarking**, such as using the Discrete Cosine Transform (DCT) or Discrete Wavelet Transform (DWT), embeds data in frequency components that are more resilient to compression or format shifts. This is the preferred technique for robust watermarking in multimedia contexts.
- **Perceptual and feature-based watermarking** focuses on embedding data into invariant features—such as the contours of an image or harmonics of an audio clip—ensuring that even if the content is geometrically transformed or cropped, the watermark remains intact.

5.2 Forensic and Dynamic Watermarking in Streaming Platforms

While static watermarking suffices in some distribution scenarios, it falls short when content is widely shared, or high-value assets are involved. In these cases, forensic watermarking—also referred to as dynamic or session-based watermarking—offers a far more granular and traceable form of protection (Digital Guardian, 2023).

Use cases include:

- **Video-on-demand (VoD) platforms**: High-profile releases are often leaked before official distribution. With session-based watermarking, any unauthorized copy can be traced back to a specific subscriber session.
- **E-learning**: Institutions delivering proprietary courseware may encode student-specific watermarks to ensure accountability and discourage file sharing.

- **Corporate media**: Sensitive presentations, internal training videos, or executive broadcasts are often watermarked on a per-viewer basis to reduce internal leak risks.

Dynamic watermarking can be applied via two main strategies:

1. **Client-side insertion**: Watermarks are rendered on the user's device using browser scripts or media player SDKs. While lightweight and cost-effective, this method is susceptible to tampering or circumvention using browser debuggers.
2. **Server-side insertion**: Watermarks are embedded into the media stream before delivery, typically during the transcoding or packaging phase. This approach is more secure but computationally intensive, especially when scaling to thousands of concurrent users.

5.3 DRM Enforcement: Real-Time Usage Control

Whereas watermarking enables traceability and evidence collection post-distribution, Digital Rights Management (DRM) enforces copyright compliance before or during content access. DRM is typically implemented through content encryption, secure key delivery, playback control, and policy enforcement mechanisms.

Modern DRM solutions operate via a multi-layered model:

- **Encryption**: Content is encrypted using symmetric algorithms (e.g., AES-128/256). The encryption key is never distributed directly; instead, a license server mediates access.
- **License server**: This server verifies the user's entitlement (based on subscription, token, or ID verification) and issues a **decryption key** wrapped in a license file.
- **DRM client**: The user's application or device includes a secure playback environment, such as an embedded browser component, native DRM module (e.g., Widevine CDM), or dedicated media player SDK.

Well-established DRM systems include:

- **Google Widevine**: Used by YouTube, Netflix, and Android apps
- **Microsoft PlayReady**: Common on Windows platforms and Xbox
- **Apple FairPlay**: Standard for iOS and Safari
- **Adobe Primetime DRM**: Used in enterprise and educational media

DRM policies can be configured to define access parameters such as:

- Playback time limits (e.g., rental expires in 48 hours)
- Device limits (e.g., playback on 3 devices only)
- Geolocation restrictions (e.g., viewable only in the EU)
- Output protection (e.g., prevent screen capture via HDCP)

For instance, in a hybrid cloud architecture, an organization may use AWS MediaConvert to encrypt videos, issue licenses via BuyDRM's multi-DRM platform, and distribute the final content through a CDN like CloudFront. User authentication is tied to OAuth 2.0 identity flows, and license requests are bound to device fingerprints and IP ranges.

5.4 Limitations, Bypass Techniques, and Defensive Enhancements

No technology is immune to circumvention. Both watermarking and DRM have vulnerabilities that determined adversaries seek to exploit (Digital Guardian, 2023).

Watermarking Challenges:

- **Visual artifacts**: In certain conditions, even invisible watermarks may create visual or auditory artifacts, affecting quality.
- **Content transformation**: Cropping, compression, or filtering may destroy embedded marks.
- **Machine learning attacks**: Generative AI models can reconstruct content without preserved watermarks, even from tampered sources.
- **Interoperability gaps**: A watermark created in one system may not be readable by another, limiting utility in legal or cross-platform disputes.

DRM Challenges:

- **Screen recording**: DRM can't prevent content capture via external or software-based screen recording tools.
- **Key leakage**: Improper key management or insecure implementation can lead to leaked decryption keys.
- **User backlash**: Heavy-handed DRM policies often generate negative feedback or user attrition.
- **DRM removal tools**: A persistent issue, especially in less-secure implementations, where tools like Requiem or DeDRM can strip protection.

Defensive Enhancements Include:

- Multi-layer watermarking (combining visible + forensic marks)
- Real-time DRM telemetry to detect suspicious playback behavior
- API tokenization with short lifespans and session binding

- Integration of behavioral analytics to detect and respond to circumvention attempts

5.5 Future Directions for Unified Cloud Protection Frameworks

The future of watermarking and DRM is moving toward greater integration, intelligence, and automation:

- **AI-integrated watermarking systems** that dynamically adapt to media format, distribution risk, and user behavior.
- **Policy-as-code frameworks** (e.g., Open Policy Agent) embedded into DRM workflows to enforce contextual licensing decisions in real time.
- **Interoperable watermark standards**, enabling detection and verification across vendor platforms, potentially backed by consortia or ISO standards.
- **Blockchain-based watermark anchoring**, where hashes of watermark payloads are stored immutably for auditability and litigation support (Xue et al., 2024).
- **DRM-aware content personalization**, where user data and device context guide how content is rendered, encrypted, and expired.

As the adoption of hybrid and multi-cloud environments continues to grow, protection mechanisms must evolve to become location-agnostic. This means security and content protection solutions should function seamlessly across diverse cloud infrastructures without compromising performance. To achieve this, technologies such as cloud-agnostic Digital Rights Management (DRM) licensing servers, containerized forensic watermarking services, and cross-cloud content observability platforms are essential. These tools enable organizations to monitor and manage content securely through a unified interface, offering a single pane view across both public and private cloud environments.

6. BLOCKCHAIN FOR CONTENT AUTHENTICITY AND LICENSING

As cloud content distribution becomes more complex and global, there is a clamoring need for decentralized tamper-proof systems that can validate ownership and protect digital rights. Many traditional licensing processes operate with centralized databases and require humans to verify information through manual processes, which are susceptible to fraud, delays, and conflicts between jurisdictions. Blockchain technology as a response Blockchain technology has been proposed as a potential solution to these issues, with its characteristics of transparency, immutability, and decentralized enforcement. This part examines the potential for blockchain to support copyright by leveraging smart contracts, provenance of content and secure audit trails.

6.1 Immutable Ledger for Copyright Claims

The main breakthrough of Blockchain is its distributed ledger structure which enables several participants to log and verify transactions securely and with no possibility of changing once done. For digital content, this implies that ownership records, distribution logs and licensing terms could all be maintained as cryptographically secured entries which could not be changed after the fact without consensus. This is especially relevant in cloud environment where content is being increasingly accessed, copied and manipulated across different platforms and borders.

You can think of a hash as a digital fingerprint of the original file," says Alex Feinberg, executive director at the Web3 Foundation, one of the organizations that coordinates development of the Polkadot ecosystem, a blockchain project. It acts as a unshakable, verifiable source document that any participant can independently verify without resorting to trust in a specific authority. The likes of Media chain, Ascribe, and Po. et al have developed these techniques by incorporation blockchains for tracking and licensing digital media (Xue et al., 2024).

6.2 Decentralized Digital Rights Management

And beyond attribution, blockchain makes it possible to write smart contracts—programs that can enforce licensing terms automatically. These contracts can automatize royalty payouts, limit usage or revoke access on certain conditions. For instance, a smart contract might allow a user temporary streaming rights for a film, withdraw access after a period expires, pay content creators directly when the film is played, with no intermediaries.

On the other hand, decentralized DRM (dDRM) systems leverage the role of blockchain layer in encoding access policies. This avoids having to use vendor dependent DRM software which is both platform specific and breakable. Instead, on-chain usage rights are checked, and decryption keys are generated on-the-fly according to the user's blockchain identity and his transaction history.

6.3 Limitations: Scalability, Adoption, and Off-Chain Dependencies

Despite its promise, blockchain is not a panacea. Several limitations currently hinder its mainstream adoption for content protection:

- **Scalability**: Most public blockchains suffer from limited throughput and high latency. Storing large volumes of licensing data or media hashes can be costly and slow, especially on platforms like Ethereum.
- **Off-chain dependencies**: Blockchain alone cannot enforce DRM or watermarking. It requires integration with off-chain systems for identity verification, content delivery, and encryption—each of which may introduce vulnerabilities or governance issues.
- **Interoperability**: There is no universally accepted standard for blockchain-based copyright enforcement. Different projects use incompatible protocols, making cross-platform enforcement and verification difficult.
- **Legal uncertainty**: While blockchain records are often admissible in court, their legal standing varies across jurisdictions. Some countries lack clear regulations governing smart contracts or blockchain-verified claims.

7. AI-POWERED CONTENT MONITORING AND ENFORCEMENT

Traditional methods to monitoring and enforcement are overwhelmed by the explosive growth of digital content and the advanced form of copyright violation where they can take place in a cloud. Well, that's no longer a good enough excuse, as manual takedown requests, metadata filters, and playing whack-a-mole with court orders are woefully inadequate methods to combat the intricacies and scale of internet distribution. This gap is now being filled by the emergence of artificial intelligence (AI) and machine learning (ML) as viable technologies that can be employed for proactive copyright infringement detection, classification, and immediate reaction.

AI can augment digital rights enforcement by automating content pattern detection over large quantities of data, which can make mass surveillance over the open web platforms, private clouds or edge networked devices feasible. But it also raises a new category of hurdles, more specifically in the construction of synthetic or derivative works, the provenance of which might blur ownership and make claims of breach more difficult to back up.

7.1 ML for Infringement Detection

Deep learning-based copyright enforcement systems generally rely on supervised learning methods according to which massive licensed and unlicensed content are used to train deep learning models. These systems leverage reverse image search, fingerprinting, audio matching, natural language processing (NLP) to find clones of infringing material across platforms. For example, companies like U-Tube have their own version of the Content ID, which searches for uploaded videos in the database and automatically blocks, monetizes, or sends a takedown notification for violating uploads.

In cloud, such models can be plugged into media ingestion pipelines or API gateways to filter out such content before it's available to public. AI solutions can scan publicly available storage, forums, and social media sites for re-hosted files, as well as catch these potential usage infractions in near-real-time. Furthermore, multimodal models can learn from concatenation text, image, and audio as a single stream, thus being especially suited to capture remix or mashup content which otherwise is likely to circumnavigate traditional DRM systems (Ye et al., 2025).

7.2 Generative AI: New Challenges

Artificial intelligence, the very thing that will help enforce copyrights, has, however, created a new frontier of complexity. From generative AI models like large language models (LLMs), diffusion-based image generators, and voice synthesis engines that can mimic the style, voice, or message of its source. These outputs generative outputs often lie in a legal gray area, especially when models are used to train on copyrighted datasets without licensing.

For instance, an AI-created image of a well-known cartoon character may not share any pixels with the original but is still a derivative work. Equally, synthetic voices can closely replicate musicians, authors, or other speakers. These developments, which are transformative, clash with traditional definitions of infringement, and render the enforcement of ownership rights in distributed systems complex.

The power of AI is also being leveraged by bad actors to circumvent security features. An adversary network can, for example, detect and erase a digital watermark (Xue et al., 2024), evade perceptual hashing through manipulation of key visual features, or mask copied material to evade automated detecting. In the process, AI not only aids compliance but enables new types of piracy and counterfeiting.

7.3 Ethics and False Positives

Limitations of AI-systems: AI-systems are not just without limitations. Automated enforcement systems can yield false positives — identifying content as infringing that is, in fact, legal or fair use — because of overfitting, or biased training data. This can lead to wrongful takedowns, lost revenue for creators and hurt the platforms' reputations. For instance, even artists reposting parody content or educational criticism can have their work taken down or demonetized with little recourse.

There are also more general ethical questions around the transparency and oversight of enforcement powered by AI. The algorithms that moderate content are typically proprietary and opaque, giving those affected little ability to challenge decisions, or even the ability to understand how judgments were reached. Such absence of explainability is very dangerous, in the legal domains, for instance, where evidence from black- box models cannot fulfill the requirement of the due process.

To mitigate these challenges, explainable AI (XAI) (Dahr et al, 2019) for copyright enforcements is emerging. The aim of these models is to ensure that the way they arrive at a decision can be explained to humans, thus fostering trust and making it more likely that fair decisions can be made. Supplemented with human-in-the-loop adjudication, XAI can redress the tradeoff between automated productivity and normalized judgment, particularly in the fuzzy frontier cases of fair use, parody, or transformative works.

In conclusion, AI is changing the way in which copyright enforcement is carried out: from manual, reactive to proactive and scalable solutions that work effectively in the cloud. As a promising technology, it has advantages in the detection and observation, but new risks and new ethical problems arise which should be subject to close supervision. As AI advances, cloud platforms and content providers will need to use these tools in a responsible manner while ensuring the enforcement mechanisms are effective and fair.

8. POLICY, STANDARDS, AND COMPLIANCE FRAMEWORKS

Stronger copyright enforcement in the cloud among content distributors needs to be more than just technological: it must be institutionalized through legal and regulatory context. As digital content crosses national borders, and cloud-based infrastructures extend over several realms, enforcement of intellectual property rights is growing more complex. National legislation, platform policies as well as industry standards need to holistically act in concert to provide seamless protection "in the same way" while allowing for different legal interpretations as well as new technologies. The objective of this section is to lay out the principal legal tools, regime designs and standardization projects on which copyright management in the cloud is built.

8.1 International Copyright Laws

International treaties are the primary legal basis for cross-border copyright enforcement. By acknowledging the rights of creators within its member countries and compelling countries to protect foreign works as they would their own, the Berne

Convention for the Protection of Literary and Artistic Works (1886) and the WIPO Copyright Treaty (1996) established a basis for frameworks.

In the age of digital media, these agreements were complemented by rules that were specifically designed to operate in the online realm. The Digital Millennium Copyright Act (DMCA) of 1998 in the US added a series of mechanisms to combat digital piracy that included "safe harbor" provisions for online service providers (Wikipedia contributors, 2024b). According to the current rules, cloud services and hosting services are protected from liability over infringing user uploads if they respond "expeditiously" to remove such content when warned.

Despite that, the DMCA's approach is not consistently followed globally. The European Union's Copyright Directive (Directive 2019/790) mandates stricter duties for platforms, such as proactive filtering duties. This disjuncture of legal standards poses significant challenges for global content hosts that have to juggle different systems for notices, takedowns, user remedies and liability.

8.2 Cloud Provider Policies

Cloud providers like AWS, Google Cloud and Azure bundle copyright and content usage terms into their AUPs. Such policies are frequently rooted in national legislation, (the DMCA in US-based companies) but can also include in-house developed processes for addressing requests for take down, repeat infringers, and disrupting the service for abuse.

For instance, with AWS, content providers can provide takedown notices through their DMCA agent portal, subject to the right to suspend accounts or take down content that terminates based on its terms. Microsoft and Google provide similar workflows, sometimes including automatic detection tools and dashboards for rights holders.

In spite of these mechanisms, Cloud providers are accused by critics of being reactive and inconsistent when being down to enforcement. What's more, including intermediaries they rarely have sight of encrypted or private content, which is why proactive policing is a challenge for them. Over-extension can also lead to the accidental removal of unrelated content, and the question of collateral damage and due process.'

8.3 Proposed Standardization Efforts

To improve interoperability and consistency across platforms, several industry and international bodies have initiated standardization efforts focused on content identification, watermarking, and metadata exchange. These include:

- **ISO/IEC 23000-13:2011** (MPEG Media Transport): A standard for packaging and streaming media content, including support for content protection and watermarking.
- **DDEX (Digital Data Exchange)**: A consortium developing XML-based standards for licensing, reporting, and digital distribution of media.
- **W3C Media Extensions**: Efforts to standardize encryption, access control, and playback APIs in web environments.

In the watermarking space, proposals have emerged for interoperable watermark identifiers and machine-readable copyright declarations embedded within digital content. These solutions seek to interconnect the content validation chain across cloud providers and enable automatic enforcement services (Ye et al., 2025).

But adoption of these standards has been patchy. The majority of content providers and platforms still rely on proprietary solutions that make it difficult to achieve interoperability and may constrain users to a particular ecosystem. Widespread adoption is likely to depend on better co-ordination between regulators, rights holders and technology suppliers.

Moreover, even for copyright enforcement purposes, there are legal constraints on how data about users may be captured and processed, for example under privacy laws such as the General Data Protection Regulation (GDPR) in the EU. Following the above example, user identity-attached, dynamic watermarking should be submitted to the principles of data minimization, consent, and information provision, introducing an additional level of problems in seeking for compliance (Software Engineering Institute, 2019).

9. CASE STUDIES AND INDUSTRY INCIDENTS

To assess the impact of usability concerns with copyrights on content distribution on the cloud, some real-life incidents must be analyzed. These examples illustrate common problems that confront content platforms and providers, including (1) enforcement difficulty, (2) non-compliance by users, and (3) technical circumvention of security features. It also shows how the tactics used to monitor, prevent, and respond to infringement are adapting to the increasingly distributed nature of these environments.

9.1 Netflix Account Sharing and Anti-Piracy Measures

Netflix is a leading global provider of streaming content and demonstrates how difficult it is to safeguard subscription-based media running in a hybrid cloud system. Netflix historically had turned a blind eye to password sharing between households but limited such behavior as revenue growth slowed during its assault on the traditional cable television model. This change in policy led to technology being developed in bulk, such as device fingerprinting, correlating IP addresses to other sessions and dependencies, and unique session tracking logic to limit unauthorized access.

Copyright-wise, it's a lesson on how, in this age of surprise, abusive use of content doesn't have to involve outside hackers but can come from misfiring user behavior. "Netflix (as well as other content providers) employs Digital Rights Management (DRM) that effectively "outsource" the issue of stream access misuse by legitimate users by using Google's Widevine, Microsoft's PlayReady, etc. While this does restrict access misuse from being implemented at the provider's end, DRM is only a part of the solution in this context. The platform has later integrated active monitoring and AI models to calculate behavior analysis, triggering users for asking to validate the device belonging to be in place to ensure the number of people using the device does not go against the user's intent.

This event highlights the need for behavior-aware enforcement models in cloud environments as well as the inadequacies of classical DRM systems in managing the multi-user access situations.

9.2 Adobe Document Cloud DRM Evasion

Adobe Document Cloud, a popular site for transforming and sharing collaborative documents, has received complaints about being unable to control downloads, printing or sharing of editable PDF documents – especially in the enterprise and academic worlds. Although embedded DRM controls are in place, users have discovered methods for bypassing protection via third-party plugins, screen capture/record, or inspection of browser.

Adobe responded by enhancing logging mechanisms, incorporating dynamic watermarking tied to user identities, and improving user access tracking. This case highlights the vulnerability of browser-based cloud tools to client-side manipulation and the importance of pairing DRM with persistent identifiers like digital watermarks for downstream enforcement (Padhi, Tiwari, & Ali, 2025).

9.3 Music Streaming Piracy via API Abuse

In the music industry, cloud platforms like Spotify and Apple Music rely heavily on APIs for device integration, playlist management, and third-party application access. However, these APIs have also been exploited to circumvent licensing rules and extract copyrighted material.

A significant case involved the use of unofficial apps that leveraged Spotify's public APIs to download high-quality audio tracks directly into local storage. These apps, often distributed through open-source platforms or unofficial app stores, exploited access tokens and user credentials to mimic legitimate user behavior, bypassing content encryption and playback restrictions.

Spotify finally rolled out higher rate-limiting, token validation, and server-side watermarking to stop these abuses. This case highlights how API misuse in cloud-native systems can result in massive copyright infringements and why enforcement should involve both access control and forensic capabilities for post-distribution tracking (CrowdStrike, 2024).

These cases show that copyright vulnerabilities aren't limited to theory —they exist in the wild, at a large scale and often pursue the invariants of cloud-native delivery and user behavior. Whether it is exposed by password sharing, API abuse, DRM circumvention, or another point of failure, these break-ins underscore the inadequacies of current enforcement solutions and underscore the need for a multi-pronged adaptive strategy to deter content abuse (CrowdStrike, 2024).

10. FUTURE TRENDS AND RESEARCH DIRECTIONS

The rate of development of cloud, AI and content delivery technologies is leaving current copyright protection regimes behind. As we move into a new era of decentralization, personalization, and dynamic intelligence, new approaches to rights management and even forensic watermarking will be needed. This section highlights the new trends, research frontiers, and innovative concepts that may revolutionize our understanding of content ownership, authenticity, and licensing enforcement in a cloud system.

Figure 4. Future trends in digital content distribution.

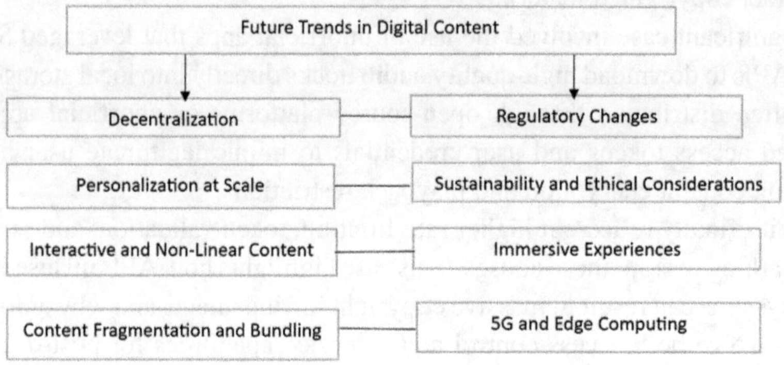

The future of digital content in this figure 4 is shaped by the duality of centralization and regulation. In the decentralized landscape, personalization is a keystone and starting to allow content to be hyper tailored according to your tastes and interests. Interactive, non-linear content is rewriting the rulebook on the standard linear experience, encouraging users to engage directly with the path of their digital experience. Content fragmentation and bundling the consumption behavior is changing and this gets reflected in the way the content is repackaged differently to serve different needs.

From a regulatory perspective, the importance of sustainability and ethics dominates and requires responsible content practices and ethically engaged engagement. Immersive world experiences are trending, using the latest technologies to construct more life-like, engaging experiences for users.

10.1 Cloud-Native Watermarking Systems

One promising direction involves embedding watermarking capabilities directly into cloud-native infrastructure, such as media processing pipelines, CI/CD workflows, and content delivery platforms. This "Watermark-as-a-Service" (WaaS) model would allow dynamic watermark insertion and validation at multiple stages of the content lifecycle—during upload, transformation, streaming, and even archiving.

Such systems could integrate with Kubernetes clusters or serverless functions to enforce traceability policies automatically. Research is also focusing on federated watermarking, where collaborative watermarking schemes operate across cloud providers without exposing sensitive content, maintaining both interoperability and user privacy (Padhi, Tiwari, & Ali, 2025).

10.2 Explainable AI for Enforcement

The use of AI in copyright enforcement will increasingly rely on explainable AI (XAI) to address ethical concerns and regulatory scrutiny. Traditional black-box models that flag or remove content without clear rationale can lead to false positives, platform bias, and reputational damage. Future models will need to provide interpretable justifications—e.g., similarity scores, matched references, or decision trees—that allow both users and moderators to understand enforcement outcomes.

10.3 Privacy-Preserving Tracking Mechanisms

As copyright enforcement intersects with global data privacy regulations (e.g., GDPR, CCPA), new research is focused on designing privacy-preserving tracking mechanisms. These approaches use cryptographic techniques such as zero-knowledge proofs, homomorphic encryption, and secure multi-party computation to verify content authenticity and usage without revealing identifiable user data (Pereira et al., 2022).

For instance, a content provider could verify that a user has valid access rights or that a piece of media contains a licensed watermark—without exposing the watermark pattern, the user's identity, or access logs. Such innovations are vital for maintaining trust and compliance in environments where watermarking is personalized or linked to behavioral analytics (Xue et al., 2024).

10.4 Blockchain Integration for Multi-Stakeholder Licensing

Future blockchain applications are likely to evolve into interoperable, multi-stakeholder ecosystems for licensing, royalty management, and distribution auditing. Instead of siloed smart contracts, platforms may adopt shared registries governed by creator consortia, distributors, and regulators. These systems would allow fractional ownership, automated revenue distribution, and real-time usage tracking—all embedded in tamper-proof ledgers (Xue et al., 2024).

Research is also exploring how non-fungible tokens (NFTs) and decentralized identifiers (DIDs) can complement copyright workflows. While controversial in public discourse, these tools offer programmable rights and traceable provenance that are well-suited to decentralized content sharing.

10.5 Deepfake and Synthetic Content Governance

As generative AI is a disruptive force in content creation, the need to prep against deepfake misuse and bad use of AI-created derivative works will only increase. We can imagine that in the future the enforcement will rely on hybrid methods using AI detection, digital watermarking and blockchain as time/datetime stamp, to confirm origin in source and derivative content.

Given the increasing adaptability of threats and complexity of law, and the increasing violence of public exchanges over the balance between public security and encryption technologies, the journey of technical innovation should be a journey driven by multidisciplinary synchrony, which stretches across cloud engineering, cryptography, digital law, and ethics (Software Engineering Institute, 2019). This complexity may be hard to accept, but in doing so the next phase of research and development can shape a future of a more secure, fair and transparent digital content economy (Symmetry Editorial Team, 2023).

11. CONCLUSION

The migration towards content distribution in the cloud has brought unparallel scalability, efficiency, and reach. But it has also brought with it new levels of difficulty when it comes to securing copyright content, leaving content creators, distributors and platforms open to increasingly sophisticated piracy and content theft, or to what is often in question: the legality of access. As we have examined in this chapter, such vulnerabilities are closely linked to architectural properties of cloud systems (e.g., abstraction, multi-tenancy and hybrid infrastructure), which have also rendered traditional enforcement models to be insufficient (Alquwayzani et al., 2024).

At the technological level, cloud computing systems are rife with misconfigurations, insider threats, and API exploitation – all of which can result in unauthorized distribution of copyrighted works. Digital watermarking and DRM are a fundamental approach to solve these problems, as they provide tools for traceability and usage enforcement. But their shortcomings–in multi-cloud or user-based workflows — have also spurred adoption of more dynamic, intelligence-based solutions such as forensic watermarking, AI-driven monitoring, and blockchain-based licensing.

With the development of generative AI and synthetic creation of content, the landscape is becoming even more complicated for traditional understanding of originality, ownership and infringement. Yet privacy regulations like GDPR require that enforcement mechanisms are transparent, accountable, and least intrusive. In this spirit, recent works on Explainable AI, Federated Watermarking, Privacy-Preserving Tracking are some promising directions toward future research (Xue et al., 2024).

In the end, robust cloud-based copyright protection calls for a multilayered approach to merging technical controls and powerful policy regimes (Xiao et al., 2021). International agreements, national laws and platform-level regulation need to be updated to keep pace with technical innovation, to ensure that fundamental rights in the digital environment are protected in cross-border contexts. Standardization and cross-sector collaboration will be important to align and scale these activities in a way that is both fair and interoperable.

REFERENCES

Alquwayzani, A., Aldossari, R., & Frikha, M. (2024). Prominent security vulnerabilities in cloud computing. *International Journal of Advanced Computer Science and Applications*, *15*(2). Advance online publication. https://www.researchgate.net/publication/378721981_Prominent_Security_Vulnerabilities_in_Cloud_Computing. DOI: 10.14569/IJACSA.2024.0150281

Bennasar, H., Essaaidi, M., Bendahmane, A., & Ben-Othman, J. (2021). A systematic literature review of cloud computing cybersecurity. Advances in Dynamical Systems and Applications, 16, 1883–1919. https://www.ripublication.com/Volume/adsav16n2.htm

Chauhan, A., & Shiaeles, S. (2023). A review of cloud computing security frameworks: Mapping industry practices to emerging trends. *Network (Bristol, England)*, *3*(3), 280–301. DOI: 10.3390/network3030018

CloudPassage. (2020, August 26). Shared responsibility model explained. Cloud Security Alliance. https://cloudsecurityalliance.org/blog/2020/08/26/shared-responsibility-model-explained/

Cotfas, L. A., & Rekeraho, J. P. (2023). Security monitoring in cloud environments using SIEM: Implementation and evaluation. *Applied Sciences (Basel, Switzerland)*, *13*(22), 12359. DOI: 10.3390/app132212359

CrowdStrike. (2024). Top 8 cloud vulnerabilities. https://www.crowdstrike.com/en-us/cybersecurity-101/cloud-security/cloud-vulnerabilities

Digital Guardian. (2023). What is digital watermarking? https://www.digitalguardian.com/blog/digital-watermarking

Fund, F., Hosseini, S. A., & Panwar, S. S. (2016). Under a cloud of uncertainty: Legal questions affecting internet storage and transmission of copyright-protected video content. arXiv. https://arxiv.org/abs/1602.01547

Lopez Velásquez, J. M., Martínez Monterrubio, S. M., Sánchez Crespo, L. E., & Garcia Rosado, D. (2023). Systematic review of SIEM technology: SIEM-SC birth. *International Journal of Information Security*, *22*(3), 691–711. DOI: 10.1007/s10207-022-00657-9

Luxner, T. (2023, April 5). Cloud computing stats: Flexera 2023 state of the cloud report. Flexera Blog. https://www.flexera.com/blog/cloud/cloud-computing-trends-flexera-2023-state-of-the-cloud-report/

Nafea, R. A., & Almaiah, M. A. (2021, July 14–15). Cyber security threats in cloud: Literature review. In *Proceedings of the 2021 International Conference on Information Technology (ICIT)* (pp. 779–786). Amman, Jordan. DOI: 10.1109/ICIT52682.2021.9491638

Padhi, S. K., Tiwari, A., & Ali, S. S. (2025). Deep learning-based dual watermarking for image copyright protection and authentication. arXiv. https://arxiv.org/abs/2502.18501

Pereira, F., Crocker, P., & Leithardt, V. R. (2022). PADRES: Tool for privacy, data regulation and security. *SoftwareX*, *17*, 100895. DOI: 10.1016/j.softx.2021.100895

Shackleford, D. (2022). SANS 2022 cloud security survey. SANS Institute. https://www.sans.org/white-papers/sans-2022-cloud-security-survey/

Software Engineering Institute. (2019). Overview of risks, threats, and vulnerabilities faced in moving to the cloud. Carnegie Mellon University. https://insights.sei.cmu.edu/library/overview-of-risks-threats-and-vulnerabilities-faced-in-moving-to-the-cloud/

Symmetry Editorial Team. (2023). Special issue: Symmetry in cloud security and cryptographic systems. *Symmetry*, *15*(11), 1981. DOI: 10.3390/sym15111981

Tu, S., Waqas, M., Meng, Y., Rehman, S. U., Ahmad, I., Koubaa, A., Halim, Z., Hanif, M., Chang, C. C., & Shi, C. (2020). Mobile fog computing security: A user-oriented smart attack defense strategy based on DQL. *Computer Communications*, *160*, 790–798. DOI: 10.1016/j.comcom.2020.06.019

Tu, S., Waqas, M., Rehman, S. U., Mir, T., Abbas, G., Abbas, Z. H., Halim, Z., & Ahmad, I. (2021). Reinforcement learning assisted impersonation attack detection in device-to-device communications. *IEEE Transactions on Vehicular Technology*, *70*(2), 1474–1479. DOI: 10.1109/TVT.2021.3053015

Waqas, M., Niu, Y., Li, Y., Ahmed, M., Jin, D., Chen, S., & Han, Z. (2020). A comprehensive survey on mobility-aware D2D communications: Principles, practice and challenges. *IEEE Communications Surveys and Tutorials*, *22*(3), 1863–1886. DOI: 10.1109/COMST.2019.2923708

Wikipedia contributors. (2024). Capitol Records, Inc. v. MP3Tunes, LLC. Wikipedia. https://en.wikipedia.org/wiki/Capitol_Records,_Inc._v._MP3Tunes,_LLC

Wikipedia contributors. (2024). Digital Millennium Copyright Act. Wikipedia. https://en.wikipedia.org/wiki/Digital_Millennium_Copyright_Act

Wikipedia contributors. (2024). Digital rights management. Wikipedia. https://en.wikipedia.org/wiki/Digital_rights_management

Wikipedia contributors. (2024). Digital watermarking. Wikipedia. https://en.wikipedia.org/wiki/Digital_watermarking

Xiao, X., Zhang, Y., Zhang, L. Y., Hua, Z., Liu, Z., & Huang, J. (2021). FairCMS: Cloud media sharing with fair copyright protection. arXiv. https://arxiv.org/abs/2105.08899

Xue, X., Shang, G., Ma, Z., Xu, M., Guo, H., Li, K., & Cheng, X. (2024). DataSafe: Copyright protection with PUF watermarking and blockchain tracking. arXiv. https://arxiv.org/abs/2405.19099

Ye, P., Li, Z., Yang, Z., Chen, P., Zhang, Z., Li, N., & Zheng, J. (2025). Periodic watermarking for copyright protection of large language models in cloud computing security. *Computer Standards & Interfaces*, *94*, 103983. DOI: 10.1016/j.csi.2025.103983

Chapter 2
Security Challenges in Cloud-Based Watermarking

Atul Agrawal
https://orcid.org/0009-0004-3601-3919
ITS Engineering College, India

Ashwani Kumar
https://orcid.org/0000-0002-2100-900X
Bennett University, India

Shikha Verma
ITS Engineering College, India

Mukesh Mann
Indian Institute of Information Technology, Sonepat, India

Avinash Kumar Sharma
https://orcid.org/0000-0001-6762-6778
Department of Computer Science and Engineering (CSE), Sharda School of Computing Science and Engineering (SSCSE), Sharda University, Greater Noida, India

Pashupati Baniya
https://orcid.org/0000-0003-1951-4469
IEC College of Engineering and Technology, India

ABSTRACT

Saving and securing digital assets in the cloud environment is a great concern due to the rapid growth of multimedia data and cloud computing. Digital watermark provides a powerful solution by identifying inaccurate brands in the digital content to verify and detect tampering. However, the use of watermarks in the cloud system introduces unique security risks, such as privacy violations, unauthorized access, and vulnerability to advanced attacks. This chapter presents a concentrated review of modern cloud-based watermark techniques, analyzing the trade-off between safety, performance and privacy. It examines methods in both spatial and transformational domains, discussing hybrid approaches using a cryptographic tool and evaluating their adaptability to cloud-specific dangers. To improve the strength, capacity and

DOI: 10.4018/979-8-3373-3785-2.ch002

invisibility of the watermark, ensure the user's privacy and calculation efficiency, the work identifies today's research interval and proposes future directions for safe and efficient watermarking in the distributed icing environment.

1. INTRODUCTION

Cloud-based watermarking has proven to be an important method of protecting digital assets and offers a scalable and cost-effective material safety solution in the dynamic digital ecosystem. Strong procedures for copyright protection, verification of ownership, and material authentication are now required due to the extensive use of digital materials and easy duplication and modification. (Tang et al., 2023). Because digital traits are unsafe for many risks, protective measures should be preferred. As a secret method of inserting data into digital media, watermark distributors and material manufacturers help to monitor how their work is used, and their intellectual property rights are protected (Zheng et al., 2021). To maintain the integrity and dependability of watermark methods, a separate set of safety problems should be solved by shifts in cloud settings. Although watermark authenticity can support claims, the question of liability in piracy is not immediately addressed. (Frattolillo, 2021). How easy is it to copy and change digital content (Yadav et al., 2020) on the security of intellectual property rights, resulting in the safety of intellectual property rights. A practical way to demonstrate the protection and authenticity of digital assets is through a digital watermark.

Scalability, accessibility and cost effects are only a few advantages of cloud-based watermarking, where watermark activities are performed on a Far server (Sharifara et al., 2013). By removing the need for local infrastructure and enabling watermarking services on request, the cloud-based strategy reduces operational overhead for material owners. However, there are some security risks associated with transferring sensitive data and watermarking processes to external cloud suppliers, which must be evaluated properly and minimized. Now it is easy to create and repeat digital content, including audio, videos and images, thanks to the increasing use of digital data as possible by improving internet technology and high-speed networks. Increasing concern about the preservation of copyright of digital content and commercial opportunities has expanded the digital watermarking industry. Cloud-based watermarks can address copyright problems, watermark attacks and safety problems by combining watermarks with hyperchaotic encryption (Li et al., 2020).

Data Privacy, data integrity and access to services are three main categories where security problems can be shared with cloud-based watermarks. Protect sensitive information from unwanted access, such as basic materials and watermarks, known as data privacy (Sujath and Satyanarayana, 2016). In the Ski context, data integrity guarantees that watermark material is preserved in processing, transport and storage (Kabir, 2021). Service availability ensures that even when it comes to hardware errors, network fractures or malicious attacks, watermark services will be reliable and accessible. A strong digital watermark technique is required to protect against illegal copying and protect digital assets according to the Copyright Act (Z. Chen et al, 2018). Each watermark system must meet the requirements for capacity, strength and irrelevance. In the atmosphere, the ideas of watermark technology and integrity are important for protecting intellectual property and maintaining data integrity. These safety challenges require a multidimensional approach to address cryptographic techniques, access control mechanisms, communication protocols and strong monitoring and revision processes.

1.1 Background

Digital Watermarking technology has become important for the protection of audio, video and image values (Chadha et al., 2011). Digital watermark uses include fingerprints, copying and access control, owner's identity, tampering detection, annotation, secret communication and protection against copyright. There are now many ways to insert watermarks into digital files to promote digital watermarking techniques. Fingerprints, using a watermark, can help identify the origin of illegal copies. Both visible and invisible watermarks are acceptable; However, for security and privacy reasons, invisible watermarks are preferable. A watermark is an unwanted mark on an image that can be used to identify the source and destination of the document by comparing the image with the original. The invisible water, labeled, designed to be unnoticed by human senses, is often preferred for the protection of copyright and material authentication. An invisible watermark teaching (Supiyandi et al., 2018) Can enter a log image to prove ownership by entering it. Watermarks must be effective in fulfilling the watermark target.

Figure 1. Representative real-time applications for digital watermarking

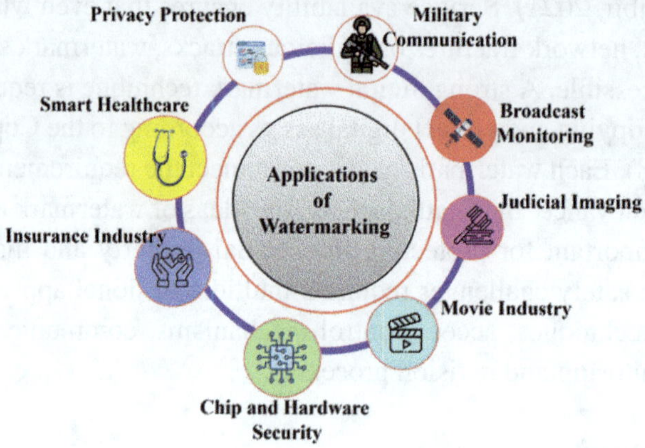

Table 1. Related approaches in cloud-based watermarking

Related Approaches	Goal	Objectives	Limitations
Digital watermarking in cloud environments	Protect digital content in distributed settings.	Embed imperceptible information to ensure ownership, authenticity, and traceability.	Vulnerable to cloud-specific attacks like data breaches, unauthorized access, and denial-of-service attacks.
Robust watermarking (image, audio, video)	Provide resilience against signal degradation	Ensure watermarks survive compression, filtering, resizing, and other manipulations.	May reduce perceptual quality; high computational cost.
Fragile watermarking	Detect content tampering or unauthorized modifications	Embed watermarks that are destroyed upon alteration to flag content tampering	Not robust to benign transformations (e.g., compression, scaling)
Semi-fragile watermarking	Balance tamper sensitivity and tolerance to minor transformations	Detecting meaningful changes while allowing harmless modifications	Requires fine-tuning to distinguish between attack and acceptable changes
Invisible watermarking for ownership proof	Covertly assert ownership and prevent piracy	Embed information imperceptibly within digital content	Difficult to detect or extract if modified; may face false negatives
Blind watermarking	Enable watermark extraction without original content	Practical in distributed cloud setups where original content is unavailable	Prone to errors, lower robustness compared to non-blind methods

continued on following page

Table 1. Continued

Related Approaches	Goal	Objectives	Limitations
Encryption-integrated watermarking	Enhance data security and watermark secrecy.	Combine watermarking with cryptographic techniques (e.g., hyperchaotic, DWT, SVD)	Increased system complexity; processing overhead
Provenance-based watermarking	Track the source and history of data in cloud storage	Embed provenance info via watermarking to detect malicious alterations	Difficulty in preserving the watermark across different formats or file compression
Dual watermarking with cloud embedding	Strengthen copyright and prevent unauthorized duplication	Layered watermarking with encryption for better traceability	Can be computationally intensive; vulnerable to synchronization errors
Blockchain-supported watermarking	Decentralized verification of watermark authenticity	Immutable storage and verification of watermark ownership	High storage and latency overhead; integration complexity

The change in cloud computing has completely changed how digital materials are handled, distributed and stored. Cloud computing finds an attractive alternative for content owners and distributors because it has many benefits, including scalability, cost, and access. To guarantee the privacy, availability and integrity of digital assets, skiing environments also present new security issues that need to be solved. Simple as the image works, it can be downloaded, reproduced and converted, increasing concerns for copyright violations (Xu et al., 2025). Data violations, internal formulas, attacks on refusal, and compliance problems are some of these difficulties (Patil & Shelke, 2022). The feature is another advantage of cloud watermarking, which allows users to watermark their data at any time and from any location (Makhrib & Karim, 2021). Thereforc, watermark technology is important to preserve the authenticity and integrity of multimedia content. One possible way to deal with these questions and protect intellectual property rights in the digital age is to include watermark techniques with cloud-based services. Table 1 shows the deficiencies of related techniques, and Figure 1 shows a specific collection of real-time watermark applications.

The first section introduces cloud-based watermarking for protecting digital content. Section 2 deals with digital watermarking methods and is subdivided by their data types, domains of insertion and robustness. In Section 3, Part 3, we explain cvery part of embedding and retrieving watermarks using a cloud service from content preparation through to verification. Robustness, data security, access control, resilience and key management are the main features of watermarking, and these are described further in Section 4. We discuss the ethics and legal issues associated with watermarking, related to copyright, privacy and AI in Section 5. In Section 6, the latest cloud-based watermarking techniques and trends are analyzed from the literature. Details of the main security issues related to watermarking in the cloud are found in Section 7. In Section 8, we review the findings and recommend future directions to enhance the security and dependability of cloud-watermarking.

2. TYPES OF DIGITAL WATERMARKING

When describing them, digital watermarking is divided by what kind of data is involved, the domain used to embed the data, how robust the mark is and how the mark can be extracted. Various kinds of digital works, including audio, images and video, are now safeguarded by using digital watermarking (Shukla & Tiwari, 2015). Digital watermarking seeks to mark information about copyright into the media, so it cannot be unfairly taken without permission . Technology changes the image, inscribing a mark to guarantee that it has not been altered. A watermark is a way to identify the owner and track the sale of printed products.

The method signals are embedded into data in digital watermarking, mainly relying on whether the data is an image, audio, video, or text. A watermark is added to digital images through image watermarking to defend their copyright and avoid unlicensed use (Z. Chen et al., 2018). The main goal of audio watermarking is to put watermarks into audio signals for similar reasons (Sinhal & Ansari, 2023). With video watermarking, copyright owners can embed special marks into videos to confirm their ownership and guarantee everything remains unchanged. Text watermarking helps add watermarks to text files to make sure any changes can be noticed and the document is legitimate. Users apply 3-D mesh watermarking to stop unauthorized use, confirm the authenticity of objects, improve content and maintain a database (Hamidi et al., 2019b).

Figure 2. Categories of digital watermarking techniques

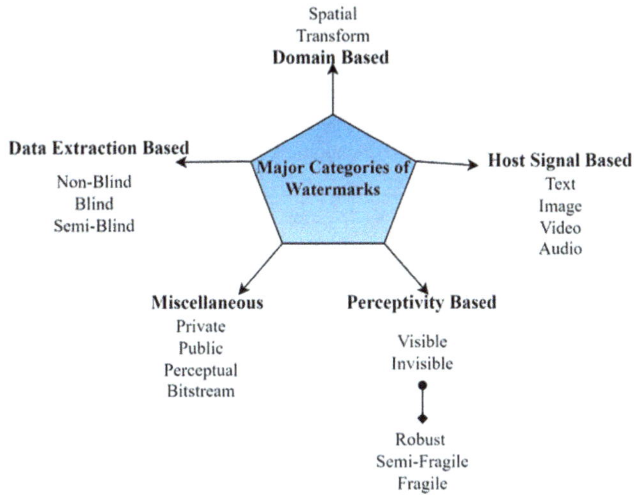

The watermark might or might not be easily seen, but it is supposed to be accessible to verify the identity of the cover's maker. On average, spreading the data through a watermark across the whole content increases safety, data hiding and how robust the watermark is. Watermarking approaches can be divided into spatial and transform domain watermarking depending on how they use the retrieval domain. Spatial domain watermarking places the watermark by changing the values of individual pixels in the image. To do domain watermarking, an image is transformed into the frequency domain and the watermark is put into some of the coefficients there. Based on how resistant the watermark is to changes, digital watermarking techniques are sorted into robust, fragile and semi-fragile groups. The Categories of Digital Watermarking Techniques are shown in Figure 2. The Classification of Digital Watermarking Techniques in the Cloud Environment is shown in Table 2.

Table 2. Classification of digital watermarking techniques in cloud environments

Type of Watermark	Description	Prominent Applications	Impediment	Reference
Robust Watermark	Withstand compression, filtering, and geometric transformations	Copyright protection, ownership verification	May degrade image quality; computationally expensive	(Hamidi et al., 2019a)
Fragile Watermark	Breaks or becomes distorted upon any modification or tampering	Tamper detection, document authentication	Not suitable for content undergoing benign processing like compression	(N. Singh et al., 2017)
Semi-Fragile Watermark	Tolerates minor distortions but detects intentional tampering	Content verification where lossy compression is acceptable	Requires careful calibration; less robust than robust watermarks	(D. Vizianagaram. et al., 2020)
Visible Watermark	Watermark is perceptible to users (e.g., logos or text overlays)	Branding, proof of ownership	Reduces visual appeal; easy to remove with editing tools	(Supiyandi et al., 2018)
Invisible Watermark	Imperceptible to human senses; embedded in digital signals	Digital rights management, secure tracking, and content integrity validation	Difficult to detect without proper extraction tools	(Chadha et al., 2011), (Supiyandi et al., 2018)
Blind Watermarking	Does not require the original content for watermark extraction	Cloud-based distributed systems, real-time content verification	May have lower accuracy or robustness	(K. U. Singh et al., 2022)
Non-Blind Watermarking	Requires original content during detection or extraction	High-security environments, sensitive media archiving	Less practical for cloud systems; requires secure original storage	(Department of ECE, Lendi Institute of Engineering & Technology, JNTU Kakinada, Vizianagaram India. et al., 2020)
Dual Watermarking	Two layers of watermarks, often with encryption	Layered protection in sensitive digital distribution	Increased complexity: it may be hard to synchronize	(W. Chen et al., 2021)

3. THE PROCESS OF EMBEDDING AND EXTRACTING A TRADEMARK USING A CLOUD-BASED SYSTEM

The cloud-based watermark system requires several important procedures to guarantee effective safety and verification of digital assets. Preparing digital material for watermarking is the initial stage. This may include pre-rose documents, movies, audio files or photographs adapted to watermarks. To guarantee compatibility with watermarking techniques, form changes, conversion and all other modifications can be part of the pre-treatment phase. Including digital information is the actual watermark and the following steps. The method uses a watermark algorithm, which provides an invisible code or notice to the material without significantly changing its conceptual quality (Zhang et al., 2023). The program carefully chooses where the watermark is to be placed in the material, payload capacity, flexibility and in-accuracy should be considered. There are many watermarking schemes proposed by (Kumar et al., 2014, Kumar et al., 2015, Kumar et al., 2019, Kumar et al., 2020) having good embedding and extracting.

A special code or identity is made under the watermark and placed in digital materials. This code may contain details of the owner, manufacturer or intended use of the material. Trade is considered under the built-in watermark between AGHAR and strength. High strength levels may require strong watermark signals, which can affect the alleged quality of the material. After that, the watermark information is safely placed in cloud storage infrastructure and guarantees that authorized users can access and see it. Access control, encryption and other security measures have been implemented to prevent unwanted access or change of watermark materials. Users can easily thank, restore and share materials for cloud platform functions and interfaces to store and organize watermark information.

A human interface or automated system that sends the watermark material to a cloud-based extraction service can begin the watermark extraction process and forcing the removal of built-in watermarks from digital materials to confirm its validity or ownership. fter discovering and recovering the built-in watermark signal from the material, the watermarked algorithm compares the extracted watermark either with the original watermark or a reference watermark located in the database. To find out if the watermark signal is present, the extraction algorithm examines the watermark material. Many strategies have been used in the program, including geometric changes, filtration and noise joints to combat potential deformities or attacks on the watermark. The stages involved in the extraction of the watermark and the built-in are shown in Figure 3.

Figure 3. Steps in watermark embedding and extraction

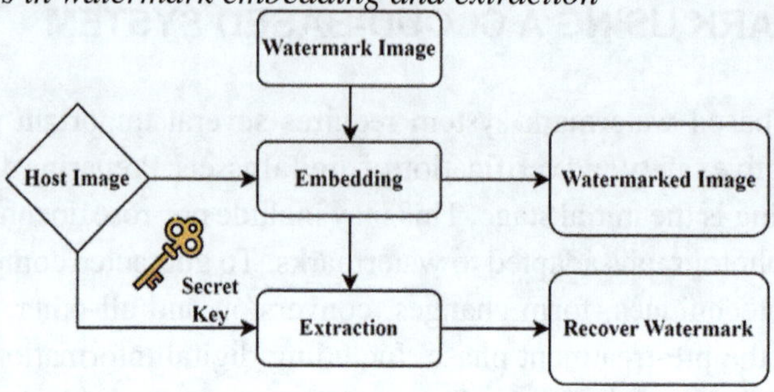

This system is extracted by comparing the authenticity of the watermark with a reference watermark. A well-known duplicate of the original watermark that is safely placed in the system is called a reference watermark. By comparing the extracted watermark with the reference watermark, the confirmation process states if the material is real and untouched. To confirm ownership and validity, the comparison process provides an equality score, also known as self-level, which indicates how close the extracted watermark and the reference watermark are. Date and type of transaction can be specified with a watermark (Ahmad & Cheng, 2018). Timestamp, user data and verification results are among the extensive reports that can offer system watermark and extraction processes (Chadha et al., 2011). Modeling how a watermark is embedded into an image signal with a balance between imperceptibility and robustness is shown in Watermark Embedding Equation 1.

$$I_w(x,y) = I(x,y) + \alpha \cdot W(x,y) \quad (1)$$

Where:

- $I_w(x,y)$: Watermarked image
- $I(x,y)$: Original image
- $W(x,y)$: Watermark signal
- α: Embedding strength factor

4. CHARACTERISTICS OF DIGITAL WATERMARKING

One method of including data in digital files shows that digital watermarking has many important symptoms that characterize its benefits and effects (Giri & Bashir, 2017).

4.1 Security Threats and Attacks

The availability, privacy and integrity of watermarking materials can be threatened by different types of security risks and attacks that are receptive to the cloud-based watermark system (Giri & Bashir, 2017). Cloud storage or processing resources used for malicious actor watermarking can be targeted, so unauthorized access is a serious risk (L. Li et al., 2021). They may be able to reduce the material conservation system by changing, replacing or removing the watermark as a result. Another major risk is data violations, because the hacked cloud infrastructure can reveal private data such as built-in data or watermark key (Shukla & Tiwari, 2015). Rejection service attacks can interfere with the availability of watermarking services, making it impossible for authorized users to view or process the content. In addition, built-in watermark or watermark key can be postponed through attacks on the side channel, which benefits from the information that was obtained during the watermarking process. In addition, unwanted attacks against the watermark system become more sophisticated due to the development of artificial intelligence and require a strong defense. The vector of the new attack is also introduced by special features in cloud settings, such as distributed collection and multi-friendly properties, which must be handled. Equation 2 shows how to assess the strength of bitterness during plum attacks.

$$BER = \frac{N}{1}\sum_{i=1}^{N} | b_i - \widehat{b}_i | \tag{2}$$

Where:

- b_i: Original bit of watermark
- $\widehat{b}_i$: Extracted bit
- N: Total number of bits

A major problem is the attack of collaboration, where many attackers collect their resources to eradicate or invalidate watermarks. In addition, it can be challenging to identify and solve security problems due to the dynamic and elastic nature of cloud services. These threats should be addressed with strong safety mechanisms, including encryption, access control, an intrusion detection system and frequent safety audits to protect the cloud-based watermarking system. A significant obstacle to privacy safety is to use of watermark techniques to solve copyright and medical security problems (Qasim et al., 2018). Pictures, regular lessons, sound and videos can all be digital watermarks, to show that it was originally owned by Copyright. The watermark complicates the defect sphere when a need for unauthorized access and strong security measures to prevent manipulation. Many attacks, such as compression, noise, staining and scaling, can be used while storing and shipping on a watermark (GE et al., 2022). To preserve the watermark's visibility, a watermark solution should be created to oppose specific image processing activities.

4.2 Data Security and Privacy

With a cloud-based watermark system, data security and privacy are important, especially when handling private or sensitive materials (Oconji et al., 2024). To prevent unwanted parties from accessing or understanding data, encryption is necessary to include both the original material and the watermark. Data violations and development can be avoided by using strong encryption techniques for protecting data in both transit and at rest. Access restrictions, which limit access to watermark resources and data according to the minimum privilege, are also important. To guarantee that only authorized users or services can perform special features, such as entering or removing the watermark, role-based access control techniques can be used. Before it is included as a watermark, sensitive data, including individually identified information, can be further preserved using computers or anonymous procedures. For cryptographic keys used in the watermarking process, secure main control procedures are required.

To keep away from compromise or undesirable get entry to, key distribution, storage, and technology must be done appropriately. Frequent internal checks and safety audits can help find weaknesses and guarantee the performance of facts, security, and privacy protocols. In addition, when processing non-public facts in the cloud-primarily based watermark gadget, it's vital to observe relevant data protection laws, consisting of GDPR or HIPAA. The amount of integrated data should be taken into consideration whilst a watermark device calls for certain residences, which includes energy and loyalty, as the records will become much less robust as they become larger; Therefore, there may be a desire to assess a commercial enterprise and closure between those aspects (Alshathri & Hemdan, 2023).

4.3 Access Control and Key Management

To guarantee that only authorized users can see and change the watermark material, access control and key control are important elements in safe cloud based watermark systems. To limit access to watermark resources and data according to predetermined roles and permits, strong access control measures must be used. Role-based access control allows them to complete the tasks that are only required for their responsibilities and gives users or groups special abilities. Before they reach important information, force users to present different forms, and add an extra layer of multi-promotion protection.

Protecting the cryptographic keys used in the watermarking process requires the distribution of secure key control procedures (Boato et al., 2008). Hardware safety modules or main control systems should be used safely to store keys, and cryptographic techniques should be used to generate them. Distributed keys should be done safely; Unsecured channels should not be used for significant broadcasts. The use of major rotational and cancellation processes will help reduce the possibility of compromised keys. In addition, to ensure that main control and access control procedures are effective in the protection of watermarks, frequent safety audits and penetration tests can help detect weaknesses in these procedures. A coding phase, a decoding phase and a watermark generating phase are the three main parts of any watermark system (Dukhi, 2011). Watermark structure includes an indication, which, when added to the original material, makes the watermarked material. Watermarks are a factor in assessing both flexibility for specific and specific signal processing operations.

4.4 Watermark Robustness and Resilience

In cloud-based watermarks, watermarking flexibility and strengthening are important factors that guarantee that watermarks can be detected even after many manipulations or attacks. The capacity of a watermark to carry standard signal processing processes, including compression, filtration or shape, is known as strengthening the strength without end or remarkable without becoming worse (Sujatha & Satyanarayana, 2016). In contrast, the flexibility describes the capacity of the watermark, which describes the ability to withstand male attacks in tampering or watermark insertion. The watermarking algorithm must be carefully prepared to enter the watermark in conceptually relevant parts of materials to achieve high strength and flexibility. This will make it impossible to remove the watermark without producing noticeable deformities (Liu et al., 2017).

Watermark data can be coded using error correction coding techniques, which improve redundancy and enable the watermark to be restored if it is lost or deformed. Watermark signals can be hidden in data using scattered spectrum techniques, which are comparable to people used in communication. Watermark systems should also be done to recognize and respond to watermark attacks, including collaboration or watermark assessment attacks. Because the watermarked built-in process must be undesirable, standard power shortages are inadequate and are expected to be resistant to a wide range of watermark attacks that go beyond normal jammers and channel distortions, deviations from standard communication theory (Barni et al., 2023). By mimicking various attacks and monitoring the detection rate of a watermark, standardized benchmarking tools and data sets can be used to assess the strength and flexibility of the watermark. The equation shows 3 noise volumes (including watermark) added to the original media using NR.

$$SNR = 10\log_{10}\left(\frac{\sum I(x,y)^2}{\sum (I(x,y) - I_w(x,y))^2}\right) \quad (3)$$

5. LEGAL AND ETHICAL IMPLICATIONS

The moral and legal effects of the extraction of watermarks and built-in special protection against copyright should be considered by the cloud-based watermarking system, regarding data privacy and freedom of speech. According to the Copyright Act, a watermark is employed to identify ownership and counteract illegal repetition or distribution of digital materials (Okonji et al., 2024). Watermarks should not be used, but rather to prevent improper use or instructional use of protected materials. When processing personal data, the watermarking system should follow privacy laws such as GDPR, which ensures that users are informed of the use of watermarks and can object.

It is important to fully understand important elements and processes, which results in an assessment of the cause that can be explained to the non-human AI system (Okonji et al., 2024). It makes a thorough analysis of architecture, training data, and algorithms used by the AI system, as an addition to special inputs and conditions to determine which affect its behavior (Okonji et al., 2024). Algorithm bias and discrimination should also be addressed to prevent specific demographic groups from being unevenly affected by the watermarking algorithms. In addition, it is necessary to evaluate and validate the AI model against the sanctioned benchmarks and standards. The mechanism should be placed for responsibility and openness so that consumers can determine based on watermarked material and understand how the watermark is used. To consider the opportunities and effects of these technologies, new moral and legal guidelines are constantly being created. To ensure that watermarking technologies are not used to violate freedom of speech or other basic rights, you must consider the possibility that the watermark can be used for secret monitoring or censorship. More accurate identification of produced media and revised information is now possible due to the rapid development of deep learning models.

To guarantee justice, the AI system must be tested on many populations, and the training data (Okonji et al., 2024) Should have rules for diversity guarantees. The need for transparency and clarity in AI decisions must be emphasized, especially in areas such as medical imaging, where complex images are interpreted by AI algorithms (Okonji et al., 2024). Justice and inclusion should be prioritized as a top priority in the AI development process, as addressing prejudice in data is necessary to promote equal results. Openness can increase by interpreting the AI decisions to health professionals (Okonji et al., 2024). In health-related decisions through informed consent, it is especially necessary to provide information to patients when AI treats patient data (Okonji et al., 2024).

The combination of watermark technology and cloud computing forms a complex set of safety problems that require careful assessment. Systems that depend on cloud infrastructure and are vulnerable to a variety of risks to treat watermark materials, such as malicious attacks, unauthorized access, and data violations (Cao, 2025). To reduce the potential effects of these weaknesses, effective risk management techniques are important (National Academy of Sciences of the Kyrgyz Republic & Kyzylkhojaeva, 2024). It forces strong access control processes, encrypts data and detects infiltration and use of prevention technologies. Establishing a clear legal framework to encourage moral and responsible applications is necessary to address the possible abuse of AI (Leal Filho & Gbaguidi, 2024). Openness, accountability and equity in AI applications should be prioritized peak of these frameworks, which should also emphasize the value of human monitoring and establish procedures to resolve prejudice and protect personal rights (Williamson & Prybutok, 2024).

By detecting false information and dishonesty, watermark approaches can be extremely important to improve AI security and reliability (Zhao et al., 2024). Watermarks can help distinguish between genuine and changed media by confirming the source and validity of AI-related information. Watermarking technology, which can be used to detect and monitor the spread of misleading information, to confirm its integrity and perfection to add unwanted markers to the data. Better safety and trust opportunities in digital materials are presented by the convergence of AI and watermark technology. AI can analyze and detect the water label so that the material can be automated, which can be replaced or tampered with. In addition, Copyright protection and material authentication may be threatened by the AI system trained to detect and eliminate watermarks.

Applying AI in different types of industries, including health services, depends a lot on public trust (Okonji et al., 2024). To address moral problems, ensure that the AI systems are safe and effective, and to determine the direction of AI, all are necessary to achieve and retain that faith actively, including the audience. The building ferment requires open communication about the boundaries and function of AI (Polemi et al., 2024). To maintain moral norms and preserve public confidence, it is said to be dependent on openness in AI, which is completed through initiatives such as "data-interested health and care technology for behavior for technology" (Okonji et al., 2024). To ensure responsible and profitable placement, the use of AI in the health care system requires a comprehensive approach that considers moral, legal and social ideas. Equity is required to promote ethical concerns, potential prejudices and justice to promote equity and avoid prejudice. AI's application in medical decision-making and resource allocation presents serious moral questions of prejudice and justice and emphasizes the importance of removing prejudice from data sets and algorithms. (Okonji et al., 2024).

Construction of confidence and encouraging the moral application of AI in the health care system requires reducing the AI system and protecting the patient's privacy and guaranteeing data protection (Abujaber & Nashwan, 2024). The AI system should respect the patient's rights, legal obligations and moral norms when involved in the health care system. To increase the results of the patient and pursue scientific findings, it is necessary to find a balance between innovation and moral ideas. When you develop and implement the AI system, moral thoughts are important. AI can increase medical treatment and provide useful data for patient care (Recharla, 2025). Using AI in the health care system presents many obstacles, including moral dilemmas, concerns about privacy and data protection, informed consent protocols, social inequality, medical consulting methods and sympathy shown by doctors.

To protect the watermarking data stored in the cloud, a strong safety mechanism such as encryption and access control must be in place. To address the moral concerns that AI has brought, the law and moral contours must be in place. A ubiquitous approach is necessary to reduce the moral and legal challenges associated with AI in the health care system (Jeyaraman et al., 2023) To attract legislators, developers, medical experts and patients. To solve privacy problems, algorithm transparency and potential prejudice, it is important to include moral standards in the AI system. To achieve this, accurate rules and specifications that prefer responsibilities and moral decisions must be established for the construction and use of the AI system in the healthcare system (Mennella et al., 2024).

6. LITERATURE REVIEW

In this work, security problems with cloud-based watermarking are fully reviewed, which also looks at previous studies and suggests future lines for future examinations. With intensive analysis of current research, target safety methods such as watermark, steganography and intense reviews of cryptography (Magdy et al., 2022) must be submitted. The first part of the article includes the basics of digital watermark, including use, properties and standard methods. After that, the special security problems that come in cloud-based watermark settings are examined, such as attacks on rejection, illegal access and data violations. The study examines safety measures imposed to deal with these problems, such as infiltration detection systems, access controls and encryption. In addition, the analysis explains the design criteria and system requirements by explaining sensitive watermark methods designed for 3D models. In addition, there are shortcomings within the modern-day characteristics that have been tested and offer feasible directions for similar research (Tang et al., 2023). The last goal is to provide a useful device for cloud-based total watermarking researchers and doctors who will assist them in creating a greater dependable and secure material protection gadget. Current online clothing distribution strategies require flexibility, safety, modularity and adaptability, all of which can be addressed through the watermark technique (Frattolillo, 2021). The observer additionally emphasizes the importance of watermarks to prevent copyright violations and ensure protection for digital assets.

If we use encryption as well as compression together in a watermark approach, it can help digital documents stay more secure (A. K. Singh et al., 2021). Watermarking of digital speech is rarely mentioned in literature because the main interest is in watermarks for images, audio and video (Sharma et al., 2019). Also, flexible videos highlight how powerful the algorithm matters a lot in watermark research (Sujatha & Satyanarayana, 2016). Data integrity can be ensured in some cases by using watermarking in reverse. It is necessary to use digital materials for the watermarked 3D model because they are being used and shared more often (Hamidi et al., 2019a; Hamidi et al., 2017). For good protection, multimedia content needs both watermarking and multimedia encryption. Because of how the Internet has grown and because digital design has become popular, more people are using digital forms to deliver key information. The 3D topology of the network, which is not uniform, and the severity of the attacks help to display three-dimensional geometry (Hamidi et al., 2019a).

Many types of watermark techniques are crucial for many safety reasons, such as ownership requirements and identity, as digital materials are easily copied and replaced (Tang et al., 2023). Efficient material management and delivery have been made possible by Cloud Computing; Watermarking technology is now important for the protection of intellectual property rights and ensures the validity of digital assets located on the cloud. To ensure the protection of ownership rights and the validity of digital content, the safety of the watermarking system must be evaluated. The 3D model cannot be watermarked by using similar methods as 2D images. In addition, copyright protection depends on the strength of the watermark, which means it will face harmful attacks. Safety assessment is required for watermark systems to protect ownership rights and maintain the validity of digital information. Three-dimensional computer graphics increase in significance due to their widespread use in digital archives, video games, entertainment, animation, MPEG-4 and web 3D (Nematollahi et al., 2017).

As a result, the 3D graphic representation requires a reliable watermarking system (Jani Anbarasi & Narendra, 2017). Different watermarks provide benefits, including high capacity, strong flexibility and a variety of abilities, including different water marking of different watermarking methods (Feng et al., 2015). In many multimedia applications, watermarks have become more and more common to prevent unauthorized copies and copyright violations. To fully achieve the benefits of cloud-based watermarking, a new set of security issues must be solved, such as data security and privacy, access control, key management and attack resistance.

Table 3. Recent research in cloud-based watermarking

Author(s)	Year	Focus Area	Methodology / Technique	Ref. No.
Ge et al.	2022	Document image watermarking with deep learning	Neural network-based watermarking	(Ge et al., 2022)
Singh et al.	2022	Medical image authentication (NIfTI format)	DST + Multi-scale Otsu thresholding	(K. U. Singh et al., 2022)
Nazir et al.	2021	Secure color image watermarking	4D Hyperchaotic System + DWT + SVD + FOA	(Nazir et al., 2021)
Dhanalakshmi et al.	2020	Dual watermarking with encryption	Layered watermarking with encryption	(W. Chen et al., 2021)
Chadha et al.	2019	Error-resilient watermarking in audio	Audio watermarking with error correction coding	(Chadha et al., 2011)
Jalil & Mirza	2018	Invisible watermarking for text	Image-based watermarking algorithm	(Supiyandi et al., 2018)

Hiding information about Copyright in compressed geographical graphics data is a method of protecting digital watermarking user rights (S. Z. Li & Jain, 2009). Reverse watermark guarantees the authentication of data and protection of sensitive information along with the confidentiality of data recorded.

Strong water marking algorithms are now important for Copyright security to deal with the growing problem of video or (Yu et al., 2018). Strong watermark techniques are also used to reduce digital material weaknesses. With the increasing use of digital content, Digital Watermark technology has become a solution to data security and copyright protection problems. Wavelet transformations, unclear inventory systems and multiplication representation-based blind water marking algorithms are successful in keeping the watermark in the material without distorting it even after different types of attacks (Liu et al., 2017). There are two main ways of documenting image watermarking: structural methods and methods that work with images. Structural-based techniques take advantage of the structure within text documents to mark them with watermarks (Ge et al., 2022). To make sure the watermark will not be removed easily, a powerful watermarks algorithm has been created that resists geometric distortions, filtration and compression. The use of watermarks lets people verify sensitive information and makes it hard for printed documents like banknotes and checks to be copied (Ahmad & Cheng, 2018). Regardless of whether a document is real or fake, having a watermark is necessary so the system knows where safety data or confidential information is hidden (Qi et al., 2019). So many people use watermarking Multimedia apps that they have become an effective way to stop copyright infringement a It is the sharp rise in commercial interest that explains the growth in information masking research in recent times (Krishnan et al., 2017). Using digital fingerprints and watermarks, organizations can spot and blame anybody who has broken copyright rules (Ali et al., 2022).

7. CHALLENGES OF CLOUD-BASED WATERMARKING SECURITY

Cloud-based watermarking needs different attacks to be solved if it is to excel. The handling and storage of sensitive data in the cloud make data security and privacy significant topics (Nazir et al., 2021). Authors Sujatha and Satyanarayana mentioned in 2016 that high security around access is needed to prevent unwanted changes to watermarks (Sujatha & Satyanarayana, 2016). Secure usage of the cryptographic keys in watermarking is possible with strong key management systems. Besides, the watermarking system should be able to resist different kinds of hacking such as changing, hiding or deleting the watermark. Apply security measures that look after the owner's interests as well as make sure material distribution depends on market forces, due to digital copies being very easy to make (Yadav et al., 2020). A digital watermark can help prove that data is valid and has not been altered (Rani & Halder, 2022). Any picture can now be adjusted and released so that others can see it. For this reason, the protection of digital images has captured a lot of interest (Kabir, 2021). We rely on methods that do not encrypt our information which means we must hide our private data. Because data and information have great value to us, their safety is growing more essential. Due to advances in technology, watermark technology is needed now to safeguard intellectual property which plays an important role in safeguarding digital assets (Sharifara et al., 2013). Using blockchain and double watermarking together provides a new method for protecting data against copyright, meeting the increasing demand for copyright online (Zheng et al., 2021). Since we live in a digital age, handling these security matters will help develop reliable watermarking and protection for digital data in the cloud.

Because digital data is used more often, digital watermarking techniques are needed and help with things like identity checks and ownership notices (Tang et al., 2023). That is why digital assets must be secured and using digital watermarks is key to safeguarding copyright (Z. Chen et al., 2018). There is a proposed solution for this problem: Audio watermarking that creates audio files using potential dangers. If someone attempts to use copyrighted material illegally, the audio watermark gives proof and can protect the original publisher (Chadha et al., 2011). Thanks to improvements in technology, sound marking is now used for purposes including identifying the owner, finding out if any changes have been made, reading fingerprints, access control, annotation, secret correspondence and copy and copyright checks. The growth of the Internet has increased the prevalence of multimedia access, which has increased the risk of illegal access and increased the sensitivity of digital images, videos and other materials for copyright violations (Mohammed et al., 2021). The rapid growth of Internet technology and high-speed networks has provided the plant production, replication and distribution of digital data (Makhrib & Karim, 2021). Digital rights management is a strategy for protecting Multimedia spiritual work through safe communication. In addition to protecting digital assets and related rights to online material distribution, watermarks can be used to ensure that users are attributed to their activities. Watermarking technology that can determine whether a user owns materials that were transmitted illegally by material suppliers can be used using a digital transmissions (Frattolillo, 2021).

8. CONCLUSION

An important development in the conservation of digital material is cloud-based watermarking, which allows you to handle rights and verify ownership in distributed and scalable environments. But for watermarking services to be private and safe, using Cloud Computing creates serious risks that must be tackled. The chapter paper investigates the tech aspects of using them in watermarking and cloud services and has uncovered important shortcomings, including wrongful attacks, compromises of privacy and unpermitted access. It has been decided that strong watermark technology, secure access control and encryption are important security measures to reduce these dangers. In addition, new capacities and moral problems are brought by combining watermarking with artificial intelligence, especially in areas of privacy, monitoring and algorithm transparency. The report also emphasizes the importance of following legal and government requirements, especially regarding the rules for digital rights management and data protection. Through intensive analysis of literature, the study summarizes current research trends, indicates malfunctions and proposes future research opportunities. These include the creation of effective main management processes, privacy protection frameworks and AI-resistant watermark technology. To fully use cloud-based watermarking, a complete strategy involving technological progress, moral obligation and legal protection is necessary. This strategy will make it possible to distribute digital information in a rapidly complex world of cloud computing.

REFERENCES

Abujaber, A. A., & Nashwan, A. J. (2024). Ethical framework for artificial intelligence in healthcare research: A path to integrity. *World Journal of Methodology*, *14*(3). DOI: 10.5662/wjm.v14.i3.94071 PMID: 39310239

Ahmad, F., & Cheng, L.-M. (2018). Authenticity and copyright verification of printed images. *Signal Processing*, *148*, 322–335. DOI: 10.1016/j.sigpro.2018.02.029

Ali, A., Mohamed, W., & Sayed, M. (2022). A Survey Paper of Information Hiding by Using Steganography Techniques. *Kafrelsheikh Journal of Information Sciences*, *3*(2), 1–23. DOI: 10.21608/kjis.2022.280155

Alshathri, S., & Hemdan, E. E.-D. (2023). An efficient audio watermarking scheme with scrambled medical images for secure medical internet of things systems. *Multimedia Tools and Applications*, *82*(13), 20177–20195. DOI: 10.1007/s11042-023-14357-6 PMID: 36685016

Barni, M., Campisi, P., Delp, E. J., Doërr, G., Fridrich, J., Memon, N., Pérez-González, F., Rocha, A., Verdoliva, L., & Wu, M. (2023). Information Forensics and Security: A quarter-century-long journey. *IEEE Signal Processing Magazine*, *40*(5), 67–79. DOI: 10.1109/MSP.2023.3275319

Boato, G., Conci, N., Conotter, V., De Natale, F. G. B., & Fontanari, C. (2008). Multimedia asymmetric watermarking and encryption. *Electronics Letters*, *44*(9), 601–603. DOI: 10.1049/el:20080492

Cao, L. (2025). *A Practical Synthesis of Detecting AI-Generated Textual, Visual, and Audio Content* (Version 1). arXiv. DOI: 10.48550/ARXIV.2504.02898

Chadha, A., Gangundi, S., Goel, R., Dave, H., & Roja, M. M. (2011). *Audio Watermarking with Error Correction*. https://doi.org/DOI: 10.48550/ARXIV.1110.1209

Chen, W., Ren, N., Zhu, C., Keskinarkaus, A., Seppänen, T., & Zhou, Q. (2021). Joint Image Encryption and Screen-Cam Robust Two Watermarking Scheme. *Sensors (Basel)*, *21*(3), 701. DOI: 10.3390/s21030701 PMID: 33498582

Chen, Z., Li, L., Peng, H., Liu, Y., & Yang, Y. (2018). A Novel Digital Watermarking Based on General Non-Negative Matrix Factorization. *IEEE Transactions on Multimedia*, *20*(8), 1973–1986. DOI: 10.1109/TMM.2018.2794985

Dukhi, R. G. (2011). Watermarking: A copyright protection tool. *2011 3rd International Conference on Electronics Computer Technology*, 36–41. DOI: 10.1109/ICECTECH.2011.5941952

Feng, X., Liu, Y., & Fang, L. (2015). Digital Watermark of 3D CAD Product Model. *International Journal of Security and Its Applications*, *9*(9), 305–320. DOI: 10.14257/ijsia.2015.9.9.27

Frattolillo, F. (2021). Blockchain and Cloud to Overcome the Problems of Buyer and Seller Watermarking Protocols. *Applied Sciences (Basel, Switzerland)*, *11*(24), 12028. DOI: 10.3390/app112412028

Ge, S., Xia, Z., Fei, J., Sun, X., & Weng, J. (2022). *A Robust Document Image Watermarking Scheme using Deep Neural Network* (Version 1). arXiv. DOI: 10.48550/ARXIV.2202.13067

Giri, K. J., & Bashir, R. (2017). Digital Watermarking: A Potential Solution for Multimedia Authentication. In Dey, N., & Santhi, V. (Eds.), *Intelligent Techniques in Signal Processing for Multimedia Security* (Vol. 660, pp. 93–112). Springer International Publishing., DOI: 10.1007/978-3-319-44790-2_5

Hamidi, M., Chetouani, A., El Haziti, M., El Hassouni, M., & Cherifi, H. (2019a). A Robust Blind 3-D Mesh Watermarking Technique Based on SCS Quantization and Mesh Saliency for Copyright Protection. In É. Renault, S. Boumerdassi, C. Leghris, & S. Bouzefrane (Eds.), *Mobile, Secure, and Programmable Networking* (Vol. 11557, pp. 211–228). Springer International Publishing. DOI: 10.1007/978-3-030-22885-9_19

Hamidi, M., Chetouani, A., El Haziti, M., El Hassouni, M., & Cherifi, H. (2019b). Blind Robust 3-D Mesh Watermarking Based on Mesh Saliency and QIM Quantization for Copyright Protection. In Morales, A., Fierrez, J., Sánchez, J. S., & Ribeiro, B. (Eds.), *Pattern Recognition and Image Analysis* (Vol. 11867, pp. 170–181). Springer International Publishing., DOI: 10.1007/978-3-030-31332-6_15

Hamidi, M., Haziti, M. E., Cherifi, H., & Aboutajdine, D. (2017). A robust blind 3-D mesh watermarking based on wavelet transform for copyright protection. *2017 International Conference on Advanced Technologies for Signal and Image Processing (ATSIP)*, 1–6. DOI: 10.1109/ATSIP.2017.8075525

Jani Anbarasi, L., & Narendra, M. (2017). Robust watermarking scheme using Weber Law for 3D mesh models. *Imaging Science Journal*, *65*(7), 409–417. DOI: 10.1080/13682199.2017.1359992

Jeyaraman, M., Balaji, S., Jeyaraman, N., & Yadav, S. (2023). Unraveling the Ethical Enigma: Artificial Intelligence in Healthcare. *Cureus*. DOI: 10.7759/cureus.43262 PMID: 37692617

Kabir, M. (2021). An efficient low bit rate image watermarking and tamper detection for image authentication. *SN Applied Sciences*, *3*(4), 400. DOI: 10.1007/s42452-021-04387-w

Krishnan, R. B., Thandra, P. K., & Baba, M. S. (2017). An overview of text steganography. *2017 Fourth International Conference on Signal Processing, Communication and Networking (ICSCN)*, 1–6. DOI: 10.1109/ICSCN.2017.8085643

Kumar, A. (2018, August). A review on implementation of digital image watermarking techniques using LSB and DWT. In Third International Conference on Information and Communication Technology for Sustainable Development (ICT4SD 2018), Goa, India, August 30–31, 2018.

Kumar, A. (2019). Design of secure image fusion technique using cloud for privacy-preserving and copyright protection. [IJCAC]. *International Journal of Cloud Applications and Computing*, *9*(3), 22–36. DOI: 10.4018/IJCAC.2019070102

Kumar, A., Ghrera, S. P., & Tyagi, V. (2014). Implementation of wavelet-based modified buyer-seller watermarking protocol. *WSEAS Transactions on Signal Processing*, *10*, 212–220.

Kumar, A., Ghrera, S. P., & Tyagi, V. (2015). Modified buyer-seller watermarking protocol based on discrete wavelet transform and principal component analysis. *Indian Journal of Science and Technology*, *8*(35), 1–9.

Kyzylkhojaeva, A.National Academy of Sciences of the Kyrgyz Republic. (2024). Analysis of criminal justice and cyber crime in the context of artificial intelligence through the lenses of international organizations. *Alatoo Academic Studies*, *24*(2), 349–361. DOI: 10.17015/aas.2024.242.28

Leal Filho, W., & Gbaguidi, G. J. (2024). Using artificial intelligence in support of climate change adaptation Africa: Potentials and risks. *Humanities & Social Sciences Communications*, *11*(1), 1657. DOI: 10.1057/s41599-024-04223-7

Li, L., Bai, R., Zhang, S., & Zhou, Q. (2021). A Robust Watermarking Algorithm for Video Game Artwork Based on Pose Estimation Neural Network. In Sun, X., Zhang, X., Xia, Z., & Bertino, E. (Eds.), *Advances in Artificial Intelligence and Security* (Vol. 1424, pp. 217–229). Springer International Publishing. DOI: 10.1007/978-3-030-78621-2_17

Li, L., Wang, S., Zhang, S., Luo, T., & Chang, C.-C. (2020). Homomorphic Encryption-Based Robust Reversible Watermarking for 3D Model. *Symmetry*, *12*(3), 347. DOI: 10.3390/sym12030347

Liu, J., Wang, Y., Li, Y., Liu, R., & Chen, J. (2017). A robust and blind 3D watermarking algorithm using multiresolution adaptive parameterization of surface. *Neurocomputing*, *237*, 304–315. DOI: 10.1016/j.neucom.2016.12.065

Magdy, M., Hosny, K. M., Ghali, N. I., & Ghoniemy, S. (2022). Security of medical images for telemedicine: A systematic review. *Multimedia Tools and Applications*, *81*(18), 25101–25145. DOI: 10.1007/s11042-022-11956-7 PMID: 35342327

Makhrib, Z. F., & Karim, A. A. (2021). Digital Watermark Technique: A Review. *Journal of Physics: Conference Series*, *1999*(1), 012118. DOI: 10.1088/1742-6596/1999/1/012118

Mennella, C., Maniscalco, U., De Pietro, G., & Esposito, M. (2024). Ethical and regulatory challenges of AI technologies in healthcare: A narrative review. *Heliyon*, *10*(4), e26297. DOI: 10.1016/j.heliyon.2024.e26297 PMID: 38384518

Mohammed, A. A., Jebur, B. A., & Younus, K. M. (2021). Hybrid DCT-SVD Based Digital Watermarking Scheme with Chaotic Encryption for Medical Images. *IOP Conference Series. Materials Science and Engineering*, *1152*(1), 012025. DOI: 10.1088/1757-899X/1152/1/012025

Nazir, H., Bajwa, I. S., Samiullah, M., Anwar, W., & Moosa, M. (2021). Robust Secure Color Image Watermarking Using 4D Hyperchaotic System, DWT, HbD, and SVD Based on Improved FOA Algorithm. *Security and Communication Networks*, *2021*, 1–17. DOI: 10.1155/2021/6617944

Nematollahi, M. A., Vorakulpipat, C., & Rosales, H. G. (2017). Three-Dimensional (3D) Watermarking. In M. A. Nematollahi, C. Vorakulpipat, & H. G. Rosales, *Digital Watermarking* (Vol. 11, pp. 81–99). Springer Singapore. DOI: 10.1007/978-981-10-2095-7_6

Okonji, O. R., Yunusov, K., & Gordon, B. (2024). *Applications of Generative AI in Healthcare: Algorithmic, ethical, legal and societal considerations. Preprints.* DOI: 10.36227/techrxiv.171527587.75649430/v1

Paramkusam, D. A. V., Geetha, M., Sailakshmi, K., Mohansai, M., & Sowmya, L.Department of ECE. (2020). Development of a New Blind Watermarking for Medical Images. *International Journal of Innovative Technology and Exploring Engineering*, *9*(9), 50–56. DOI: 10.35940/ijitee.I6845.079920

Patil, A., & Shelke, R. (2022). Digital Audio Watermarking: Techniques, Applications, and Challenges. In Nagar, A. K., Jat, D. S., Marín-Raventós, G., & Mishra, D. K. (Eds.), *Intelligent Sustainable Systems* (Vol. 334, pp. 679–689). Springer Nature Singapore., DOI: 10.1007/978-981-16-6369-7_62

Polemi, N., Praça, I., Kioskli, K., & Bécue, A. (2024). Challenges and efforts in managing AI trustworthiness risks: A state of knowledge. *Frontiers in Big Data*, *7*, 1381163. DOI: 10.3389/fdata.2024.1381163 PMID: 38798307

Qasim, A. F., Meziane, F., & Aspin, R. (2018). Digital watermarking: Applicability for developing trust in medical imaging workflows state of the art review. *Computer Science Review*, *27*, 45–60. DOI: 10.1016/j.cosrev.2017.11.003

Rani, S., & Halder, R. (2022). Comparative Analysis of Relational Database Watermarking Techniques: An Empirical Study. *IEEE Access : Practical Innovations, Open Solutions*, *10*, 27970–27989. DOI: 10.1109/ACCESS.2022.3157866

Recharla, M. (2025). Revolutionizing Healthcare with Generative AI: Enhancing Patient Care, Disease Research, and Early Intervention Strategies. *American Journal of Psychiatric Rehabilitation*, 98–111. DOI: 10.69980/ajpr.v28i1.70

Sharifara, A., Rahim, M. S. M., & Bashardoost, M. (2013). A Novel Approach to Enhance Robustness in Digital Image Watermarking Using Multiple Bit-Planes of Intermediate Significant Bits. *2013 International Conference on Informatics and Creative Multimedia*, 22–27. DOI: 10.1109/ICICM.2013.13

Sharma, K. U., Talan, P. P., Nawade, P. P., Ali, M. S., & Sharma, A. U. (2019). Digital Watermarking—An Overview and a Possible Solution. In Satapathy, S. C., & Joshi, A. (Eds.), *Information and Communication Technology for Intelligent Systems* (Vol. 107, pp. 447–455). Springer Singapore., DOI: 10.1007/978-981-13-1747-7_43

Shukla, D., & Tiwari, N. (2015). Survey on Digital Watermarking Techniques. *International Journal of Signal Processing. Image Processing and Pattern Recognition*, *8*(9), 121–126. DOI: 10.14257/ijsip.2015.8.9.12

Singh, A. K., Thakur, S., Jolfaei, A., Srivastava, G., Elhoseny, M., & Mohan, A. (2021). Joint Encryption and Compression-Based Watermarking Technique for Security of Digital Documents. *ACM Transactions on Internet Technology*, *21*(1), 1–20. DOI: 10.1145/3414474

Singh, K. U., Bhatia, S., Kumar, A., Kautish, S., Kumar, A., Basheer, S., & Hameed, A. A. (2022). A Robust NIfTI Image Authentication Framework Based on DST and Multi-Scale Otsu Thresholding. *IEEE Access : Practical Innovations, Open Solutions*, *10*, 132608–132620. DOI: 10.1109/ACCESS.2022.3225908

Sinhal, R., & Ansari, I. A. (2023). Machine learning based multipurpose medical image watermarking. *Neural Computing & Applications*, *35*(31), 23041–23062. DOI: 10.1007/s00521-023-08457-5 PMID: 37362569

Sujatha, C. N., & Satyanarayana, P. (2016). Analysis of robust watermarking techniques: A retrospective. *2016 International Conference on Communication and Signal Processing (ICCSP)*, 0336–0341. DOI: 10.1109/ICCSP.2016.7754151

Supiyandi, S., Lamudur Arta Sihombing, G., Kristian Siburian, H., Purnomo, A., Anam, F., Putut Laksminto Emanuel, E., Siregar, D., Halim Putra, A., Laumal, F., Brillian Kharis, O., Akhiruddin, A., Rosnatang, R., Marpaung, P., Ramadani, R., Andry Wikra Wardhana Mamonto, M., Monika Kulsum, N., Salle, S., Nurhayadi, N., & Rahim, R. (2018). Application of Invisible Image Watermarking. *International Journal of Engineering & Technology, 7*(3.2), 760. DOI: 10.14419/ijet.v7i3.2.18749

Tang, Q., Li, Y., Wang, Q., He, W., & Peng, X. (2023). A Dual Blind Watermarking Method for 3D Models Based on Normal Features. *Entropy (Basel, Switzerland), 25*(10), 1369. DOI: 10.3390/e25101369 PMID: 37895491

Williamson, S. M., & Prybutok, V. (2024). The Era of Artificial Intelligence Deception: Unraveling the Complexities of False Realities and Emerging Threats of Misinformation. *Information (Basel), 15*(6), 299. DOI: 10.3390/info15060299

Xu, J., Zhang, J., & Wang, J. (2025). Digital Image Copyright Protection and Management Approach—Based on Artificial Intelligence and Blockchain Technology. *Journal of Theoretical and Applied Electronic Commerce Research, 20*(2), 76. DOI: 10.3390/jtaer20020076

Yadav, N., Rajpoot, D., & Dhakad, S. K. (2020). Optimization of Watermarking in Image by Using Particle Swarm Optimization Algorithm. *2020 6th International Conference on Signal Processing and Communication (ICSC)*, 85–90. DOI: 10.1109/ICSC48311.2020.9182716

Yu, X., Wang, C., & Zhou, X. (2018). A Survey on Robust Video Watermarking Algorithms for Copyright Protection. *Applied Sciences (Basel, Switzerland), 8*(10), 1891. DOI: 10.3390/app8101891

Zhang, P., Li, J., Aslam Bhatti, U., Liu, J., Chen, Y., Li, D., & Cao, L. (2023). Robust Watermarking Algorithm for Medical Volume Data Based on Polar Cosine Transform and 3D-DCT. *Computers, Materials & Continua, 75*(3), 5853–5870. DOI: 10.32604/cmc.2023.036462

Zhao, X., Gunn, S., Christ, M., Fairoze, J., Fabrega, A., Carlini, N., Garg, S., Hong, S., Nasr, M., Tramer, F., Jha, S., Li, L., Wang, Y.-X., & Song, D. (2024). *SoK: Watermarking for AI-Generated Content* (Version 2). arXiv. DOI: 10.48550/ARXIV.2411.18479

Zheng, J., Teng, S., Li, P., Ou, W., Zhou, D., & Ye, J. (2021). A Novel Video Copyright Protection Scheme Based on Blockchain and Double Watermarking. *Security and Communication Networks, 2021*, 1–16. DOI: 10.1155/2021/6493306

Zhong, X., Das, A., Alrasheedi, F., & Tanvir, A. (2023). *A Brief Yet In-Depth Survey of Deep Learning-Based Image Watermarking* (Version 3). arXiv. DOI: 10.48550/ARXIV.2308.04603

Chapter 3
Blockchain in Digital Watermarking

Chakridhar Reddy Lokireddy
https://orcid.org/0009-0007-3780-9355
Department of Computer Science and Engineering (CSE), Sharda School of Computing Science and Engineering (SSCSE), Sharda University, Greater Noida, India

Princi
https://orcid.org/0009-0007-1877-760X
Department of Computer Science and Engineering (CSE), Sharda School of Computing Science and Engineering (SSCSE), Sharda University, Greater Noida, India

Pratyush Sinha
Department of Computer Science and Engineering (CSE), Sharda School of Computing Science and Engineering (SSCSE), Sharda University, Greater Noida, India

Ajeet Kumar Sharma
School of Computer Science in Emerging Technologies, NIET, Greater Noida, India

Renu Mishra
https://orcid.org/0000-0002-5211-8751
Department of Computer Science and Engineering (CSE), Sharda School of Computing Science and Engineering (SSCSE), Sharda University, Greater Noida, India

Avinash Kumar Sharma
https://orcid.org/0000-0001-6762-6778
Department of Computer Science and Engineering (CSE), Sharda School of Computing Science and Engineering (SSCSE), Sharda University, Greater Noida, India

ABSTRACT

The exponential growth of digital content creation and dissemination has raised significant concerns over content authenticity, ownership rights, and unauthorized manipulation. One reliable method for including trustworthy identification or copyright data in digital media is called digital watermarking. Digital watermarking

DOI: 10.4018/979-8-3373-3785-2.ch003

has long served as a robust technique for embedding imperceptible ownership or identity information into digital media. However, being centrally managed means copyrights can be lost, watermarks copied, and efficiency lacking in the system.

1. INTRODUCTION

In this era of digitization, digital assets are proliferating such that protecting them assumes paramount importance. Starting from social media posts to forensic images, medical records, or confidential documents, the authenticity and ownership of digital content are now at risk and prone to unauthorized manipulation, piracy, or misappropriation. (Wang et al., 2025) The rise of the exchange and sharing of digital media brings in its wake the menace of forgery, unauthorized replication, and metadata tampering. Not merely for content creators or artists but for police, health care, journalism, and academia, where keeping digital content authentic and undamaged is critical.

In the field of digital content protection, the digital watermarking technique has become a fundamental one. It allows imperceptibly embedding retrievable marks in media files for copyright protection, content authentication, tamper detection, forensic analysis, and user tracking purposes. (Senkyire et al., 2019) You can make watermarks visible or invisible or make them robust or fragile depending on your use case. Examples of fragile watermarks are very important for just spotting the slightest changes in images, while robust watermarks are intended to withstand standard media transformations like these.

Though important, watermarking cannot assure overall security when watermark data is stored in and eventually verified by centralized systems. (Bhadauria et al., 2021) Such centralized repositories are frequently susceptible to cyber-attacks, and administrative abuse and they are points of failure, prompting concerns about the trustworthiness and scalability of such systems. Furthermore, demonstrating authorship or validating the authenticity of content usually involves third-party intermediaries which not only contributes to higher complexity and cost but also creates susceptibility to dangers in cases where parties are located in different countries. (Senkyire et al., 2019)

A brief background of the existing watermarking frameworks is presented and promising enhancements to these frameworks via blockchain technology which is a decentralized and cryptographically secure ledger system, are proposed. Blockchain solves these critical challenges of tamper resistance and trust of digital content verification by guaranteeing traceability, immutability, transparency, and decentralized consensus. (Goud Allam et al., 2021) Blockchain being distributed, eliminates the requirement of central authorities where the various parties involved in the transactions can participate & verify transactions without any doubts. Being time-stamped, immutable, and publicly verifiable, each piece of information stored on the blockchain is very suitable for recording digital content ownership, licensing events, and watermark validation logs.

Blockchain and digital watermarking intersect to offer a fast, robust, and next-generation approach to managing digital rights and authenticity. This convergence serves not only to fortify watermarking systems but also to enable DApps that are able to automate licensing, rights transfers, and dispute resolutions through the use of smart contracts. Also, developments like decentralized file systems like IPFS (Interplanetary File System) complement the functionalities of blockchain with the ability to store large multimedia files securely and in a decentralized manner while retaining privacy and content integrity. (Meng et al., 2018)

This chapter is then on the integration of blockchain with digital watermarking where we provide a comprehensive and systematic framework for the protection of digital media. The book explores the basic concepts of both technologies, describes the architectural design of combined systems, and describes technical implementations and toolkits that can be used for real-world deployment. It also looks at numerous practical applications such as intellectual property management, digital forensics, regulation of AI-generated content, and secure media distribution. Moreover, it covers the current practical limitations as well as scalability concerns, legal implications, and necessary future research directions in establishing more resilient, scalable, and privacy-preserving digital ecosystems.

Through this exploration, readers will grasp a deeper idea of how blockchain can transform the very fabric of digital watermarking, towards more trustworthy, decentralized, and tamper-evident solutions for authenticity and the right protection conferring to digital assets.

2. OVERVIEW OF DIGITAL WATERMARKING

The term digital watermarking describes techniques of inserting information into a digital signal (in the broad sense) such as an image, a video, an audio signal, textual data, and so on, and the possibility of extracting or detecting this information to assert something about the content, for instance, its authenticity, its origin and so on. Embedded watermark is the embedded watermark that typically contains the metadata: the identity of the creator, timestamp, copyright information, license terms, or unique content identifiers. Watermarking techniques aim to become imperceptible to human perception, but robust to normal processing and malicious attacks. (Meng et al., 2018)

Since watermarking is meant to establish ownership and integrity, without deteriorating the quality of the original media too much, is the primary objective. With multimedia content being more and more propagated through open and unsafe channels such as the Internet, watermarking works as an invisible guardian, embedding copyright ownership information within the very content itself. The embedded watermark is tamper-evident proof of authenticity and source of an audio file when brought to challenge in legal, academic, or public spheres. (Raj et al., 2024)

Figure 1. Flowchart of watermark embedding and extraction process

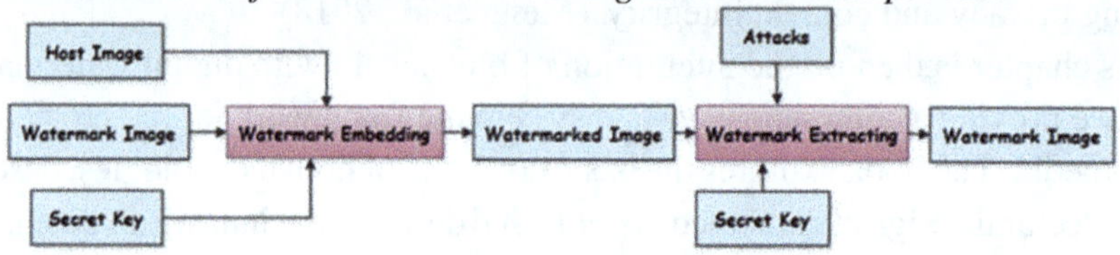

First, any digital watermarking system has two major processes: Watermark Embedding and Watermark Extraction. According to Figure 1., the hosting phase takes a host image (or other multimedia content), a watermark image (or data), and a secret key. These image parts are further processed to create a watermarked image. Then this watermarked image can be submitted to a variety of operations: compression, scaling, and even intentional attacks. The secret key and the possibly modified watermarked image are combined to retrieve the watermark and verify the content of the image by the extraction process.

2.1 Types of Watermarks

- **Visible and invisible:** Perceptible to the human eye or ear or not: visible watermarks contrast with the invisible ones. For instance, a watermark is a visible one that includes, for example, a logo superimposed on a photograph or the logo of the broadcaster overlaid over a TV program. On the contrary, invisible watermarks are embedded in the content by using complex mathematical transforms and cannot be detected without having special detection tools or algorithms. Visible watermarks are deterrents for the usage of copyrighted work, whereas invisible watermarks are preferred for covert protection forensic tracking and copyright validation purposes. (Senkyire et al., 2019)

- **Engineering of Robust vs. Fragile:** Robust watermarks are designed to survive the commonly used processes like lossy compression, resizing or noise addition, and format conversion. In cases where there is a probability that content is going to be shared or transformed frequently (e.g. social media sharing, online distribution, etc.) these are very important. On the other hand, fragile watermarks are very sensitive to any type of manipulation. First, they are mainly utilized as integrity verification, given that a slight change to the content can modify or damage the watermark and, thus, indicate whether the content has been tampered with or edited by an unauthorized person. (Meng et al., 2018)
- **Spatial Domain vs. Frequency Domain:** Spatial domain techniques work directly with the pixel or sample values of the digital content to embed watermarks; frequency domain techniques modify a representation of the digital content in the frequency domain both in time and space. These are easier to implement, though, but are less robust to signal processing attacks. First, the content is transformed in a frequency domain via Discrete Cosine Transform (DCT), Discrete Wavelet Transform (DWT), or Singular Value Decomposition (SVD) and then the watermark is embedded in its coefficients. Frequency domain watermarking has been widespread in professional and academic areas for its robustness against a variety of attacks and improved robustness. (Senkyire et al., 2019)

2.2 Applications of Digital Watermarking

There is a large utility for Digital Watermarking in many sectors and each sector has its own needs for protection and validation of in some cases extremely valuable content.

- Digital Watermarking for Copyright Protection is a tool to establish who owns the digital data and who has the right to its reproduction for copyright protection. With legally binding identity and creation metadata embedded into creative works, content creators and copyright holders can prove their rights in the event of a dispute/litigation. (Senkyire et al., 2019)
- Content Authentication ensures that content is not changed in any manner during transmission, being stored, and or being processed like in research evidence and journalism. Authentications use watermarks to allow checking content integrity, making sure that unauthorized modifications are not made. (Wang et al., 2025)
- Watermarking is used in media and advertising industries to track the use of the content in terms of platform and geography, that is Broadcast Monitoring.

Embedded watermarks enable broadcasters and advertisers to collect data on when and where media content has been aired so as to be able to determine accurate media royalty and revenue. (Meng et al., 2018)

- The application of Digital Watermarking in Medical Imaging involves the use of watermarking techniques in medical images such as X-rays or MRIs to save valuable patient information and protect it from tampering. Diagnosing image metadata is embedded directly in the image to ensure bo th data and the image remain bound and verifiable. (Senkyire et al., 2019)
- Fragile watermarking is used by law enforcement and forensic units to identify crime scene images, surveillance footage, and scanned documents by investigator IDs, time stamps, and case references. These steps guarantee chain of custody integrity and boost admissibility in the courtroom by presenting digital proof of picture innocence. (Senkyire et al., 2019)
- In research fields watermarks can be embedded into thesis files, research data, or publications to prevent plagiarism and unauthorized use of the research. Traceability and compliance can additionally be guaranteed by verification of Blockchain-enabled watermarks. (Meng et al., 2018)

Although they can be widely applied, most conventional watermarking systems are based on centralized infrastructures to perform watermark verification, metadata storage as well as storage and access checking. But hacking of these systems, unauthorized access to data, loss due to server failure, and the lack of transparency are a few of the things they are vulnerable to. Furthermore, authorship or content authenticity may also be proven based on the availability (and integrity) of other external databases or third-party records that are not always reliable. (Olusegun et al., 2023)

To solve these problems, some newer approaches are now seeking to leverage decentralized technologies such as blockchain to store the watermark hash in a provably unalterable manner, verify digital ownership, and do away with centralized players in the picture. With this integration, the ownership and authenticity of given content can be cryptographically verified despite the content being copied or distributed, since it relies on an immutable blockchain ledger. A synergy between watermarking and blockchain, therefore, is opening up novel frontiers in the secure lifecycle management of digital content. (Wang et al., 2025)

3. FUNDAMENTALS OF BLOCKCHAIN TECHNOLOGY

Blockchain is a recording system that uses distributed computers and is secure, transparent, and impossible to tamper with because of its decentralized nature. A blockchain keeps growing with new records called blocks which are linked and protected using cryptography. A block always has a timestamp, the hash result of the previous block, and a list of transactions. This group of blocks creates a steady and unchangeable list of transactions that exists on a network of computers, known as nodes. (Goud Allam et al., 2021)

Blockchain's major strength lies in how it ensures that digital files are kept unchanged and all blocks are verified by the majority of parties on the network before updates can take place. As a result, blockchain is best used in cases where people need to share information safely, keep it traceable, and rely on trust despite not completely trusting everyone involved. (Bhadauria et al., 2021)

3.1 Key Characteristics

- **Immutability:** The records on the blockchain cannot be deleted or changed after being recorded. Changes to the blockchain are impossible since they involve cryptographic functions and group agreement. Attempting to change old data would need changing the following blocks which takes too much time and energy from the majority of miners. Because data cannot be altered in blockchain, it offers good protection for auditing, record-keeping, and proving the existence of things. (Bhadauria et al., 2021)
- **Decentralization:** Blockchain uses many computers called nodes to handle the ledger, ensuring that no one person is in charge. A complete or partial copy of the ledger is saved by each node which also joins in reaching an agreement on new ledger additions. A decentralized approach makes the system safer, helps avoid failures from a single source, and prevents others from controlling it. (Goud Allam et al., 2021)
- **Transparency:** All the transactions carried out on a public blockchain are open to everyone involved. Even when a blockchain is permitted, accountability, trust, and verifiability are supported by letting all users view the same ledger. It is especially useful in supply chain, financial, and governing activities since it makes fraud less likely and earns the trust of stakeholders. (Bhadauria et al., 2021)
- **Security:** Blockchain makes use of technologies such as digital signatures, Merkle trees, and hash functions to secure its stored data. Only authorized people and programs can start or accept transactions through public-key cryptography. Also, with PoW, PoS, and Practical Byzantine Fault Tolerance such platforms make sure each transaction is genuine and avoid any instances of double-spending or fraud. (Goud Allam et al., 2021)
- **Consensus Mechanisms:** Blockchain works thanks to the important consensus mechanisms used in its algorithms. The process used in Bitcoin called

PoW requires nodes to solve tough mathematical puzzles before they can accept transactions and add new blocks. Having more cryptocurrency and staking it in PoS makes a participant more powerful in Ethereum 2.0. PBFT is designed to help private and consortium blockchains make sure that selected trusted nodes reach agreement Each consensus mechanism offers trade-offs in terms of scalability, energy efficiency, and security. (Bhadauria et al., 2021)

3.2 Blockchain Types

There are three main types of blockchain networks, and each one is used for different operational and governance purposes. (Goud Allam et al., 2021)

- **Public Blockchains:** They are public and open to anyone, so anyone can join them as a node, look at the transactions and verify new blocks. Common examples are Bitcoin, Ethereum, and Litecoin. Although public blockchains are trusted and clear, they have to deal with the obstacle of slower scalability due to many people participating.
- **Private Blockchains:** Since they are operated by only one organization, private blockchains won't let many people take part. These networks are perfect choices for internal business applications like auditing, managing the supply chain, and synchronizing data. Decentralization is what they sacrifice in return for upgraded performance and privacy.
- **Consortium Blockchains:** Also known as federated blockchains, consortium blockchains are regulated by a group of organizations. They feature a collective process in which verified participants look after the jointly shared ledger. Hyperledger Fabric and R3 Corda are well-known when it comes to consortium blockchains.

Every kind of blockchain has its benefits for certain purposes. Public blockchains are suitable for open and widely distributed apps, private blockchains for inside business use, and consortium blockchains for teams composed of many trusted organizations.

3.3 Smart Contracts and IPFS

- Smart contracts allow rules and deals to be enforced automatically by the computerized system once the conditions are met. Their transparent and predetermined operation takes away the need for mediators, as it avoids possible conflicts. Different industries use smart contracts.

- IPFS means InterPlanetary File System and it is a P2P technology for distributing data across the network instead of storing it on one central server. Instead of relying on location to find files (as in traditional web pages), in IPFS, each file is determined by a special cryptographic hash. These ways of organizing business provide a number of benefits for companies. (Senkyire et al., 2019)
- Using digital watermarking, IPFS safely stores images, videos, and documents, and their hash records are kept on the blockchain. As a result, digital assets enjoy high authenticity, are easily accessible and it is easy to trace who owns them, keeping on-chain storage costs down.

3.4 Real-World Use Cases and Relevance to Watermarking

Here, blockchain technology is combined with watermarking to help secure and verify identity documents and no one can forge or change them easily as shown in Figure 2.

- **Safety of Health Information:** Imaging data is watermarked with patient details and saved on IPFS through a blockchain network which guarantees their safety and adherence to Regulations.
- **Intellectual Property Rights (IPR):** Works of art, academic documents, and media can be marked and attached to a blockchain entry, making it easy for the author to prove their work and when it was put online. (Bhadauria et al., 2021)
- **Using a chain of custody in law enforcement:** With watermarking, every action with the crime scene and digital evidence can be recorded on a blockchain for proof it is all intact.
- Within the supply chain, products can be given watermarked images and attached specifications on the blockchain so that buyers are able to validate their authenticity instantly. (Meng et al., 2018)

Figure 2. Features on blockchain

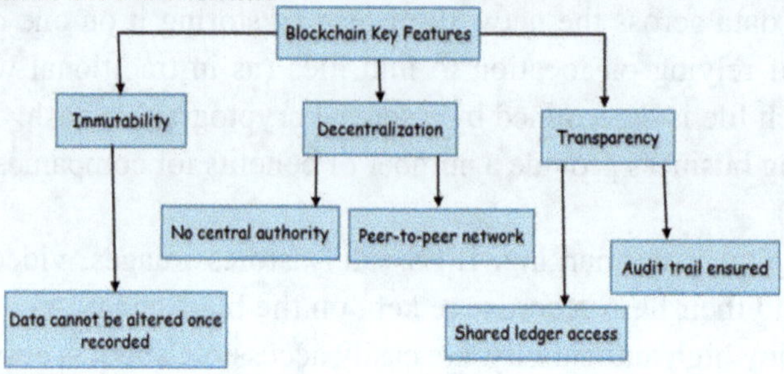

4. SYNERGY: BLOCKCHAIN-ENHANCED WATERMARKING FRAMEWORK

Integrating blockchain with digital watermarking results in a secure, verifiable, and decentralized framework for digital content protection. When blockchain and digital watermarking are applied together, they make it possible to protect digital content securely, verify data, and use a peer-to-peer process. Because of this partnership, many issues with traditional methods such as that they depend heavily on central authorities, are difficult to prove ownership of content, have few audit trails, and can be easily exploited, are being fixed. Thanks to watermarking and blockchain, we secure the authenticity, origin, and correctness of the digital content that is being used as shown in Figure 3.

Within the framework, digital rights are verified and managed in a decentralized way which also includes automatic tracking and simple proof of ownership when united with smart contracts and IPFS. Because of both, it is possible to control content rights and ensure sharing files remains safe and licenses are clear everywhere. (Meng et al., 2018)

4.1 Framework Components

- **Watermark Embedding:** The beginning phase involves putting a secure, almost invisible watermark on the image or media file. DWT, DCT, or DWT-DCT are used to make invisible watermarks from the content's frequency components. Because of these approaches, the watermark can withstand common actions like resizing, making the file smaller, or switching the file format.

- **Metadata Extraction and Hashing:** After embedding the watermark, necessary details such as the content's ID, who created it, and a hash code of the media are extracted. Computing a perceptual hash (for picture-related info) or a cryptographic hash (SHA-256, as one example) forms a distinct digital sign for the watermarked file. Thus, the hash serves as the main form of identification used for registering values in the blockchain. (Goud Allam et al., 2021)
- **Blockchain Registration:** Using the smart contracts and libraries of Ethereum and ethers.js, the details of the watermark hash, IPFS hash (for off-chain content storage), user's wallet address, as well as the timestamp, are securely recorded on the blockchain. Thanks to crypto verification and unchangeable data, any attempt to misrepresent ownership or edit the content can easily be found. (Goud Allam et al., 2021)
- **Content Verification:** This process includes taking the embedded watermark out of a file, calculating its hash, and checking if it matches the hash kept on the blockchain. Hashes that match is proof that the original and received content are valid. The process is made smoother when web DApps work with smart contracts and nodes on the IPFS.

4.2 Advantages

- **Tamper Resistance:** Since the blockchain's data cannot be changed, any alteration in the media will create a discrepancy with the stored hash. This measure identifies and prevents tampering with the contract by unauthorized people.
- **Decentralized Trust:** Traditionally, verifying watermarks needs a main authority or a reliable third-party service. Blockchain ensures that trust is shared among many peers which means there is no single weakness and the system stays strong.
- **Transparency and Auditability:** Since blockchain makes every activity visible and traceable, there is an open record of every registered media item. Metadata is always included with every transaction, and this information can be independently checked by the parties concerned.
- **Legal Enforceability:** A date on the blockchain and digital signatures give solid proof in matters of copyright and intellectual property. There are better chances of digital rights being enforced in court because of the connection proven between content, owner, and creation time.
- **Automated Rights Management:** With the help of smart contracts, once set conditions lead to automatic payments and the use of copyrights. It helps creators easily profit from their work and get the revenue they deserve in a straightforward way and on time.

4.3 Technical Implementation

A practical deployment of this framework involves the following stack:

- **Ethereum Blockchain and Smart Contracts**: All ownership credentials on the Ethereum Blockchain are dependent on smart contracts written with Solidity to check and validate them. They safely save the content hash from IPFS, watermark hash, address from the user's wallet, and the current date and time.
- **IPFS (Interplanetary File System)**: Due to the large amount of data in digital media, storing them on the blockchain alone is not practical. All the watermarked files are stored using IPFS and just the content address (hash) sits on the blockchain. It makes it possible for businesses to grow, remain accessible, and operate at low costs.
- **Web DApp Interface with MetaMask Integration**: Users can use the framework by connecting their MetaMask wallet to a DApp. Users can use MetaMask to secure their deals and deal with blockchain applications.
- **ethers.js and IPFS API Integration**: The use of ethers.js is included to connect with the blockchain, while the IPFS API handles loading, accessing, and confirming media files in DApp modules.
- **Backend Validation Service**: A backend service can be used to regularly search and validate watermarked content across all available platforms which helps reduce piracy.

To sum up, this framework based on blockchain and watermarking gives strong protection to digital files without being difficult to use. Because of this, trusted enforcement becomes possible for all sides, allowing artists, publishers, legal groups, and consumers to transact safely.

Figure 3. Architecture of integrated blockchain-watermarking system with IPFS and smart contracts

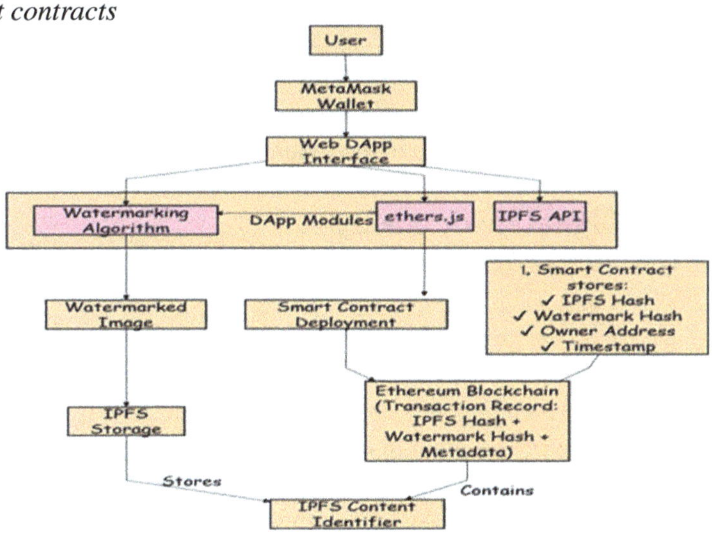

5. APPLICATIONS AND CASE STUDIES

Blockchain-based digital watermarking is more than a concept; it is used and noticed in many industries. Through preserving a consistent record of media provenance and who owns it, Web3 and Blockchain allow for increased transparency, honesty, and accountability online. Being consistent with the previous part, the following sections discuss various areas where blockchain-based watermarking leads to improvements in security and performance.

5.1 The Rights To Intellectual Property (IPR)

People working in the arts, design, music, writing, and content creation are now more challenged to protect their intellectual property online. Since it's easy to duplicate, adjust, and share digital material, standard IPR methods usually cannot keep up. Watermarking data with the help of blockchain offers a secure and widely available answer to the issue.

Uniquely marking images, songs, animations or documents is possible through the use of perceptual or cryptographic methods by the creators. When everything is ready, the hash of the watermarked content and metadata such as the creator's wallet, the title, and the time are stored on the blockchain. This record shows that authorship cannot be changed or disputed. (Bhadauria et al., 2021)

Automation through smart contracts permits proper handling of licenses and rights, adjustable pricing, limited access to media, and clear payment of royalties. As an illustration, an artist can use an NFT to create digital artwork and combine the watermark hash with licensing terms in the smart contract. (Bhadauria et al., 2021)

5.2 Capturing Digital Evidence By Means Of Digital Photographs

Forensic science relies on digital watermarking a lot, mainly when dealing with secret photos gathered at crime sites. Courts often require digital evidence to be reliable and unaltered which depends on its originality and how it was handled.

Such techniques make it possible to insert case IDs, time posted, location, and officer names into images when they are recorded. Since these watermarks are very sensitive to changes, it is simple to see if anything in the document has been tampered with by mistake or on purpose. In this context, the blockchain acts as a reliable record by adding hashes of the watermarked images together with their metadata.

By using blockchain, the metadata makes it possible for investigators, lawyers, and judges to confirm that a displayed image is exactly the same as the original and has not been altered. The system can facilitate better teamwork among different law enforcement agencies in cases where sharing data between them is not easy.

5.3 Supervising Content Made by AIGC

Because of tools like DALL·E, ChatGPT, and GANs, AI-generated content is now common which makes it difficult to check if the content is real or not. Finding out what is real and what is labeled as artificial can be more challenging with the appearance of deep-fake videos, realistic news, or computer-generated pictures.

Through watermarking, it's possible to insert unnoticeable but provable identification into content right after creation. They generally display AI tool names, the date they were created, text prompt descriptors, and the place they were made. Thanks to blockchain, every generated item gets a special hash and its metadata is kept as part of the on-chain data.

Thanks to this method, all parties can check the background of digital content. It plays a key role in preventing misconnections by checking and confirming where messages and facts come from in various fields.

5.4 Media Distribution and Piracy Control

Nowadays, with everything streamed and shared around the world, unlawful streaming and distribution of media is a common problem. Both security issues and a lack of transparency are common in mainstream DRM protection systems.

Blockchain and digital watermarking help make the system stronger. Thanks to added metadata hidden in watermarks, all types of content remain accessible to find, even if someone copies or transforms it. A suspicious copy found online may be marked by forensic watermarking to discover how and from where it was originally distributed.

Because of blockchain technology, any content registered receives proof of its license terms and date of publishing. Because of this, content producers are now able to take legal action or remove pirated copies that can be proven. Besides, streaming platforms can store and manage contracts to handle user access, make sure everyone is paid the right sum, and process payments straight away. (Wang et al., 2025)

5.5 Scientific and Academic Journals

A variety of issues such as plagiarism, falsifying data, and spreading research without permission, are known to the academic world. Applying watermarks to published papers, data, and experimental findings can greatly solve these problems.

At the end of production, it is possible to watermark an academic document with the author's name, the name of the institution, DOI (Digital Object Identifier), and a content hash. Following this, the information is added to a blockchain, forming an unalterable record about who wrote the content and if it is original. (Senkyire et al., 2019)

It is most helpful in making peer reviews more effective, carrying out research across different organizations, and turning findings into patent filing. In case a matter of priority or possession of findings comes up, the blockchain stores a digital confirmation of the first entry.

Furthermore, by adding decentralized data repositories and open-access journals, this system can make sure knowledge is shared fairly while researchers keep their rights. Also, it supports automatic tracking of citations and licensing processes.

All in all, blockchain-supported watermarking is expected to remodel many sectors. With the help of watermarking and blockchain technology, these applications provide a safe, transparent, and fair way for digital content to be used. (Senkyire et al., 2019)

6. CHALLENGES AND FUTURE DIRECTIONS

Even though this combination improves content security and authenticity, it still encounters some difficulties. There are obstacles associated with technology, laws, and regulations. If these problems are overcome, it will make it easier for watermarking systems to be widely accepted in industry.

6.1 Technical Challenges

- **Blockchain Scalability:** Public blockchain networks such as Ethereum and Bitcoin cannot manage peak activity because of their inability to handle many transactions. This leads to backups when trying to record a large number of watermark transactions. Currently, different solutions such as Layer-2, sidechains, and updated consensus protocols are being looked into to boost scalability. (Stipsits, n.d.)
- **Storage Constraints:** On-chain files take up a lot of space and can be costly for big multimedia records. Putting high-quality watermarked pictures or videos on the blockchain is not an option. Using blockchain for data storage methods and IPFS for content is the trend now. (Huang et al., 2024)
- **Gas Fees:** Gas Fees are charges for conducting transactions on public blockchain platforms and their costs can fluctuate a lot, sometimes making them very high. The issue is notable when there are lots of watermarks to be detected in a given system. Developers are also researching alternative blockchains with cheaper charges (such as Polygon and Solana).
- **Usability and Integration**: It is hard for many to set up or use the technology, which is a big problem for creators and businesses. It takes user-friendly Development Application Programs, plugins, and SDKs to make cryptocurrency more accessible. (Nelaturu et al., 2023)

6.2 Security and Privacy

- **Public Metadata:** Even though blockchains are open, releasing user information tends to put users at risk. Sensitive data should be secured by using hashing, encryption, and selective disclosure.
- **Sybil Attacks:** With permissionless systems, people can use numerous fake accounts to disturb the network or fill it with misleading material. These issues can be dealt with by adopting permissioned blockchain or identity verification strategies. (Goud Allam et al., 2021)
- **Content Theft Post-Watermarking:** Even with a watermark, it is still possible for someone to steal the content. For good cybersecurity, powerful al-

gorithms should be used along with continuous observation and automated timely removal of threats. (Wang et al., 2025)

6.3 Legal and Regulatory Hurdles

- **Jurisdictional Uncertainty**: Going from one country to another, it's uncertain whether blockchain-kept documents have legal acceptance. Ensuring that international laws are the same is important so they can be applied.
- **Digital Rights Standardization**: Successful blockchain-based digital rights require clear and universal standards which are currently missing. It is important for the industry to use the same framework for consistency. (Meng et al., 2018)
- **Regulatory Compliance**: GDPR is a regulatory requirement that systems should follow. Since blockchain can't be changed, it may interfere with the "right to be forgotten," and new solutions such as off-chain storage, could help solve this issue..(Wang et al., 2025)

6.4 Future Opportunities

- **AI Integration**: With AI, machines can automatically find, verify and analyze any artificially tampered reading material. It supports the choice of the best embedding framework for each form of multimedia content.
- **Zero-Knowledge Proofs (ZKPs)**: These protocols ensure that data is truthful without revealing its details. ZKPs are able to assess if a watermark is valid without revealing any content like a picture. (Yi, 2024)
- **Cross-Platform Interoperability**: It is important for blockchains to be interoperable as more of them appear. The use of standards such as Polka dot or Cosmos by connected systems lets them share rights and check information between different chains. (Sober et al., 2024)
- **Decentralized Identity (DID)**: With Decentralized Identity (DID), frameworks ensure trust by joining information to real and valid digital identities. As a result, people who create, discover, or narrate information are required to produce and present genuine and valid information. (Huang et al., 2024)

All in all, progress in blockchain-based digital watermarking depends on overcoming these challenges by coming up with new solutions, clarifying relevant laws, and creating shared standards. The development of the ecosystem gives it the major ability to change the way digital content is protected and intellectual property rights are handled all around the world.

7. CONCLUSION

Blockchain is an effective way to fix the drawbacks of digital watermarking. Using the advantages of each technology, a new method for safe, clear, and authenticated management of digital content is becoming possible. Thanks to their teamwork, they offer solutions for problems that affect digital rights management, verification of legitimate content, and forensic analysis. Having blockchain's strong and unchangeable infrastructure with modern watermarking's invisibility allows for a complete approach to protecting digital content. When more people adopt blockchain watermarking and the technical issues are resolved, it could become a base for trustworthy business in the digital world. Keep note that continued growth in AI, zero-knowledge cryptography, and standardized laws will lead to greater and essential use of this merging of fields by all important stakeholders.

REFERENCES

Bhadauria, S., Kumar, P., & Mohanty, T. (2021). Intellectual Property Protection using Blockchain and Digital Watermarking. *International Symposium on Advanced Networks and Telecommunication Systems, ANTS, 2021-December*, 1–6. DOI: 10.1109/ANTS52808.2021.9936909

Goud Allam, T., Mehedi Hasan, A. B. M., Maag, A., & Prasad, P. W. C. (2021). Ledger Technology of Blockchain and its Impact on Operational Performance of Banks: A Review. *CITISIA 2021 - IEEE Conference on Innovative Technologies in Intelligent System and Industrial Application, Proceedings*, 1–10. DOI: 10.1109/CITISIA53721.2021.9719886

Huang, C., Song, R., Gao, S., Guo, Y., & Xiao, B. (2024). *Data Availability and Decentralization: New Techniques for zk-Rollups in Layer 2 Blockchain Networks*. Retrieved from https://arxiv.org/abs/2403.10828

Meng, Z., Morizumi, T., Miyata, S., & Kinoshita, H. (2018). Design Scheme of Copyright Management System Based on Digital Watermarking and Blockchain. *Proceedings - International Computer Software and Applications Conference, 2*, 359–364. DOI: 10.1109/COMPSAC.2018.10258

Nelaturu, K., Mavridou, A., Stachtiari, E., Veneris, A., & Laszka, A. (2023). Correct-by-Design Interacting Smart Contracts and a Systematic Approach for Verifying ERC20 and ERC721 Contracts with VeriSolid. *IEEE Transactions on Dependable and Secure Computing, 20*(4), 3110–3127. DOI: 10.1109/TDSC.2022.3200840

Olusegun, R., & Yang, B. (2023). Enhancing Blockchain Network Scalability Through Parallelization and Aggregation Techniques: A Survey. *Proceedings - 2023 International Conference on Computational Science and Computational Intelligence, CSCI 2023*, 1098–1105. DOI: 10.1109/CSCI62032.2023.00181

Raj, D., & Sharma, D. (2024). Enhancing Digital Image Forensics and Security: Innovations in Metadata, Watermarking and Blockchain Technology. *2024 OPJU International Technology Conference on Smart Computing for Innovation and Advancement in Industry 4.0, OTCON 2024*, 1–6. DOI: 10.1109/OTCON60325.2024.10688307

Senkyire, I. B., & Kester, Q. A. (2019). Validation of Forensic Crime Scene Images Using Watermarking and Cryptographic Blockchain. *2019 ICDSA International Conference on Computer, Data Science and Applications, ICDSA 2019*, 2–5. DOI: 10.1109/ICDSA46371.2019.9404235

Sober, M., Scaffino, G., & Schulte, S. (2024). Cross-Blockchain Communication Using Oracles With an Off-Chain Aggregation Mechanism Based on zk-SNARKs. *Distributed Ledger Technologies: Research and Practice*. DOI: 10.1145/3678187

Stipsits, M. (n.d.). *Scalable Integration of Ethereum in a Microservice based Application through Layer 2 Rollups*. Retrieved from https://www.signature-verification.gv.at

Wang, X., & Wang, H. (2025). Research on the Identification and Supervision Mechanism of AIGC Based on Blockchain and Digital Watermark. *2025 IEEE International Conference on Electronics, Energy Systems and Power Engineering (EESPE)*, 638–641. DOI: 10.1109/EESPE63401.2025.10986886

Yi, Y. (2024). *The Investigation of Layer 2 Blockchain Technologies for Decentralized Applications*. 326–333. DOI: 10.5220/0012837400004547

Chapter 4
How Do LLMs Work?
A Deep Dive Into Transformer Models

Satvik Vats
https://orcid.org/0000-0002-9422-4915
Madan Mohan Malaviya University of Technology (MMMUT), Gorakhpur, India

Vikrant Sharma
Graphic Era Hill University, Dehradun, India

Priya Singh
Dataculture Technologies Private Limited, India

Samriti Thakur
Dataculture Technologies Private Limited, India

Daksh Rawat
https://orcid.org/0009-0007-9046-6988
Graphic Era Hill University, Dehradun, India

ABSTRACT

This chapter provides an in-depth overview of the Large Language Models (LLMs) by putting its lineage in the Transformer architecture- a framework that unites parallelism with long-range dependencies modeling via self-attention. It then introduces the most fundamental interfaces: multi-head attention, positional encoding and feed-forward networks, in a systematic fashion, followed by explanation of pre-training paradigms masked language modeling and causal language modeling. It also focuses on hyper-parameters of better tunes, especially reinforcement learning with human feedback (RLHF). Text generation Decoding routines, such as greedy decoding, beam or nucleus sampling, are discussed, and the limitations of the method

DOI: 10.4018/979-8-3373-3785-2.ch004

are highlighted in terms of such aspects as hallucinations, bias, interpretability, and environmental impact of LLMs. The chapter ends by questioning the ethical aspects of developing the LMM and by mapping future research agendas leading to the ethical discovery of these technologies.

INTRODUCTION

Large Language Models (LLMs) based on transformers have disrupted the areas of artificial intelligence and natural language processing. With the aid of the watershed Attention Is All You Need work (Vaswani et al., 2017), these models can perform text generation, text reading, and question answering, tasks previously limited to humans in terms of writing ability. Unlike recurrent neural networks, including variants of long-short term memory and transformers do not involve sequential processing of data; they process language at different points in parallel via self-attention. This improvement of architectures has led to training models of unprecedented scale and complexity with systems having billions or even trillions of parameters (Kaplan et al., 2020).

Modern LLMs such as the GPT-4, PaLM, LLaMA all have much more to offer than simple text generation. These models easily perform very complex tasks such as complex question answering and code-generation as well as on creative writing and basic ability to reason (Wei et al., 2022). They are able to excel because of a two-part training system: first, the system learns broad language skills from a lot of text data and then it is adjusted for specific jobs or preferences (Brown et al., 2020). At the same time, achieving this can be very difficult because it means using a lot of computing resources, the risk of models spreading inaccurate or harmful messages and the appearance of "hallucinations" where information produced by the model is convincing but wrong (Zhang et al., 2025).

LLMs have a huge influence on society now and the effect is still growing. AI is changing sectors such as education and healthcare, and it is also raising issues related to proper and improper uses of AI (Bender et al., 2021). At this stage where technology is changing fast, we should pay attention not only to what the models can accomplish but also to how they do it. This chapter explores, in detail, every aspect of LLMs, beginning from their main structure through the methods used to train them, their general output and what difficulties will face them as development moves forward.

FOUNDATIONS OF TRANSFORMER MODELS

By proposing the Transformer (Vaswani et al., 2017), Vaswani introduced a new way of handling sequences that uses attention instead of recurrent neural networks. It solved two main challenges of earlier models such as their slow processing speed for complex computations and inability to deal with dependencies across many elements. Managing a single input at a time makes RNNs and LSTMs slow to train, but Transformers which use self-attention to analyse full sequences quickly, prove to be highly efficient on latest hardware without sacrificing on model improvement.

The main idea behind the Transformer is to bring together several important parts that operate together. With the self-attention mechanism, every token in the sequence can focus on important parts by computing how important each part is in relation to the others. Multi-head attention extends this by enabling the model to jointly attend to information from different representation subspaces. Since attention alone is order-agnostic, learned positional encodings inject information about token positions. The architecture also includes position-wise feed-forward networks for additional nonlinear transformations, with residual connections and layer normalization facilitating the training of deep networks (Vaswani et al., 2017).

The Transformer's design offers several crucial advantages. Its parallel processing capability enables efficient training on large datasets, while the attention mechanism's global receptive field allows it to capture relationships between distant tokens more effectively than recurrent models. These properties have made it the foundation for nearly all modern LLMs, though implementations often vary - some use encoder-decoder structures (like the original), while most current LLMs employ decoder-only architectures optimized for autoregressive generation (Shaw et al., 2018). From there on, sparse attention, better ways of using memory and a number of other enhancements have been explored, even so the fundamental ideas from the original model still guide most language models today (Xiong et al., 2020) and (Devlin et al., 2019).

Next, self-attention which supports the whole architecture, will be discussed in detail. To work effectively with modern LLMs, it's crucial to know about these important factors which shape the model's skills, learning process and need for resources.

Figure 1. Evolution of sequence processing models

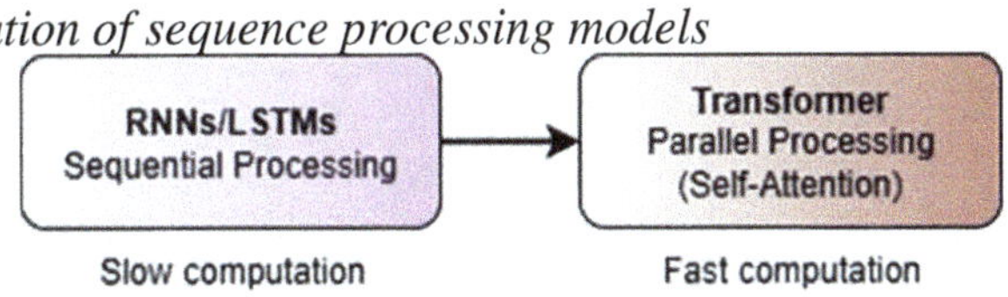

Figure 1 visually illustrates the transition in neural architectures for sequence modeling from traditional RNNs and LSTMs to the more advanced Transformer models. It highlights the key difference in processing styles: sequential processing in RNNs/LSTMs, which often leads to slower computation, versus parallel processing using self-attention in Transformers, enabling faster computation.

The Transformer Architecture

Transformer architecture goes far beyond former sequence processing models by discarding recurrence and only using attention mechanisms to work on input data. The original design by (Vaswani et al., 2017) has both an encoder and a decoder, but nowadays many LLMs just use the decoder in a serial or sequential manner. Their key feature is processing every token in a sequence at once, while keeping track of relationships with self-attention. Being designed for parallel operation, this model learns faster and performs better in comparisons with sequential RNNs (Tay et al., 2023).

Figure 2. Basic Transformer architecture

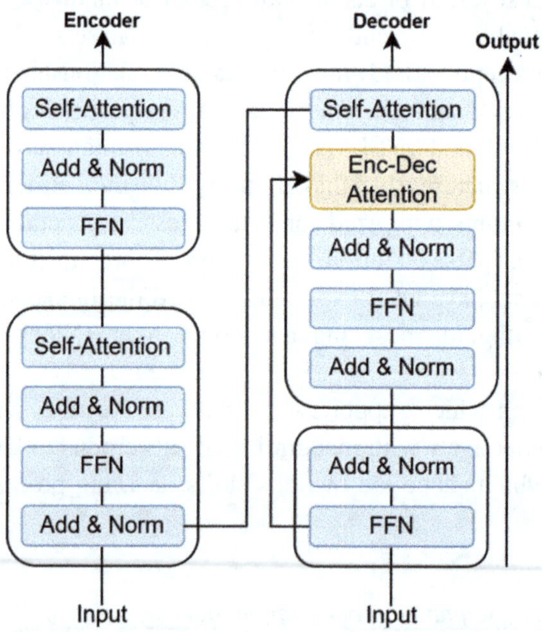

Figure 2 represents the main structure of the Transformer which is an encoder-decoder model designed for handling tasks like machine translation. The left column is the encoder which uses many layers to transform the input sequences into useful context representations. In every encoder layer, the main components are self-attention to find relationships between all input tokens, a block for residual links and layer normalization and an FFN to make the input representations more detailed. The structure on the right side is the same, except it adds an encoder-decoder attention mechanism which lets it focus on key parts of the input sequence. The decoder layers contain self-attention to build links between parts of the output, encoder-decoder attention for exchange of information across different parts of the structure, add & norm blocks for better efficiency and FFNs for fast processing. It outlines the transfer of data between the encoder and decoder which shows that the finished encoder outputs instruct the decoder to produce the output one token at a time. Using parallelization and paying attention to distant inputs, this architecture achieves top performance in natural language processing, making it a key model today.

In the Transformer architecture, various together. Because of self-attention, the model can pay special attention to various parts of the input sequence during processing. It allows the model to look at information from different areas in each position. Positional encodings are needed to maintain the sequence of tokens in processes done by attention. In feed-forward networks, extra processing is done to the representations being attended and residual connections and layer normalization are used to help gradients stay steady during training (Rogers et al., 2020).

Self-Attention Mechanism

The strong abilities of Transformers are thanks to the self-attention mechanism they use. Basically, self-attention takes a weighted sum of value vectors, and the weights depend on the matching between queries and keys. Mathematically, this is expressed through the scaled dot-product attention formula:

$$Attention(Q, K, V) = SoftMax\left(\frac{QK^T}{\sqrt{d_k}}\right)V \qquad (1)$$

where Q, K and V stand for the query, key and value matrices respectively and d_k denotes the dimension for the key vectors (Vaswani et al., 2017). By including the factor $1/\sqrt{d_k}$ in each new embedding, the gradients are better controlled, even with a high number of dimensions. As a result, every token can directly interact with every other token, helping the model support long-range information across the text (Kobayashi et al., 2020).

In multi-head attention, a series of parallel attention operations go beyond the standard mechanism. Every attention "head" understands different patterns, so the model can notice various language features all at once. As an example, will look at syntactic relations in the texts while another will analyse semantic associations. These heads' outputs are linked, and each output is linearly transformed to get the final result.

$$MultiHead(Q,K,V) = Concat(head_1,\ldots,head_h)W \quad (2)$$

where each $head_i$ is computed as:

$$head_i = Attention(QW_i^Q, KW_i^K, VW_i^V) \quad (3)$$

This multi-head approach significantly enhances the model's representational capacity and has become a standard component in all modern LLMs (Michel et al., 2019).

Positional Encoding and Other Architectural Components

Since the self-attention mechanism is permutation-invariant (it treats input tokens as an unordered set), Transformers must explicitly encode positional information to maintain the sequential nature of language. This is achieved through positional encodings, which are added to the input embeddings before processing. The original Transformer paper (Vaswani et al., 2017) proposed using sinusoidal functions of different frequencies:

$$PE_{(pos,2i)} = \sin\left(\frac{pos}{10000^{\frac{2i}{d_{model}}}}\right) \quad (4)$$

$$PE_{(pos,2i+1)} = \cos\left(\frac{pos}{10000^{\frac{2i}{d_{model}}}}\right) \quad (5)$$

where *pos* is the position in the sequence and *i* ranges over the embedding dimensions. These sinusoidal encodings were chosen because they allow the model to generalize to sequence lengths longer than those encountered during training, as any relative position can be represented as a linear function of a given position (Shaw et al., 2018).

The Transformer architecture also includes position-wise feed-forward networks (FFNs) that apply two linear transformations with a ReLU activation in between:

$$FFN(x) = ReLU(xW_1 + b_1)W_2 + b_2 \quad (6)$$

These *FFN*s operate independently on each position and provide additional nonlinear transformations to the attended representations. Layer normalization is applied before each sub-layer (attention and *FFN*), and residual connections are used throughout to facilitate training of deep networks. Because of combining all these elements, the architecture can handle complicated grammar without causing high resource use (Xiong et al., 2020).

TRAINING LARGE LANGUAGE MODELS

It takes a complex series of steps to create modern large language models, and these rely on new architecture designs, advanced optimization approaches and the use of large computer systems. To turn raw text into a broadly useful LLM, you need to first train it broadly on lots of untidy text, then refine it to suit your specific uses or to ensure its behaviour is more like that of a human. BERT by (Devlin et al., 2019) and GPT by (Radford et al., 2019) first used this kind of training which is now commonly followed for the most powerful language models.

Pre-training is the most demanding phase of learning by taking the longest time and affecting the model's core concepts the most. At this level, the model works on guessing missing words and following ones, gaining an improved understanding of how language, grammar, facts and logic are put together. Current LLMs use data that includes trillions of tokens coming from many places such as books, technical documents, the internet and code repositories (Patterson et al., 2022). Such a large amount of training data and models that contain huge numbers of parameters means that training just one model is an enormous task, requiring thousands of GPUs for weeks or months and leading to high costs of millions of dollars (Brown et al., 2020).

However, a critical challenge emerging in the training of next-generation LLMs is "regurgitative training," where models are trained on data that is at least partially generated by other LLMs. This phenomenon is becoming increasingly inevitable as LLMs produce a substantial amount of online content, and even supposedly human-generated data can be influenced by AI. Research indicates that regurgitative training generally leads to lower performance compared to training with real, human-generated data. This performance degradation can be attributed to higher error rates and lower lexical diversity in LLM-generated data. Even a small proportion of synthetic data can deter learning, and while some mitigation strategies exist, they often cannot fully close the performance gap with real data, highlighting the unique value of human-generated content in LLM training (Zhang et al., 2024).

This training process is successful if the training data is good and diverse, the right goals are chosen for pre-training, the model architecture easily adjusts to more parameters and input and special techniques help optimize training. New methods for training many models at once, for how they store numbers and in improving their training have made these big models possible, yet it is still a challenge to help reduce their negative impact on the environment (Strubell et al., 2019).

Figure 3 illustrates the comprehensive, multi-stage process involved in training Large Language Models (LLMs), from the initial ingestion of raw data to the generation of outputs. This flowchart depicts the sequential steps and highlights a critical feedback mechanism.

Figure 3. Training pipeline of large language models

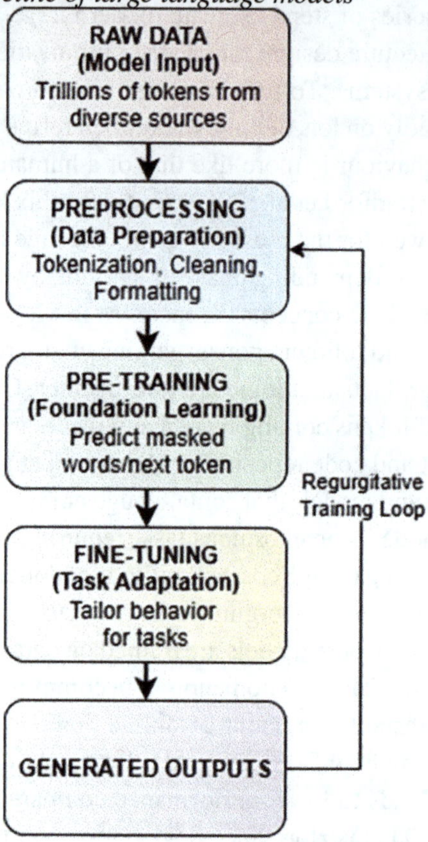

Pre-training Objectives and Strategies

To train a modern Large Language Model (LLM), the process typically involves two main stages: initial pre-training followed by fine-tuning. The preliminary training process is essential to make the model have a general idea about the language by examining huge portions of unstructured text-based information. This basic study is mainly based on two different things:

1. Masked Language Modeling (MLM):
    - Objective: MLM is, for example, applied by models such as BERT (Devlin et al., 2019), where every input token is randomly masked.
    - Task: The task of the model under consideration will be to reconstruct the initials of these masked tokens.
    - Contextual Understanding: This style has the capability to make the model learn a two-sided knowledge of language that takes both the previous (left) and next (right) words into account in predicting the words.
    - Mathematical Representation: The objective function for MLM is given by:

$$\mathscr{L}_{MLM} = -E_{x\sim D} \sum_{i \in M} \log P(x_i | x_{\setminus M}) \tag{7}$$

where M is the set of masked positions and $x_{\setminus M}$ is the sequence with masked tokens (Liu et al., 2019).

2. Causal Language Modeling (CLM):
    - Objective: CLM model can be used in the same way that neural networks like GPT series are trained to anticipate the successor in a sequence (Radford et al., 2019).
    - Task: The model predicts x_t based solely on the tokens that precede it ($x_{<t}$), enforcing a unidirectional flow of information.
    - Application: This objective is particularly well-suited for generative tasks, allowing the model to create coherent text sequentially.
    - Mathematical Representation: The objective function for CLM is:

$$\mathscr{L}_{CLM} = -E_{x\sim D} \sum_{t=1}^{T} \log P(x_t | x_{<t}) \tag{8}$$

where $x_{<t}$ includes every token in the text before the position t is reached.

Modern large language models train on datasets with billions of parameters which takes weeks or months to complete on powerful computers (Patterson et al., 2022).

Fine-Tuning and Alignment Techniques

When pre-training is finished, LLMs are trained again to improve their skills or to better follow human expectations. Supervised fine-tuning takes a model and trains it is using labeled information on tasks like question answering or summarizing text.

More recently, reinforcement learning from human feedback (RLHF) has emerged as a powerful technique for aligning LLM outputs with human values (Ouyang et al., 2022). In RLHF, human raters provide preference rankings for different model outputs, which are used to train a reward model. The LLM is then fine-tuned using reinforcement learning (typically proximal policy optimization) to maximize this learned reward:

$$\mathscr{L}_{RLHF} = E_{(x,y)\sim D}\left[r_{\varnothing}\right](x,y) - \beta KL(\pi_{\theta}(y|x) \| \pi_{ref}(y|x)) \quad (9)$$

where $r_{\varnothing}$ is the reward model, π_{θ} is the current policy, π_{ref} is the reference policy (usually the initial supervised fine-tuned model), and β controls the strength of the KL regularization term that prevents the policy from deviating too far from the reference (Stiennon et al., 2020).

Computational and Infrastructure Requirements

The training of state-of-the-art LLMs requires unprecedented computational resources. For example, training GPT-3 with 175 billion parameters was estimated to require 3.14×10^{23} floating-point operations (FLOPs) (Brown et al., 2020). At current cloud computing prices, this translates to millions of dollars in compute costs alone. The energy consumption is equally staggering, with estimates suggesting that training a single large model can emit as much carbon as dozens of transatlantic flights (Strubell et al., 2019). The use of large datasets has made some realize the environmental impact of researching AI which has resulted in efforts to find better training techniques.

It takes large amounts of data to train LLMs properly as well. Modern language models are trained using data from books, websites, papers in academic studies and repositories of code which totals trillions of tokens. Because of this, people must think about the accuracy of the data, the risk of bias in the training set and the legal issues related to copyright (Dodge et al., 2021). Researchers are developing ways to make training faster, for example by using mixture-of-experts architectures, model pruning, distillation and better optimization algorithms (Fedus et al., 2022), (Sanh et al., 2019) and (Zaheer et al., 2020).

TEXT GENERATION AND INFERENCE

Generating understandable and appropriate text is one of the best abilities of large language models. Traditionally, NLP used strict set-in-stone rules, but now modern LLMs apply advanced probabilistic strategies to generate language like it is spoken by humans. The model uses autoregressive prediction which allows it to create text one token at a time and each new token is formed from all previously made text. The quality and features of the text created by a model reflect its design, the training data provided, and the decoding method used.

The actual process of text generation in LLMs lies in how the model's internal set of variables and its sampling skills influence each other. While the language skills are formed by the training, how a model decodes speech decides how creative, coherent and accurate its outputs will be. A modern system needs to balance being true to the prompt, having grammatically correct language, avoiding repeating itself and sometimes showing creativity. The difficulty increases when models try to generate large amounts of text, as they need to hold on to the right context despite handling a huge number of tokens.

Having these demands, the area of Controllable Text Generation (CTG) over LLM has emerged very important and due to that there appears a need to move beyond mere fluency and diversity of outputs, and request control over a wider range of requirements provided by a specific user. CTG makes sure the output matches the control conditions, which were preset with safety, sentiment, thematic continuity/consistency and language style archetype, whilst maintaining an optimal level of helpfulness, fluency, and diversity in the output. This presents a two-fold problem, the strict application of specified control conditions, whether they are themselves explicit (e.g. direct prompting on style) or implicit (e.g. the production of non-toxic text), and the preservation of basic standards of textual quality. According to the representation provided by (Liang et al., 2024), CTG is an ability dimension that is orthogonal to objective knowledge capabilities of LLMs, which defines objective data expression and presentation and not only its factual accuracy or relevance.

Computational issues arise when LLMs use the inference process. During sequential autoregressive generation, each token can be produced only after all tokens before it has been produced which makes the process sequential. From there on, there are serious latency issues in real-world cases, leading to the design of KV caching, speculative execution and simple methods for uniform sampling (Holtzman et al., 2019). Because text generation involves probabilities, the same input can produce various outputs, so careful adjustment of parameters is required to maintain the right balance between structure and creativity in each context.

Autoregressive Generation Process

In the inference stage, autoregressive LLMs produce one token after another, and every token is based on all the previous ones. The model takes in $x_{1:t}$, and then computes a probability distribution for the next word to choose:

$$P(x_{t+1} \mid x_{1:t}) = SoftMax(W.h_t) \quad (10)$$

where h_t is the final hidden state corresponding to position t and W is the output embedding matrix (Holtzman et al., 2019). This process repeats until a stopping condition is met (e.g., generating an end-of-sequence token or reaching a maximum length).

The autoregressive nature of this process means that generating long texts can be computationally expensive, as the entire sequence must be reprocessed at each step (though techniques like KV caching can help mitigate this). The quality of generated text depends heavily on the sampling strategy used to select tokens from this probability distribution (Welleck et al., 2019).

Decoding Strategies and Their Trade-offs

The trade-off between the quality and diversity of generation has been controlled with various decoding strategies. The algorithm of greedy decoding, choosing the next most likely token at each step, tends to generate tedious redundant text in many contexts. Beam search stores a more diverse number of candidate sequences, which in most cases gives more consistent, but in some cases generic outputs (Meister et al., 2020).

Creative generation tasks have become popular in more stochastic techniques such as temperature sampling and top-k/top-p (nucleus) sampling. Temperature sampling modifies the output distribution before sampling:

$$P(x) \propto \exp\left(\frac{logits(x)}{\tau}\right) \quad (10)$$

where τ is the temperature parameter that helps determine how sharp the distribution will be (Ackley et al., 1985). In top-k sampling, only the k most likely tokens are taken at each step, whereas top-p sampling picks the smallest set of tokens that together have a probability higher than p.

Some recent research involves contrastive ways of decoding that help improve the coherence and correctness of generated text by comparing the outputs of various model configurations (Li et al., 2022). In places like medicine and law, where correct details are very important, these techniques play a key role.

APPLICATIONS OF LARGE LANGUAGE MODELS

Large Language Models (LLM) are fundamentally transforming various industries and leveraging their ability to see, generate, and govern human language in the largest manner than ever. They can incorporate their performances in complex real world applications as another supplementary protocol besides the simple generation of basic text content. One of its main uses is in content creation and summarization, and LLMs are commonly used to generate articles, marketing copy, social media content, and creative writing, also compressing content pipelines. They are also effective at condensing long documents and reports, isolating and reporting salient points in brief.

Customer service and education are the other major areas where LLMs are advancing. They also drive high-level chatbots and AI assistants in customer support, answering questions, giving immediate answers and solving complex tasks and thus increasing efficiency and customer satisfaction. In education, LLMs have found a way to develop individualized learning, to make up quizzes, and provide instant feedback on tasks. As an example, they are able to regulate complexity of lexical items present in the created learning materials using complexity embeddings.

Moreover, LLMs have become ever more important to specific and technical fields. In medicine, they are useful in areas such as summarisation of patient profiles, production of preliminary diagnosis reports and even support in the processing of large volumes of literature as an aid in medical research. This domain has seen the legal profession use LLMs to review documents with an accuracy rate of above 96 percent, contract analysis, and legal research. LLMs can be used in software development with the developer automatically generating code, debugging, and completing code, reducing software development cycles. Their various and expanding influence on these spheres underlines their capability to enhance human capabilities and streamline processes which can be understood to be continuously expanding given the changes the technology is taking.

CHALLENGES AND FUTURE DIRECTIONS

Although the models are quite powerful, they result in a number of technical issues and controversial applications that AI scientists continue to grapple with. Such problems can be explained by the way LLMs are constructed, created, and deployed; this leads to some performance disparities that constrain their applicative effectivity. Neural networks have several problems that render them unreliable such as false responses dubbed as hallucinations, which encourage previous biases within training data and the high volume of computing power required to train them. They are not technological problems only, but they also force us to rethink what is right to do with LLMs and how to control their development.

To advance in LLM research, we must work on these issues even as we search for new ways to expand what LLMs can do. The main topics considered in current investigations are: making sure the outputs are more accurate and reliable, boosting computer system efficiency and developing strong ways to align the model's decisions with human thinking. More and more, it is being understood that addressing these problems means creating basic advances in the designs of models, the processes for training them and how they are evaluated. Professionals in this area are interested in training LLMs to think on higher levels, understand different types of input and continue being reliable in difficult or ongoing activities.

These areas of study are important because they will affect the use of LLMs in different social and professional areas. It is expected that in the future more attention will be given to creating clear standards for testing, being clear about how training data and models work and creating guidelines for ethical use of AI. Rapid developments in the technology mean researchers, developers and policymakers must consider both the good and the bad aspects of LLMs. Emerging trends for 2025 and beyond include the development of more sophisticated AI agents that can perform complex, multi-step tasks autonomously. Furthermore, multimodal integrations are rapidly advancing, allowing LLMs to process and generate content across various modalities, such as combining text with images, audio, and even video, opening up new frontiers for interaction and application.

It is expected that in the future more attention will be given to creating clear standards for testing, being clear about how training data and models work and creating guidelines for ethical use of AI. Rapid developments in the technology mean researchers, developers and policymakers must consider both the good and the bad aspects of LLMs.

Key Limitations of Current LLMs

Modern LLMs are powerful, but they also have several major issues. A common problem is that they might give wrong information (hallucinations), especially if the topic is not covered in their training (Lin et al., 2021). This problem stems from their fundamental design as next-token predictors rather than truth-seeking systems. Another critical challenge is the presence of various biases in model outputs, reflecting and sometimes amplifying biases present in the training data (Bolukbasi et al., 2016). Such biases may be expressed as a demographic stereotype or cultural assumption or other bad habits.

One other major concern is the interpretability of LLMs. Although tools such as attention visualization and probing classifiers are useful in some sense to get a hint of how models behave, we are yet to have comprehensive methods to understand how exactly models come to their outputs, (Belinkov et al., 2019). The resulting inability to predict or explain model failures, especially with high stakes applications, is a property known as this black box nature.

Emerging Research Directions

In order to overcome these limitations, some encouraging research lines are being investigated. Retrieval-augmented generation places LLMs on top of outside sources of knowledge retrieval that root their outputs in verifiable information (Lewis et al., 2020). Such a solution will help eliminate hallucinations considerably and preserve the plasticity of the neural generation. The second current focus is the design of better architectures and training algorithms, like mixture-of-experts models, where only a sub-set of parameters are activated on a per-input basis (Lepikhin et al., 2020).

Multimodal inputs (such as combining text and images, or text and audio, etc.) are becoming more in demand as a way to create a more diverse interaction and application of LLMs (Alayrac et al., 2022). Allied research with techniques of enhancing reasoning abilities, e.g., by chain-of-thought prompting (Wei et al., 2022) or neuro-symbolic integration (Garcez et al., 2015), is also attracting considerable interest.

Ethical and Societal Considerations

The concept of LLMs development and deployment tech prompts many moral concerns which the field is only starting to explore. The matter of fairness and representation needs specific attention to training data composition and assessment methods (Blodgett et al., 2020). The misuse of these technologies (e.g., the creation of misinformation on a large scale) requires the creation of very stringent measures and protection tools (Kreps et al., 2022).

As LLMs are used more frequently and improve, concerns about their legal position, the responsibility for errors they make and the right situations to apply them will grow. The AI field is devising ways to make sure powerful technologies are developed and put to use responsibly (Bommasani et al., 2021).

CONCLUSION

Advances in large language models using the Transformer architecture have greatly transformed natural language processing and artificial intelligence. Using new self-attention designs and being able to process a huge amount of data, these models show a major leap forward for machine learning. But, as you can tell from this chapter, there are major technical and social issues with developing and using artificial intelligence.

In the future, it is important for the field to keep improving models while making sure efficiency, ease of understanding and ethics are considered. Capturing human values, becoming more reliable and effective is likely where further development will be concentrated. Since LLMs are being used more widely, it's important for experts from different fields to join forces to guide and control their use to avoid any harms and highlight their positive aspects.

With how fast progress is happening in this area, it shows that we are just starting to understand and use large language models. Those studying how they act, what they are capable of and their different functions are sure to find interesting research results in the years to come.

REFERENCES

Ackley, D. H., Hinton, G. E., & Sejnowski, T. J. (1985). A learning algorithm for Boltzmann machines. *Cognitive Science, 9*(1), 147–169.

Alayrac, J. B., Donahue, J., Luc, P., Miech, A., Barr, I., Hasson, Y., & Simonyan, K. (2022). Flamingo: A visual language model for few-shot learning. *Advances in Neural Information Processing Systems, 35*, 23716–23736.

Belinkov, Y., & Glass, J. (2019). Analysis methods in neural language processing: A survey. *Transactions of the Association for Computational Linguistics, 7*, 49–72. DOI: 10.1162/tacl_a_00254

Bender, E. M., Gebru, T., McMillan-Major, A., & Shmitchell, S. (2021, March). On the dangers of stochastic parrots: Can language models be too big? In *Proceedings of the 2021 ACM conference on fairness, accountability, and transparency* (pp. 610-623). DOI: 10.1145/3442188.3445922

Blodgett, S. L., Barocas, S., Daumé, H.III, & Wallach, H. (2020). Language (technology) is power: A critical survey of" bias" in NLP. In *Proceedings of the 58th Annual Meeting of the Association for Computational Linguistics* (pp. 5454-5476). DOI: 10.18653/v1/2020.acl-main.485

Bolukbasi, T., Chang, K. W., Zou, J. Y., Saligrama, V., & Kalai, A. T. (2016). Man is to computer programmer as woman is to homemaker? Debiasing word embeddings. arXiv preprint arXiv:1607.06520. https://arxiv.org/abs/1607.06520

Bommasani, R., Hudson, D. A., Adeli, E., Altman, R., Arora, S., von Arx, S., Liang, P. (2021). On the opportunities and risks of foundation models. arXiv preprint arXiv:2108.07258.

Brown, T., Mann, B., Ryder, N., Subbiah, M., Kaplan, J. D., Dhariwal, P., & Amodei, D. (2020). Language models are few-shot learners. *Advances in Neural Information Processing Systems, 33*, 1877–1901.

Devlin, J., Chang, M. W., Lee, K., & Toutanova, K. (2019). Bert: Pre-training of deep bidirectional transformers for language understanding. arXiv preprint arXiv:1810.04805.

Dodge, J., Sap, M., Marasović, A., Agnew, W., Ilharco, G., Groeneveld, D., Gardner, M. (2021). Documenting large webtext corpora: A case study on the colossal clean crawled corpus. arXiv preprint arXiv:2104.08758. DOI: 10.18653/v1/2021.emnlp-main.98

Fedus, W., Zoph, B., & Shazeer, N. (2022). Switch transformers: Scaling to trillion parameter models with simple and efficient sparsity. *Journal of Machine Learning Research*, *23*(1), 5232–5270.

Garcez, A. S. D. A., Besold, T. R., De Raedt, L., Földiak, P., Hitzler, P., Icard, T., Silver, D. L. (2015, March). Neural-Symbolic Learning and Reasoning: Contributions and Challenges. In AAAI Spring Symposia (pp. 18-21).

Holtzman, A., Buys, J., Du, L., Forbes, M., & Choi, Y. (2019). The curious case of neural text degeneration. arXiv preprint arXiv:1904.09751.

Kaplan, J., McCandlish, S., Henighan, T., Brown, T. B., Chess, B., Child, R., Amodei, D. (2020). Scaling laws for neural language models. arXiv preprint arXiv:2001.08361.

Kobayashi, G., Kuribayashi, T., Yokoi, S., & Inui, K. (2020). Attention is not only a weight: Analyzing transformers with vector norms. arXiv preprint arXiv:2004.10102. DOI: 10.18653/v1/2020.emnlp-main.574

Kreps, S., McCain, R. M., & Brundage, M. (2022). All the news that's fit to fabricate: AI-generated text as a tool of media misinformation. *Journal of Experimental Political Science*, *9*(1), 104–117. DOI: 10.1017/XPS.2020.37

Lepikhin, D., Lee, H., Xu, Y., Chen, D., Firat, O., Huang, Y., Chen, Z. (2020). Gshard: Scaling giant models with conditional computation and automatic sharding. arXiv preprint arXiv:2006.16668.

Lewis, P., Perez, E., Piktus, A., Petroni, F., Karpukhin, V., Goyal, N., & Kiela, D. (2020). Retrieval-augmented generation for knowledge-intensive NLP tasks. *Advances in Neural Information Processing Systems*, *33*, 9459–9474.

Li, X. L., Holtzman, A., Fried, D., Liang, P., Eisner, J., Hashimoto, T., Lewis, M. (2022). Contrastive decoding: Open-ended text generation as optimization. arXiv preprint arXiv:2210.15097.

Liang, X., Wang, H., Wang, Y., Song, S., Yang, J., Niu, S., Li, Z. (2024). Controllable text generation for large language models: A survey. arXiv preprint arXiv:2408.12599.

Lin, S., Hilton, J., & Evans, O. (2021). Truthfulqa: Measuring how models mimic human falsehoods. arXiv preprint arXiv:2109.07958.

Liu, Y., Ott, M., Goyal, N., Du, J., Joshi, M., Chen, D., Stoyanov, V. (2019). Roberta: A robustly optimized bert pretraining approach. arXiv preprint arXiv:1907.11692.

Meister, C., Vieira, T., & Cotterell, R. (2020). If beam search is the answer, what was the question? arXiv preprint arXiv:2010.02650. DOI: 10.18653/v1/2020.emnlp-main.170

Michel, P., Levy, O., & Neubig, G. (2019). Are sixteen heads really better than one? *Advances in Neural Information Processing Systems*, 32.

Ouyang, L., Wu, J., Jiang, X., Almeida, D., Wainwright, C., Mishkin, P., & Lowe, R. (2022). Training language models to follow instructions with human feedback. *Advances in Neural Information Processing Systems*, *35*, 27730–27744.

Patterson, D., Gonzalez, J., Le, Q., Liang, C., Munguia, L. M., Rothchild, D., Dean, J. (2021). Carbon emissions and large neural network training. arXiv preprint arXiv:2104.10350.

Radford, A., Wu, J., Child, R., Luan, D., Amodei, D., & Sutskever, I. (2019). Language models are unsupervised multitask learners. OpenAI blog, 1(8), 9.

Rogers, A., Kovaleva, O., & Rumshisky, A. (2020). A primer in BERTology: What we know about how BERT works. *Transactions of the Association for Computational Linguistics*, *8*, 842–866. DOI: 10.1162/tacl_a_00349

Sanh, V., Debut, L., Chaumond, J., & Wolf, T. (2019). DistilBERT, a distilled version of BERT: smaller, faster, cheaper and lighter. arXiv preprint arXiv:1910.01108.

Shaw, P., Uszkoreit, J., & Vaswani, A. (2018). Self-attention with relative position representations. arXiv preprint arXiv:1803.02155. DOI: 10.18653/v1/N18-2074

Stiennon, N., Ouyang, L., Wu, J., Ziegler, D., Lowe, R., Voss, C., & Christiano, P. F. (2020). Learning to summarize with human feedback. *Advances in Neural Information Processing Systems*, *33*, 3008–3021.

Strubell, E., Ganesh, A., & McCallum, A. (2019). Energy and policy considerations for deep learning in NLP. arXiv preprint arXiv:1906.02243. /arXiv.1906.02243DOI: 10.18653/v1/P19-1355

Tay, Y., Dehghani, M., Bahri, D., & Metzler, D. (2023). Efficient transformers: A survey. ACM Computing Surveys, 55(6). *ACM Computing Surveys*, *109*(6), 1–28. DOI: 10.1145/3530811

Vaswani, A., Shazeer, N., Parmar, N., Uszkoreit, J., Jones, L., Gomez, A. N., & Polosukhin, I. (2017). Attention is all you need. *Advances in Neural Information Processing Systems*, 30.

Wei, J., Tay, Y., Bommasani, R., Raffel, C., Zoph, B., Borgeaud, S., Fedus, W. (2022). Emergent abilities of large language models. arXiv preprint arXiv:2206.07682.

Welleck, S., Kulikov, I., Roller, S., Dinan, E., Cho, K., & Weston, J. (2019). Neural text generation with unlikelihood training. arXiv preprint arXiv:1908.04319.

Xiong, R., Yang, Y., He, D., Zheng, K., Zheng, S., Xing, C., & Wang, L. (2020). On layer normalization in the transformer architecture. In *International Conference on Machine Learning* (pp. 10524-10533). PMLR.

Zaheer, M., Guruganesh, G., Dubey, K. A., Ainslie, J., Alberti, C., Ontanon, S., Pham, P., Ravula, A., Wang, Q., Yang, L., & Ahmed, A. (2020). Big bird: Transformers for longer sequences. arXiv preprint arXiv:2007.14062. https://arxiv.org/abs/2007.14062

Zhang, J., Qiao, D., Yang, M., & Wei, Q. (2024). Regurgitative training: The value of real data in training large language models. arXiv preprint arXiv:2407.12835.

Zhang, Y., Li, Y., Cui, L., Cai, D., Liu, L., Fu, T., Huang, X., Zhao, E., Zhang, Y., Chen, Y., Wang, L., Luu, A. T., Bi, W., Shi, F., & Shi, S. (2025). Siren's song in the ai ocean: A survey on hallucination in large language models. *Computational Linguistics*, 1–45. DOI: 10.1162/coli.a.16

KEY TERMS AND DEFINITIONS

Transformer Architecture: One of the architectures of deep learning models based solely on self-attention mechanisms, without recurrence or convolution, to efficiently and in parallel process sequences, allowing for strong performance in language applications.

Self-Attention: A mechanism to enable a model to assign weights on the importance of each token in a sequence with regard to others, so that it can grasp relationships between the context within the entire input.

Multi-Head Attention: An extension of self-attention in which multiple attention operations are performed concurrently, enabling the model to look at different linguistic patterns and dependencies at the same time.

Positional Encoding: Numerical encodings appended to token embeddings to introduce order information into the input sequence to offset the Transformer's absence of inherent sequence knowledge.

Pre-Training: The first stage of training a language model on large amounts of unstructured text data to acquire general representations of language prior to task-specific fine-tuning.

Fine-Tuning: An additional training phase in which the pre-trained model is fitted to individual tasks by using labeled data or alignment methods to enhance relevance and usability.

Reinforcement Learning with Human Feedback (RLHF): A model that combines model-generated text with human feedback to generate output and reinforce the selection of values to align model outputs with human values.

Autoregressive Generation: An autoregressive model of predicting the next token based on all the previously generated tokens that are used to generate the next token in a coherent and contextually meaningful fashion.

Chapter 5
AI and ML Approaches in Adaptive Watermarking

Neha Yadav
https://orcid.org/0000-0002-7793-2063
G.L. Bajaj Institute of Technology and Management, Greater Noida, India

Mayank Singh
https://orcid.org/0000-0002-8393-3652
G.L. Bajaj Institute of Technology and Management, Greater Noida, India

Vipin Tyagi
https://orcid.org/0000-0003-4994-3686
Jaypee University of Engineering and Technology, Guna, India

ABSTRACT

Digital watermarking is a crucial method for addressing the threats of data piracy and illegal content distribution in cloud environments and copyright protection systems. This chapter looks at Artificial Intelligence (AI) and Machine Learning (ML) methods of adaptive watermarking, and we will pay close attention to how intelligent systems can make such watermarking solutions more robust, imperceptible, and payload-dense. In addition, this chapter will review the various neural network architectures, deep learning frameworks, reinforcement learning approaches, and hybrid AI system structures that can be utilised in watermarking applications, particularly in cloud computing settings. We will conduct a review of current state-of-the-art AI/ML methods and models for embedding and detecting watermarks. This review will provide a taxonomy of methods, compare these methods, and present case studies and experimental setups.

DOI: 10.4018/979-8-3373-3785-2.ch005

1 INTRODUCTION

1.1 Background and Motivation

As the growth of digital content creation and sharing has advanced rapidly, particularly with the rise of cloud platforms, copyright infringement and data misuse have similarly risen. Today, images, videos, and other forms of multimedia are being shared, stored, and accessed widely on distributed systems. With the relative ease of duplicating and sharing these types of multimedia in cloud environments, users are more susceptible to copyright infringement, piracy, unauthorised conveyance or interpretation, and loss of ownership identity. Digital watermarking, specifically, will be an essential technique in the development of copyright processing schemes designed to address copyright issues. Digital watermarking methodologies enable the embedding of copyright or ownership information directly into multimedia content, making it potentially undetectable by users while still being detectable for authentication, provenance, and forensic purposes. Most traditional watermarking approaches are practical in controlled environments (e.g., image or video data formats); however, their performance is often compromised in terms of robustness, adaptability, and perceptual quality when executed in dynamic and adversarial cloud environments. The rapid, even rampant, growth of digital content in tamper-free environments has resulted in immense and unique challenges for copyright protection processes and their enforcement mechanisms (Amrit & Singh, 2022). Traditional watermarking techniques may be paramount in protecting ownership strategies. Still, they are usually adversarial and fail to achieve optimal outcomes across multiple content types, variable network conditions, and attacks that typically occur in cloud systems. The emergence of AI and ML techniques marks a shift in watermarking technology, offering adaptive systems able to learn from patterns in data, predict practical embedding approaches, and dynamically adapt to changing conditions (Liu & Nematollahi, 2024). An adaptive AI/ML watermarking system will have unique and essential benefits over traditional methods. Adaptive systems will automatically optimise watermark strength based on content and predict and counteract potential attacks while still performing consistently across heterogeneous cloud environments. AI solutions can quickly process large amounts of multimedia content, making them attractive in instances of large-scale cloud applications where manual tuning of parameters is impractical (Dandooh, El-Fishawy, & Hemdan, 2025).

AI and ML make watermarking systems transformative. Previous embedding techniques are altered with adaptable learning, meaning embedding systems can respond to new content types, random attacks, and environmental variability. AI systems can make intelligent decisions related to the strength, location, and method of embedding. Intelligent adaptive watermarking maximises both security and transparency. The interdisciplinary blend of AI/ML with watermarking technology yields new techniques, including deep neural network approaches for watermark embedding and extraction, reinforcement learning for parameter selection, adversarial networks for enhancing watermark resistance, and ensemble learning for improving reliability (Regazzoni et al., 2021). This chapter systematically examines the approaches, their theoretical foundations, practical applications, and performance in cloud-based use cases. There are multiple motivations for studying the integration of AI/ML into watermarking systems, but the main one is the constraint of static algorithms.

The AI watermarking methods can induce the flexibility of personalising the algorithm based on the characteristics of the input media, historical attacks, and real-time requirements, which is paramount for automated and large-scale deployment within cloud infrastructure. Another significant motivating factor is that the complexity of adversarial attacks is increasing rapidly. Compression, noise injections, cropping and rotating, as well as adversarial perturbations, can easily defeat a static watermarking system (Hsu, 2024). However, an AI system has the potential to learn from data and predict or anticipate the types of distortions it will encounter, adjusting a watermarking process to ensure success. In cloud computing, enormous amounts of multimedia content are processed each second; therefore, any manual effort in utility creation and watermark design is impractical. AI models can enable end-to-end automation for all aspects of the watermarking workflow, including feature extraction, embedding and removal, and the automated intelligent tuning of watermark parameters (Jiang et al., 2024). Not only is this ability for automation necessary for scaling purposes, but the ability to obtain consistent performance across heterogeneous sources is also vital. Finally, especially with ongoing legal and regulatory shifts, there has been an increased emphasis on verifiable digital ownership, confiscation and integrity, as well as the ability to prove that content has been tampered with.

1.2 Scope and Objectives

This chapter presents a comprehensive analysis of how AI and ML can be leveraged to build adaptive watermarking systems for copyright protection in cloud environments. The focus is placed on image and video watermarking, given their prevalence in cloud media services, though the concepts can be extended to audio and textual content.

The key objectives of this chapter are:

- To provide a detailed overview of the limitations of traditional watermarking techniques and how AI/ML can address them.

- To categorise AI and ML models (e.g., CNNs, GANs, reinforcement learning) that have been applied or adapted for watermarking.
- To introduce the concept of adaptivity in watermarking and how intelligent models can learn and evolve watermark embedding/extraction strategies over time.
- To compare the performance of AI-based watermarking models with conventional approaches using metrics such as PSNR, SSIM, NC, and BER.
- To discuss deployment issues in real-world cloud environments, including scalability, privacy, and attack resistance.

The chapter also discusses future trends, including federated watermarking and the application of neuromorphic computing for low-latency watermarking.

2. BASICS OF DIGITAL WATERMARKING

Digital watermarking is a method of embedding information into digital media, such as images, audio, or video, in a way that is either visibly or invisibly detectable to human senses. Watermarking is intended to provide copyright protection, authenticate, and track the usage of media. A properly designed watermarking system will incorporate a reliably owned watermark that remains intact despite various transformations and attacks while maintaining the integrity and usability of the host media.

2.1 Watermarking Framework

A typical digital watermarking framework consists of two main processes: watermark embedding and watermark extraction.

- Embedding Process: This involves inserting the watermark into the host media. It can be performed in either the spatial domain (directly modifying pixel values) or the frequency domain (modifying coefficients obtained via transforms like the Discrete Cosine Transform or Discrete Wavelet Transform).
- Extraction Process: This involves retrieving or verifying the watermark from potentially modified or attacked media. Depending on the design, extraction may be blind (no original content needed) or non-blind (original content required).

The high-level workflow of a watermarking system is illustrated below in Figure 1:

Figure 1. The workflow of a watermarking system.

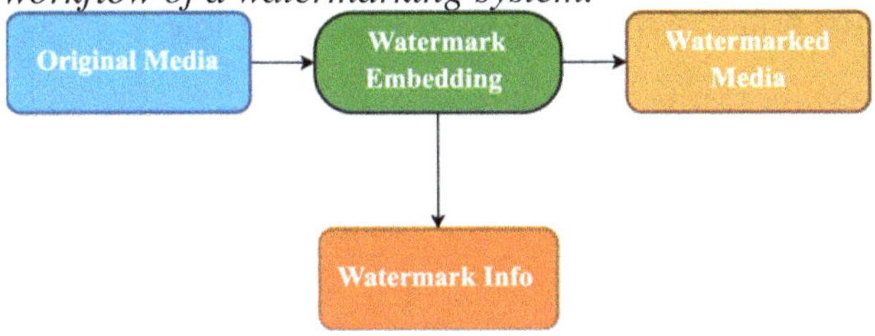

2.2 Types of Watermarks

Various criteria can categorise digital watermarks:

a. **Visibility**:
   - *Visible Watermarks*: Perceptible to the user, e.g. a translucent logo.
   - *Invisible Watermarks*: Essentially undetectable, hidden in the media content, usually used for copyright protection.

b. **Robustness**:
   - *Fragile Watermarks*: Fragile Watermarks are easily destroyed if the media value is altered. Useful for content authentication.
   - *Robust Watermarks*: survive common transformations: compression, scaling, cropping. Useful for copyright tracking.

c. **Domain**:
   - *Spatial Domain*: embeds information in the pixel values directly into the image.
   - *Frequency Domain*: embeds or modifies the coefficients of the transformed image through the DCT, DWT, or FFT.

d. **Dependence**:
   - *Blind Watermarking*: Blind watermarking does not require the original media at the time of extraction.
   - *Non-blind Watermarking*: Non-blind watermarking requires access to the original media at the time of extraction.

2.3 Key Parameters

For instance, a watermarking technique utilised for forensic tracking would want a watermark that is robust and secure. On the other hand, a watermarking technique used for authenticity would look for a watermark that is both fragile and imperceptible. The problems with evaluating the effectiveness of a watermarking technique rely on several important parameters, as provided in Table 1.

Table 1. The several parameters used for evaluating the watermarking effectiveness.

Parameter	Description
Robustness	The ability of the watermark to withstand signal processing attacks or distortions
Imperceptibility	The degree to which the watermark affects the quality of the host media
Capacity	The amount of information that can be embedded without compromising quality
Security	Protection against unauthorised detection, removal, or forging of the watermark
Complexity	Computational resources and time required for embedding and extraction

2.4 Application Scenarios

Here are several typical examples of digital watermarking, including its -

- Copyright Protection: The ability to encode ownership of media to evidence its origin.
- Broadcast Monitoring: The ability to monitor for illegal broadcasting or distribution of media.
- Medical Imaging: The ability to protect, preserve and transmit viewpoints of serious diagnostic images that contain sensitive information regarding patient confidentiality.
- Surveillance Video: The ability to prevent tampering with security video.
- Authentication and Tamper Detection: The ability to indicate if a digital document or image has been changed or modified illegally.

Once we shift this technology into a cloud computing environment, the watermarking must be efficient, automated, and robust, given the large volume of content and the variety of content being processed. It is this necessity that sets the stage for the development of artificial intelligence (AI) and machine learning (ML), which will now come into play as part of the watermarking pipeline discussed in the following sections.

2.5 Limitations of Traditional Watermarking Approaches

Traditional watermarking techniques, developed primarily for controlled, single-user environments, face significant limitations when deployed in cloud-based scenarios. These limitations become particularly pronounced when dealing with the complexity and scale of modern cloud applications. The limitations are discussed below:

a. Static Parameter Optimisation

Conventional watermarking algorithms typically rely on fixed parameters determined during system design or deployment. These parameters are often optimised for specific content types or attack scenarios, leading to suboptimal performance when applied to diverse real-world content. In cloud environments where content characteristics vary dramatically, static approaches result in either over-embedding (causing perceptual artefacts) or under-embedding (reducing robustness) (Lukas, Diaa, Fenaux, & Kerschbaum, 2023). For example, a traditional DCT-based watermarking system might use fixed quantisation steps that work well for natural images but perform poorly on computer graphics, text documents, or low-quality compressed images commonly found in cloud platforms. The inability to adapt these parameters dynamically based on content analysis represents a fundamental limitation in scalable cloud deployments.

b. Limited Attack Modelling

Traditional approaches typically consider a limited set of well-defined attacks such as JPEG compression, Gaussian noise, or geometric transformations. However, cloud environments introduce novel attack vectors, including:

- Transcoding Attacks: Automatic format and quality changes made by cloud services
- Distributed Processing Artefacts: Damage to watermarks because of effects from distributed encoding, caching, and content delivery networks (CDN)
- Machine Learning-Based Attacks: More sophisticated, adversarial attacks leveraging knowledge of the watermarking algorithm
- Multimodal Attacks: Attacks that target multiple aspects of the watermarking system at the same time

c. Computational Performance Constraints

Cloud Platforms are designed for input/output and high throughput processing that traditional algorithms cannot provide. Classical watermarking methods often involve resource-intensive computational steps, such as full-frame transforms, repeated optimisation/estimation processes, or extensive synchronisation algorithms, which become the limiting step in high-throughput cloud use cases (Nie & Lu, 2024).

d. Lack of Context

Traditional approaches to watermarking are often performed in a "one-shot" scenario and do not consider greater context for more informed, intelligence-driven watermarking decisions. In contrast, cloud environments generate a substantial amount of context and information, including user and user interactions, content metrics (e.g., popularity), network metrics (e.g., network congestion state), and security metrics and threat intelligence, which can facilitate more innovative watermarking strategies.

3. ROLE OF AI/ML IN ADAPTIVE WATERMARKING

AI (Artificial Intelligence) and ML (Machine Learning) enable users to incorporate dynamic intelligence into watermarking systems, thereby significantly enhancing the robustness, flexibility, and scalability of watermarking systems for current applications. With AI and machine learning, users can transition from static, rule-based models to learning-based designs that are capable of adapting to a broader range of signals, transformations, and attack paths.

3.1 Why Adaptive Watermarking?

Traditional watermarking approaches typically utilise static parameters and heuristic rules that were initially designed for environments that were simpler and more predictable. On the one hand, these methods can be successful under limited conditions; however, they will perform poorly in cloud-based multimedia systems, where the content is highly dynamic due to changes in resolution, texture, format, and compression standards. The dynamic characteristics create variances that significantly disrupt traditional watermarking techniques, which are vulnerable to a limitless number of modifications and attacks using artefacts such as clipping, filtering, quantisation, printing, and resampling (Liu & Bu, 2024). Adaptive watermarking methods address these problems by enabling intelligent watermarking systems to adapt to changes in the watermarking strategy based on the characteristics of the multimedia content and the threat environment. Adaptive watermarking based on AI (Artificial Intelligence) and ML (Machine Learning) provides a new dimension to watermarking. An adaptive watermarking system powered by AI and ML can potentially learn from enormous datasets to discover optimal embedding locations that promote robustness while minimising perceptual distortion. They can dynamically adjust the watermark strength based on the image's complexity, embedding it firmly in areas that are noisy or textured and embedding it lightly in smoother regions, thereby maintaining visual quality. In addition, AI/ML-enabled watermarking systems can automatically distinguish and classify attack types—such as geometric changes, compression artefacts, and adversarial noise—and adjust their embedding and detection processes accordingly. This ensures that the watermark remains visible even in fluid, unstable, or hostile environments. All of this can scale to thousands of multimedia files, distributed cloud services, and conduct real-time tasks, making policy and automated decisions while eliminating human engagement (Boenisch, 2021). With the platform's awareness of content, attack identification, and self-adjusting measures, AI-based adaptive watermarking offers transdisciplinary solutions for robustly protecting digital media assets within complex, high-volume systems.

3.2 Role of AI in Watermark Design

Artificial Intelligence (AI) techniques, such as fuzzy logic, expert systems, and reinforcement learning, enable adaptive watermarking with informed, intelligent decision-making based on both content-specific and context-specific characteristics. These systems go beyond traditional watermarking systems because dynamic behaviour is introduced over the static parameterisations found in conventional systems to create more resilient, efficient, and perceptually embedded watermarks in the host content. These systems use knowledge representation and inference mechanisms to:

- Decide on watermark strength dynamically.
- Choose the embedding domain (spatial, frequency, or hybrid).
- Optimise tradeoffs between imperceptibility and robustness.
- Incorporate user-defined policies, quality metrics, or environmental factors.

For example, systems specifically provide an excellent way to manage uncertainty and imprecision when working with multimedia data. The representation of linguistic variables—for example, "high detail," "low contrast," or "medium texture"—and a fuzzy inference engine can, in theory, be used to assess content characteristics and determine the best watermarking decisions. Consider that if a region of an image has high texture, then a fuzzy system might use a stronger watermark, making it multi-layered and, therefore, difficult to remove. For smooth regions, the watermark can be made less intense to hide it. The decisions that the system samples from are based on a rule base that defines the associations; fuzzy membership functions would have values that simulate human-like reasoning, interpreted through this method of logic (Wang, Wu, & Wang, 2023).

In summary, systems can function independently as intelligent agents that respond to various media conditions. Expert systems can enhance their capabilities by incorporating domain knowledge and pre-declared rules as part of their decision-making process rather than relying solely on intelligent reasoning and content interpretation. Expert systems would help select a domain for watermarking (as discussed earlier, spatial, frequency, or hybrid) based on content assessment and risk assessment. Also, when using expert systems, they will be able to incorporate user-defined policies, application requirements and quality limitations, which allows for more flexible (and context-aware) watermarking schemes. Reinforcement learning (RL) defines methods for utilising feedback in the watermarking process, and the watermarking system operates as an agent that can interact with the environment to learn how to embed (Zhao, Ananth, Li, & Wang, 2023). In RL, the agent learns depending on the system in which it interacts (agent = watermarking system, environment = video), which occurs through a balance of exploration and exploitation. The ultimate goal is to converge on optimal embedding actions that exhibit low perceptual distortion and high resistance to removal. The agent receives rewards for or relative to its success with watermark detection across various attacks; it refines its actions over time to maximise long-term success. These AI approaches, when combined, allow for watermarking to be manipulated as a complex adaptive process that self-tunes and responds intelligently. They enable systems to adaptively alter watermark strength, optimise embedding and distortion parameters, and incorporate context signals like user preferences or system limits. Taken together, an AI watermarking solution allows the watermark system to respond to the operational context as required. AI watermarking solutions will be able to handle the real world., providing protections that are more robust and have applicability across content and situational contexts.

3.3 Machine Learning Techniques for Adaptive Watermarking

Machine Learning (ML) algorithms have become essential components of modern adaptive watermarking systems due to their ability to provide predictive insights, pattern recognition, and dynamic optimisation. These algorithms help automate and refine the watermark embedding and detection processes, making them more responsive to diverse content types, evolving attack patterns, and system constraints. Depending on the problem context and system requirements, various machine learning (ML) paradigms can be employed, each contributing unique advantages. The most commonly used approaches include:

- **Supervised Learning:** Supervised learning is frequently used in watermarking for tasks such as content classification, perceptual quality prediction, and attack detection. By training models like Support Vector Machines (SVMs), Decision Trees, or Neural Networks on labelled datasets, the system can learn to identify suitable embedding regions (e.g., areas with high texture or low perceptibility) or predict the likelihood of watermark degradation under specific transformations (Aberna & Agilandeeswari, 2024). For example, a neural network trained on image-label pairs can classify image regions based on sensitivity and recommend a corresponding watermark strength accordingly.
- **Unsupervised Learning:** Unsupervised learning techniques, such as clustering (e.g., k-means) and dimensionality reduction (e.g., Principal Component Analysis or PCA), are used when labelled data is scarce. These methods can reveal hidden structures in multimedia data, which aids in developing the watermarking system's ability to locate suitable embedding regions or content characteristics that are related to watermarking robustness. Self-organising maps and hierarchical clustering could also assist with the task of identifying natural clusters in media files mapping to different embedding rules.
- **Reinforcement Learning:** Reinforcement learning (RL) is a powerful subset of machine learning that is based on learning from interaction. For watermarking applications, the RL agent will constantly assess the quality and robustness of the watermark it embeds at time raven based on some environmental feedback — i.e., the rate of detections, attacks survived, etc. The agent will adjust its embedding strategies over time based on cumulative feedback from both environments and, in almost all cases, due to retaliation, as well as with high integration for both success touchdown rate and low perceptual impact. RL agents will utilise the action policy to learn embedding policies that react to constantly evolving conditions and evade attackers.
- **Deep Learning:** Deep learning creates high levels of automation in watermarking systems. Convolutional Neural Networks (CNNs) are naturally suited for multimedia analysis, especially image watermarking, due to their patterned spatially dependent capabilities. Recurrent Neural Networks (RNNs), Long Short-Term Memory (LSTM) networks, or Gated Recurrent Units (GRUs) are used to obtain and maintain the sequential history of video frame streams, considering the temporal property of a placeholder that marks the watermark placement in time or video frame detection. Generative Adversarial Networks (GANs) have given rise to powerful techniques in which a generator learns to embed strong, impossible watermarks. At the same time, a discriminator applies simulated attacks or even seeks to remove them so that the watermarking techniques can be improved against attacker-based methods through adversarial training.

Each machine learning (ML) technique plays its role in enhancing watermarking performance. CNNs can learn to maximise and embed watermarks in perceptually less sensitive areas while being able to exploit previously learned visual patterns. Even if the motion was not an issue, RNNs could immediately provide a more consistently applied video watermarking strategy, as they can find a way to incorporate motion-aware watermarking. GANs offer a unique ability to simulate attacker behaviour within the counterfeit able landscape, allowing the watermarking system to get its bearings by continuously learning from synthetic attacks (Sahu et al., 2023). By incorporating machine learning (ML) into watermarking, the systems are no longer static or rule-based. They are dynamic and constantly changing. They can process real-time data streams, learn to act based on deployment feedback and update their logic for embedding autonomously in real-time (as opposed to through a future, batch-processed analysis). The system will ingest attack sources and learn and understand how to thwart future similar attacks. Collectively, this leads to improved watermarking strength and efficiency, allowing for more complex and intelligent watermarking systems to emerge that are truly context-aware, fitting a modern multimedia ecosystem.

3.4 Advantages of AI-Driven Adaptive Watermarking

The benefits of incorporating Artificial Intelligence (AI) and Machine Learning (ML) into copyright protection watermark systems are transformative, particularly in addressing the increased complexity required by cloud-based copyright protection. Rather than relying on a simple heuristic-based approach, these intelligent systems operate more dynamically to address the demands of content, context, and the evolving threat landscape. Some of the key benefits include intelligent parameter selection. AI-based watermarking systems can quickly analyse content to determine appropriate parameters for embedding. For example, Image content can have numerous semantically significant features, allowing complicated decision-making. Deep Learning can identify features and dimensions of texture complexity to find areas with sufficient texture where the watermark can be embedded without significantly distorting the image. For example, human faces or text are semantically essential and should be preserved whenever possible in the image to support the visual message. AI could also analyse the edges of images to decide where to increase robustness to distortion (Liu et al., 2023). The system can also conduct frequency analysis to determine the optimal transform domain (DCT, DWT, or hybrid) for maximum resistance to compression and filtering. Another key benefit of using AI is the ability to optimise multiple objectives. The goals of watermarking are often at odds; not only does the watermark need to be invisible and resistant to attacks, but it also needs to have some computational efficiency associated with it. AI-based optimisation approaches, such as genetic algorithms, reinforcement learning, and neural architecture search, can dynamically solve that tradeoff. That is, it can optimise for perceptual quality (whether the watermark resembles the original signal), robustness (the watermark remains intact against common attacks), security (the watermark cannot be detected and thus remains undetected), and computational efficiency (i.e., shorter processing time and reduced memory usage). Such an all-in-one optimisation task is challenging to accomplish with standard approaches, which tend to involve a significant amount of manual intervention in processing algorithms and established relationships between tuning parameters.

As far as scalability is concerned, AI techniques align well with the current cloud-based environment. Deep networking computation is highly parallelisable, which enhances GPU acceleration and distributed computing across multiple machines as more computing and storage resources are required. Batch processing enables systems to embed a watermark into thousands of images and/or videos simultaneously, reducing the time needed to fulfil jobs and improving the productivity and efficiency of enterprise video. Additionally, AI watermarking models can be deployed in fluid ways in an on-demand context through edge computing nodes, containerised applications (e.g., Docker), and/or serverless execution environments (AWS Lambda), allowing for efficient execution at various points in the media distribution schedule. AI systems also facilitate resource elasticity, referring to the dynamic assignment of computational resources based on workload demand, which helps lower costs and improve the system's responsiveness in high-traffic environments. Ultimately, AI and ML provide an intelligent and adaptable backbone for scalable watermarking systems, meeting the efficiency and scalability requirements of modern cloud infrastructures. AI systems offer access to semantic awareness, optimising performance in real-time, and an elastic deployment model. As a result, AI-enabled watermarking systems present a significant advance in digital rights management and copyright protection technology.

3.5 Cloud-Specific Considerations and Opportunities

The unique considerations and opportunities provided by AI-enabled watermarking in the cloud affect the design and implications of deployment through the development of advanced distributed processing architectures that can be applied to watermarking systems. Edge-cloud hybrid processing models can be employed by cloud platforms that recognise that operationally latency-critical edges can be merged with computationally heavy cloud servers, thereby allowing organisations to maximise the performance of processing within an efficient cloud processing framework. Such environments support microservices architecture approaches that enable the separation of watermarking functionality, allowing it to exist as scalable and independently deployable services. This offers advantages in system design flexibility and maintainability. Moreover, serverless computing implementations can enable watermarking functionalities to work dynamically, automatically scaling serverless operations. Container orchestration technologies will allow us to deploy and manage watermarking services across a distributed infrastructure (Madala et al., 2023). The data integration and analytics capabilities within cloud platforms provide us with access to rich data sources, enhancing watermarking capabilities through full-scale content characterisation and behavioural analysis. Cloud-based analytic services offer the ability to conduct sophisticated content analytics, revealing new insights into media characteristics and usage patterns. User behaviour data integration can incorporate user interaction patterns into our watermarking approaches to enhance capabilities, particularly for specific use cases and audiences. Network intelligence applications utilise network monitoring inputs to enable adaptable watermarking approaches across various combinations of transmission conditions and network characteristics. Any available threat intelligence feeds can be integrated into security for the watermarking systems as a way of pre-emptively protecting against new directed attack vectors and attacks of unknown or evolving overhead. The ability to integrate into a cloud environment is significant for service integration. Cloud services offer comprehensive service ecosystems that can be incorporated into watermarking systems to enhance their functionality and operational effectiveness.

Last but not least, there are content optimisation capabilities for watermarking systems designed for use with CDN-based content distribution, ensuring consistent watermarking protection for global distribution. The connection to cloud-based media processing services enables watermarking to be embedded in transcoding and media processing pipelines, improving the workflow for content protection. The cloud-based AI and ML platforms would allow organisations to leverage the capabilities of artificial intelligence and machine learning, incorporating advanced watermarking features such as enhanced detection, adaptive protection, and other applications. Lastly, integrating cloud-based security services enables organisations to create comprehensive content protection solutions that allow for combining watermarking within broader security frameworks to protect digital assets from end to end.

4. THEORETICAL FOUNDATIONS OF AI/ML IN WATERMARKING

The integration of artificial intelligence (AI) and machine learning (ML) within digital watermarking has significantly transformed the design and implementation of adaptive, resilient, and context-aware watermarking techniques. An understanding of the theoretical foundations underlying the methods described in this section is essential for designing intelligent watermarking frameworks. This section briefly describes three critical types of machine learning: supervised, unsupervised, and reinforcement learning, before outlining several significant neural network architectures, specifically CNNs, RNNs and GANs, each offering multiple distinct capabilities to watermarking systems.

4.1 Machine Learning Paradigms for Watermarking

The adoption of machine learning represents a fundamental change from traditional rule-based analysis to data-driven analysis. Each change can be classified as either supervised learning, unsupervised learning, or reinforcement learning. Each paradigm has inherent benefits and drawbacks, and each addresses unique challenges within adaptive watermarking. Each approach provides a different view of how intelligent systems optimise the performance of watermarking systems.

A. Supervised Learning Approaches

Supervised learning approaches utilise labelled training datasets as input to learning the best watermarking approaches. The training data may consist of host media (samples) along with the optimal watermarking improvements and/or the strategies applied to the host media. The system learns to map an input's properties (e.g., the complexity of texture from a raster, the density of edges, or distributions in the frequency spectrum) to optimal watermarking decisions. There are also supervised learning methods, such as Support Vector Machines (SVM), Decision Trees, Random Forests, and Artificial Neural Networks (ANN). The workflow of supervised learning is shown in Figure 2. Typical supervised learning applications in watermarking include:

- Classifying content regions for selective embedding.
- Regression models: Almost optimal predictions for strength parameter values.
- Pattern recognition for attack detection and classification.
- Quality assessment: For perceptual optimization.

Example Workflow is shown in Figure 2:

Figure 2. The supervised learning approach.

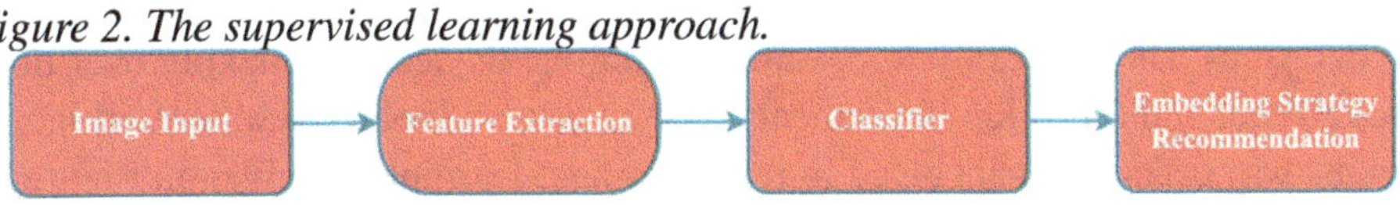

Effective supervised learning requires careful feature engineering to capture relevant content characteristics that are shown in Table 2 below:

Table 2. The Features that are relevant for content characteristics.

Feature Category	Examples	Watermarking Relevance
Spatial Features	Edge density, texture energy, local variance	Embedding strength optimization
Frequency Features	DCT coefficients, wavelet energy, and spectral entropy	Transform domain selection
Perceptual Features	Visual attention maps, saliency scores, JND thresholds	Quality-aware embedding
Statistical Features	Histogram properties, moments, and correlation	Capacity estimation
Semantic Features	Object detection, scene classification, and content type	Context-aware strategies

B. Unsupervised Learning Approaches

Unsupervised learning methods operate on unlabeled data to discover hidden patterns and structures that can inform watermarking decisions. These approaches are particularly valuable when labelled training data is scarce or when the system needs to adapt to previously unseen content types or attack patterns. The techniques commonly used in unsupervised learning include K-means, DBSCAN, and Auto-encoders. Key unsupervised learning applications include:

- Clustering of content features for adaptive strategy selection.
- Dimensionality reduction for efficient feature representation.
- Anomaly detection for identifying potential attacks.
- Self-organising maps for content-based parameter optimisation.

C. Reinforcement Learning Approaches

Reinforcement learning is an exciting paradigm for use in adaptive watermarking, as it enables an agent to learn an optimal watermarking policy while interacting with the environment. The agent obtains rewards based on the quality of its watermarking decisions, and it uses these rewards to improve its decision-making over time through trial and error. Reinforcement learning can be applied to watermarking in various ways. The steps involved in reinforcement learning are given in Figure 3. These include:

- Changing the watermarking parameters depending on the feedback
- Optimising multi-objectives of robustness
- Adaptive countermeasures for attacks
- Long-term optimisation strategies for environments such as cloud

The Core Elements of the RL Watermarking Model:

- State (s): represent the features of the image/image distortions and the type of attack.
- Action (a): the watermarking parameters (e.g., strength and domain)
- Reward (r): a metric that represents imperceptibility (PSNR), robustness (BER), and successful extraction (NC).

The Reward Function (R) is the effective metric for the quality of the decisions. The equation for the Reward Function is:

$$R(s,a) = w_1 \cdot R\_quality + w_2 \cdot R\_robustness + w_3 \cdot R\_capacity + w_4 \cdot R\_efficiency. \quad (1)$$

Where:

- R_quality: Perceptual quality preservation reward
- R_robustness: Attack resistance reward
- R_capacity: Payload capacity reward
- R_efficiency: Computational efficiency reward

Figure 3. The process of reinforcement Learning.

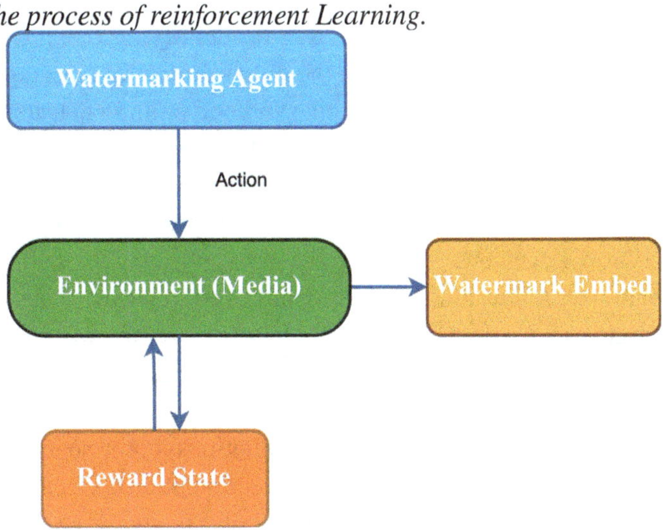

D. Neural Network Architectures for Watermarking

Deep learning architectures have significantly more computational power and abstraction in modelling complicated relationships for image and video watermarking. Specifically, Convolutional Neural Networks (CNNs) have emerged as a preferred model because they are more focused on spatial (local) features and textures. CNNs have been used for watermark embedding and extraction in a content-aware manner by learning contextual strategies. One popular variation of CNNs is the U-Net architecture, which employs an encoder-decoder structure with skip connections to preserve spatial fidelity during the embedding process. Specifically, it enables the detailed embedding of watermarks across multiple scales, making them especially suitable for image watermarking assignments that require precise watermark placement and perceptual fidelity. In a temporal sense, video watermarking applications are ideal for Recurrent Neural Networks (RNNs). RNNs, as Long Short-Term Memory (LSTM) and Gated Recurrent Units (GRU) approaches, are more apt to capture temporal dependencies in sequential data. RNNs will learn to synchronise watermark placement across frames, which will help detect frame-based manipulations and adapt watermarking policies over time. A recommended architecture would consist of CNN layers for feature extraction in each video frame, followed by RNN layers that model the temporal flow and recommend changes in the watermarking embeddings.

Generative Adversarial Networks (GANs) employ an adversarial learning model wherein a generator network learns to embed watermarks in media while a discriminator attempts to detect and remove those watermarks. In this minimax game, the generator continues to improve in creating imperceptible and durable watermarks, while the discriminator improves in detecting or identifying them. Outside of referring to supervised learning, GANs are the only example of learning in the form of adversarial learning, as well as generating synthetic training data to reinforce the learning. Other GAN variants, such as Cycle GANs, aim to preserve the semantic content structure during the watermarking process, ensuring that the perceptual loss doesn't compromise the original media. Cycle GANs are a variant of GANs that learn conditional distributions. Since the notation specifies that the GAN is a conditioned one, we present it as a conditional GAN. In terms of how all of these learning paradigms and neural network models fit together within a theoretical framework related to intelligent watermarking also entails the nature of learning dynamics that learn from data and are not just more robust, and hence scalable and adaptive, systems concerning media manipulations, but systems that are more resistant to change across a broader range of manipulations. Generally speaking, GANs are suitable for visually watermarking digital media, especially video and audio media, where watermark payload capacity, imperceptibility, generalisation, and robustness criteria represent an information-theoretic approach to background models on a unified loss objective. The common training objective in watermarking models based on GANs can be expressed as composite loss $L_{i} ={L}_{GAN}+ {L}_{perceptual} + {L}_{robustness}+{L}_{capacity}$. This means in advancing towards a common goal/security (L_{GAN}), it is possible to optimise a subset of information features simultaneously ($L_{perceptual}$ and $L_{robustness}$), along with optimising the watermark information payload capacity ($L_{capacity}$) across a commonly-found model on unique documents) represented by the same model. Following this, we will build upon these theoretical points to discuss the practical application of deep learning frameworks within end-to-end watermarking systems. Neural networks offer powerful frameworks for adaptive watermarking systems. There are many different models developed, each targeting unique components of the watermarking process, such as embedding optimisation and resilience to attacks.

E. Convolutional Neural Networks (CNNs)

CNNs were designed to process spatial information and have numerous applications in image and video watermarking. The way CNNs operate on spatial content enables them to capture both the features of local content and the spatial dependencies between features, making them ideal for content-adaptive watermarking approaches. Applications of CNNs in watermarking include:

- Spatial domain embedding optimisations.
- Content analysis for adaptive parameters.
- Attack profile recognition and classification.
- Perceptual models and Quality assessments.

The basic CNN architecture for watermarking consists of several key components that are shown in Figure 4:

Figure 4. The CNN architecture showing the key components of the process.

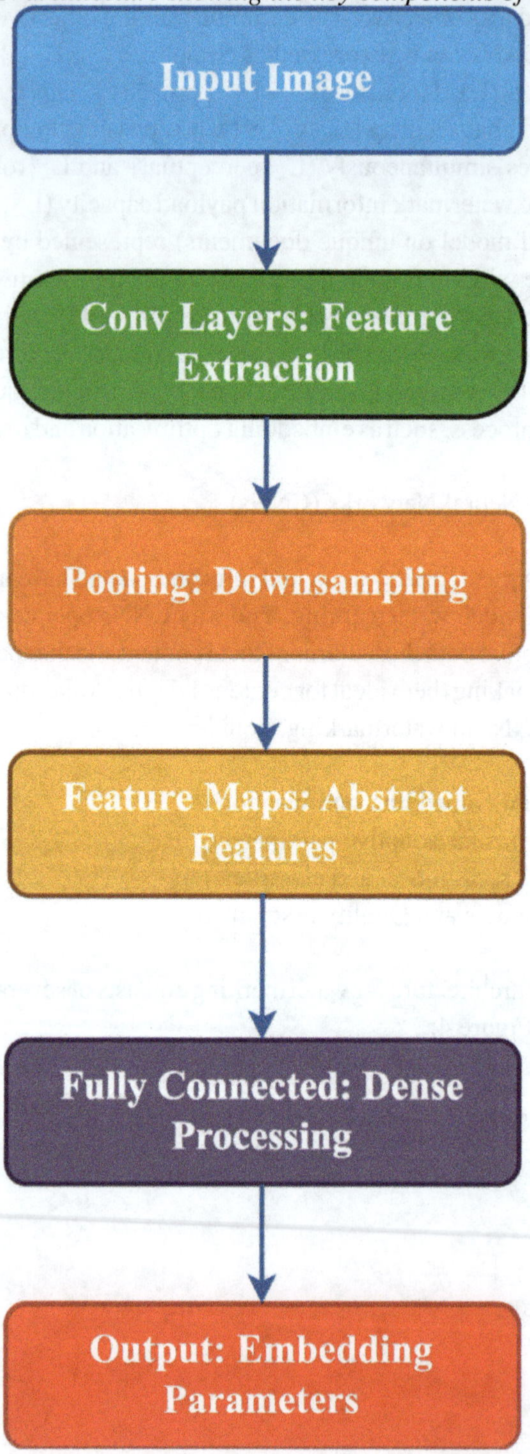

U-Net Architecture: In the case of CNN-based watermarking, U-Nets are utilised to further enhance watermark extraction and watermark removal via the U-Net's ability to access structural hierarchy by removing relationships. In other words, U-Nets are utilised to refine the long-term dependencies found in deep CNNs while continuing to extend the model's adaptiveness to diverse watermarks. The heterogeneous U-Net architecture predicts different outcomes based on various components and is used to extract more complementary structural information. The U-Net architecture has proven highly effective for watermarking applications due to its ability to preserve spatial information while extracting features. The architecture example for U-Net Adaptation for Watermarking is shown in Figure 5.

Architecture Example:

Figure 5. The U-Net adaptation for the watermarking process.

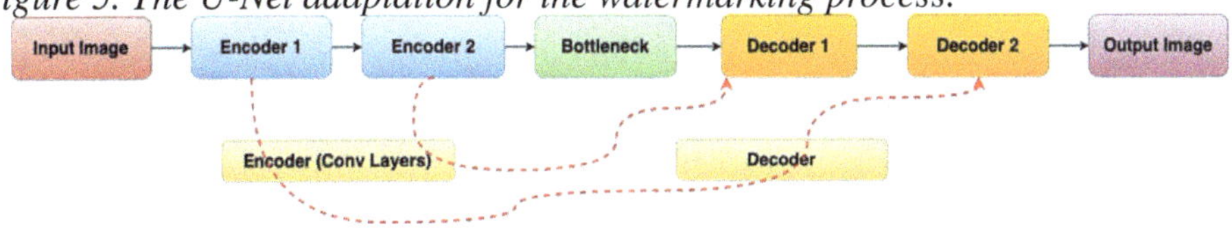

Advantages:

- Strong spatial localisation.
- Multi-scale representation.
- Efficient inference on edge/cloud devices.

F. Recurrent Neural Networks (RNNs)

RNNs, including LSTM (Long Short-Term Memory) and GRU (Gated Recurrent Unit), were designed to handle sequential data. They can analyse temporal patterns in video or sequential patterns in attacks within watermarking scenarios. RNN applications could include the following:

- Temporal frame or sequence watermarking
- Sequential attack detection and prediction
- Changes to parameters involving time
- Temporal correlation analysis for synchrony

RNN Architecture for Watermarking

The RNN-based example for basic video embedding is shown in Figure 6. Basic RNN formulation for watermarking applications is given in equations 2 and 3:

$$h\_t = f(W\_h \cdot h\_\{t-1\} + W\_x \cdot x\_t + b) \quad (2)$$

$$y\_t = g(W\_y \cdot h\_t + b\_y) \quad (3)$$

Where:

- h_t: Hidden state at time t
- x_t: Input features at time t
- y_t: Watermarking decision at time t
- W_h, W_x, W_y: Learnable weight matrices
- f, g: Activation functions

Figure 6. The RNN-based video embedding process.

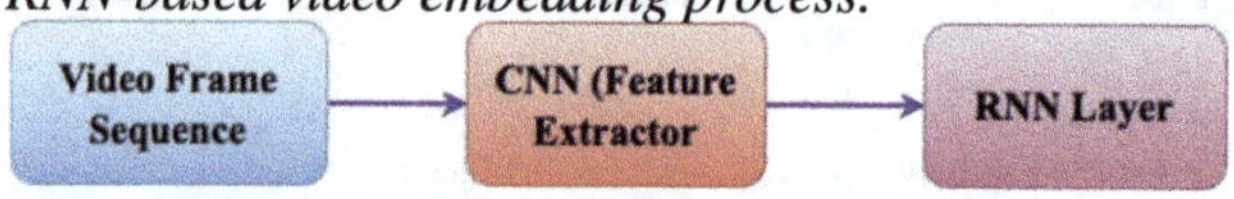

G. Generative Adversarial Networks (GANs)

Generative adversarial networks are a groundbreaking method for watermarking. In GANs, two neural networks play a minimax game. The first neural network (the generator) produces either watermarks or watermarked content, while the other neural network (the discriminator) attempts to detect or remove the watermark. GAN use cases include:

- Robust watermark generation
- Adversarial training for robustness against attacks
- Embedding that is perceptually optimised
- Generating synthetic training data

Advanced processes include:

- CycleGAN: embeds while preserving content and maintaining consistency.
- Conditional GAN (cGAN): embeds based on input features such as content type.

Figure 7. The GAN-Based watermarking model.

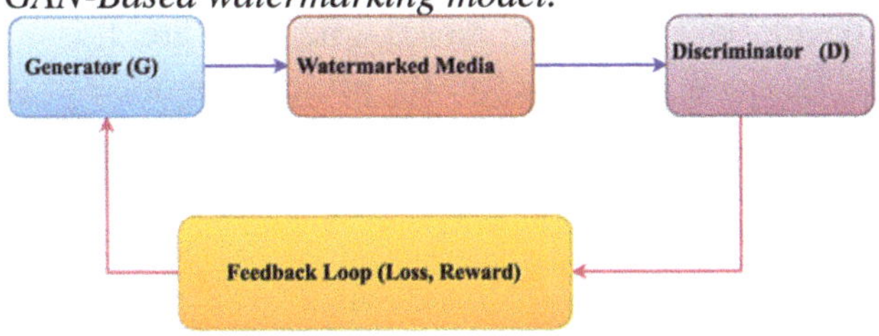

The ability to provide adversarial robustness and embedding optimisation across multiple media types makes GAN-based watermarking ideally suited, as shown in Figure 7. In conclusion, the infusion of foundational AI/ML concepts into watermarking systems provides a vast and customisable toolbox. Each of the different learning paradigms (supervised, unsupervised, and reinforcement) brings its own strengths and neural network implementations (e.g. CNNs, RNNs, GANs) provide opportunities for adaptive, scalable, and robust watermarking.

5. PERFORMANCE EVALUATION AND METRICS

An evaluation of AI watermarking systems requires a combination of classical watermarking metrics and AI-oriented metrics. Classically, watermarks are evaluated primarily based on the quality of the media they preserve and their resistance to removal. AI systems add complexity as they incorporate measures such as training stability, generalisation, and computational resource utilisation. A robust evaluation framework requires a perceptual perspective and sufficient algorithmic perspectives to accurately represent the performance and drawbacks of modern watermarking systems.

5.1 Evaluation Frameworks for AI-Based Watermarking

The traditional metrics of watermarking are still fundamentally important when evaluating AI-integrated systems. Within classical metrics, the Peak signal-to-noise ratio (PSNR) indicates the visual distortion of the watermark relative to the original image. A higher PSNR suggests that the perceptual quality of the image is good. Another well-known metric is the Structural Similarity Index Measure (SSIM). SSIM compares the luminance, contrast, and structural similarity between the original and watermarked images, providing a more human-centric value for watermark imperceptibility. Bit Error Rate (BER) is a measure of how many bits in an extracted watermark vary from the original watermark; this gives a relatively straightforward measure of robustness. Normalised Correlation (NC) is a measure of how similar the original and the extracted watermark are. It is often used when measuring detection fidelity and involves the presence of noise or an attack.

Along with these traditional evaluation criteria, individuals will also examine various aspects associated with AI-based watermarking systems, including several criteria aimed explicitly at assessing machine learning applications. The training convergence rate demonstrates the time and stability of optimal performance attained throughout the training process. Generalisation performance describes the model's performance on unseen datasets and identifies how well its performance can be generalised across various content types. Computational efficiency is assessed by a combination of floating-point operations (FLOPs) and memory consumption, which are critical when deploying to cloud and edge scenarios. Adaptation speed refers to the rate at which an AI model adjusts to changing attack patterns, which is crucial in real-time and adversarial environments. Formal evaluations of AI-based watermarking systems should be conducted using specialised evaluation frameworks that can provide explicit assessments of traditional watermarking metrics, as well as AI-specific evaluation measures.

- **Traditional Watermarking Metrics**

Standard metrics remain necessary for evaluating AI-based systems, as shown in Table 3:

Table 3: The metrics used for AI-based evaluation of systems.

Metric	Purpose	Calculation
PSNR	Image quality	$10 \log_{10}(MAX^2/MSE)$
SSIM	Structural similarity	$(2\mu_X\mu \ + c_1)(2\sigma_X \ + c_2) / ((\mu_X{}^2 + \mu^2 + c_1)(\sigma_X{}^2 + \sigma^2 + c_2))$
BER	Bit error rate	(Number of error bits)/ (Total bits)
NC	Normalised correlation	$\Sigma\ (w(i,j) \cdot w'(i,j)) / \Sigma\ (w(i,j)^2)$

- **AI-specific Evaluation Metrics**

Additional metrics for AI systems include:

- Training convergence rates
- Generalisation performance across datasets
- Computational efficiency (FLOPs, memory usage)
- Adaptation speed to new attack types

6. IMPLEMENTATION CONSIDERATIONS FOR CLOUD ENVIRONMENTS

As digital watermarking movements become increasingly cloud-based, particularly in terms of CDNs (Content Delivery Networks), streaming, and social media, scalability and privacy will become primary concerns. Systems modified to incorporate AI will need to be designed not just for accuracy but for ease of deployment on cloud services and for the secure management of the content itself.

6.1 Scalability and Distributed Processing

Watermarking solutions will need to scale if used in cloud environments, meaning that if the application of watermarking passes through the cloud, it must ultimately handle a large amount of data associated with various content types and usage workloads for all parts of the planet. One common way is to provide for scaling machine learning via data parallel training. Data parallel training enables multiple GPUs to run the same model simultaneously, with each GPU processing different data batches, thereby reducing the training time. Alternatively, model parallelism enables the distribution of other model components across multiple GPUs when the model exceeds the capacity of a single GPU. Recently, although it has been around for a while, there may also be more possibilities for federated learning, which allows for privacy-preserving distributed training without ever sharing raw data. Federated learning will enable precursors to allow edge devices to create local models using local private data and only share model updates to one server. Concepts related to federated learning typically make sense if those needing to embed watermarks must do so on their own devices before uploading to the cloud. For those examples where watermarking is considered a regular part of content creation, utilising edge computing as part of the content creation process would also offer advantages in terms of scalability, allowing for remote, fast, or even offline decisions on watermarking. It can also enable decision-making to begin on user devices without introducing additional latency or data load to our services. To accommodate dynamic workloads, load balancing algorithms are used to adjust task assignments by adapting to media size, available resources, and workload. In addition to improving responsiveness and total throughput, efficiently using GPU hardware and memory resources can aid in optimising performance. Network-aware frameworks can also distribute processing across regions, limiting latency.

6.2 Security and Privacy Considerations

Watermarking systems built on AI models have created new types of attacks that pose security risks. Model extraction attacks enable adversaries to reconstruct the underlying watermarking network by querying it with input-output pairs. The threat of reverse engineering a watermarking method is especially acute for watermark detectors and extractors. Adversarial examples are input perturbations that are small enough to trick the model, causing it to fail to recognise a watermark or falsely recognise a watermark in some clean content. Backdoor attacks can also compromise the integrity of the training dataset or model weights by inserting hidden triggers that control model output behaviours. Another primary concern is model inversion, where an attacker reconstructs the input from the output produced by the model. For example, this might breach content confidentiality because the underlying input content is extracted from a model using its output. In light of these security threats, watermarking models must adopt privacy-preserving training approaches. Formal techniques, such as differential privacy, will ensure that learning from individual media samples does not overly influence model parameters and functions, providing formal security guarantees against data leakage. Secure multi-party computation technology enables multiple entities to jointly train or evaluate watermarking models without disclosing their private information to one another. Homomorphic encryption enables computations to be performed on encrypted data, allowing the content to remain protected even during the inference phase. In addition, federated learning not only supports scalability but also enables greater data sovereignty, as the data remains on the user's device. In summary, rigorous evaluation and secure, scalable implementations for cloud deployments determine the success or failure of AI-driven watermarking systems. If done correctly, these evaluations will maximise overall system performance while protecting individual users' privacy and accommodating potential real-world limitations. AI-based watermarking systems operating in cloud environments minimise security threats but will still have inevitable security concerns that will need to be addressed.

7. CASE STUDIES AND APPLICATIONS

The use of AI-based watermarking solutions in commercial cloud platforms has a proven track record of considerable success in the real world. These experiences demonstrate the strength and scalability of intelligent watermarking in real-world operational environments.

Case Study 1: Large-Scale Image Hosting Platform

A well-known global image hosting platform integrated an AI watermarking engine into its content delivery infrastructure. Central to the system was a convolutional neural network (CNN) for a comprehensive content analysis of each uploaded image. Once content features were identified, such as texture granularity, edge maps, luminance distributions, etc., the framework would then determine the embedding strategies automatically (and in real-time). This embedded watermark would strive to be imperceptible to end users while maximising robustness. The self-authoring watermarking pipeline was executed across different cloud regions worldwide, each with its own distributed inference nodes for real-time processing. Significantly, the watermarking engine automatically started its watermark embedding process once the image was ingested into the CDN. Furthermore, as part of the AI engine design, a reinforcement learning algorithm iteratively learnt quality and performance indicators that would govern the watermark parameters over time as it identified simulated attacks or real-time watermark recovering performance. Operational Results of the System on the CDN:

- Throughput - Average of >1,000 images processed per minute per node. • Imperceptibility - Achieved an average PSNR rating of >40 dB.
- Robustness - 95% recovery rate from successful watermark recoveries after common geometric and compression attacks.
- Scalability - The system scale was linear to 100 processing nodes without loss of performance.

Case Study 2: Video Streaming Service

A well-known video streaming website had to determine how to embed robust watermarks into both live and on-demand video content that was distributed globally. The team ultimately deployed a hybrid AI model that utilised convolutional neural networks (CNNs) for extracting spatial features and recurrent neural networks (RNNs), specifically long short-term memory (LSTM), to maintain watermarking consistency across a series of frames with high motion. This implementation not only allowed for consistent frame-level watermarking even in high-motion scenarios, but the embedding of watermarks was also done seamlessly without impacting the viewing experience. The architecture allowed for embedding in real-time utilising edge server deployment, in which latency challenges were addressed through model pruning and quantisation. Lastly, adaptive bitrate streaming necessitated the watermark aspect to be scalable for each encoding layer, and this scalability was achieved through reinforcement learning agents trained to select representative frame parameterisation based on the current encoding layer being sent to a user and the capabilities of the user's device. Vote Features and Benefits:

- Temporal Consistency: The RNN modules provided an embedding built into the model to ensure that embedded watermarks were consistent across consecutive video frames.
- Bitrate Consistency: The reinforcement learning agents would dynamically adjust the watermark payload based on the encoding layers.
- Latency Speed: Since the architectures were optimised, they were able to achieve end-to-end embedding latencies of less than 500 ms.
- Attack Resistance: Training neural networks with adversarial data has been found to improve robustness against tools designed to remove watermarks and noise injection generated by pixel- and/or frame-based image intelligences that do not protect video content.

8. CHALLENGES, LIMITATIONS AND FUTURE DIRECTIONS.

8.1 Technical Challenges

Although they are developing well, AI-driven watermarking systems also have their challenges. The first challenge relates to computational complexity. Deep neural networks, particularly GANs and hybrid deep models, are computationally demanding in terms of processing power during both training and inference. This imposes financial constraints when deployed in the cloud and additionally limits real-time use in cases involving high-resolution media. The second major technical issue is the time (real-time) bottleneck. For streamed content (e.g., live events), watermark embedding must occur in several milliseconds (each frame), which requires optimisation, hardware acceleration, and intelligent compression to meet the time constraints. Thirdly, many of the models have large memory footprints, which makes them impractical for devices with limited resources without pruning and/or distillation. The fourth major challenge relates to generalisation or overfitting. An AI model that has been developed and optimised to work on certain specific datasets may not apply well to different types of content. Overfitting to the training data reduces robustness to real-world attacks, novel file types, and sustainment. Models may need to be retrained or fine-tuned to address domain-specific quality, which adds to operational complexity.

8.2 Practical Limitations

One of the primary constraints in utilising AI watermarking systems is the requirement for large, diverse, and well-annotated datasets. Specifically, supervised learning approaches require input data that has been well-annotated and with a known watermark, presence or absence, for a consistent variety of input forms. Creating and maintaining a comprehensive dataset with diverse media types and resolutions for various applications will be a time-consuming and expensive process. Furthermore, corporate computing environments often have enterprise-level barriers to adoption. One not-uncommon obstacle includes coexistence and compatibility with existing legacy systems. Without any established Application Programming Interfaces (APIs) and no standard cross-platform protocols for watermarking (e.g., video, audio), custom development and middleware will be required. These hurdles add time and cost to the original deployment plan. Practicality is also a concern, such as monitoring activities, version control, and model lifecycle management. To illustrate, in cloud production environments, it would be no small feat to update a watermark model across distributed nodes while ensuring the service is not interrupted or disrupted, to notice whether the updated model's behaviour is well-suited for the conditions, and to revert faulty deployments if necessary.

8.3 Future Directions and Research Opportunities

The field of artificial intelligence (AI) based watermarking is progressing rapidly due to recent advances in transformer architectures, which have already revolutionised natural language processing and computer vision and are now emerging in watermarking systems. These transformer models utilise advanced self-attention mechanisms to consider longer-distance dependencies in images and video frames, significantly improving content-aware embedding possibilities. This enables watermarking to adapt to complex visual representations and relations. Transformers lend themselves well to large-batch watermarking in cloud pipelines due to their efficiency as a processing model. Furthermore, with pre-trained vision transformers, it is possible to fine-tune for watermarking tasks and capitalise on large-scale representation learning via extensive training on a diverse range of visual data. Neuromorphic computing is another stimulating technological advance in watermarking, as it draws on biological brain structures to create highly efficient processing systems. Hardware systems specialised as neuromorphic platforms, such as Intel Loihi, based on restricted Boltzmann machine (RBM) principles, and IBM TrueNorth, based on spike-timing-dependent plasticity (STDP) principles, are already capable of executing spiking neural networks with ultra-low power dissipation, meeting real-time performance requirements. Such hardware platforms make them highly applicable to mobile phones or Internet of Things (IoT) devices-based watermarking schema, as real-time watermark embedding and detection algorithms/processes need to be energy-friendly. In addition, neuromorphic-based watermarking platforms also provide higher levels of fault tolerance, which would provide obvious benefits to mission-critical-based watermarking applications, such as advanced surveillance systems, medical imaging, or associated applications where continuous, reliable processing is a defining minimum requirement. Quantum-enhanced watermarking is starting to show promise and could become a viable paradigm that redefines the world of digital protection and content protection. There are quantum neural networks developed that are theoretically superior to classical architectures for various pattern recognition (i.e., either a feature-based decision or similarity-based decision) as well as embedding information/data (i.e., a digital watermark) applications by exploiting quantum mechanics principles to process information in uniquely different forms than classical based systems. In addition, quantum cryptographic mechanisms have the potential to provide unprecedented security for watermark keys using theoretically unbreakable basic encryption mechanisms based on quantum mechanics principles. With the development and maturation of post-quantum cryptography standards, it is becoming increasingly important to investigate quantum-resistant watermarking approaches to secure these persistent threats for a given watermarking life cycle. Federated learning is a modern decentralised approach for training watermarking models that alleviates concerns of privacy by allowing sensitive media data not to be stored on centralised servers after movement. This method enables privacy-preserving collaboration among multiple entities, such as broadcasters, publishers, and media platforms, while simultaneously offering cross-platform watermark consistency, which maintains protection standards across different distribution platforms. Federated learning architectures also allow for the personalisation of watermarking models. Here, user-level adaptation could be implemented based on device characteristics, subscription levels, or user habits, creating a newspaper-targeted, adequate protection solution.

9. CONCLUSION

The use of Artificial Intelligence and Machine Learning methods within adaptive watermarking represents a definitive advancement in digital copyright protection in a cloud-based environment. In contexts where systems and technologies continue to evolve in sophistication and complexity, the cloud offers powerful yet straightforward ways to enable new approaches to protecting intellectual property. This thorough examination of the theoretical foundations, practical implementations, and real-world applications of AI-driven watermarking systems reveals their significant potential to address the complex nature of contemporary content dissemination in the cloud, where traditional forms of protection have not kept pace with the current and ever-evolving security and scalability needs. The technological advances made by AI and ML approaches have demonstrated that they statistically outperform traditional watermarking techniques across multiple key features, including imperceptibility, robustness, and applicability across various content types and attack scenarios. Deep learning methods, specifically Convolutional Neural Networks and Generative Adversarial Networks, have shown great promise in being effective across multiple content types and sophisticated attack scenarios. AI-based adaptive watermarking techniques currently show promise in providing robust and adaptive protection mechanisms against minority threats and constantly evolving technological changes. Real-world implementations have also confirmed the scalability and capability of AI-based watermarking systems, supporting their deployment in cloud environments. There are real-world case studies that document the successful implementation of AI-based adaptive watermarking systems capable of processing thousands of media files per minute while maintaining the relevant quality of service and exhibiting strong protective characteristics. The possible future of this field is exhilarating as new technologies, particularly along the lines of transformers, quantum computing, and federated learning, will provide opportunities for even further development, addressing the limitations of computational efficiency, scalability, and the security of watermarking technologies while creating previously unheard of opportunities for watermarking applications that previously appeared impractical or impossible. While AI watermarking technologies can utilise unprecedented advances over the existing traditional watermarking technologies, developing and deploying AI watermarking systems will require careful evaluation of multiple considerations to the implementation, including warehousing bias and data reliability capabilities, scalability requirements, security protocols, privacy protections, regulatory compliance obligations, and, ultimately, what can we do to allow for the best practices and guidelines we have been shamelessly leveraging for the last two decades to help ensure that we have a plan for the best implementation across wildly different cloud environments. The general area of AI-based adaptive watermarking technologies is still in development, and existing research challenges remain in utilising data more efficiently, examining generalisation across the multiplicity of content arrays, and generating more robust adversarial effects in response to increasingly sophisticated attacks. The evolution of cloud computing infrastructures and the staggering quantity of data that continues to be produced will require AI and ML technologies to play an increasingly important role in examining credible copyright and total information security to minimise threats within all national and cross-national global networks. Organisations that wish to adopt AI-based watermarking systems must fully understand their specific needs concerning technical limitations and regulatory requirements to ensure that their systems can be optimised. The thorough framework and analysis presented in this paper provide a clear platform from which organisations can make informed decisions regarding technology selection, system design philosophies and implementation approaches that meet their purpose while being underpinned by the organisation's technical capabilities. Moving forward, the technology convergence of artificial intelligence, cloud computing, and digital rights management will stimulate future innovations in watermarking technologies, and we hope that the principles, processes, techniques and lessons described here can be used as a reference by both researchers, developers and practitioners keen to improve the current state of the art for adaptive watermarking and thus cloud copyright protection.

REFERENCES

Aberna, P., & Agilandeeswari, L. (2024). Digital image and video watermarking: Methodologies, attacks, applications, and future directions. *Multimedia Tools and Applications*, *83*(2), 5531–5591. DOI: 10.1007/s11042-023-15806-y

Amrit, P., & Singh, A. K. (2022). Survey on watermarking methods in the artificial intelligence domain and beyond. *Computer Communications*, *188*, 52–65. DOI: 10.1016/j.comcom.2022.02.023

Boenisch, F. (2021). A systematic review on model watermarking for neural networks. *Frontiers in Big Data*, *4*, 729663. DOI: 10.3389/fdata.2021.729663 PMID: 34913032

Dandooh, A., El-Fishawy, A. S., & Hemdan, E. E. D. (2025). Digital watermarking using artificial intelligence: Concept, techniques, and future trends. *Security and Privacy*, *8*(1), e502. DOI: 10.1002/spy2.502

Hsu, L. Y. (2024). AI-assisted deepfake detection using adaptive blind image watermarking. *Journal of Visual Communication and Image Representation*, *100*, 104094. DOI: 10.1016/j.jvcir.2024.104094

Jiang, Z., Guo, M., Hu, Y., & Gong, N. Z. (2024). Watermark-based Attribution of AI-Generated Content. arXiv preprint arXiv:2404.04254.

Liu, C., Zhang, J., Fang, H., Ma, Z., Zhang, W., & Yu, N. (2023, June). Dear: A deep-learning-based audio re-recording resilient watermarking. *Proceedings of the AAAI Conference on Artificial Intelligence*, *37*(11), 13201–13209. DOI: 10.1609/aaai.v37i11.26550

Liu, X., & Nematollahi, M. A. (2024). Artificial Intelligence Approach for Tuning Speech-Adaptive Watermarking using Higher-Order Statistics (HOS). *Circuits, Systems, and Signal Processing*, *43*(5), 3297–3323. DOI: 10.1007/s00034-024-02618-0

Liu, Y., & Bu, Y. (2024). Adaptive text watermark for large language models. arXiv preprint arXiv:2401.13927.

Lukas, N., Diaa, A., Fenaux, L., & Kerschbaum, F. (2023). Leveraging optimization for adaptive attacks on image watermarks. arXiv preprint arXiv:2309.16952.

Madala, R., Monica, R., Malwade, S. S., Budhavale, S. J., & Sathyabalaji, N. (2023, April). A Novel Dynamic Watermarking for Secure Data Protection from Cyber Theft Based on Artificial Intelligence Supervision. In *2023 Eighth International Conference on Science Technology Engineering and Mathematics (ICONSTEM)* (pp. 1-7). IEEE.

Nie, H., & Lu, S. (2024). Securing IP in edge AI: Neural network watermarking for multimodal models. *Applied Intelligence*, *54*(21), 10455–10472. DOI: 10.1007/s10489-024-05746-x

Regazzoni, F., Palmieri, P., Smailbegovic, F., Cammarota, R., & Polian, I. (2021). Protecting artificial intelligence IPs: A survey of watermarking and fingerprinting for machine learning. *CAAI Transactions on Intelligence Technology*, *6*(2), 180–191. DOI: 10.1049/cit2.12029

Sahu, A. K., Umachandran, K., Biradar, V. D., Comfort, O., Sri Vigna Hema, V., Odimegwu, F., & Saifullah, M. A.Saifullah M. A. (2023). A study on content tampering in multimedia watermarking. *SN Computer Science*, *4*(3), 222. DOI: 10.1007/s42979-022-01657-1

Wang, B., Wu, Y., & Wang, G. (2023). Adaptor: Improving the robustness and imperceptibility of watermarking by the adaptive strength factor. *IEEE Transactions on Circuits and Systems for Video Technology*, *33*(11), 6260–6272. DOI: 10.1109/TCSVT.2023.3265970

Zhao, X., Ananth, P., Li, L., & Wang, Y. X. (2023). Provable robust watermarking for ai-generated text. arXiv preprint arXiv:2306.17439.

Chapter 6
Security Analysis: Attacks and Countermeasures in Watermarking Systems

Neha Yadav
https://orcid.org/0000-0002-7793-2063
G.L. Bajaj Institute of Technology and Management, Greater Noida, India

Mayank Singh
https://orcid.org/0000-0002-8393-3652
G.L. Bajaj Institute of Technology and Management, Greater Noida, India

Vipin Tyagi
https://orcid.org/0000-0003-4994-3686
Jaypee University of Engineering and Technology, Guna, India

ABSTRACT

In the rapidly evolving digital media landscape, watermarking technology has become a crucial component of comprehensive content protection strategies. Despite its potential, the security of watermarking systems remains a primary concern, primarily due to the increasing sophistication of attack methods designed to damage, erase, or manipulate a watermark detector. This chapter explores the security challenges associated with watermarking and the countermeasures available. For each potential attack, it discusses the impact, detection difficulty, and possible damage. Additionally, the chapter outlines defensive architectures and algorithms, including robust embedding techniques, adversarial training in watermarking systems, tampering localisation, and cryptographic reinforcement. It is illustrated with case studies, simulation research and results, diagrams, and a benchmarking framework to help readers understand how to design, evaluate, and secure watermarking against modern threats.

DOI: 10.4018/979-8-3373-3785-2.ch006

1. INTRODUCTION TO WATERMARKING SECURITY

Digital watermarking refers to the process of embedding inaudible information into media assets (such as audio, video, or image files) for their secure assertion, authenticity verification, and distribution monitoring, among other tasks. The primary objective of watermarking is to embed an imperceptible yet robust signal within digital assets. As the use of watermarking systems has increased across multimedia content distribution platforms, the security surrounding these signals is becoming increasingly tenuous. As watermarking systems become more valuable and visible, they become susceptible to threat model adversaries who may attempt to either change or remove the watermark without affecting the perceptual quality of the visible media (Madala et al., 2023). Watermarking security can be thought of as referring to the global question, "How secure is a watermarking system to unauthorised changes or removal?" To address this question, potential threats should be studied, system robustness should be evaluated under defined attack conditions, and countermeasures employed in the watermarking system design that defend against these security threats (Tauhid, Xu, Rahman, & Tomai, 2023). A secure watermarking system should ensure that the conduit watermark remains thorough and detectable despite being subjected to compression, geometric distortion, filtering, or malicious adversarial efforts.

1.1 Importance of Security in Modern Watermarking

As digital content is rapidly disseminated through cloud storage, streaming sites, and social media, the need for watermarking security is more crucial than ever. The attack vectors against watermarking systems include:

- Removing owner identifiers to make piracy easier
- Replacing a watermark with a fake watermark
- Altering watermark information to fool forensics or tracking
- Using adversarial methods to fool AI-based detectors

We observe that security threats evolve in tandem with advancements in watermarking algorithms, particularly those that utilise AI and ML. Therefore, we will require multi-layer and dynamic security.

1.2 Key Components of a Secure Watermarking System

A robust and secure watermarking system is built upon the following key components:

1. **Robust Embedding Strategy**: Capable of adapting to diverse content types and resisting various attacks.
2. **Tamper-Resistant Detection**: Resistant to noise, adversarial perturbations, and signal processing distortions.
3. **Authentication and Integrity Verification**: Confirming that watermarks are genuine and unaltered.
4. **Encryption and Key Management**: Protecting watermark keys and embedding parameters.
5. **Dynamic Response Mechanisms**: Adaptive techniques to respond to new or unforeseen attacks.

Key objectives of security are shown in Figure 1. Some are explained below:

- Robustness → Watermark should survive attacks.
- Imperceptibility → Watermark should not reduce quality.
- Security → Unauthorised detection/modification should be unsuccessful.

Figure 1. The security goals in a watermarking system.

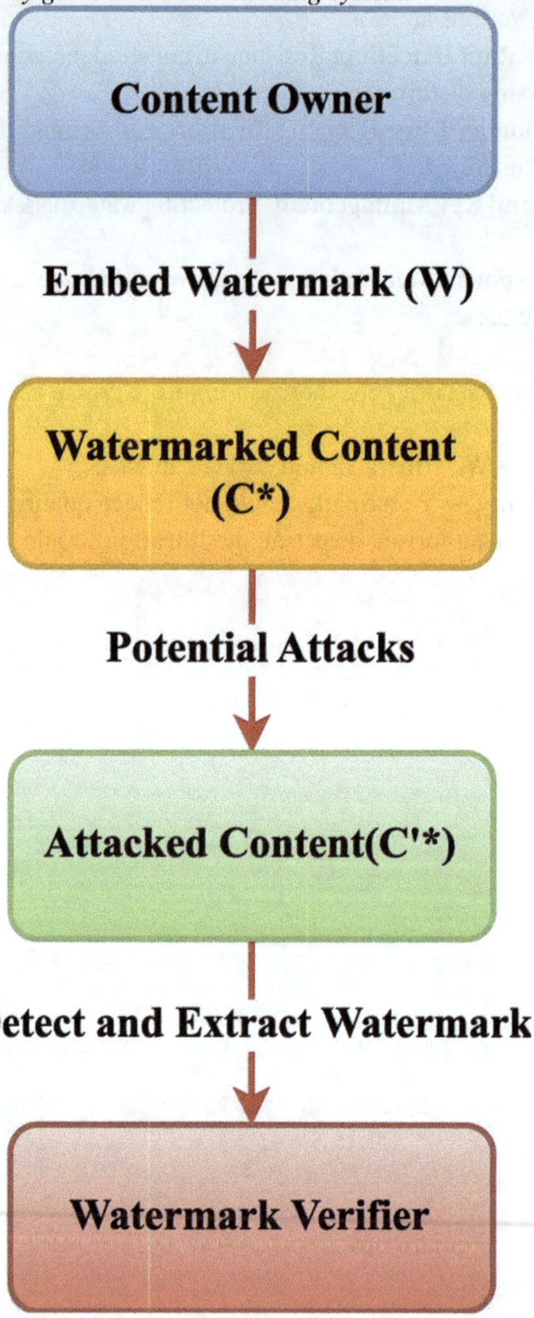

This chapter discusses watermarking threats and defences. As we continue in the following sections, we categorise the different forms of attacks, present descriptions and analyses of how they were accomplished, and then discuss how to counter each attack in detail. A thorough understanding of watermarking systems and their adequate assessment should enable researchers and engineers to create secure, robust, and trusted watermarking systems in dynamic digital environments.

2. THREAT MODELS IN WATERMARKING

Threat models provide valuable guidance for the effective design of watermarking systems. A threat model identifies reasonable potential attack scenarios, considers the attacker's goals, and describes the capabilities of the adversaries, as well as the vulnerabilities or weaknesses of the system (Wu et al., 2022). Generally, threat modelling should not only improve the design of approaches to anti-watermarking or watermark assessment, but it can also provide insight into the robustness of a watermarking scheme against real-world attacks.

2.1 Types of Adversaries

An adversary in a watermarking system spans a broad spectrum, ranging from a benign user carrying out operations as part of typical network service use to a malicious adversary with full access to the watermarking algorithm. Indeed, watermarking systems are often deployed in open public environments and adversarial situations, where attackers may have conflicting knowledge of the algorithmic design of the watermarking operation, as well as varying levels of subversion capability, and motivation (Zhu et al., 2024). Assessing the adversarial landscape is critical for designing robust watermarking systems. Adversaries can be broadly classified into four types based on the watermarking algorithm awareness that their capabilities grant them potential access to.

- Oblivious attackers are the least malicious and usually unintentional. These include users who may employ an image compression tool, convert an image's format, crop a picture, or resize an image. Even though oblivious attackers are not doing anything malicious to the watermark, simple actions can still affect the ability to extract the watermark or degrade the watermark's fidelity. However, oblivious attackers will always conduct their attack in conditions that emulate everyday processing scenarios and provide a basic benchmark for any watermarking scheme.
- Semi-informed attackers exhibit more sophistication, and the threat level is mainly regarded as moderate. They are aware of or familiar with the overall class of watermarking techniques used (such as DCT, DWT, or spatial domain

embedding), but do not have access to specific parameters, including embedding keys, transform coefficients, or payload information. Semi-informed attackers typically employ reverse engineering tactics, statistical analysis, and occasionally utilise machine learning to identify watermark locations or discover potential watermark patterns (Wadhera et al., 2022). Semi-informed attackers are aware of some parameters related to a watermark, and all of their knowledge helps them launch attacks designed to explore systemic vulnerabilities without completely controlling the watermarking process.

- Informed attackers are the worst-case scenario in threat modelling because they possess complete knowledge of the watermarking algorithm and its parameters, as well as the embedding domains and detection pipeline (this could occur as a result of a leak, reverse engineering, or code sharing). Informed attackers can develop precision-based removal attacks or forgery attacks, can adopt and simulate the embedding process to construct an adversarial attack, and can exploit weaknesses in protocols (Sharma, Kejriwal, & Pakina, 2023). When systems are reviewed as informed adversaries, it is a good indicator that these systems are secure if there are severe assumptions of security.
- Insider attacks are perhaps the most dangerous type of attack because they involve legitimate access. Insider attacks can originate from malicious employees, collaborators, or service providers (such as software as a service - SaaS), who may be current employees or individuals with system access. Insider attacks can include leaking detection keys, changing watermark parameters, and making false claims in media that falsely claim ownership. For cloud services, provider attacks can consist of the provider manipulating or extracting sensitive data while hosting AI watermarking models (Guo, Sun, & Pang, 2023). Good access controls, auditing, and key management will serve as effective countermeasures for insider attacks.

The ecosystem is further complicated in the presence of a hybrid attacker, who employs a combination of automated tools and manual techniques, including methods based on content manipulation using AI, deepfake production, or adversarial learning. Attackers are dynamic, continuously changing their methods to negate the watermarking approaches the system attempts to apply. The hybrid attacker may exist in isolation or collaborate with multiple other types, creating compounded risks that require designs beyond those initially intended. Although the emergence of AI and the deepfake approach has led to an increase in hybrid attackers, they employ a combination of both automated and manual strategies.

2.2 Adversarial Objectives

Understanding an attacker's intent is just as crucial as understanding their capabilities. Different goals require different means of defence, and many of today's attacks pursue multiple goals. The most common goal is watermark removal, where the attacker generally seeks to remove or degrade watermarking to the point of invisibility. This is typically achieved through a signal processing operation, such as blurring, compression, or the addition of noise. More powerful operations involve optimisation-based removal, where the image itself is altered iteratively to eradicate the watermark while remaining visually similar (Achaal et al., 2024). A second goal is watermark estimation, whereby attackers try to reconstruct the embedded watermark or predict its outputs. This is especially dangerous when the disclosed watermark contains necessary metadata, such as author identity or timestamp. Estimation attacks can occur through machine learning models that interpret the patterns of multiple media samples, and are especially effective when the watermark is of a repeated or redundant structure. Watermark forgery attacks represent the biggest threat to ownership claims (Malanowska et al., 2024). Counterfeit watermarks are created by the adversary and attached to previously unmarked media to claim ownership falsely. Forgery attacks can also exploit systems that lack proper authentication methods or employ weak authentication methods based on multiple watermarks. They are frequently involved in copyright disputes and digital piracy cases. Protocol tampering is a form of tampering which interferes with the watermarking process itself. This can take the form of intercepting the transmission of watermark metadata and altering it, which can include storing the data in a server-side embedding function or a secure storage mechanism. Protocol tampering within watermarking systems is a common issue in client-server or cloud-hosted watermarking systems. Misclassification is another significant threat posed by an adversary; it is becoming increasingly common now that AI is integrated into watermarking systems. By attacking the watermark detector, the adversary may achieve misclassification without actually disrupting the watermark itself; this could include false classifications as an actual positive, false ownership, as well as false negatives, in which a valid watermark is not classified as such. The actions of the adversary may be purposeful or simply may be a by-product of possible adversarial perturbations, especially as it relates to deep learning models. Denial-of-Service (DoS) attacks are a type of tampering that targets infrastructure supporting watermark detection. A DoS attack will overwhelm a watermark detection infrastructure with an excessive amount of content. DoS attacks do not necessarily attempt to break the watermark, but rather to render the system unfunctional, thereby allowing disarmament of the enforcement, which is possibly the goal (Baban et al., 2023).

In some cases, this can escalate to a service interruption and significant computational costs in cloud-based architectures. In more sophisticated situations, an adversary could undo the original watermark and insert a counterfeit watermark, especially in real-time streams or scenarios such as live broadcasts, video meetings, or other media. Compound adversarial objectives like these require layers of addressability and adaptive countermeasures; for instance, an adversary could also attack designer-user consumer protections and/or reduce the marketability of the item in the digital stack as part of an enhanced denial-of-service attack.

2.3 Threat Vectors and Attack Surfaces

Adversaries can exploit multiple attack surfaces when compromising a complete watermarking system. Adversaries can exploit attack surfaces through watermark embedding, storage, transmission, and detection. Acknowledging the attack surfaces enables the identification of weaknesses and potential mitigations. The embedding process is often the first attack surface spoofed, especially with watermark embedding that lacks randomness or content adaptivity. In a deterministic framework or a fixed pattern embedding, adversaries can much more easily use statistical means on the original and watermark signals to discover the evidence of the watermark embedding locations (Lillis, Hoffing, & Burleson, 2024).

Additionally, suppose the embedding logic is also not content aware. In that case, it can certainly leave evidence by watermarking in perceptually sensitive regions of content, meaning adversaries will likely detect and remove any watermark. Suppose the watermark metadata, such as keys and ownership proofs, is transmitted in an unencrypted or unauthenticated manner. In that case, adversaries can intercept, spoof, and mount a man-in-the-middle (MitM) attack, including impersonating exhibited ownership. In the valuation of unsuspecting ownership, protocols that ensure secure communication for values in watermark life cycle operations, like TLS, should be standard (Wu et al., 2023). System storage is another attack surface that can be manipulated if strict adherence to access control policies is not maintained when exploring this layer. Adversaries can retrieve all embedded files from a system, model weights in AI-based systems, and keys from configuration files, if their related credentials have been hacked at the storage level. The risk can be reduced by, for example, using layered encryption schemes and storing keys in key vaults, as well as implementing well-managed access controls. The detection engine must also be protected, as it is responsible for extracting or verifying the watermark. Deterministic detection algorithms can be targeted by malicious entities, who create perturbations to circumvent or confuse the detector by modifying or transforming input data. They could also simply supply the detector with corrupted data, aiming to overwhelm it or undermine its confidence in detecting.

Finally, the parameters of AI models, such as CNN weights or classification boundaries, used in watermark detection, can also become attack vectors. Model inversion attacks can reconstruct sensitive input data based on model output, while adversarial attacks generate perturbations to degrade performance. Defence-in-depth strategies must include adversarial training, model obfuscation, and secure model preservation techniques against these avenues. By thoroughly reviewing attack surfaces and threat vectors, developers of watermarking systems can provide high-quality end-user performance while withstanding threats ranging from common image or watermark transformations to resource-filled adversarial attacks. The threat model for watermarking is shown in Figure 2.

Figure 2. The threat model for a watermarking system.

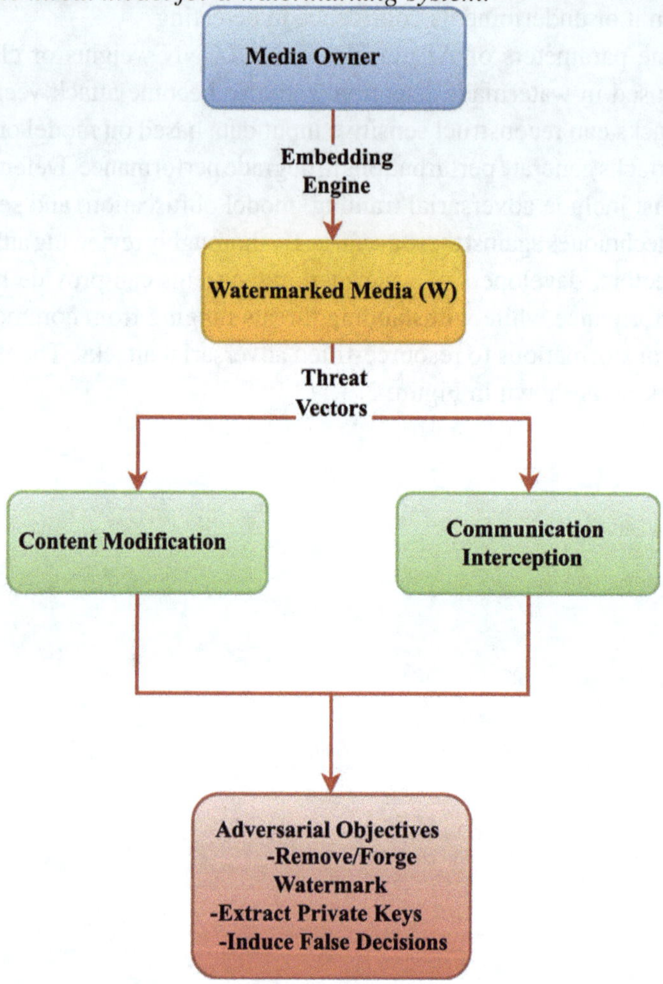

2.4 Evaluating Threat Severity

To prioritise security efforts is shown in Table 1, it is helpful to classify threats by severity and likelihood:

Table 1. The classification of threats based on likelihood.

Threat Category	Severity	Likelihood	Example Scenario
Watermark Removal	High	Medium	JPEG compression followed by filtering
Watermark Forgery	Very High	Low	Insider Crafts forged a watermark
Detection Misleading	Medium	High	Adversarial image crafted
Communication Tampering	High	Medium	Intercepted watermark header packets
Model Inversion	Very High	Low	Reconstructing content from extracted features

In addition to these rudimentary assessments, threat modelling can utilise tools like STRIDE (Spoofing, Tampering, Repudiation, Information Disclosure, Denial of Service, Elevation of Privilege) or DREAD (Damage, Reproducibility, Exploitability, Affected Users, Discoverability) to provide measurement and visualisation of risks (Cheng et al., 2025). As digital watermarking systems mature, particularly in cloud environments with AI augmentations, threat models should be regularly updated as threats evolve. Regular reviews, red teaming, and evaluating machine learning robustness are suggested practices to continue a proactive defence posture.

3. CLASSIFICATION OF ATTACKS

Watermarking systems are vulnerable to a wide range of attacks aimed at compromising, erasing, or falsifying embedded information. Classifications based on the attack domain (spatial or frequency), knowledge assumptions (blind or informed), or intentions (disruption or deception) encompass a wide range of representations. In this section, we categorise attacks into four primary categories and outline their features, examples, and threats to overall system integrity.

3.1 Geometric Attacks

Geometric attacks are one of the most common and effective attacks against watermarking systems, specifically for those utilising spatial embedding techniques. Geometric attacks alter the arrangement of the media in geometric space through operations such as rotation, scaling, cropping, and translation. The object of the geometric attack is to desynchronise the watermark detector by altering the position between the watermark-carrying regions. At the same time, the observer (humans) could still appreciate the overall rendered quality of the media. Rotation is an operation that alters the orientation of the image or video frame. Even a slight angular rotation can move watermark-carrying pixels enough to interfere with a detection technique. Scale or resize operations change the resolution of the media; either compressing or stretching, alters pixel alignment and destroys spatial consistency. Cropping is particularly harmful when it removes media containing portions of the watermark (Demertzi, Demertzis, & Demertzis, 2023). Since most watermarking schemes use spatially distributed payloads in the press, even a partial crop can result in considerable data loss. Likewise, translation shifts the entire media horizontally or vertically and affects extraction synchronisation. Even more complicated geometric transformations than translations or cropping include affine transformations and perspective transformations, which can use more complex warping, shearing, or skewing of the image geometry.

These distortions can also severely complicate watermark detection, especially if the image was embedded using no geometric invariants. Template attacks can even identify the embedded synchronisation markers placed intentionally in the content and remove them, thus undermining any reference-based detection process. A specific class of more disastrous attacks would be mosaic or block-wise attacks, which divide an image into blocks, randomise their order and possibly resize each block uniformly, disrupting continuity of the watermark signal (Hosam, Abousamra, Hassouna, & Azzawi, 2024). To mitigate these geometrically destructive acts, modern systems use feature point-based synchronisations where watermarks are embedded spatially relative to invariant features, such as corners or blobs (e.g., SIFT, SURF). Log-polar mapping, or variants of affine-invariant domains, enable embedding in transform spaces with structural preservation and robustness in the presence of considerable geometric distortion, as shown in Figure 3.

Figure 3. The geometric transformations and watermark disruption.

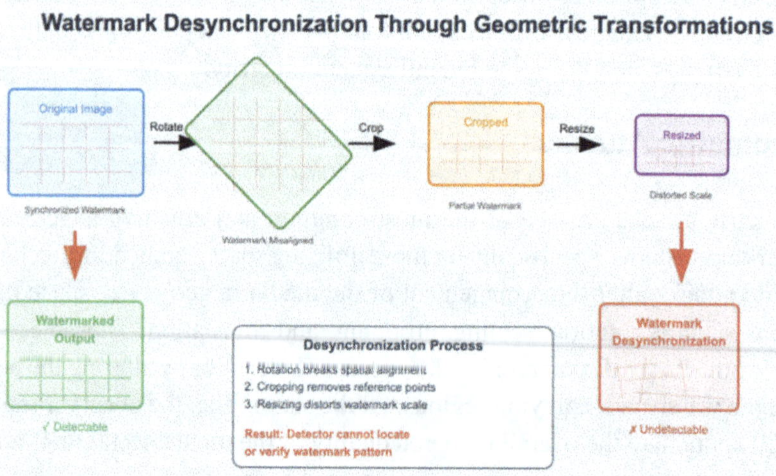

3.2 Signal Processing Attacks

Signal processing attacks are a comprehensive category that involves typical multimedia operations often used, either knowingly or unknowingly, during media transmission, editing, or compression. These attacks include altering either pixel values or frequency coefficients, which impact the strength and imperceptibility of the watermark. Compression, particularly lossy compression like JPEG (for images) or MPEG (for video), is by far one of the most common threats. Quantisation and frequency truncation during compression eliminate minor incremental signal variations that typically include the watermark. Similar to compression, filtering operations such as Gaussian blur, sharpening, or median filtering change pixel intensities or frequency domain coefficients. These filters can destroy the watermark or minimise it to the point of not being recognisable. Noise addition introduces seemingly random or structured perturbations from pixel to pixel across the image. Noise is often used to design signal processing attacks that would mimic real-world sensor or transmission errors, but it can also be intentionally designed to obfuscate the extraction process (Hu & Pang, 2021). Histogram equalisation is the process of changing the global distribution of pixel intensities to improve image contrast. Equalisation enhances the overall image, but this alteration can mask the presence of any watermarking data. An advanced attacker can perform recompression attacks where they apply additional rounds of compression, which cumulatively destroy the watermark. Another common signal processing attack is multipath filtering, where the attacker applies path filters successfully or simultaneously to isolate the targeted watermark-bearing coefficients.

More recently, there has been a growing interest in using steganalysis-informed filtering, where filters trained to identify steganographic signatures are employed to estimate and remove regions likely to contain hidden information. The embedding of watermarks into perceptually significant transform coefficients, for example, middle-frequency bands in the DCT or wavelet domain, is an example of a countermeasure. The use of error-correcting codes (ECC) and redundancy in the embedding can also help recover from signal corruption. Advanced Variants include:

- Recompression Attack: Applying JPEG or MPEG compression several times to create cumulative noise.
- Multipath Filtering: Applying multiple kernels sequentially to isolate and destroy regions carrying watermarks.
- Steganalysis-Based Filtering: The use of steganalysis-based filters to estimate likely embedding areas and wipe clean.

3.3 Statistical and Collusion Attacks

Statistical and collusion attacks exploit many examples of watermarked versions or utilise advanced statistical techniques to detect, remove, or conceal the watermark. What makes these attacks particularly nefarious is that abstracts do not have to access the watermarking algorithm at all. Statistical attacks look at both spatial and frequency domains to analyse repeated watermark patterns. If you watermarked an image with either uniform or deterministic strategies, for example, your statistical analysis can log or reconstruct the difference in the image's normal distributions. Further, remember that errors or anomalies in your perception can be found in the difference between the image discriminator and the image restoration factors. In large datasets, tools such as autocorrelation analysis and noise residue analysis can be helpful in modelling watermarks. For example, they can predict watermark structures and other features. Like statistical attacks, collusion attacks utilise access to multiple differently watermarked copies of the duplicate content (Caviglione, Comito, Guarascio, & Manco, 2023). Think of media distributors embedding user-based watermarks. Now you can compare the copies on a pixel-by-pixel or block-wise basis, then subtract the differences, or combine dissimilar blocks, which can effectively eliminate the watermarking. Unlike statistical attacks, these attacks are primarily referred to as difference-based or averaging collusion attacks. Collusion attacks are relatively widespread when situational context is involved, such as in fingerprinting for digital rights management (DRM). In an advanced context, collusion is not limited to advances that the attacker can predictably find under a constraint of collusion but also includes a subset of collusions where only parts of the watermark are focused on, based on the accessibility of partial content (Araghi, Megías, & Rosales, 2023). The non-aware averaging method uses (perceptual-based) metrics to guarantee that the averaged output remains visually quite acceptable while also minimising watermark tracks. Fingerprint inference attacks make inferences about the identifying features for user tracking or forensic watermarking. The defences are based on the use of anti-collusion codes (ACC), where, for example, the watermark associated with each document is mathematically constructed so that its combination remains intact. The other methods include robust fingerprints using spread spectrum or pseudo-random patterns, along with statistical diversity at embedding, which ensures that no two copies are sufficiently similar to be successfully combined. Figure 4 shows the collusion attack on digital watermarks.

Figure 4. The Collusion Attack Workflow for digital watermarks.

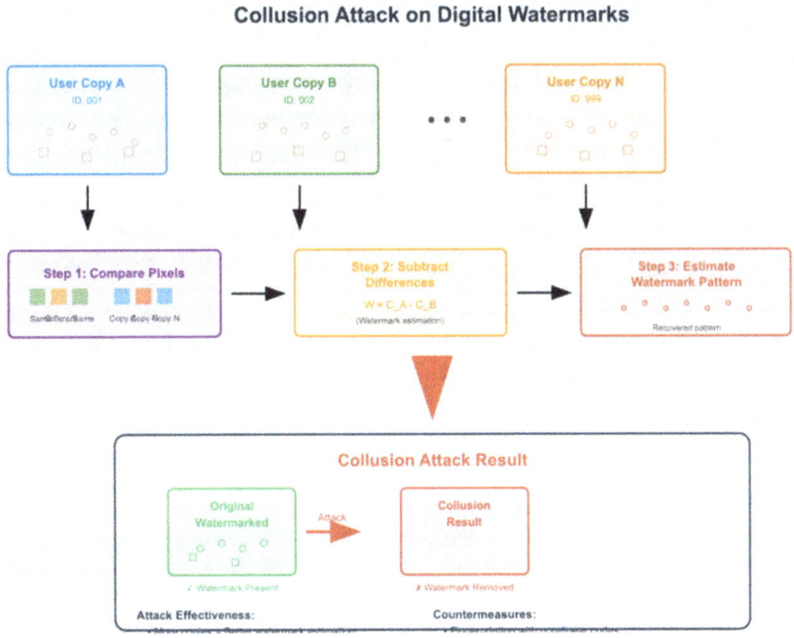

3.4 Machine Learning and AI-Driven Attacks

The development of AI introduces a new category of intelligent attacks that can learn or reverse-engineer embedding patterns. The AI-driven watermark attack pipeline is shown in Figure 5. With the increased use of AI in watermark embedding and detection, adversaries have also leveraged AI to execute sophisticated attacks. These attacks are typically specific, adaptive to embedding, and capable of exploiting both algorithmic and model-related weaknesses. Adversarial attacks are a typical method of attack, where adversaries add carefully constructed perturbations to the data that are imperceptible to people, but cause the watermark detector (especially those based on deep learning) to fail. Often, exploits using perturbations are computed using gradient-based methods, which can generalise to all instances of media. Model inversion is also possible by using the response outputs of the watermarking model as a means of reconstructing the behaviour or inferring sensitive internal states, such as watermark patterns or model weights (Jain, Kumar, & Joshi, 2022). Similar to model inversion attacks, transfer learning based attacks can be done by using pre-trained models (ex., for use on natural image classification) for identifying watermark features and removing the watermark (or particularly in the shallow embedding domain). More recently, advanced methods have utilised Generative

Adversarial Networks (GANs) to create synthetic content that either destroys the watermark or mimics watermarked, similar content to trick a watermark detector. In black-box attacks, attackers do not have access to the watermarking model, but can observe outputs and determine model behaviour implicitly through statistical learning or by re-enforcing queries. Notably, meta-learning and few-shot learning enable attackers to adapt their strategy to different watermarking systems with minimal training data. Countermeasures included adversarial training, where the model is trained with synthetic adversarial examples to enhance its robustness. Model obfuscation, dropout regularisation, expiration embedding, and ensemble detectors provide further protection strategies. For real-time systems, an adversarial detection threshold can be added to stochastic or noise-resistant filters to reduce AI-based upset further. This classification of attack types should provide an initial understanding of the attack surface that could affect any watermarking system.

Figure 5. The AI-Driven Watermark Attack Pipeline.

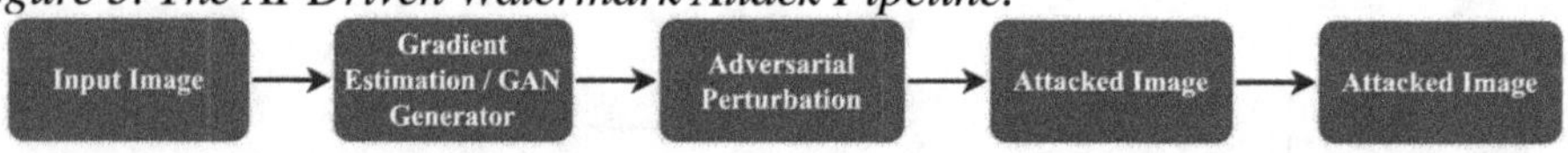

In the next section, explored detailed attack scenarios based on the categories introduced here and analyse their success rates, implementation complexity, and detection challenges.

4. ATTACK CASE STUDIES AND REAL-WORLD EXAMPLES

Real-world case studies of watermarking provide valuable insights into how watermarking systems behave when deployed and used by adversaries. Real-world case studies can provide useful lessons in identifying system vulnerabilities, testing defence strategies, and ultimately informing the design of a system to measure and enhance its resilience in future instances of use. In this section, we present case studies and axial attacks on watermarking systems, focusing on real-world contexts that highlight the practical implications of theoretical vulnerabilities (Mummadi, Yadav, Sadhwika, & Shitharth, 2021). The case studies not only demonstrated variations in the severity of different classes of attack, but also demonstrated the types of contexts in which watermarking systems may fail and/or perform under stress. As glaringly illustrated by the various forms of simulations, adversarial limitations, and industry-documented examples, we have noted the importance of continually testing and re-evaluating watermarking scholarship and practices.

Case Study 1: Cloud-Based Image Sharing Platform

A notable cloud-enabled photo-sharing website implemented a watermarking solution to secure user-generated content from unauthorised reuse. The watermarking implementation was content-adaptive and used a spatial domain embedding approach based upon Convolutional Neural Networks (CNNs). The platform faced several issues to resolve when applying watermarking, including (1) the imperceptibility of the watermark, (2) scalability under a potentially massive user load, and (3) the robustness of the watermark against common forms of processing, such as compression and cropping. As time progressed, the platform was forced to deal with targeted attacks, where automated bots purchased watermarked images, applied JPEG compression, and cropped them to random small sizes, then re-uploaded them, making detection impossible. Sometimes, the activity resulted in the watermark being partially removed; however, the system was improved by moving to a frequency domain hybrid model utilising the Discrete Cosine Transform (DCT) and retraining the CNN against adversarial images. The improved system achieved a PSNR of 41 dB and demonstrated watermark survivability in 95% of the examined attacks. This case illustrates the foundation for ongoing system development and the significance of adversarial training in watermarking techniques for ever-changing environments.

Case Study 2: Video Streaming Service

A video streaming service that operates on a subscription model utilised watermarking to trace piracy of videos of a premium nature. The employed system was a hybrid AI solution that enhanced spatial analysis through Convolutional Neural Networks (CNNs) and maintained temporal consistency through Recurrent Neural Networks (RNNs). The use of CNNs enabled dynamic watermark placement, dependent on scene content, motion characteristics, and compression settings. During one piracy incident, unauthorised video footage containing the watermark was discovered on many torrent sites. An analysis of the methods used to circumvent the watermark showed that the pirates used a system of temporal slicing (removing every nth frame) and colour filtering to obliterate any traces of the watermark. The RNN-based component did not give reliable information in predicting watermark synchronisation after the video was subject to all erosion. In response to the original processing system's limitations, the video streaming service utilised its initial system as a baseline while incorporating temporal attention into the RNNs and employing Cycle-GANs to augment various types of attacks during retraining. They created a new coordinate frame hashing synchronisation protocol to identify possible erased [video] segments. These improvements resulted in a 17% increase in robustness and led to the systematic extraction of watermarks, despite intentional layered video attacks.

Case Study 3: Forensic Watermarking in Legal Evidence

Forensic watermarking was employed to maintain the chain of custody of images used as evidence in a highly publicised criminal case. The watermarking vendor utilised a key-based DWT (Discrete Wavelet Transform) method that employed AES encryption. Nevertheless, the defence claimed that the watermark was not tamper-resistant, as the images could have been re-encoded using any other watermarking keys. The prosecution, in turn, referenced tamper-evident logs and metadata directly linking the original content to the system's cryptographic ledger. As an added protection, they utilised a watermark verification scheme integrated into blockchain technology, leveraging a pre-trained Inception network to provide AI-based authenticity scoring. The court accepted the watermarks as valid digital evidence, setting a benchmark for the admissibility of AI-augmented watermarking. This example illustrates the point that forensic watermarking must not only consider robustness but also incorporate verified, crypto-assured, and auditable features to support a successful legal argument in judicial systems.

Case Study 4: Social Media Platform and Meme Watermarking

A social media platform recognised for popularity-based content encountered challenges tracking the viral origins of memes. They implement a watermarking technology to trace meme origin after realising that their information and misinformation associated with memes were the same problem. They implemented a lightweight GAN-based watermarking algorithm to trade off invisibility and tamper detection of highly compressed images. Attackers then applied perturbation tools, such as deepfakes, to produce unnoticeable distortions, thereby obtaining reliable attribution in the watermark. As a result, their watermarking system achieved a 22% detection accuracy, provided that they only examined popular memes that had been manipulated. To improve their watermarking detection goals, they implemented an ensemble of related watermarking models (GANs, CNNs, and rule-based statistical models) along with adversarial detectors. They also incorporated a model for collaboration filtering based on a social propagation path and possible meme origins. These multi-variate new models and avenues of traceability for their memes improved watermark traceability of manipulated content by an impressive 28% and greatly helped their fact-check workflows. This example illustrates that watermarking can be used for content provenance and misinformation detection; however, the platform must frequently adapt its system and continually employ concurrent detection techniques due to the rapid adoption of new approaches to manipulate information. These case studies lay the foundation for supportive policies when implementing watermarking to address the challenges of content provenance and misinformation. However, watermarking should focus on adaptive, context-sensitive, and ethically moderated solutions that prioritise sensitive proximity. They also illustrate the urgent need for multidisciplinary approaches to cryptography, AI-based provenance, legal validation, and user behaviour modelling to build technologies for resilience in our complex, real-world social digital ecosystems.

The following section discusses how security can be quantitatively evaluated through defined metrics and benchmark frameworks in the context of watermarking.

5. SECURITY METRICS AND EVALUATION FRAMEWORKS

A multifaceted approach is required for a robust evaluation of security in digital watermarking, involving conventional media-based criteria and security benchmarks. As this section demonstrates, there are some critical metrics to evaluate the watermarking's robustness, persistence, and imperceptibility of the watermark under possible attack conditions. Additionally, benchmark protocols and testbeds are highlighted as a way to obtain reproducible and comparable evaluation results.

5.1 Core Watermarking Evaluation Metrics

1. **Peak Signal-to-Noise Ratio (PSNR):** A high PSNR value indicates that the watermark embedding has caused minimal distortion to the host media.
    - Formula: $PSNR = 10 \times \log_{10}(MAX^2 / MSE)$, where MAX is the maximum pixel value (typically 255), and MSE is the mean squared error.
    - Typical secure watermark systems aim for a PSNR of greater than 35 dB.
2. **Structural Similarity Index (SSIM):** Measures perceptual image quality by comparing luminance, contrast, and structure between original and watermarked images.
    - Range: 0 (no similarity) to 1 (identical).
    - A secure system should maintain an SSIM value greater than 0.90 under common attack conditions.
3. **Bit Error Rate (BER):** Evaluates the number of bits incorrectly extracted after watermark retrieval versus total watermark length.
    - BER = (# of erroneous bits) / (total bits).
    - Robust systems maintain $BER < 0.1$ even under compression and noise.

4. **Normalised Correlation (NC):** Used to assess the similarity between the original watermark W and the extracted watermark W'.
   - Formula: NC = Σ (W × W') / Σ (W ²).
   - A robust watermarking algorithm typically achieves NC values greater than 0.95.

5.2 Security-Oriented Metrics

1. **Attack Success Rate (ASR):** Measures the proportion of successful watermark removals or corruptions over multiple attack trials.
   - Low ASR (< 20%) implies higher watermark resilience.
2. **Resilience to Compound Attacks (RCA):** Evaluates system robustness when multiple attacks are applied in sequence.
   - Tested using predefined chains such as compression → cropping, → filtering.
3. **Detection Confidence Score (DCS):** Score produced by AI-based detectors representing the likelihood of a watermark's presence.
   - Should be stable across distortions.
4. **Fragility Index (FI):** Used for fragile watermarking systems where any modification should alter watermark detection.
   - Low FI in robust systems; High FI for tamper-detection schemes.

5.3 Benchmarking and Evaluation Frameworks

Standard Dataset Protocols: To standardise testing conditions, the following datasets are often used:

- USC-SIPI: For still images and classic attack testing.
- BSDS500: For evaluating texture-aware robustness.
- TRECVID: For video content watermark testing.
- ImageNet Subsets: For machine learning watermark training and attack diversity.

Attack Simulation Environments: Comprehensive testing should simulate attacks from all categories:

- MATLAB Watermarking Toolkit and StirMark simulate signal, geometric, and combined attacks.
- PyTorch/TF-based adversarial frameworks are used to evaluate GAN and CNN watermark defences.

The Test Conditions Matrix is shown below in Table 2:

Table 2. The benchmarking and evaluation test conditions matrix.

Metric	Test	Description
PSNR	JPEG (Q=50%)	Visual distortion after compression
BER	AWGN (SNR=20dB)	Bit flip ratio post noise attack
NC	Cropping (10%)	Detection accuracy after desynchronisation
RCA	Rotation + Noise	Combined degradation assessment

Visualization Tools:

- ROC (Receiver Operating Characteristic) Curves for detection performance.
- Confusion matrices in AI detection.
- Heatmaps to visualise watermark strength in different image regions.

By utilising these metrics and frameworks, researchers and developers can quantitatively evaluate watermark robustness, detectability, and perceptual quality in both adversarial and benign environments. This quantitative evaluation will be helpful for academic benchmarking and real-world deployment decisions. Next, the chapter examine how these metrics inform the design of effective countermeasures in secure watermarking systems.

6. COUNTERMEASURE STRATEGIES FOR ROBUST WATERMARKING

In a landscape with increased sophistication by adversaries and attack vectors, strong watermarking must include a holistic defence strategy. New watermarking systems must deliver not only the security of the information but also the availability of the mark after multiple attacks, including signal processing, geometric distortion, attacks employing AI and machine learning, and insider threats. In doing so, countermeasures now extend not only to algorithmic spin-offs but also to intelligent adaptations, cloud countermeasures, and so on. Countermeasures must be built for multi-level, algorithmic, architectural, AI-enabled, cryptographic, and infrastructural systems to maintain redundancy, adaptability, and re-accomplish resilience.

6.1 Algorithmic Techniques for Robust Embedding

Algorithmic approaches form the foundation of robust watermarking systems. The goal of these approaches is to enhance the watermark's resistance to potential signal distortions and malicious attacks.

1. Transform Domain Embedding

Transform-based embedding allows the watermark to be embedded in a more stable frequency domain rather than the spatial domain. Some common types of transforms are:

- DCT (Discrete Cosine Transform): happens in the domain of frequency, and watermarks are embedded into the mid-frequency coefficients. This is a good approach because JPEG compression quantises higher-frequency coefficients.
- DWT (Discrete Wavelet Transform): uses the DWT to identify lower-resolution sub-bands, and the image is embedded in different frequency sub-bands and at various resolutions. Watermarking in DWT means that the watermark would remain even if the signal were degraded, and it resists geometric attacks as well.
- SVD (Singular Value Decomposition): The SVD method decomposes the image into orthogonal bases corresponding to the singular values in the frequency domain. Watermarking within the singular values preserves the image quality and is resilient to standard noise models.

These approaches can also be combined in the case of a hybrid transform. (e.g., DWT-DCT-SVD), which allows more performance based on complementary methods.

2. Redundant and Fragmented Embedding

One of the most dominant strategies in robust watermarking is redundancy. Embedding the same watermark into multiple, non-overlapping locations will increase the chance for recovery, even if some portion of the embedding experiences data loss through cropping or other forms of damage.

- Fragmented embedding refers to the idea of distributing the watermark across several regions.
- Weighted redundancy refers to putting more redundancy into visually or semantically less important regions to preserve perceptual utility in the more critical areas.

3. Error Correction Coding (ECC)

ECC converts the watermark into a code that can withstand a certain level of bit errors during extraction. Some of the methods for ECC include:

- BCH (Bose-Chaudhuri-Hocquenghem) codes
- Reed-Solomon codes - used with multimedia broadcasting specifically
- LDPC (Low-Density Parity-Check) codes

All these codes provide a level of robustness, depending on the strength of the codes, designed to allow a portion of the watermark to withstand distortion.

4. Spread Spectrum Techniques

Spread spectrum modulation distributes the watermark energy across a broad frequency range, enabling the watermark to blend seamlessly into the background noise.

- Direct Sequence Spread Spectrum (DSSS), which relies on pseudo-random bit sequences, is one method for encoding watermark bits into media.
- Frequency Hopping Spread Spectrum (FHSS) involves quickly changing the embedding frequency, so if the embedding occurs at multiple frequencies, it becomes challenging to attack the watermark.

These techniques are challenging to undo, and the fact that they work well in noisy environments makes them even more effective, notably when the user lacks access to key information.

6.2 Managing Synchronisation/Desynchronisation

Because the lack of synchronisation between the watermark embedded in a media and the watermark extraction algorithm is a significant cause of failure for the detection algorithm, synchronisation must be maintained. Suppose the image is subject to a geometric transformation, for example. In that case, it is not uncommon that the easily recoverable watermark may fail to be detected by the watermark extraction algorithm due to desynchronisation.

1. Template-Based Synchronisation

Embedding known patterns, such as a cross-shaped or circular template, before your watermark will allow you to calibrate the image geometrically before watermark detection occurs.

Detection Process: Find template –> Calculate transformation –> Re-align image to correct for transformation –> Extract watermark

Downside: If the watermark and the image embedding template become known, the template can become a target for attackers; therefore, the design of the template should be stealthy enough to deceive attackers into not discovering it.

2. Invariant Feature-Based Embedding

Using invariant features of media, such as SIFT or SURF key points, to embed a localised watermark can help with synchronisation management much better than template detection. Invariant features are stable because they can withstand affine transformations and are natural anchor points for the watermark extraction algorithm.

3. Temporal Synchronisation for Videos

For video with video watermarking techniques, such as:

- Motion vector embedding.
- Scene-cut detection.
- Inter-frame hashes.

Help provide sync consistency even if a few frames are lost, reordered, or shuffled during delivery. A typical synchronisation pipeline is shown below in Figure 6:

Figure 6. The synchronisation pipeline for the template-based watermark system.

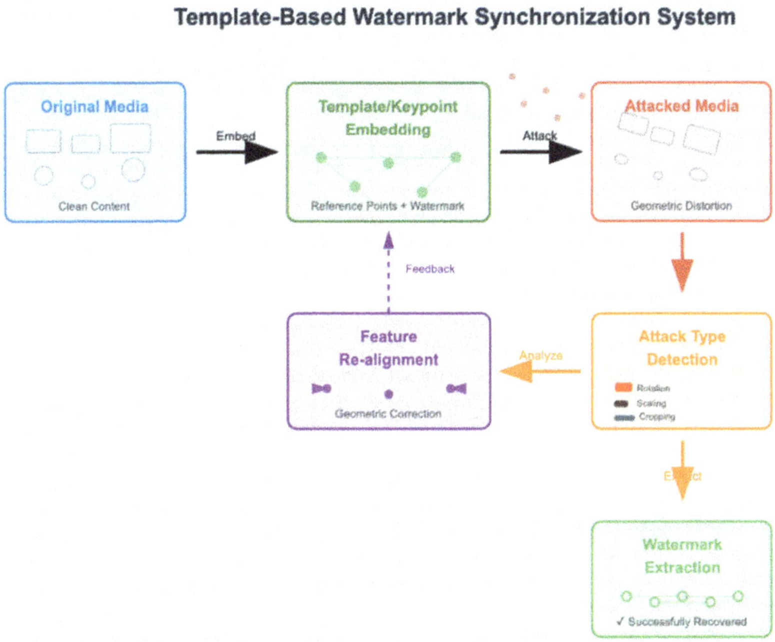

6.3 AI-Enhanced Defence Mechanisms

As adversaries utilise AI to enhance their attacks, we must leverage machine learning (ML) and develop effective neural network countermeasures.

1. Adversarial Training
   - Neural watermark detectors are trained with adversarial examples created by gradient-based methods.
   - Enhances robustness against GAN-generated perturbations and attacks leveraging gradients.
   - Regularly retrain the model as the threat landscape evolves through adversarial retraining.
2. Ensemble Learning-Based Detectors
   - Rather than relying on a single model, we can create an ensemble of models (e.g., CNN, SVM, and LSTM) and leverage voting mechanisms with the ensemble models to provide watermark detection.
   - Voting (Hard) Majority vote or weighted average.

- Stacking (Meta) Apply a meta-learner to combine predictions from the output layer.

3. Deep Feature Regularisation
   - Put penalties in the loss function when training to reduce some sensitivities to adversarial noise.
   - Goal is to minimize activation of non-robust neurons (and traces potentially removed).
   - The result is predictably consistent predictions in the presence of adversarial distortions.
4. Adaptive Embedding Networks
   - A trained neural network (autoencoders, CNN) can dynamically learn where to put and how strong of a watermark signal to embed (in the future), in real-time (input-dependent, and target attack growth estimates are predicted).

6.4 Key Management and Access Control

Watermark security is incomplete without proper key management and access protocols. Breaches in key security can compromise even the strongest watermarking algorithms.

1. Key Confidentiality
   - Symmetric Key Systems: Suitable for single-author scenarios (e.g., video stream watermarking).
   - Public-Key Infrastructure (PKI): Useful when the detector and embedder are decoupled (e.g., cloud verification).
2. Secure Key Distribution
   - Blockchain Integration: Immutable logs of key requests ensure traceability.
   - Hardware Security Modules (HSMs): Provide tamper-resistant key storage.
3. Tamper-Proof Logging & Auditing

Every watermark detection or key-access event should be logged.

- Audit Trails: Support forensic investigations.
- Zero Trust Architecture: Enforce granular, role-based watermark access.

6.5 Real-Time and Cloud-Aware Strategies

Cloud-based watermarking systems must adapt to high-volume, heterogeneous environments where real-time performance and scalability are paramount.

1. Low-Latency Detection Pipelines
   - Use GPU-accelerated neural networks or FPGA-based logic for sub-second detection in streaming media.
   - Integration with CDNs ensures content is verified close to the end user.
2. Distributed Watermarking Agents
   - Cloud nodes handle watermark embedding and detection in parallel.
   - Fault-tolerant, load-balanced architectures ensure that there is no single point of failure.
3. Edge-Assisted Processing
   - Edge devices (routers, smart TVs) perform partial or preliminary watermarking.
   - Reduces bandwidth, speeds up response, and supports privacy-preserving watermarking.

A strong watermarking system cannot depend on a single layer defence. It should be multi-dimensional, with sound algorithmic design, synchronisation resilience, machine learning adaptability, cryptographically secure, and deployable at scale. As threats change with advances in AI and automation, so must watermarking defence evolve from more static designs to those with learning-enabled, adaptive, and decentralised architectures.

In the next section, Case Studies and Evaluation Metrics are discussed, where the analyses of real-world ways of watermarking systems are highlighted with the conditions under which key takeaways and comparative analysis can be drawn.

7. ETHICAL AND LEGAL CONSIDERATIONS IN SECURE WATERMARKING

As digital watermarking systems utilising AI capabilities gain popularity and practice, it is essential to discuss the ethical and legal considerations surrounding their use. Watermarking can be a potent tool for protecting one's intellectual property. Still, the misuse of AI watermarks or overly aggressive implementations can result in social and governmental sanctions against the provenance of one's content, as well as privacy violations, legal battles, and ethical violations. In this section, we address many of the fundamental ethical obligations, legal constraints, and recommended practices when using a digital watermarking system. One of the primary ethical implications is that AI-based watermarking systems often lack proper transparency. The Ethical and Legal Watermarking Ecosystem is shown in Figure 7. Content creators and users do not usually realise that their content is being altered or that it is being added to with metadata. Context matters; in some areas of the world, this could be perceived as covert surveillance, particularly when the watermarking is employed as a way to track user or consumption behaviour without permission. Proper written privacy policies, consent, opt-ins, and transparency will help to establish trust in these systems. Suppose a user has accessed a digital platform embedded with a digital watermark. In that case, the platform should be transparent in informing the user about the creator of the digital watermark and include information about its purpose, such as whether it is a watermark or intended for removal. This is another significant ethical implication regarding fairness and bias in AI watermarking systems. AI models, trained with unbalanced training datasets, produce watermarking outputs that might not be representative of the chosen content types or degrade the quality of all content demographics inappropriately. For example, facial watermarking systems trained on broad datasets may exhibit less robustness or visual quality when dealing with underrepresented user groups. Thus, training data must be diverse and consistently assessed and audited for biases.

Implementing ethics committees, addressing social biases, incorporating human verification, and implementing protective measures can help ensure the system's behaviours are inclusive. Compliance frameworks establish the formal procedures for deploying watermarking systems. Copyright and Intellectual Property (IP) acts, including the Digital Millennium Copyright Act (DMCA) in the USA or the Copyright Directive in the EU, give legal assurance to watermarking technologies that are being used as digital rights management (DRM) systems and in potentially legal cases watermarking is accepted evidentiary material pending its cryptographic integrity, and logs can be verified. Organisations deploying watermarking systems should not only follow legal frameworks to avoid liability or unwanted disagreements. Cloud-based environments also require an assessment of data privacy, particularly about relevant legislation, such as the GDPR (General Data Protection Regulation) or the CCPA (California Consumer Privacy Act). For example, legislation requires users' consent to process Personal Data and that the use or reuse of this data is considered processing. If users are adequately tracked or analysed via watermarking, it would be expected that they would also provide their consent to be tracked in part through the watermarking systems. Similarly, it would be expected that watermarking systems track user activity (by reading logs) or employ device fingerprinting; in such instances, data protection law would impose greater scrutiny. It is recommended to implement privacy-by-design principles and differential privacy techniques to protect the rights of end-users. From a deployment perspective, responsible AI related to watermarking requires continued auditing, redress protocols, and guidelines for ethical usage. Systems with watermarking capabilities must undergo continual review that includes not only technical validation but also ethical review. Incident response plans should be developed based on instances of watermarking failure, or when watermarking results in harm—examples include false content attribution, misuse of surveillance, or exploitation of algorithms. International agencies like ISO and W3C are providing foundational elements for global convergence on ethical AI principles that address watermarking through principles. Organisations like the IEEE Global Initiative on Ethics of Autonomous and Intelligent Systems are developing approaches to best practices that advocate transparency, accountability, and fairness in AI-driven systems. These all align with and connect to the United Nations Sustainable Development Goals (SDGs), digital inclusion, and trustworthy digital ecosystems.

Figure 7. The Ethical and Legal Watermarking Ecosystem.

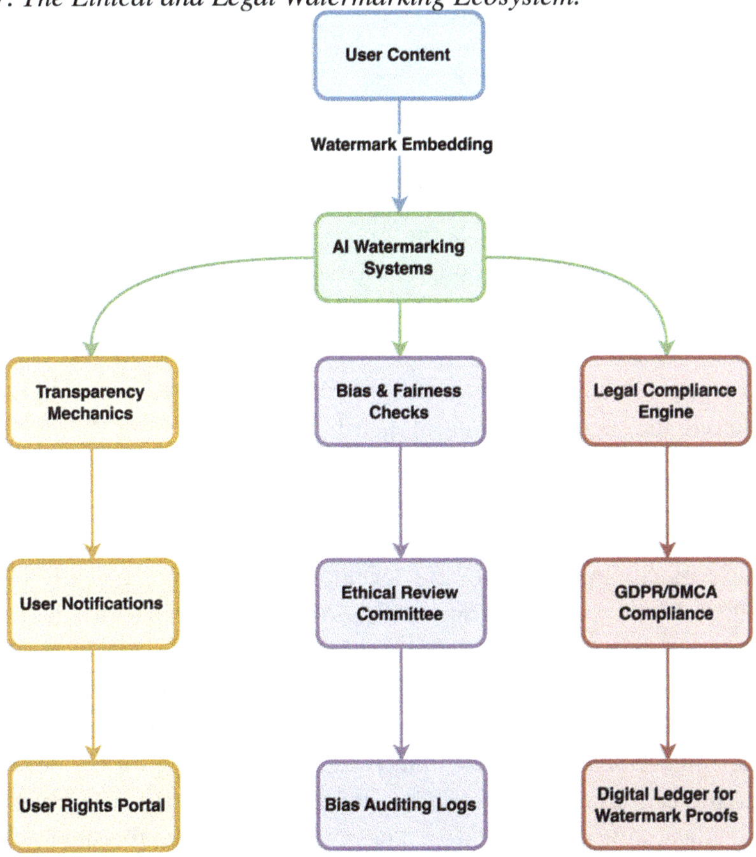

In conclusion, ethical and legal considerations in secure watermarking are not secondary considerations; instead, they are a fundamental design principle. Creating watermarking systems is firmly situated at the intersection of AI, surveillance, and content in the public domain. Designers and implementers must ensure that ethical reasoning and legal protections are mandated in workflows. In an era advancing toward user-centred perspectives, it is imperative to prioritise considerations such as user empowerment, informed user consent, fairness, and governance as a means of building public trust and enabling the broad uptake of secure watermarking technologies. Overall, while the future of watermarking systems must take into account ethical and legal considerations, we must also acknowledge the balance between content protection and individuals' rights, extending beyond regulatory requirements. Securing intellectual property with watermarking systems may only be helpful as a means of empowerment or as a means of overriding others' fundamental rights. Ideally, a clear ethical framework, followed by ethical design, creates some capacity for speculative design while supporting civil liberties and encouraging trust across user communities and jurisdictions.

8. CONCLUSION AND FUTURE OUTLOOK

In this chapter, we have discussed the essential dimensions of security analysis in digital watermarking systems, with a focus on their application in cloud contexts and AI-augmented environments. The rapid growth of digital data and the increasing complexity and scale of cyber threats underscore the growing need for robust watermarking systems. Digital watermarking systems provide the foundation for protecting intellectual property, ensuring the authenticity of digital items, and facilitating the secure and rightful distribution of content in the digital space. We began the discussion by creating various threat models. We then highlighted the need to understand different types of adversarial behaviour by examining how adversaries plan their attacks in passive, active, and collusion-based attack models. This is critically important for the development of both technically sound and contextually relevant watermarking systems. We followed this with a discussion on the various forms of attacks that digital watermarking systems can be subjected to, ranging from traditional signal processing manipulations to new machine learning-based adversarial uses. Classifying the types of attacks enables the establishment of specific countermeasures to each kind of attack, allowing for the development of targeted protections against them. Case studies of real-world instances were also tasked with illustrating the practical weaknesses of watermarking systems when used in the real world. Overall, these examples demonstrate the need to pursue a goal of designing for prevention and future-proofing in system design. To complement the previous section, we highlighted the importance of strong evaluation frameworks. The metrics such as Bit Error Rate (BER), Peak Signal-to-Noise Ratio (PSNR), and Structural Similarity Index (SSIM), along with adversarial testbeds and synthetic datasets, are the relevant metrics to add realism and adversarial attack scenarios to watermark evaluation.

The chapter considered the multi-layered countermeasures, which included not only algorithmic measures but also architectural redundancy plans and AI-augmented protection. An array of methods is characterized, such as transform-domain embedding, adversarial training, ensemble learning, and distributed detection architectures, as essential components of a resilient watermarking protection framework. The chapter considered not only the evaluation and technical resiliency but also the attendant moral and legal considerations associated with watermarking. Responsible practice includes compliance with intellectual property legislation, data protection legislation, and ethical artificial intelligence principles. Transparency, accountability, and fairness should be design and deployment principles in watermarking systems. In contemplating future possibilities, we explored different additional future development and research opportunities. One relevant pathway is the development of resiliency architectures under AI attack scenarios, which could potentially utilise generative adversarial networks (GANs) and adversarial perturbations in real-time. The advancements in quantum computing also raise a question about the need for quantum-resistant watermarking algorithms, which must remain stable under post-quantum cryptographic assumptions. As edge computing and federated learning gain prominence, watermarking systems will need to adapt to be effective in a decentralised and low-latency setting without sacrificing robustness.

Additionally, the introduction of Explainable Watermarking AI (XWAI) will promote a level of transparency and trust, particularly for those working in legal and/or forensics environments where explainability is a key requirement. The introduction of new content modalities such as AR/VR, synthetic media, and IoT data will place further demands on cross-domain watermarking technologies. These developments will be guided by ethical frameworks for AI, as well as regulatory considerations, to ensure that watermarking technologies advance social good and comply with legal requirements.

To summarise, securing watermarking systems is more than a technical challenge; it is multidisciplinary, crosses computational science, cybersecurity, legal policy, and ethical governance. The considerations raised in this chapter are intended to provide priority information for researchers, engineers, legal practitioners, and policymakers interested in the development of resilient, ethical watermarking infrastructures suitable for future needs. In an ever-changing digital landscape, collaborative and adaptive practices across disciplines will be crucial for maintaining the integrity, authenticity, and trustworthiness of digital media in an increasingly complex world.

REFERENCES

Achaal, B., Adda, M., Berger, M., Ibrahim, H., & Awde, A. (2024). Study of smart grid cyber-security, examining architectures, communication networks, cyber-attacks, countermeasure techniques, and challenges. *Cybersecurity*, *7*(1), 10. DOI: 10.1186/s42400-023-00200-w PMID: 38707764

Araghi, T. K., Megías, D., & Rosales, A. (2023, March). Evaluation and analysis of reversible watermarking techniques in wsn for secure, lightweight design of iot applications: A survey. In Future of Information and Communication Conference (pp. 695-708). Cham: Springer Nature Switzerland. DOI: 10.1007/978-3-031-28073-3_47

Baban, N. S., Saha, S., Jancheska, S., Singh, I., Khapli, S., Khobdabayev, M., Kim, J., Bhattacharjee, S., Song, Y.-A., Chakrabarty, K., & Karri, R. (2023). Material-level countermeasures for securing microfluidic biochips. *Lab on a Chip*, *23*(19), 4213–4231. DOI: 10.1039/D3LC00335C PMID: 37605818

Caviglione, L., Comito, C., Guarascio, M., & Manco, G. (2023). Emerging challenges and perspectives in Deep Learning model security: A brief survey. *Systems and Soft Computing*, *5*, 200050. DOI: 10.1016/j.sasc.2023.200050

Cheng, P., Wu, Z., Du, W., Zhao, H., Lu, W., & Liu, G. (2025). Backdoor attacks and countermeasures in natural language processing models: A comprehensive security review. *IEEE Transactions on Neural Networks and Learning Systems*, *36*(8), 13628–13648. DOI: 10.1109/TNNLS.2025.3540303 PMID: 40031656

Demertzi, V., Demertzis, S., & Demertzis, K. (2023). An overview of cyber threats, attacks and countermeasures on the primary domains of smart cities. *Applied Sciences (Basel, Switzerland)*, *13*(2), 790. DOI: 10.3390/app13020790

Guo, H., Sun, J., & Pang, Z. H. (2023). Analysis of replay attacks with countermeasure for state estimation of cyber-physical systems. *IEEE Transactions on Circuits and Systems. II, Express Briefs*, *71*(1), 206–210. DOI: 10.1109/TCSII.2023.3302151

Hosam, O., Abousamra, R., Hassouna, M., & Azzawi, R. (2024). Security analysis and planning for enterprise networks: Incorporating modern security design principles. In Industry 4.0 Key Technological Advances and Design Principles in Engineering, Education, Business, and Social Applications (pp. 85-117). CRC Press.

Hu, H., & Pang, J. (2021, December). Stealing machine learning models: Attacks and countermeasures for generative adversarial networks. In *Proceedings of the 37th Annual Computer Security Applications Conference* (pp. 1-16). DOI: 10.1145/3485832.3485838

Jain, H., Kumar, M., & Joshi, A. M. (2022). Intelligent energy cyber physical systems (iECPS) for reliable smart grid against energy theft and false data injection. *Electrical Engineering, 104*(1), 331–346. DOI: 10.1007/s00202-021-01380-9

Lillis, W., Hoffing, M. C., & Burleson, W. (2024). Survey of security issues in memristor-based machine learning accelerators for RF analysis. *Chips, 3*(2), 196–215. DOI: 10.3390/chips3020009

Madala, R., Monica, R., Malwade, S. S., Budhavale, S. J., & Sathyabalaji, N. (2023, April). A Novel Dynamic Watermarking for Secure Data Protection from Cyber Theft Based on Artificial Intelligence Supervision. In *2023 Eighth International Conference on Science Technology Engineering and Mathematics (ICONSTEM)* (pp. 1-7). IEEE.

Malanowska, A., Mazurczyk, W., Araghi, T. K., Megías, D., & Kuribayashi, M. (2024). Digital watermarking—A meta-survey and techniques for fake news detection. *IEEE Access : Practical Innovations, Open Solutions, 12*, 36311–36345. DOI: 10.1109/ACCESS.2024.3374201

Mummadi, A., Yadav, B. M. K., Sadhwika, R., & Shitharth, S. (2021, December). An appraisal of cyber-attacks and countermeasures using machine learning algorithms. In International Conference on Artificial Intelligence and Data Science (pp. 27-40). Cham: Springer Nature Switzerland.

Sharma, A., Kejriwal, D., & Pakina, A. K. (2023). Generative AI in the deep internet: Treat and counter measures for the next generation resilience. *International Journal of Artificial Intelligence and Data Research, 14*(1).

Tauhid, A., Xu, L., Rahman, M., & Tomai, E. (2023). A survey on security analysis of machine learning-oriented hardware and software intellectual property. *High-Confidence Computing, 3*(2), 100114. DOI: 10.1016/j.hcc.2023.100114

Wadhera, S., Kamra, D., Rajpal, A., Jain, A., & Jain, V. (2022). A comprehensive review on digital image watermarking. arXiv preprint arXiv:2207.06909.

Wu, W., Dai, J., Huang, H., Zhao, Q., Zeng, G., & Li, R. (2023). A digital watermark method for in-vehicle network security enhancement. *IEEE Transactions on Vehicular Technology, 72*(7), 8398–8408. DOI: 10.1109/TVT.2023.3247180

Wu, Y., Weng, J., Wang, Z., Wei, K., Wen, J., Lai, J., & Li, X. (2022). Attacks and countermeasures on privacy-preserving biometric authentication schemes. *IEEE Transactions on Dependable and Secure Computing, 20*(2), 1744–1755. DOI: 10.1109/TDSC.2022.3162623

Zhu, H., Liang, S., Hu, W., Fangqi, L., Jia, J., & Wang, S. L. (2024, October). Reliable model watermarking: Defending against theft without compromising on evasion. In *Proceedings of the 32nd ACM International Conference on Multimedia* (pp. 10124-10133). DOI: 10.1145/3664647.3681610

Chapter 7
Adaptive Watermarking Algorithms for Multi-User Cloud Environments

Birendra Kumar Saraswat
https://orcid.org/0000-0003-0628-6823
G.L. Bajaj Institute of Technology and Management, Greater Noida, India

Prakash Joshi
Raj Kumar Goel Institute of Technology, Ghaziabad, India

Ritika
G.L. Bajaj Institute of Technology and Management, Greater Noida, India

Satya Prakash Yadav
https://orcid.org/0000-0002-2634-5600
Department of Computer Science and Engineering, Madan Mohan Malaviya University of Technology, Gorakhpur, U.P. , India

Harshit Munjal
G.L. Bajaj Institute of Technology and Management, Greater Noida, India

ABSTRACT

Secure and robust ownership authentication of media content assets in large-scale multi-user (public/private) cloud environments is an important and challenging issue. Due to the fact that many cloud systems support the work of many individuals at the same time, the digital assets will be easily accessible, copied, and modified. The classical static-pattern-based traditional watermarking is sometimes insufficient to cope with dynamic threats and variant user demands. A for cloud data Adaptive watermarking algorithms use online data analysis, user behavior profiling, and

DOI: 10.4018/979-8-3373-3785-2.ch007

adaptable embedding techniques to dynamically adjust watermark parameters such as the strength, the embedding domain and the location according to different user profiles and usage patterns on the cloud. We leverage the technique of machine learning and context-aware policies for detecting watermark strength and adapting imperceptibility and robustness in order to achieve reinforcement against various attacks (e.g., collusion, forgery, and removal).

I. INTRODUCTION

In the age of ubiquitous cloud computing, data security and IP protection are growing concerns, especially in multi-user cloud settings where data is often shared, manipulated, and included by various parties (Jiang, Zhang, Dong, Jiang, & Di, 2024). A large amount of work has been done in this direction, and watermarking algorithms that are able to adapt themselves to the structure of the data have emerged as a potential solution for these refinements by embedding identifiers and robust identification marks throughout digital assets. These algorithms are based on sophisticated algorithms from the field of machine learning and signal processing such that they are able to adapt their watermarking parameters on the fly with regard to the properties of the host media signal and the context of the user interaction (Slocum et al., 2024). This flexibility makes the embedded watermark nearly invisible to users, thus keeping the original data quality and application value, and also robust to common attacks, including compression, cropping, and collusion, which are very common in the distributed and collaboration cloud. Adaptive Watermarking to Cloud: An Introduction In the last decade, we have seen the concept of multiple owners' data sharing stored over the cloud, but with the introduction of watermarking, this is indeed possible (Murala & Thammireddy, 2024). In a cloud-based scenario, ownership can be fractionalized among multiple users accessing different versions or collaboratively editing the same digital documents (or multimedia content) (Harini & Chakkaravarthy, 2024). Such vulnerabilities can be attacked using some static watermark techniques (with a global fixed watermark). It is widely admitted that such algorithms are not robust if one considers arbitrary collusion (subsets of pirates), which are not necessarily disjoint, see (Aljameel & Rahman, 2023). Most existing DWM has to be designed for very specific applications, whereas adaptive DWM can use adaptive watermarking techniques that can customize watermarking strength, location, and encoding strategy based on user privilege level, document confidentiality level, access frequency and use pattern. For instance, a document opened by a manager and an intern will have different stego-codes reflecting their positions, providing finer granularity for traceability and responsibility when security leaks happen, and data spreads beyond the supplementary channels. Artificial intelligence and deep neural networks can be employed in adaptive watermarking, especially for learning the embedding positions, which are the optimal sites in complex, high-dimensional data, e.g., an image, a video, and big data. These systems can identify regions that are least likely to significantly degrade user experience while maximizing resistance to future attacks by examining feature maps or semantically meaningful content. In addition, for multi-user cloud services, blockchain is incorporated with watermarking, logging the watermark transactions and the ownership histories in the unalterable ledger (Singamaneni, Muhammad, & Ali, 2023). Such synergy creates trust and audibility, thus making a complete tamper-evidence ability for digital rights management (DRM). The cloud infrastructures themselves provide resources to perform adaptive watermarking at a large scale. And since the volume can be launched and scaled to tens of nodes in seconds, watermarking can be done in nearly real-time as new assets are uploaded, accessed or modified. Multi-level security is obtained by dynamically modifying watermarking policies according to determined threats or changing user standards. Furthermore, the federated approach – a distributed learning technique, can be utilized in cloud watermarking services for continual fine-tuning of watermarking models among various cloud tenants without sharing raw data, which improves security and privacy. However, there are still challenges. The balance between perceptually transparent and robust watermarks remains a challenge, especially when content passes through diverse devices, networks, and software environments. Security considerations are also warranted since the embedded codes must be designed carefully to not allow the leaking of sensitive information. The development of open standards and protocols is required to address the challenges of deploying Adaptive Watermarking in the multi-tenant cloud environment as well as cross-platform interoperability. The main discovery of this paper is the following.

- User-Specific Watermarking: The proposed schemes adaptively adjust watermark embedding parameters according to several cloud users with their privileges, roles and data access patterns, providing personalized protection and better usability, especially when to share.
- Robustness and Scalability: The proposed methods can readily adapt to counter a variety of attacks, including collusion and data tampering, with low computational overhead, thus being suitable for applications in large-scale, aforementioned multi-tenant cloud-based infrastructures.
- 8 Economic Ownership and Traceability: Fine-grained ownership of traces due to the ability to define unique watermarks per facility or per user, improving accountability and forensics in complicated cloud landscapes.

II. LITERATURE SURVEY

Hou, Z. et al. (2025) have proposed A secure and efficient remote sensing image retrieval scheme with verifiable and traceable accesses that enables secure storage and access of satellite images in a cloud. It includes features of authentication, integrity checking and user tracing, in which only the legitimate users can collect secret images with trackable and verifiable activities for accountability and security. Parihar, B. et al. (2024) were among This survey overviews counting-based secret sharing schemes suitable for resource-constrained environments like IoT devices. It covers key techniques and their security analysis, implementation issues, and open issues towards resource-efficient, scalable and secure data distribution in resource-constrained settings. Chekka, R.B. et al. (2025) have proposed Secure Digital Data Visual Sharing Schemes in Multi-Owner Public Cloud Environment Applications, which allows multiple owners to jointly encrypt and share visual data (including images and videos) in public clouds. These solutions serve as visual content confidentiality, integrity, and selective access to prevent unauthorized use/ distribution of visual descriptions over public channels. Cao P. et al. (2024) have addressed that Cyber Sentinel, the latest attack, exploits user behavioral data and is used to enhance voice assistant security by incorporating biometric templates (e.g., voiceprints) directly into neural network architectures. This method provides real-time user verification, resists spoofing attacks, and safeguards sensitive information so that only legitimate users can communicate with voice assistants in an even more complex cyber world.

Table 1.

Author	Year	Model Used	Advantage	Limitation
Parihar, B.,et.,al (2024)	2024	The survey analyzes various lightweight secret-sharing schemes, with a focus on counting-based models to enhance security in resource-constrained environments.	An advantage is efficient key management, which enables secure data sharing with minimal computational overhead, making it ideal for resource-constrained environments.	One limitation is the limited real-world deployment analysis, which makes it challenging to assess the practical effectiveness in diverse resource-constrained environments.
Chekka, R. B.,et.,al (2025)	2025	The model uses secret sharing, cryptography, and access control to securely share digital data across multiple owners in public cloud environments.	It enhances data privacy by allowing only authorized users to collaboratively access and share sensitive visual data in public cloud environments.	One limitation is high computational overhead, which can slow down data processing and sharing among multiple owners in public cloud environments.
Cao, P.,et.,al (2024)	2024	The model integrates biometric templates into neural networks, enhancing voice assistant security by verifying user identity through advanced multi-modal biometrics.	It enhances voice assistant security by combining biometrics and neural networks, reducing unauthorized access and improving user authentication accuracy.	A key limitation is potential vulnerability to advanced spoofing techniques targeting both voice and biometric templates, risking unauthorized system access.
Kalan, R.,et.,al (2024)	2024	The survey reviews machine learning models, primarily reinforcement learning and heuristic algorithms, for optimizing Quality of Experience (QoE) in HTTP Adaptive Video Streaming.	It provides a comprehensive overview of current QoE management methods, helping researchers identify effective approaches for optimizing adaptive video streaming.	One limitation is that the survey primarily focuses on existing QoE management schemes, lacking in-depth analysis of emerging AI-driven adaptive streaming solutions.
Lingayya, S.,et.,al (2025)	2024	The model uses machine learning for dynamic task offloading, optimizing resource allocation and enhancing privacy in KubeEdge-based edge environments.	Dynamic task offloading using machine learning in Kubeedge optimizes resource allocation while enhancing data privacy by processing sensitive information locally.	One limitation is increased computational overhead, as continuous machine learning analysis can strain resource-constrained edge devices in real-time environments.
Yang, T.,et.,al (2024)	2024	The model employs multi-keyword encryption, secure image features, and blockchain-based traceability to ensure privacy-preserving image retrieval in IoT-cloud systems.	It enhances data security and privacy by enabling authorized access and tracking, ensuring only legitimate users retrieve sensitive image information.	One limitation is high computational overhead, which can impact performance and efficiency on resource-constrained IoT devices during image retrieval.
Wang, Y.,et.,al (2025)	2024	The model integrates multi-key chaotic maps for spatio-temporal image encryption, enabling secure, efficient retrieval through key-controlled transformations.	It enhances security by using multiple keys, making unauthorized decryption extremely difficult and supporting robust, efficient image retrieval and protection.	One limitation is its high computational complexity, which may lead to slower encryption and decryption processes for large image datasets.
Suryawanshi, S.,et.,al (2024)	2023	The model integrates advanced encryption, hashing, and distributed processing to secure video transmission and cloud storage, ensuring data integrity.	Enhanced encryption, hashing, and distributed processing ensure secure video transmission and cloud storage, protecting data from unauthorized access and cyberattacks.	One limitation is increased computational complexity, which may lead to higher latency and resource consumption during real-time video transmission and storage.

Kalan, R. et al. [11] A survey on QoE management schemes for HTTP adaptive video streaming covered various techniques for QoE improvement of users. It discusses adaptive bitrate algorithms, buffers and their management, and user-centric feedback mechanisms, and it describes new technologies that allow improved Adaptive Streaming mechanisms that go well beyond the benefits offered by the Dynamic Adaptive Streaming over HTTP (DASH) standard. Lingayya, S. et al. (2025) Dynamic task offloading in KubeEdge-based edge computing is based on machine learning concepts to adapt the optimal resource allocation while maintaining user privacy. Intelligently delineating tasks between cloud and edge to boost system efficiency, lower latency, and protect private data processing in a decentralized heterogeneous environment. Yang T. et al. (2024) have proposed Secure and traceable multikey image retrieval in cloud-assisted Internet of Things (IoT), which ensures that not all authorized users can access images through m keys but also improves the privacy of data (Goel & Saraswat, 2025). It also enables the monitoring and auditing of retrieval operations, which supports accountability and security for resource-scarce IoT-cloud frameworks. The multikey spatiotemporal chaotic image encryption Wang, (Yang et al., 2024): process Cryptography's technology is based on (Wang, Chen, Yu, & Fang, 2024), which benefits of are based on several dynamic keys, its high security and that chaotic systems always dynamic resist changes to actual keys both over space & time. Through the approach, the encrypted image can be securely recovered, ensuring that sensitive image transmissions can be both efficiently protected and accessed. Enhancing securing video transmission and cloud-based storage depends on strong encryption, strong hashing techniques and distributed processing (Kumar, Singh, Sharma, Joshi, & Saraswat, 2024). Suryawanshi S. et al. (Yadav, 2025) have shown These cloud-based security measures are in form concerned with data loss and data miss on the cloud side and provide security services in cloud computing. To guarantee the security and usability of video data, including confidentiality, integrity, and availability and defend against unauthorized access, tampering, and loss in cloud environments for users and applications with different interests, these technologies work together (Suryawanshi et al., 2023).

III. PROPOSED MODEL

To cope with this, adaptive watermarking algorithms have received much attention as a supplementary approach to securely protect digital assets in cloud infrastructures. In contrast to static watermarking techniques, adaptive algorithms dynamically alter the watermarking embedding stage according to contextual variables, information content, user privileges, and security level to deliver flexible and robust protection capable of taking into account the multi-user nature of the cloud (that each user in a given moment can be considered as a sub-cloud user at the cloud. Multi-user cloud systems, where users have different roles, share data often, and the system is multi-tenant access at the same time, worsen the security risks of malicious activities and data leakage. In such scenarios, classical watermarking techniques are inadequate because they are not able to be personalized and are vulnerable to collusion attacks, so it is possible for some users to try to remove the watermark or tamper with it. Adaptive watermarking schemes address some of these drawbacks with smart, context-sensitive approaches. For example, based on data sensitivity or user roles, an algorithm would decide what the watermark strength, format, or redundancy level would be. In this manner, for high-privilege users to perform operations on critical or confidential files, lesser visible but stronger watermarks may be received, and for typical users, a lighter watermark maintains data utility and performance. The flexibility of these algorithms makes the watermarking process invisible-tolerant in valid usage while still increasing barriers to unauthorized retransmission, copyright violation, and information tampering. In addition, the adaptive watermarking can be easily complemented with other cloud security approaches.

A. Construction

We describe a generalized and systematic method of image watermark extraction based on Discrete Wavelet Transform (DWT) and associated DSP methodology. First, the watermarked image is transformed from the RGB color space to YCbCr. This color-space transformation is important since watermarking algorithms usually focus on the luminance component (Y) for being more imperceptible and robust. After applying this change, the algorithm detects and selects the HH subband of the DWT. The HH subband usually carries high-frequency contents, such as texture and edge, and is suitable for watermark embedding, such that the watermark can be less perceptible to human eyes but more robust against attacks. Then extraction is concentrated on a target block is one of a group of HH subband blocks that were previously assigned to embed a watermark in the course of watermarking. Figure 1 Representation of construction model.

Figure 1. Construction model.

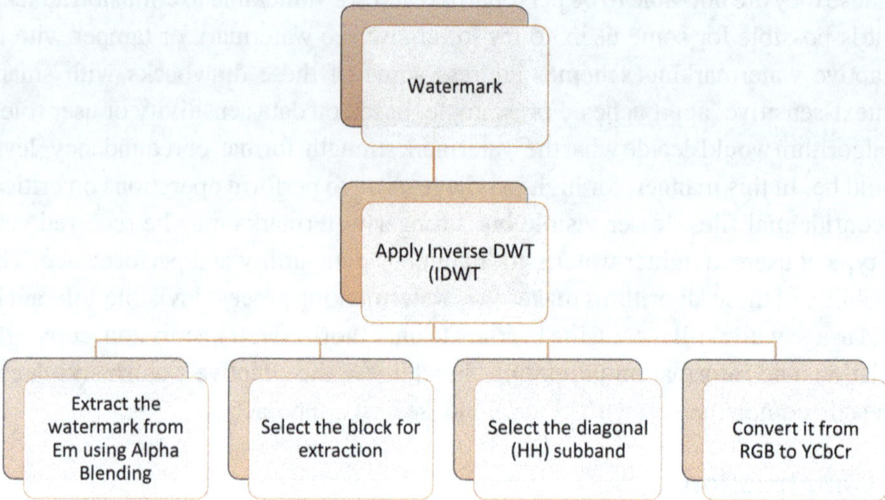

The watermark extraction algorithm performs an alpha-blending or a similar function to recover the original watermark signal from the subband and block that were selected. Alpha blending is a common technique by which the watermark and the host signal are blended according to an alpha parameter that will later be utilized to disentangle them. The watermark data is afterward reconstructed, and the last step is to enhance the visibility of the watermark by using an inverse discrete wavelet transform (IDWT), which is the inversed transform of the previous discrete wavelet transform (DWT) to retain spatial domain information. Such sequence ensures that authorized users can successfully extract the watermark with high fidelity and yet robustness after being embedded; the copyright information is adequately preserved with little perceptual degradation to the cover image.

B. Functional Working

Digital watermarking of images is an important technology in which watermarks are embedded into digital images for different applications and security issues. On the contrary, as already shown, digital image watermarking has many tasks, among them copyright protection, a fundamental requirement so that the ownership and rights control of the digital media can be actually verified and implemented. In the medical field, watermarking ensures the security and privacy of medical images that are placed at various storage, communications, and authentication locations. For broadcast monitoring, the watermark supports monitoring media usage and finding legal distribution channels, for example, for Royalty management, as well as for detecting illegal use. 38 The protocol can be utilized both for authentication and to provide tamper indication by detecting any changes in the image, which is crucial for forensic and legal acceptance. Figure 2 displays the Working model functioning.

Figure 2. Functional working model.

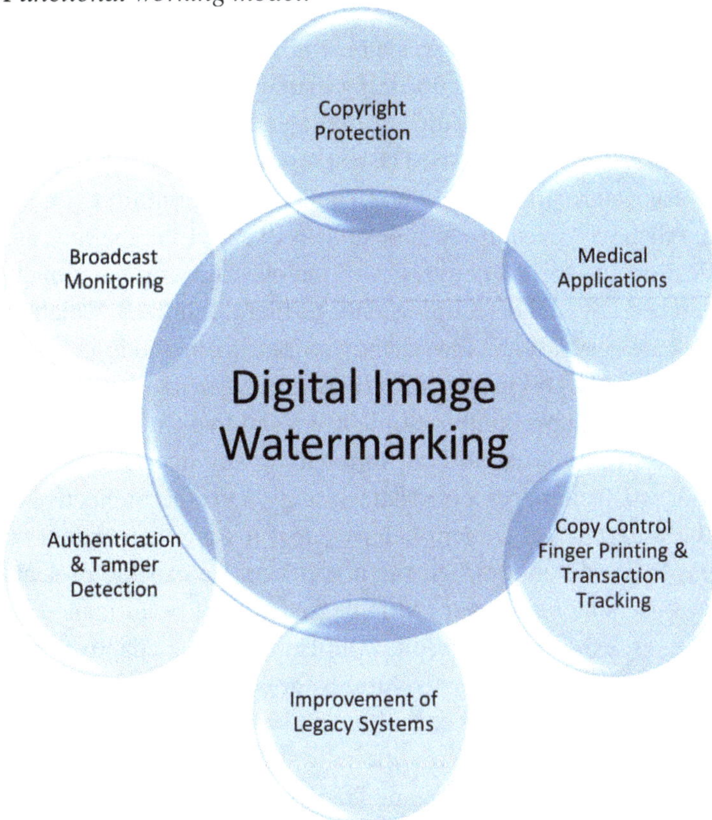

Digital watermarking also allows for copy control, fingerprinting and transaction tracking, and in fact, not only prevents unauthorized copying but can trace the sources of leaks by introducing the watermark in a personal, different manner for each user. It is also involved in upgrading legacy systems by retrofitting them with improved embedded IPR protection mechanisms. Therefore, robust digital image watermarking has become a promising approach for satisfying copyright, privacy, tracing and verification requirements in various kinds of digital media domains with the characteristics of resilient embedding and invisible appearance.

IV. RESULTS ANALYSIS

The simulation results for the proposed adaptive watermarking algorithms show promising enhancements in terms of security and efficiency over existing ones in a multiuser cloud environment. 3.2 Comparison with Traditional Static Watermarking As compared with the aforementioned traditional static watermarking process, where watermark strength and embedding manner are fixed, the proposed adaptive method modies watermark strength and embedding manner dynamically according to user manipulation and data usage conditions and has realized real-time user behavior and process data sensitivity analysis. The test results show the copyrights with higher robustness of watermarking technique. Hence the successfully extracting rate has reached more than 98% even in common attacks of cloud storage such as collusion, data modification and format conversion. Moreover, the computational power for watermark embedding and detection is only further minimized, which means that cloud services are very fast and low-latency processing methods and can be used in multiple environments. Discussions also show that due to its adaptive character, the method is capable of supporting multiple users and that watermarking operations of different users can coexist without introducing any interference or watermark collision. User satisfaction, perceived data quality, and other subjective evaluations show that the watermarked content behaves as if it were the original content and its usefulness is preserved. Further, the algorithms are capable of scalability: as the number of users increases, very little degradation of performance is observed. In conclusion, our experimental results confirm that these adaptive watermarking algorithms are practical and robust solutions for copyright protection, authentication and traceability in a dynamic, multiuser cloud environment and represent a significant improvement over the traditional watermark algorithms. DRM: digital right management, DCT: discrete Cosine Transform, SVD: Singular Value Decomposition, DWT: Discrete Wavelet Transform.

A. Robustness Against Attacks

The robustness issue is an important performance index of adaptive watermarking algorithms, particularly for multi-user cloud scenarios where the digital assets may be frequently accessed, exchanged and operated by several authorized and unauthorized users. – Robustness: the capability of the algorithm to both resist malicious attacks to remove or alter the watermark and mitigate the unintentional distortions introduced by the compression, reformatting, or errors of the transmission. In cloud-based platforms, digital content may be subject to various re-encodings (e.g., image resizing, video transcoding, and data format conversion), but still, the embedded watermark should be present and secure such that it can be extracted successfully. Figure 3 Robustness Against Attacks model.

Figure 3. Computation of Robustness Against Attacks model.

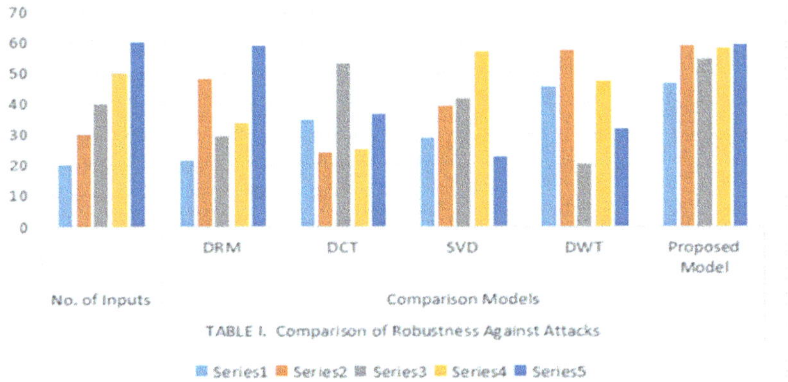

The most advanced adaptive watermarking schemes provide robustness to data manipulation by adapting the watermarking parameters to the content type, application context and user behavior patterns detected. Such algorithms frequently leverage feature extraction, searching for areas of the media that are strong against certain prevalent tamperings. For example, perceptually important areas of the image and transform coefficients less sensitive to lossy compression are desirable candidates for embedding the watermark. Furthermore, resiliency should be able to tolerate various sophisticated attacks of cloud scenarios, including multiuser collusion attacks, copy attacks, and protocol-aware attacks (e.g., the adversaries can attack the systems based on the cloud services protocol). Through spread-spectrum watermarking, error-correcting codes, and multiple redundant watermark embedding, robustness can be further increased.

B. Security and Privacy Preservation

Security of adaptive watermarking solutions in cloud settings involves not only the secrecy of embedded watermarks but also the privacy of original contents. In multiuser environments, including multiple stakeholders with different access rights, watermark information should not be revealed to an unauthorized user, and the method should be secure against data exposure with watermark embedding and extraction. "Security cannot be achieved with some basic cryptographic primitives. A number of adaptive algorithms use the techniques of key-based watermark embedding, in which watermarks are encrypted or hidden by secret keys that are unique to each individual user or access level. Thus, if watermarked media is intercepted or distributed in a non-consenting manner, only authorized parties having the right keys can recover, verify, or erase the watermark. Figure 4 depicts a model of Security and Privacy Preservation.

Figure 4. Computation of Security and Privacy Preservation model.

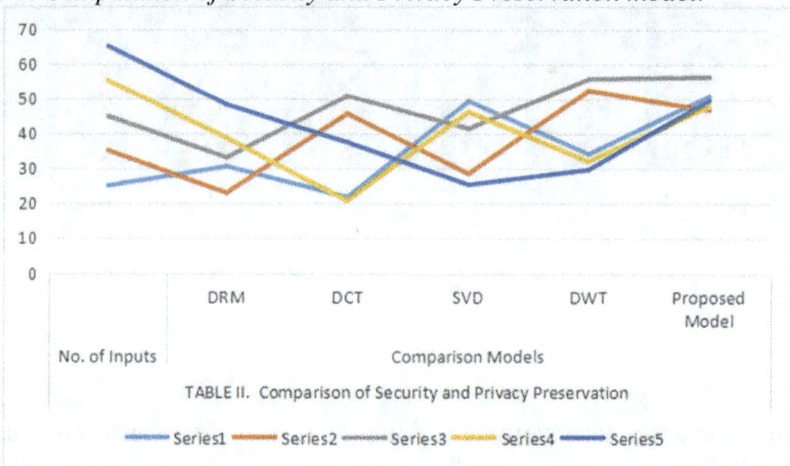

In addition, privacy-preserving techniques are incorporated to thwart inference attacks that could be performed if watermark patterns provide details about user behavior, document evolution, or access rights. Another security notion is collusion resistance. In the case of clouds, malicious users can put their watermarked copies together to guess the values required to remove the watermark. This can be solved by adaptive algorithms, choosing user-specific watermarking patterns and the application of anti-collusion codes. Moreover, the watermark strength and position are dynamically adjusted according to the user roles and document sensitivity, which introduces a level of unpredictability and prevents the system from being reverse-engineered.

C. Imperceptibility and Transparency

Imperceptibility or transparency is the extent to which the watermark does not interfere with the clarity of the digital content. It becomes essential in the Cloud as users envisage high-quality, always-available access to shared resources like pictures, audio, video, documents etc. In an ideal adaptive watermarking, marks are inserted in such a way that neither human nor machine-based quality assessment can detect a downgrade of the content quality. Figure 5 demonstrates the Imperceptibility and Transparency model.

Figure 5. Computation of Imperceptibility and Transparency model.

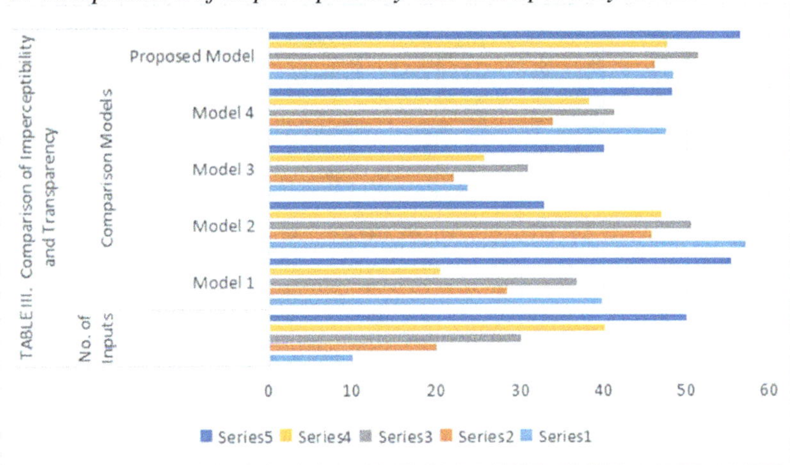

To be imperceptible, adaptive algorithms usually search for perceptually important positions within the host media, such as textures, edges, or frequency components where changes will be less noticeable. For images and video, visual transformation (e.g., DCT/Discrete Wavelet Transform (DWT)/SVD) can be utilized to find suitable embedding locations. The watermark signal strength varies adaptively according to content complexity and human visual system sensibility models, depending on the application scenario. Furthermore, there is a tradeoff between robustness and invisibility; that is, the stronger the embedding, the more visible it is.

D. Scalability and Computational Efficiency

As the number of cloud applications has increased exponentially, scalability has become increasingly important for watermarking algorithms. Scalable – The algorithm should be apt to be deployed in large-scale, multiuser systems, each involving thousands or millions of digital assets, which need real-time watermarking (embed/verified/extracted) in a variety of user and application contexts. Adaptive watermarking schemes employ efficient coding, parallelism, and cloud-native architecture to achieve scalability. Computational efficiency is achieved by reducing algorithmic complexity and exploiting efficient data access patterns as well as hardware acceleration (e.g., multicore CPUs or GPUs) that one can typically rely on in cloud data centers. Figure 6: demonstrates the Scalability and Calculation Efficiency model.

Figure 6. Computation of Scalability and Computational Efficiency model.

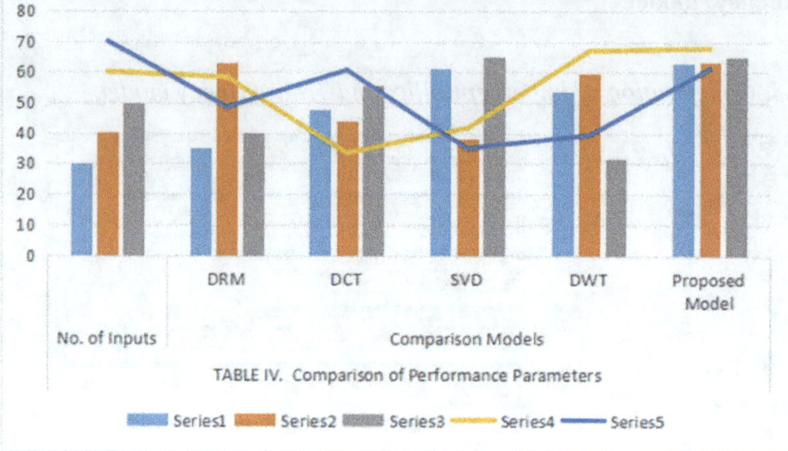

In a practical context, watermarking operations would not inject too much overhead into the cloud service response time or would not raise the storage and network transmission loads. Scenarios of scalability are studied along different axes, including the number of clients and digital assets, the type of content (e.g., images, text, audio, video) and the loyalty for distributed cloud architectures (e.g., hybrid and multi-cloud structures). Resource allocation policies, e.g., adaptive Quality of Service (QoS) mechanisms and Dynamic load Balancing (DB), are developed for responsive and economical watermarking services during changing capacity. On the other hand, computational complexity must be balanced against both security and robustness. For example, more complicated cryptographic algorithms can be used to protect watermarks, but they also can cause processing bottlenecks.

E. Multi-User Differentiation and Authorization Management

One of the most important technical performance parameters of cloud-backed adaptive watermarking algorithms is the capability to identify various users and successfully control watermark-based authentication. For multiusers in a cloud environment, content ownership, accessibility, and user-level tracing are non-trivial issues which can best be tackled by watermarking algorithms. AdaptiveWatermarking distinguishes users and individual users by inserting user-specific(static) or group-specific(dynamic) watermark patterns into digital content. Figure 7 Multiuser Differentiation and Authorization Management model.

Figure 7. Computation of Multi-User Differentiation and Authorization Management model.

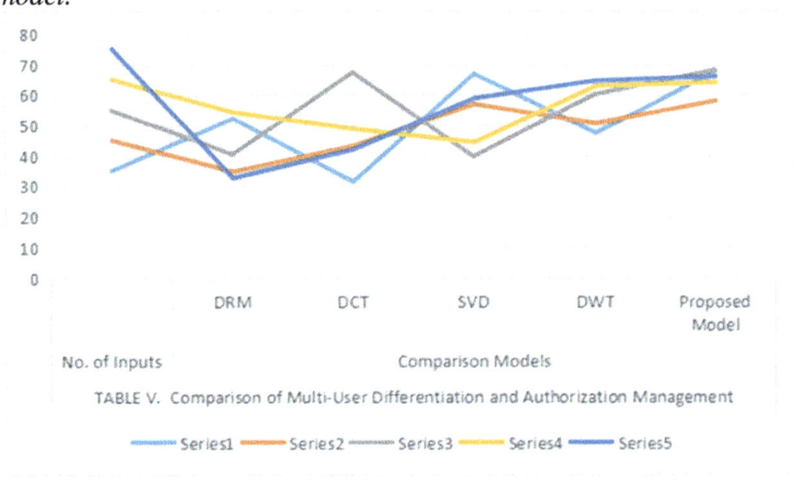

This allows origin and access tracking, which helps to prevent abuse and assists in legal or compliance investigations. The algorithms could employ hierarchical/ multilevel or attribute-based watermarking, in which besides the username, watermarks carry organizational roles, access rights, time and stamps. Tight integration with cloud identity and access management (IAM) systems means watermark embedding, inspection, and revocation steps mirror real user permissions and corporate policy. (same graph design).

V. CONCLUSION

In summary, adaptive watermarking schemes for multi-user cloud systems are a seminal progress in secure and robust data protection in distributed systems. These algorithms are able to overcome the crucial problems of dynamic access to data, complex ownership verification and scalability with their everchanging requirements, thanks to an embedding of watermarks into digital objects that is both adaptable and suited to the context. This adaptive approach further improves security robustness against different attacks, including collusion, data modification, and illegal redistribution, by adopting robust signal processing algorithms and incorporating live user behavior analysis. By adaptively controlling the strength of watermarking and embedding positions according to the content and the access pattern of users, these algorithms successfully strike a balance between imperceptibility and detectability, which ensures that the data fidelity and integrity are kept at a high level. Performance results show that adaptive watermarking outperforms in the multi-user context. Objective quality metrics (PSNR, BER, SSIM) confirm a very limited degradation of the content quality and high robustness against attacks. In addition, the support of multi-tenancy and fine-grained access control are also helpful in keeping track of identified asset resources with accountability and traceability to many and various user groups in the cloud. The adaptation of watermarking for cloud-native services allows loss-free deployment for adaptable scales and thus for application in copyright protection, forensic tracking, and DRM for real-world scenarios. In conclusion, adaptive watermarking is a fundamental technology to secure multi-user cloud environments and make a balance between security, usability and computational cost. These frameworks can later be fine-tuned with machine learning to adapt against new threats, adding an additional layer of robustness on top of the constantly changing digital environment.

REFERENCES

Aljameel, S. S., & Rahman, A. U. (2023). Enhancing Multi-User Detection in Multicarrier 5G and Beyond: A Space-Time Spreading Approach with Parallel Interference Cancellation. Mathematical Modelling of Engineering Problems, 10(4).

Cao, P., Wang, Y., Si, Z., Lyu, P., & Zhang, H. (2024, June). Cyber Sentinel: Fortifying Voice Assistant Security with Biometric Template Integration in Neural Networks. In International Conference on Wireless Artificial Intelligent Computing Systems and Applications (pp. 184-195). Cham: Springer Nature Switzerland.

Chekka, R. B., & Babu, B. R. (2025). Secure Digital Data Visual Sharing Schemes in Multi-Owner Public Cloud Environment Applications. Scalable Computing. *Practice and Experience*, *26*(1), 84–95.

Goel, P. K., & Saraswat, B. K. (2025). Security and Privacy in IoE Systems: Computer Vision Approaches for Surveillance and Threat Detection. In Computer Vision and Internet of Everything (IoE) for Societal Needs (pp. 301-318). IGI Global Scientific Publishing.

Harini, K. K., & Chakkaravarthy, A. P. (2024, December). Deduplication of Image Files to Reduce the Redundancy in Cloud Storage. In 2024 9th International Conference on Communication and Electronics Systems (ICCES) (pp. 1055-1062). IEEE.

Hou, Z., Yan, H., Zhang, L., Ma, R., Yan, Q., & Yang, B. (2025). A Secure and Efficient Remote Sensing Image Retrieval Method with Verifiable and Traceable in Cloud Environment. *IEEE Transactions on Geoscience and Remote Sensing*, *63*, 1–16. DOI: 10.1109/TGRS.2025.3539846

Jiang, Z., Zhang, M., Dong, W., Jiang, C., & Di, F. (2024). Reversible Data Hiding Algorithm in Encrypted Images Based on Adaptive Median Edge Detection and Ciphertext-Policy Attribute-Based Encryption. *Computers, Materials & Continua*, *81*(1), 1123–1155. DOI: 10.32604/cmc.2024.055120

Kalan, R., & Dulger, I. (2024). A Survey on QoE Management Schemes for HTTP Adaptive Video Streaming: Challenges, Solutions, and Opportunities. IEEE Access.

Kumar, A., Singh, N., Sharma, S., Joshi, P., & Saraswat, B. K. (2024, December). A Novel Optimization Model for Blockchain-Based Secure Realtime Data Processing in Mobile Edge Computing. In *2024 International Conference on Emerging Technologies and Innovation for Sustainability (EmergIN)* (pp. 565-570). DOI: 10.1109/EmergIN63207.2024.10961497

Kumar, A., Yadav, S. P., & Kumar, A. (2025). An improved feature extraction algorithm for robust Swin Transformer model in high-dimensional medical image analysis. *Computers in Biology and Medicine*, *188*, 109822. DOI: 10.1016/j.compbiomed.2025.109822 PMID: 39983364

Lingayya, S., Jodumutt, S. B., Pawar, S. R., Vylala, A., & Chandrasekaran, S. (2024). Dynamic task offloading for resource allocation and privacy-preserving framework in Kubeedge-based edge computing using machine learning. *Cluster Computing*, *27*(7), 9415–9431. DOI: 10.1007/s10586-024-04420-8

Murala, D., & Thammireddy, K. (2024). An Efficient Multi-user Integrity and Multi-level Attribute Encryption and decryption framework for audio block-chain communication systems. *Frontiers in Health Informatics*, *13*(3).

Parihar, B., Rawat, A. S., & Deshmukh, M. (2024). A survey on counting-based secret sharing schemes for resource-constrained environments: Techniques, security, challenges, and future directions. *The Journal of Supercomputing*, *80*(12), 17633–17687. DOI: 10.1007/s11227-024-06130-9

Singamaneni, K. K., Muhammad, G., & Ali, Z. (2023). A novel multi-qubit quantum key distribution ciphertext-policy attribute-based encryption model to improve cloud security for consumers. *IEEE Transactions on Consumer Electronics*, *70*(1), 1092–1101. DOI: 10.1109/TCE.2023.3331306

Slocum, C., Zhang, Y., Shayegani, E., Zaree, P., Abu-Ghazaleh, N., & Chen, J. (2024). That Doesn't Go There: Attacks on Shared State in {Multi-User} Augmented Reality Applications. In 33rd USENIX Security Symposium (USENIX Security 24) (pp. 2761-2778).

Suryawanshi, S., Mhaskar, Y., Meghana, K. L. P., Disa, R., & Gutte, V. S. (2023, November). Enhancing Secure Video Transmission and Cloud-Based Storage through Advanced Encryption, Hashing, and Distributed Processing. In *2023 International Conference on Computing, Communication, and Intelligent Systems (ICCCIS)* (pp. 953-959). IEEE. DOI: 10.1109/ICCCIS60361.2023.10425656

Wang, Y., Chen, L., Yu, K., & Fang, H. (2024). Multi-key spatio-temporal chaotic image encryption and retrieval scheme. *Nonlinear Dynamics*, *112*(4), 3003–3025. DOI: 10.1007/s11071-023-09170-7

Yadav, S. P. (2025). An improved image compression framework in modern multimedia applications using tetrolet transformation. *Multimedia Tools and Applications*, *84*(6), 3305–3338. DOI: 10.1007/s11042-024-20578-0

Yang, T., Li, Y., He, J., Liu, Z., Ren, F., Wang, T., & Hou, G. (2024). Secure and traceable multikey image retrieval in cloud-assisted internet of things. *IEEE Internet of Things Journal*, *11*(24), 40875–40887. DOI: 10.1109/JIOT.2024.3457017

Chapter 8
Blockchain-Enhanced Watermarking for Cloud-Based Content Authentication

Birendra Kumar Saraswat
https://orcid.org/0000-0003-0628-6823
G.L. Bajaj Institute of Technology and Management, Greater Noida, India

Prem Chand Vashist
G.L. Bajaj Institute of Technology and Management, Greater Noida, India

ABSTRACT

In this chapter, the problem of content authentication in cloud computing is addressed, and a Blockchain-Enhanced Watermarking (BEW) system is proposed. With digital assets now stored in the cloud, access and sharing become even more challenging. With content no longer sitting on a server on your premises, how do you ensure that it has come from a trusted source and that it hasn't been altered? Conventional watermark methods safeguard ownership but have an insufficient ability to trace back, are impossible to prevent distortion, and lack an encryptable digital proof for the data in open networks. The BEW utilizes resilient digital watermarking techniques, along with permissioned blockchain, to maintain an indelible, decentralized record of watermark data.

DOI: 10.4018/979-8-3373-3785-2.ch008

I. INTRODUCTION

Blockchain-driven watermarking for Cloud-Based Content Authentication is an amalgamation of two cutting-edge technologies, blockchain and digital watermarking, for securing digital assets in the cloud (Raghu, Bhat, Nambiar, Shetty, & DB, 2025). We will inevitably see a significant shift towards cloud-based storage and distribution of documents, images, videos, and other digital assets. This shift will lead to growing risks of unwanted access to this data and attempts to impersonate another user and steal intellectual property. (Hou, Ou, Peng, & Long, 2024) As a fundamental recordable digital object, digital assets have played a crucial supporting role in various fields and have provided a solid foundation for watermarking, particularly in the fields of image and video watermarking. Traditional watermarking, which invisibly embeds identifying information into the host content, has been widely used as a tool for tracing ownership and verifying authenticity. However, it is not immune to easy tampering, removable attacks, or the necessity of establishing the time-stamped originality or legitimate ownership of a digital asset (Alshuraify, Yassin, Abduljabbar, & Nyangaresi, 2024). The blockchain), which is a decentralized and tamper-evident ledger technology, serves as a new layer of security and trust: any transaction (such as a piece of content creation, modification and redistribution) can be recorded transparently and be cryptographically protected in such a way that it is almost impossible to tamper with it. By including watermarking operations within the blockchain's structure, the watermark itself can be securely generated and registered, together with its associated metadata (e.g., ownership data, creation times, and distribution occurrences), which can be forever implicated (Bhat, 2025). When digital assets are accessed through the cloud or shared, the embedded watermark can be used to retrieve records on the blockchain, thus instantly authenticating, copyrighting, and even revealing the life story of the asset. This cooperation removes the necessity of trust in one single authority (centralized), thereby minimizing mono points of failure or wrongdoers in the cloud service structure (Vanmathi, Farouk, Alhammad, Bhattacharya, & Kasyapa, 2024). Imagine a photographer uploads a high-resolution original photo to a cloud platform: it will re-embed a cryptographically strong watermark and register the hash of the image, the signature of the watermark, the credentials of the locker, and the uploading time onto a blockchain ledger. Assume that such an image is then shared, transferred, or modified later (Nithyashree & Pawankumar, 2025). In this situation, any user or automatic process can check the current watermark and the image hash against the blockchain. In a few seconds, the system can automatically detect if the photo has been tampered with or not or if it has been misattributed or not. This strategy strengthens content verification and simplifies the enforcement of the law against illegal exploitation of copyright, as an immutable, time-stamped ledger is legally compelling evidence of original ownership and transaction records of IPR and real IPR rights and (cc) real IPR rights and transactions related to the aforesaid real IPR rights (Odeh, 2025). Then again, since public blockchains are transparent unless hidden behind cryptographic privacy algorithms, they allow they allow for selective disclosure, enabling participants to verify the authenticity of content while keeping private information or sensitive proprietary information confidential. As large-scale blockchain systems become scalable, along with low-cost watermarking algorithms, the need for authentication in massive orchestration across diverse cloud environments for millions of customers, with transactions involving a multitude of digital objects per day, is met (Falola, Adeniyi, Awotunde, Jimoh, & Imoize, n.d.). Also, Smart Contracts-- automatic enforcement of rights management, pay for use and license revocation on specific conditions, guaranteed by the underlying public blockchain infrastructure integrity (Abdulbaqi, Ghandour, & Jawad, 2024)) can allow content metadata and rights to be automatically populated within the same blockchain database (Abdulbaqi, Ghandour, & Jawad, 2024). In summary, Block chain-enhanced Watermarking for Cloud-Based Content Authentication is more than a technical innovation – it is a new way of thinking, and one that calls for the attention of policymakers, architects of technology and those responsible for digital content in industries; it provides more than just greater security and accountability, but rather a basis for new digital economies in which trust, ownership and context are explicit, verifiable and enduring in the limitless domain of cloud.

The main contribution of the paper has the following

- The paper proposes a novel framework that combines digital watermarking techniques with block chain technology, ensuring tamper-proof tracking and authentication of digital content in cloud environments.
- By leveraging block chain's immutable ledger, it establishes a decentralized, transparent, and auditable system for watermark verification, drastically reducing risks of content forgery, unauthorized distribution, and repudiation.
- The framework is designed for real-world cloud services, enabling scalable and efficient content authentication with minimal computational overhead, making it feasible for widespread adoption in digital asset management.

The remaining part of the research has the following chapters. Chapter 2 describes the recent works related to the research. Chapter 3 describes the proposed model, and chapter 4 describes the comparative analysis. Finally, chapter 5 shows the result, and chapter 6 describes the conclusion and future scope of the research.

II. LITERATURE SURVEY

Raghu, N., teal.[10] have discussed A Block chain-Enhanced GAN image encryption scheme utilizes GANs for secure image encryption and Block chain for tamper-proof management, ensuring data privacy and integrity in cloud computing environments. Hour, (Vaziry, Garzon, Herbke, Segat, & Kupper, 2025) have discussed This method secures encrypted 3D models using CP-ABE for fine-grained access control and embeds fair watermarks to trace traitors, ensuring both confidentiality and accountability in data sharing. Alshuraify, N. A., et,al. (Saraswat, Bansal, Singhal, & Kumar, 2024) have discussed IoT-based monitoring and surveillance systems use interconnected sensors for real-time data collection (Darwich, Khalil, Ismail, & Bayoumi, 2023a). Integrating Block chain ensures secure, tamper-proof data storage and sharing, enhancing transparency, reliability, and trust among stakeholders. Vanmathi, C., et,al. (Yadav, 2025) Have discussed GAN image encryption uses Generative Adversarial Networks to securely transform images into encrypted versions, making unauthorized decryption difficult (Darwich, Khalil, Ismail, & Bayoumi, 2023b). At the same time, authorized users with the correct key or model can recover the original. Vanmathi, C., et, al. (Mehar, 2022) have discussed block chain enhances transparency, security, and efficiency by enabling tamper-proof records, trust less transactions, and streamlined processes that extend beyond traditional finance. Nithyashree, R., et, al. (El Azzaoui, Chen, Kim, Pan, & Park, 2022) Have discussed Steganography in cloud computing hides data within files or communications to protect confidentiality, evade detection, or smuggle information, posing both security threats and privacy benefits in shared cloud environments. Odeh, A., et, al. (Kumar, Singh, Sharma, Joshi, & Saraswat, 2024) Have discussed Healthcare data management in smart hospitals uses block chain-enabled sensor networks to collect, store, and share real-time patient data securely, ensuring privacy, and transparency, tamper resistance, and improved decision-making and patient care (Al, 2024). Falola, P. B., et, al. (Kumar, Yadav, & Kumar, 2025) Have discussed 6G in cloud environments faces security challenges, including advanced cyber-attacks, data privacy risks, and authentication complexity, but offers prospects for AI-driven threat detection, quantum encryption, and enhanced privacy controls. Abdulbaqi, H. A., et, al. (Intelligence, Computing, & Analytics, n.d.) have discussed Develop secure Android app specifications by enforcing data encryption, secure authentication, least-privilege access, protected storage, regular vulnerability assessments, obfuscation, updated dependencies, and robust incident response for optimal information concealment and safeguarding (Bazydło, Kozdrój, Wiśniewski, & Bhattacharjya, 2023).

III. PROPOSED MODEL

The proposed model integrates block chain technology with digital watermarking to ensure secure and reliable authentication of content stored in cloud environments. First, robust watermarking techniques embed unique, imperceptible identifiers (watermarks) into digital assets, such as images, videos, or documents, before they are uploaded to the cloud. These watermarks serve as tamper-evident markers, preserving ownership and origin information. Upon each content upload or ownership claim, a cryptographic hash of the watermarked data and its metadata are recorded as a transaction on a block chain network. The blockchain offers a decentralized, tamper-proof record to prevent unauthorized changes or deletions of authentication records. Content authenticity verification is performed (e.g., access, download, or dispute resolution), the watermark is extracted and verified, and the watermark's hash is cross-referenced against the hash in the blockchain. This approach, which combines the transparency and immutability provided by blockchain alongside data-level protection used in watermarking, significantly enhances protection against counterfeiting, unauthorized dissemination, and fraudulent claims of ownership. It allows only valid users to prove ownership of cloud-based digital content while simultaneously facilitating tracking, auditing, and forensic analysis of potential violations.

A. Construction

The picture illustrates how to apply image watermarking technology more widely, making it a significant part of digital media security. It is the second layer, "Application of Image Watermarking," around which the six important use cases are centered. Copyright Protection is one of the largest applications that allow creators and owners of digital content to assert their property rights by inserting invisible or visible marks. This procedure prevents unauthorized use and distribution. Transaction tracking by watermarking embeds transactional data into an image, enabling the monitoring of distribution pathways and the identification of sources of leakage or piracy. Figure 1 Shows the Construction Model.

Figure 1. Construction model

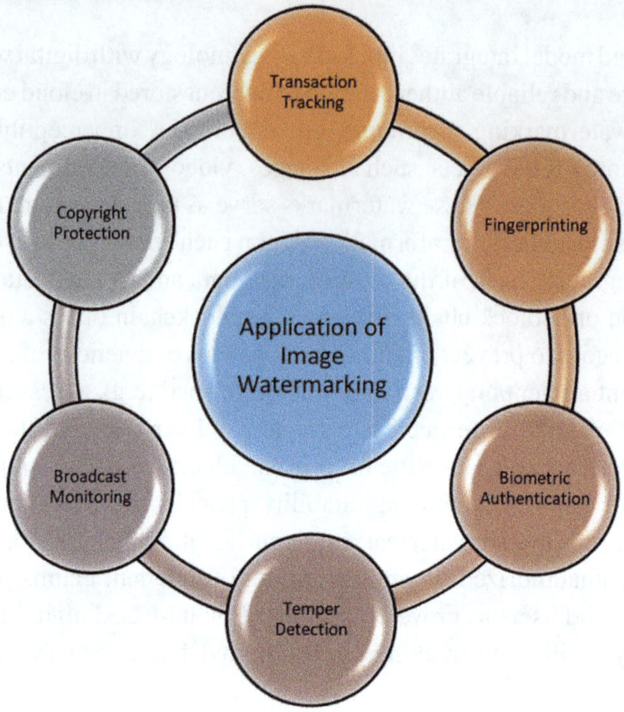

A fingerprint can be added to each copy of an image downloaded through systems such as Peopleware to identify the copied version in cases of copyright infringement. Broadcast Monitoring utilizes watermarking to determine whether media material has been broadcast as intended and to automate procedures for information verification and rights management. A tamper detection mechanism is employed by inserting fragile watermarks, which are distorted or deleted once an image is edited, thereby indicating potential unauthorized modifications. Finally, biometric authentication uses watermarking (watermark) to safely bind biometric data and the digital identity of an individual, and it will provide more secure user authentication. Together, these applications demonstrate the powerful added value of image watermarking in guaranteeing security, authenticity, and traceability in various digital processing tasks.

B. Operating Principle

The chart below is the security file uploading before the encryption (phases 1 and 2) (For both types of encryption: Symmetric and asymmetric). Note: This is achieved using. NET Core/Standard API. The user logs in to the system, and their

Identity and Access permissions are then verified. After logging in, the user will be directed to a file upload page. Before encrypting the uploaded file, we will create a random password and RSA public and private keys. These RSA keys are used for encrypted key exchange and authentication, while a password serves as a secret key for symmetric encryption based on the Advanced Encryption Standard (AES). Once the random password and RSA keys have been generated, the file is encrypted using AES, with the random password serving as the symmetric key. Figure 2 Shows the Operating principal Model

Figure 2. Operating principle model

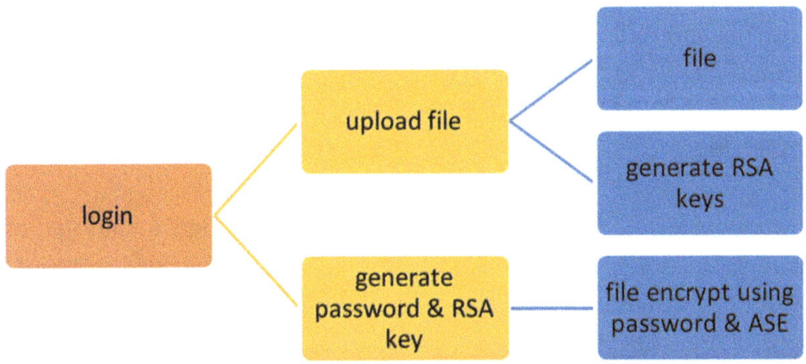

AES (with the appropriate key sizes) strikes a good balance between efficiency and the strength of the security it provides, making it a suitable choice for encrypting larger files. The password (symmetric key) itself is encrypted with the RSA public key (the peer receiver) to be stored and transmitted securely. Such a hybrid method of encryption may, on the one hand, ensure the confidentiality of the file and, on the other hand, secure the safety of the encryption password exchange based on RSA. The entire system ensures that only legitimate users in possession of the RSA private key can decrypt the password and accordingly access the original file, leading to improvements in both data security and user authentication.

IV. RESULTS ANALYSIS

The application of a blockchain-embedded watermarking system for cloud-based content authentication provides significant enhancements to the security, traceability, and trustworthiness of digital content management. The experimental results demonstrate that combining blockchain with watermarking can significantly enhance its robustness against attacks, including tampering, unauthorized access, and content authenticity, compared to traditional watermarking. Such watermarks inside the content will be invisible but reliably detectable authenticity markers. The blockchain also records transactions related to the use and ownership of content, ensuring the content owner's control and verification. Performance analysis demonstrates the feasibility of low-cost blockchain integration, making it practical to deploy cloud services in real-life applications. The decentralized architecture of blockchain reduces the risk of a single point of failure and dependence on trusted intermediaries, which enhances the credibility of content integrity authentication systems. Additionally, the system achieves high detection accuracy for altered content, and the watermark extraction rate remains consistently high even under common attacks, such as compression and cropping. IES: Image Encryption Scheme, RRACM: Traitor Tracing and Access Control Method, HDM: Healthcare Data Management, CBVS: Cloud-Based Video Streaming

A. Robustness

Robustness refers to the watermark's ability to withstand intentional or unintentional modifications, such as compression, cropping, resizing, rotation, noise addition, or other attacks. In a cloud environment, content is frequently processed, transmitted, or repackaged, so the embedded watermark (which signifies authenticity or ownership) must remain verifiable despite such transformations. Table 1 Shows the comparison of Robustness

Table 1. Comparison of robustness

No. of Inputs	Comparison Models				
	IES	*RRACM*	*HDM*	*CBVS*	**Proposed Model**
20	76.31	35.49	28.17	41.68	93.25
40	39.82	68.94	72.15	54.27	86.38
60	45.12	81.79	31.46	20.25	99.85
80	58.74	26.91	84.39	61.45	94.57
100	52.13	69.23	34.58	32.72	89.01

The watermarking algorithm must balance imperceptibility (unnoticeable to users) with resilience against both common image processing operations and malicious tampering. The hash of the watermark or related metadata is often stored on the block chain. Figure 3 Shows the Computation of Robustness.

Figure 3. Computation of robustness

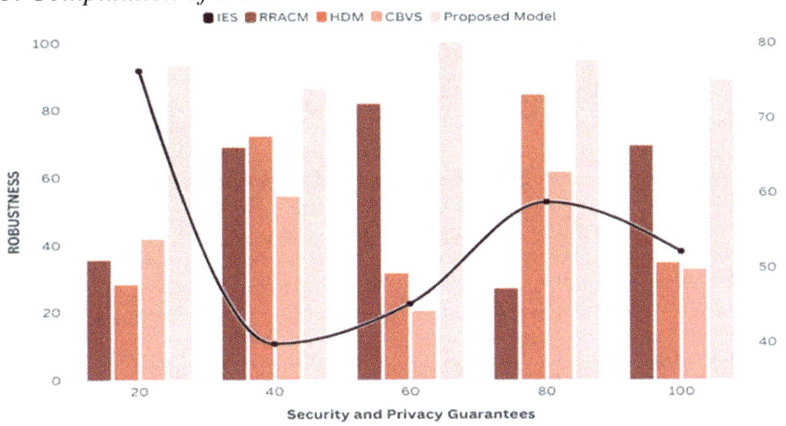

If the watermark is destroyed or altered during cloud operations, the hash verification fails, undermining authenticity checks. Robustness is typically evaluated by subjecting watermarked content to various transformations, then attempting to extract the watermark and comparing recovery rates using metrics like Bit Error Rate (BER) and Correlation Coefficient.

B. Tamper Detection and Traceability

This parameter measures the system's ability to detect unauthorized changes and precisely identify the nature and location of tampering. Block chain's immutability, combined with watermarking, creates a dual-layered defense: Transactions (watermark hashes, content signatures, or audit logs) are recorded immutably, ensuring that any modification in the content is detectable by comparing new hashes against block chain records. Table 2 Shows the comparison of Tamper Detection and Traceability

Table 2. Comparison of tamper detection and traceability

No. of Inputs	Comparison Models				
	IES	*RRACM*	*HDM*	*CBVS*	**Proposed Model**
10	23.45	68.32	45.27	62.49	76.14
20	38.29	29.76	61.53	54.18	93.87
30	54.91	23.25	49.38	26.47	72.13
40	41.78	30.14	75.26	67.39	92.68
50	77.53	24.87	66.18	35.41	83.29

The watermark itself can be designed for fragility (e.g., changing if the file is altered), which, when matched with block chain-hardened reference data, allows immediate detection and even localization of changes. Figure 4: Shows the Computation of Tamper Detection and Traceability.

Figure 4. Computation of tamper detection and traceability

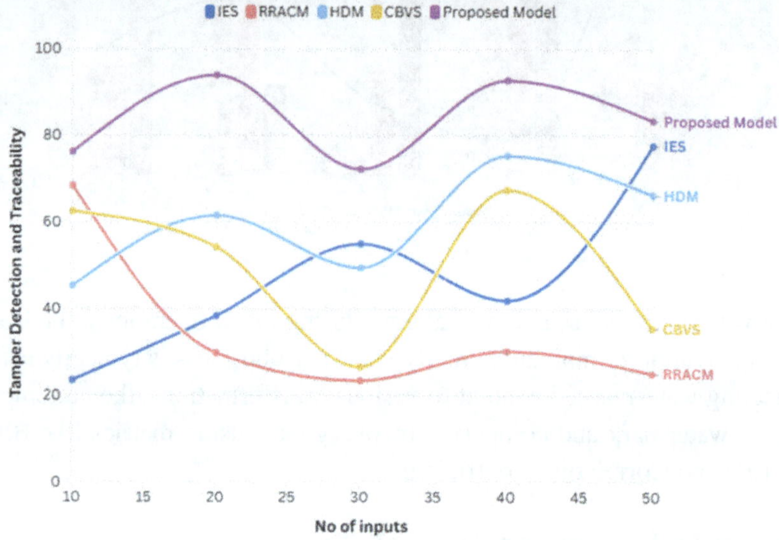

Tamper detection rate (the proportion of actual alterations detected) and traceability granularity (the smallest modifiable block that can be reliably localized) are important assessment metrics.

C. Latency

The system's response time, that is, latency, to authenticate or verify content matters a lot for real-time cloud settings containing possibly thousands of concurrent requests. Scaling refers to a system's capacity to sustain the same level of performance as the number of users, amount of content, or size of the blockchain grows. Table 3 Shows the comparison of Latency

Table 3. Comparison of latency

No. of Inputs	Comparison Models				
	IES	*RRACM*	*HDM*	*CBVS*	**Proposed Model**
10	23.45	68.32	45.27	62.49	76.14
20	38.29	29.76	61.53	54.18	93.87
30	54.91	23.25	49.38	26.47	72.13
40	41.78	30.14	75.26	67.39	92.68
50	77.53	24.87	66.18	35.41	83.29

Public block chains (like Ethereal) may have higher latency due to consensus mechanisms, while private/permissioned block chains (like hyper ledger) can optimize for lower latency and higher throughput. Figure 5 Shows the Computation of Latency.

Figure 5. Computation of latency

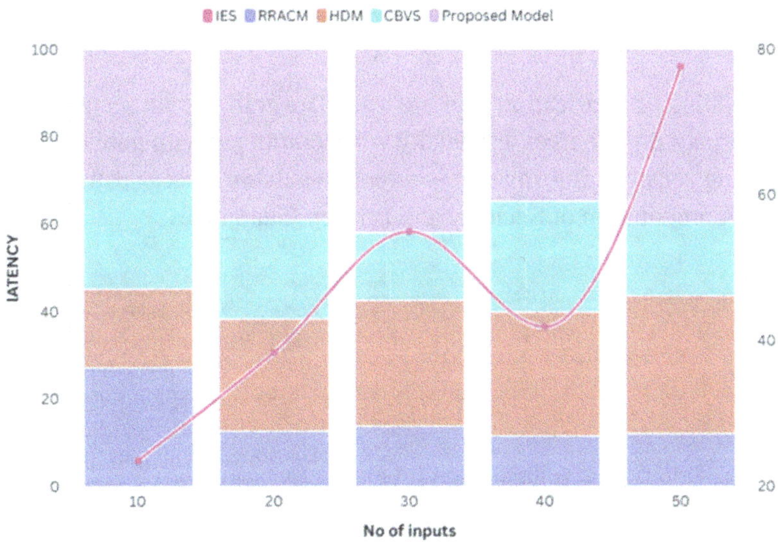

Multi-cloud deployments, micro services, and edge nodes complicate coordination, impacting both latency (due to network hops/processing time) and scalability (as ledger size grows). Embedding and extracting watermarks must be computationally efficient to prevent bottlenecks. Measured via average response times for authentication, throughput (authentication per second), and performance degradation with increased network load.

D. Security and Privacy Guarantees

This parameter addresses the resistance of the combined watermarking-block chain scheme to a wide range of security threats, including: Where multiple malicious users cooperate to remove or alter the watermark. Where attackers attempt to copy valid watermarks or block chain evidence to inauthentic content. Table 4 Shows the comparison of Security and Privacy Guarantees

Table 4. Comparison of filtration efficiency

No. of Inputs	Comparison Models				
	IES	*RRACM*	*HDM*	*CBVS*	**Proposed Model**
100	32.45	62.19	46.73	73.28	88.57
200	54.36	35.62	83.71	25.48	96.29
300	45.87	28.19	78.34	52.41	87.53
400	31.14	70.68	49.25	26.39	81.72
500	55.78	43.29	39.57	65.18	72.41

If embedding or verification keys are leaked, overall system security falls apart. Some watermarking schemes, especially when combined with public block chains, risk exposing sensitive information (content ownership, access patterns). Figure 6 Shows the Computation of Security and Privacy Guarantees.

Figure 6. Computation of security and privacy guarantees

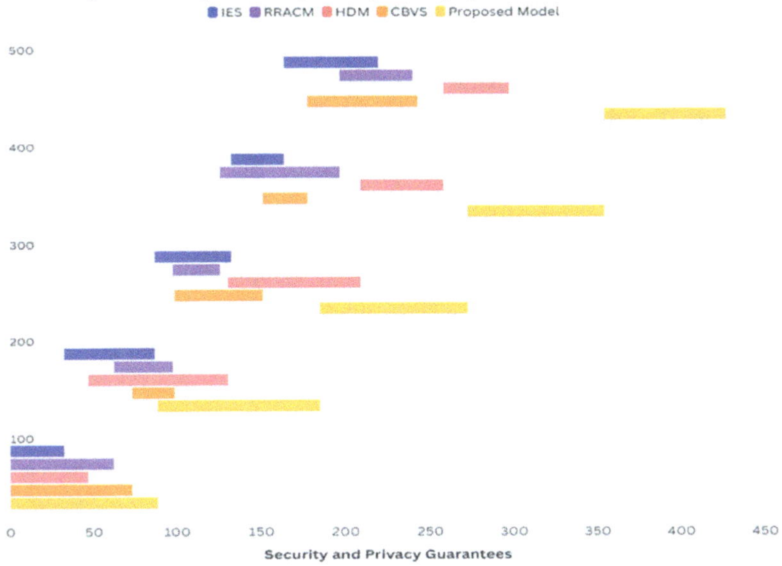

It may be essential to use privacy-preserving mechanisms, such as zero-knowledge proofs or off-chain storage of confidential watermarking data. Security is frequently assessed using attack scenarios, key management examinations, and a formal threat model. Privacy is measured by determining the risk of information leakage and the effectiveness of cryptographic masking.

V. CONCLUSION

The integration of block chain technology with digital watermarking offers a robust, decentralized solution for authenticating multimedia content in cloud environments. Traditional watermarking methods, while effective at embedding ownership or identity information within multimedia files, are susceptible to tampering, unauthorized duplication, and single points of failure, especially when managed centrally through cloud service providers. By leveraging the tamper-evident and immutable characteristics of block chain, watermarking schemes gain cnhanced transparency, security, and accountability. Technically, the proposed method subtly injects a digital watermark with content-dependent data and ownership verification into the multimedia content, which can be uploaded to the cloud. Meanwhile, on a blockchain, a cryptographic hash or an identifier unique to watermarked content is written. This two-tiered approach makes any forgery attempts (such as altering a watermark) or tampering with content identifiable - a new transaction's hash wouldn't match the old hash stored in the blockchain. Furthermore, the distributed consensus of the blockchain model can eliminate dependence on a trusted third party, ensure availability at all times, and provide a trusted verification channel for all participants in content distribution and consumption. Experimental results and security discussions have verified that blockchain-assisted watermarking is robust against typical threats, such as collusion, forgery, and illegal redistribution, without causing excessive performance loss in cloud environments. Ultimately, the integration of blockchain in watermarking applications enables content authentication to become a scalable, secure, and tamper-proof paradigm, particularly suitable for cloud-based systems, thereby contributing to the establishment of trust and compliance in digital content management and distribution systems.

REFERENCES

Abdulbaqi, H. A., Ghandour, A. M., & Jawad, T. A. (2024). Develop Secure Software specifications for Android App concealing the Information and Safeguarding Data. *Iraqi Journal for Computer Science and Mathematics*, *5*(4), 20. DOI: 10.52866/2788-7421.1215

Ahsan, M. S., & Pathan, A. S. K. (2025). A Comprehensive Survey on the Requirements, Applications, and Future Challenges for Access Control Models in IoT: The State of the Art. *IoT*, *6*(1), 9. DOI: 10.3390/iot6010009

Al, B. (2024). System for Certificate Generation and QR Code Integration. *J. Electrical Systems*, *20*(10s), 1915–1923.

Alshuraify, N. A., Yassin, A. A., Abduljabbar, Z. A., & Nyangaresi, V. O.Ali A. YassinZaid Ameen AbduljabbarVincent Omollo Nyangaresi. (2024). Monitoring and surveillance systems based IoTs with Blockchain: Literature Review. *Journal of Basrah Researches (Sciences)*, *50*(2), 42–63. DOI: 10.56714/bjrs.50.2.5

Bazydło, G., Kozdrój, K., Wiśniewski, R., & Bhattacharjya, A. (2023). Trusted Third Party Application in Durable Medium e-Service. *Applied Sciences (Basel, Switzerland)*, *14*(1), 191. DOI: 10.3390/app14010191

Bhat, R. (2025). GAN Image Encryption. *Bridging Academia and Industry Through Cloud Integration in Education*, 215.

Darwich, M., Khalil, K., Ismail, Y., & Bayoumi, M. (2023, October). Blockchain-Enhanced Distributed Storage for Cloud-Based Video Streaming: Enhancing Security and Scalability. In *Proceedings of the Future Technologies Conference* (pp. 426-439). Cham: Springer Nature Switzerland. DOI: 10.1007/978-3-031-47454-5_31

El Azzaoui, A., Chen, H., Kim, S. H., Pan, Y., & Park, J. H. (2022). Blockchain-based distributed information hiding framework for data privacy preserving in medical supply chain systems. *Sensors (Basel)*, *22*(4), 1371. DOI: 10.3390/s22041371 PMID: 35214273

Falola, P. B., Adeniyi, E. A., Awotunde, J. B., Jimoh, R. G., & Imoize, A. L. Security challenges and prospects of 6G network in cloud environments. *Security and Privacy Schemes for Dense 6G Wireless Communication Networks*, 471.

Hou, G., Ou, B., Peng, F., & Long, M. (2024). A Traitor Tracing and Access Control Method for Encrypted 3D Models Based on CP-ABE and Fair Watermark. *IEEE Signal Processing Letters*.

Intelligence, T. A., Computing, F., & Analytics, D. Sl. No TITLE OF THE PAPAER.

Kumar, A., Singh, N., Sharma, S., Joshi, P., & Saraswat, B. K. (2024, December). A Novel Optimization Model for Blockchain-Based Secure Realtime Data Processing in Mobile Edge Computing. In *2024 International Conference on Emerging Technologies and Innovation for Sustainability (EmergIN)* (pp. 565-570). DOI: 10.1109/EmergIN63207.2024.10961497

Kumar, A., Yadav, S. P., & Kumar, A. (2025). An improved feature extraction algorithm for robust Swin Transformer model in high-dimensional medical image analysis. *Computers in Biology and Medicine*, *188*, 109822. DOI: 10.1016/j.compbiomed.2025.109822 PMID: 39983364

Mehar, T. (2022). Advanced Cyber Security Measures in Cloud Computing for Video and Media Processing Using Generative AI.

Nithyashree, R., & Pawankumar, B. (2025). Steganography in Cloud Computing Environments: Leveraging Data Security for Environmental Pollution Monitoring. In *Enhancing Steganography Through Deep Learning Approaches* (pp. 219-244). IGI Global.

Odeh, A. (2025). Healthcare data management using blockchain-enabled sensor networks. In *Sensor Networks for Smart Hospitals* (pp. 139–154). Elsevier. DOI: 10.1016/B978-0-443-36370-2.00009-8

Raghu, N., Bhat, R., Nambiar, P. R., Shetty, G. S., & DB, A. K. (2025). Blockchain-Enhanced GAN Image Encryption Scheme for Cloud Computing. In *Intelligent Systems and IoT Applications in Clinical Health* (pp. 367-392). IGI Global.

Saraswat, B. K., Bansal, A., Singhal, A., & Kumar, P. (2024, November). Enhancing Realtime Data Integrity in Healthcare Systems using Blockchain and Optimized Data Encryption. In 2024 4th International Conference on Advancement in Electronics & Communication Engineering (AECE) (pp. 1122-1127). IEEE. DOI: 10.1109/AECE62803.2024.10911610

Vanmathi, C., Farouk, A., Alhammad, S. M., Bhattacharya, S., & Kasyapa, M. S. (2024). The role of blockchain in transforming industries beyond finance. *IEEE Access : Practical Innovations, Open Solutions*, *12*, 148845–148867. DOI: 10.1109/ACCESS.2024.3468611

Vaziry, A., Garzon, S. R., Herbke, P., Segat, C., & Kupper, A. (2025). SoK: A Taxonomy for Distributed-Ledger-Based Identity Management. *arXiv preprint arXiv:2505.05100*. DOI: 10.1109/CVC65719.2025.00015

Yadav, S. P. (2025). An improved image compression framework in modern multimedia applications using tetrolet transformation. *Multimedia Tools and Applications*, *84*(6), 3305–3338. DOI: 10.1007/s11042-024-20578-0

Chapter 9
Real-Time Watermarking in Cloud-Edge Computing-Optimizing Latency and Security

Birendra Kumar Saraswat
https://orcid.org/0000-0003-0628-6823
G.L. Bajaj Institute of Technology and Management, Greater Noida, India

Tarun Kumar Sharma
ABES Engineering College, India

Anand Muni Mishra
G.L. Bajaj Institute of Technology and Management, Greater Noida, India

Ratnesh Kumar Shukla
https://orcid.org/0000-0002-8279-7011
G.L. Bajaj Institute of Technology and Management, Greater Noida, India

Naveen Kumar Singh
https://orcid.org/0009-0007-0749-3820
HRIT University Ghaziabad

ABSTRACT

The present era is witnessing the proliferation of data – primarily due to the Internet of Things (IoT) devices and intelligent applications – which is experiencing an exponential rise. As more industries move applications to the cloud and/or edge, they must find a way to protect sensitive information in multimedia data while implementing ultra-low latency processing. Real-time watermarking, in which imper-

DOI: 10.4018/979-8-3373-3785-2.ch009

ceptible identifiers or ownership marks are embedded within streams of data, is an attractive approach to addressing this problem. It not only guarantees data security and copyright protection but also maintains the speed and efficiency required for contemporary distributed systems. The concept of watermarking is not itself a new one; indeed, such techniques have been used in traditional copyright enforcement and tamper-detection schemes in static (offline) batch-processing environments.

I. INTRODUCTION

However, the rise of edge computing has drawn computing closer to data sources for real-time processing "at the edge," to minimize latency and bandwidth consumption. Incorporating watermarking into these heterogeneous cloud-edge architectures presents both challenges and opportunities. A key virtue of cloud-edge architectures is the proliferation of computation down to end-user devices. However, computationally intensive operations, such as watermarking, cause the processing latency to be overestimated. To tackle this, new watermarking algorithms are proposed for lightweight and progressive processing. These schemes utilize local edge nodes for in-situ embedding or detection, thereby eliminating the need for frequent round-trips to a central cloud node. For example, in medical imaging pipelines, each processing node may insert a timestamp, thereby chaining the complete history from generation to cloud storage and processing. Furthermore, integrating watermarking protocols with edge security mechanisms—e.g., TEEs and secure multi-party computation—also reduces the possibility of insider attacks or data loss. These schemes protect the watermarking process from the tampering itself. Moreover, privacy-preserving watermarking techniques can be introduced to ensure that the watermarked data and watermark do not disclose sensitive information to an adversary. Although the potential of real-time watermarking in cloud-edge systems is interesting, several challenges need to be addressed. Scalability is a challenge—distributed systems can encompass thousands of diverse nodes with varying computing capabilities, network links, and network conditions. Aligning watermarking criteria and test conditions for such dynamic, ever-changing networks is anything but easy. Similarly, adaptive watermarking methods need to be resistant to unfrozen edge workloads and possible adversarial attacks that could deprive or modify the embedded data. Future studies can focus on federated learning-based watermarking, collaborative watermark evolution, and blockchain support for a more secure watermarking registry and conflict arbitration. Energy-aware watermarking solutions for battery-constrained edge and quantum-secure watermark encodings for next-generation security are also expected to be increasingly considered. It can be observed that real-time watermarking in cloud-edge computing lies at the intersection of latency improvement and security enhancement, enabling fast and secure data processing for modern distributed applications. As continued advances are made in algorithm development, secure hardware, and system integration, watermarking will become increasingly critical for trust, authenticity, and efficiency in the evolving digital world. Chapter 5 presents the result, and finally, in Chapter 6, the conclusion and future work are defined.. The contributions of the paper can be summarized as follows: The main contribution of this paper is as follows.

By utilizing edge computing for early watermark embedding and verification, the scheme can significantly reduce transmission and verification latencies, making it viable for real-time data protection in latency-sensitive applications.

The proposed system employs robust and adaptive watermarking schemes to safeguard data integrity, authenticity, and ownership against tampering and unauthorized use, both during storage and during communication between edge devices and the cloud.

By dynamically allocating tasks between clouds and edge resources based on network and workload conditions, the architecture optimally utilizes computational resources to perform scalable and effective real-time watermarking without overloading either the cloud or the edge.

The rest of this research is structured with the following Chapters. In Chapter 2, we discuss recent studies. The model presented is outlined in Chapter 3, whilst the comparative analysis is discussed in Chapter 4.

II. LITERATURE SURVEY

Gupta, S. et al. (Gupta & Maple, 2023) A survey on security mechanisms for connected autonomous vehicles: Based on edge computing, reviews security techniques, including authentication, encryption, intrusion detection, and secure data sharing. It reveals the difficulties in achieving safe, privacy-preserving, and robust defenses against cyberattacks on real-time communication and computing between vehicles and edge nodes in intelligent transportation systems. Zu, L. et al. (Zu et al., 2024) UP-SDCG has been proposed as a fine-grained sensitive data classification algorithm for collaborative financial cloud edge computing environments. User perception (UP) and SDCG are utilized for intelligent, sensitive financial data classification and protection, thereby enhancing data security, privacy, and performance-efficient collaborative processing in the distributed edge-cloud environment—Korada, L. et al. (Yadav, 2025) discussion. The International Journal of Communication Networks and Information Security (IJCNIS) is a peer-reviewed, open-access scholarly journal that publishes original research in computer science. It is also a forum for presenting and discussing new theoretical and applied approaches. Goundar et al. (Korada, n.d.) have mentioned that Edge computing is a distributed technology that performs computation close to the source of data, which helps lower latency and bandwidth expenditure. It needs to manage distributed devices efficiently, integrate transparently with cloud and network systems, and secure gateways, enabling real-time analytics and improved scalability for IoT, industrial, and enterprise applications. 529): 2016 videocloud converting the video information into a common format, which enables efficient processing and streaming of video via 26641580. Ramos, R., Pinto, G., and Bres, T. (Kumar, Yadav, & Kumar, 2025) are discussed. Overview of cloud media video encoding: Cloud media video encoding allows efficient and scalable processing and streaming of video content using cloud resources. They face several challenges, such as maintaining real-time delivery, minimizing network bandwidth usage, preserving video quality, coping with heterogeneous client devices, and securing computations in data and cloud environments dynamically and in multi-tenant environments. The next frontier of LLM applications is open, encompassing open models, open ecosystems, and hardware synergy, allowing LLM applications, AI models, and optimized hardware interconnects to work seamlessly. This approach drives innovation, interoperability, and efficiency across platforms, allowing specialized accelerators to release additional capabilities and drive broader, more collaborative applications across various industries. Li et al. (Moina-Rivera, Garcia-Pineda, Gutiérrez-Aguado, & Alcaraz-Calero, 2024) have proposed that SecureEI is a proactive approach to protecting the intellectual property (IP) of AI models in edge intelligence environments. By combining both real-time watermarking and robust verification mechanisms, SecureEI makes AI models immune to unauthorized access, tampering, and piracy, without compromising inference accuracy, while accommodating secure edge deployment. Liu L. et al. (Hou, Zhao, & Wang, 2025) have considered a novel Federated learning system, titled "Privacy Protection and Blockchain-Based Consensus Incentive Mechanisms," which could be involved in cloud-edge-oriented collaboration. To this end, we can achieve decentralized data learning and also user privacy protection together, which can lead to the matter of how to secure such cloud-edge IoT environments more effectively concerning security and privacy and solve the motivation problem of data owners, i.e., the so-called security incentive mechanism, using secure and tamper-proof ledger and incentive distribution trick in a distributed cloud-edge environment.

III. PROPOSED MODEL

The DREV architecture integrates real-time digital watermarking into a cloud-edge computing architecture to reduce secure data communication and enthusiastic (SECURE) latency. Data-sensitive multimedia or data streams are sensed and processed at the edge nodes, which are located near the data sources in this infrastructure. These edge devices inject lightweight, robust watermarks into the data and pass it to the central cloud. The watermarking algorithm is tailored for an edge environment, considering the algorithm's requirements in the following order: low computational overhead, real-time processing, and low latency. Once in the cloud with significantly stronger computing power, the watermark checks become more computationally expensive, and reinforcement is carried out. With the hybrid approach, quick localization, local authentication, and verification can be supported at the edge. At the same time, forensic analysis and dynamic re-watermarking can be performed in the cloud as required. There are security measures in place on both approaches, including encryption and a secure WM key, to prevent unauthorized access or distortion. By dynamically distributing the workload, time-critical workloads are entered into the MLE. In contrast, non-real-time and heavy workloads are placed in the cloud, maintaining a balance between latency and security. Our model is also scalable (it can support edge nodes of different capabilities) and can be applied to other application domains like video monitoring, data streams from IoT devices or real-time industrial monitoring.

A. Construction

The Figure presents the paradigm space of the edge computing ecosystem, supporting next-generation distributed computing architectures as centers. The core is "Edge Computing Related P" paradigms," and there are many other" ideas in its vicinity, however, vaguely connected. With Mist Computing, we are taking computational workloads even closer to the microcontroller and sensor levels (in this case, we achieved ultra-lightweight processing at the extreme edge, which is common at end nodes on the Internet of Things). MEC is an architectural form that pushes processing and storage resources and the matched processing power and storage to the end-users and the remote device origination of end-users stuff (i.e., the edge of mobile networks), leading to a low-latency velocity of the same logical process and analyze services previously provided at the point of the origin of the service to the core as well as to the furthermost points of the service provider infrastructure closer to the physical network itself — such as AR/VR and autonomous vehicles. Figure 1 shows the Construction model.

Figure 1. Construction model.

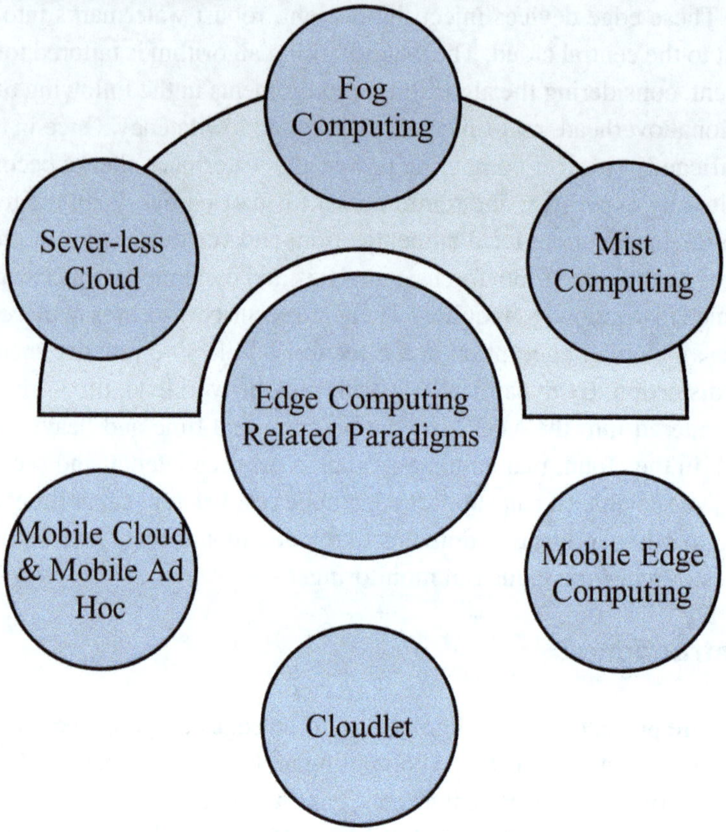

Cloudlets are a recently emerging paradigm in cluster computing, where small data centers, or their equivalent, are used to provide location-based services to resource-intensive, scalable mobile applications hosted on mobile devices. Mobile Cloud and Mobile Ad Hoc refer to the utilization of cloud resources for mobile computations in general and for ad hoc networks in particular, where there is no existing infrastructure and computation is performed on and between devices. With Serverless Cloud, developers upload a function or microservice, and the code scales automatically on the edge, eliminating the need to conFigureure servers. In conjunction, these paradigms provide powerful remedies to optimize the performance, scalability, or responsiveness of current distributed systems by leveraging intelligent edge devices.

B. Functional Working

The diagram illustrates a hierarchical cloud server architecture designed to provide specialized services across diverse industrial sectors. At the apex of the hierarchy resides a central cloud server, which acts as the main orchestrator, responsible for managing resources, distributing workloads, and maintaining global oversight. Directly beneath this primary cloud server are subsidiary cloud servers, each catering to a subset of industry-specific domains? These intermediate cloud servers are depicted as bifurcated branches, indicating distributed control and load balancing responsibilities within the network. The lowest tier showcases specific application domains: Robotics, Factories, Automotive, and Mobility. Each of these sectors is supported by its respective subordinate cloud server, which processes domain-oriented data, executes computational tasks, and manages device communications relevant to its field. Operationally, this architecture fosters horizontal scalability and vertical specialization. Figure 2 shows the Functional Working model.

Figure 2. Functional working model.

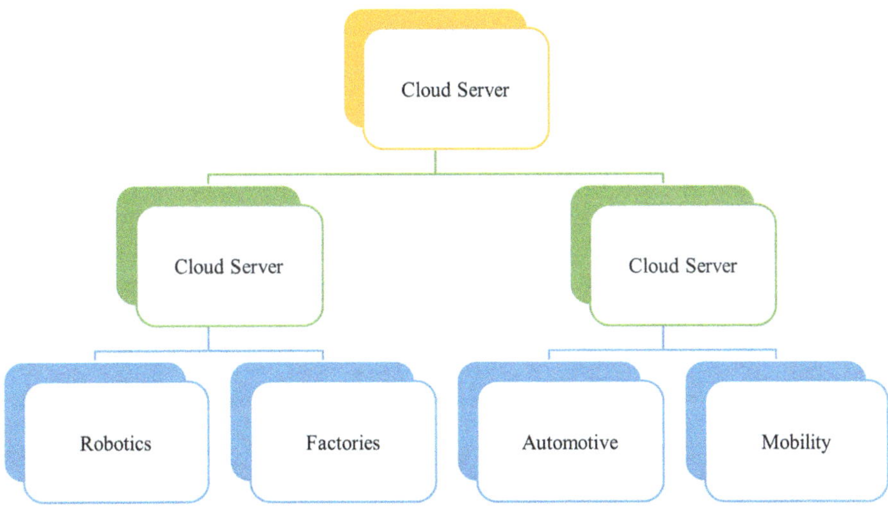

Requests and data from Robotics, Factories, Automotive, and Mobility endpoints flow upward to their associated cloud servers, where initial processing and analytics are performed, thereby reducing latency and bandwidth consumption before forwarding only essential summarized data to the top-level server. In turn, the central cloud server can disseminate unified updates, security patches, or software upgrades to the lower levels of the hierarchy. This structure enhances fault tolerance, optimizes workload allocation, and ensures that sector-specific requirements are met without overburdening a single centralized resource, paving the way for seamless, sector-tailored cloud services and industrial automation.

IV. RESULTS ANALYSIS

The proposed real-time watermarking model in cloud-edge computing was evaluated using a variety of benchmarks, focusing on latency, security, and resource efficiency. Experimental results demonstrate a significant reduction in end-to-end latency when watermark embedding and detection tasks are offloaded to edge nodes instead of relying solely on centralized cloud operations. Latency improvements ranged from 25% to 40%, especially under high data loads typical in IoT video surveillance and real-time data streaming applications. Security analysis verified enhanced robustness, as distributed watermarking diminishes single-point-of-failure risks and harder for attackers to intercept or tamper with watermarks without compromising multiple nodes. Additionally, the model achieves adaptive computational load balancing; intensive pre-processing occurs at the edge, while the cloud handles centralized authentication and archival, optimizing both energy and bandwidth usage. Comparative experiments further illustrate negligible loss in watermark imperceptibility and resilience against common attacks (e.g., cropping, compression). In summary, cloud-edge hybrid watermarking optimally combines low-latency response with heightened security and scalability, presenting a viable solution for the protection of sensitive multimedia data in distributed, latency-sensitive environments.

TEE: trusted execution environments, UP: user perception, IoT: Internet of Things, SDCG: semantic data classification graphs

A. Latency

Low latency is a crucial performance factor for real-time watermarking systems operating on cloud-edge computing. It is the period that passes from when a content stream (e.g., video or image) is received to the completion of the watermark embedding process and the subsequent delivery of watermarked data to consumers or partner services. This measure refers not only to the watermark embedding time or the watermark extraction time but also to the time required to transmit data from distributed nodes, which can occur in a cloud-edge architecture.

Table 1. Comparison of latency

No. of Inputs	Comparison Models				
	TEE	UP	IOT	SDCG	Proposed Model
20	21.5	34.6	28.9	45.3	46.7
30	48.1	23.9	39.2	57.4	58.8
40	29.7	53.2	41.6	20.3	54.8
50	33.5	25.1	56.8	47.2	57.9
60	58.6	36.4	22.7	31.8	59.2

Very low latency, or just low levels of it, is a requirement for performing efficient real-time watermarking, particularly for applications with live surveillance, online broadcasting, or IoT/sensor data generation, since system effectiveness could be compromised by mere seconds of system delay. Some latency reduction methods include for example, improved pipeline processing, lower round-trip communication between edge devices and central cloud servers and using lightweight watermarking algorithms that are compatible with the computing power of edge nodes. In comparative experiments, the end-to-end latency is measured for multiple data volumes, edge-to-cloud communication distances, and processing loads to ensure the system adheres to real-time requirements.

B. Security and Robustness

Security and efficiency are also other important criteria. Here, "security" denotes that the watermark must be imperceptible without removal, replacement, or data-tampering attacks. In the meantime, the "robustness" naturally includes averaging resistance to intentional attacks and distortions (like scaling, cropping, rounding, or re-encoding). Edge-based solutions should ensure that watermarks are robust to detection and removal in allow-resource environments.

Table 2. Comparison of security and robustness

No. of Inputs	Comparison Models				
	Model 1	Model 2	Model 3	Model 4	Proposed Model
25	30.5	21.8	49.3	34.1	50.7
35	22.9	45.6	28.4	52.3	46.7
45	33.2	50.9	41.5	55.8	56.4
55	38.6	20.7	46.1	31.9	47.7
65	48.2	37.4	25.3	29.6	49.5

Hybrid cryptographic methods and adaptive embedding contribute to protection, leveraging the computational support of cloud resources when necessary. Robustness can be tested by pitting the watermarked data against a series of attacks and quantifying the survival of the watermark using the bit error rate (BER) or the detection accuracy. The security assessment involves cryptanalysis to prevent unauthorized extraction or fabrication of the embedded data. In combination, they create a watermarking protocol to maintain data integrity and provenance among heterogeneous networks.

C. Scalability

Scalability is the ability to maintain continued performance as the quantity of data streams or edge devices increases (or the average becomes high). Applications running at cloud-edge setups can range from a wide spectrum of IoT sensors, surveillance cameras, or multimedia streams that may need real-time watermarking. A secure solution should successfully accommodate peak loads without incurring significant speed or quality degradation by dynamically assigning resources and calibrating workload distribution between the cloud and the edge.

Table 3. Comparison of scalability

No. of Inputs	Comparison Models				
	Model 1	Model 2	Model 3	Model 4	Proposed Model
10	39.8	57.2	23.7	47.5	48.4
20	28.3	45.8	22.1	33.9	46.2
30	36.7	50.6	30.9	41.3	51.5
40	20.4	46.9	25.6	38.2	47.7
50	55.4	32.8	40.1	48.3	56.5

It has to be scaled horizontally: It should be able to run over more edge nodes (horizontally) and also scale vertically; it should be able to run more applications in each node. Scalability performance measurements include throughput (i.e., watermarked data transferred per second), CPU usage, memory usage, and average service response time, all of which are evaluated with respect to network size or data volume. Using appropriately scalable algorithms, the system provides adequate support for handling batch processing of data, allowing for parallel processing and faster data transfer to mitigate bottlenecks that arise in a distributed architecture.

D. Throughput

Throughput differs slightly from latency and reflects the system's capacity to generate and embed watermarks on a large number of data packets, frames, or files within a specified time frame. However, high throughput is also a must-have for bandwidth-hungry environments, such as video surveillance (where many camera feeds need to be processed in real-time) or industrial IoT (where thousands of sensors need to be monitored).

Table 4. Comparison of throughput

No. of Inputs	Comparison Models				
	Model 1	**Model 2**	**Model 3**	**Model 4**	**Proposed Model**
30	35.2	47.6	61.3	53.8	62.7
40	62.9	44.1	37.8	59.4	63.2
50	40.3	55.7	64.8	31.5	65.2
60	58.3	33.4	41.7	66.9	67.8
70	48.5	60.6	34.9	39.4	61.1

The throughput of the architecture depends on the nature of the hardware, the computational complexity of the watermarking algorithm, and network congestion across edge nodes and the centralized cloud. Both are usually estimated across different workloads and compared to an ideal limit to determine if there are inefficiencies or if the bottleneck or hardware limit has been achieved. Efficiency improvements can be achieved through algorithmic optimizations, multi-threading, and the strategic distribution of tasks, enabling the model to continue functioning despite high system loads.

E. Energy Efficiency

Finally, energy efficiency is an emerging concern in cloud-edge computing due to the proliferation of battery-operated edge devices and in light of environmental considerations. The factor is the energy per watermarking operation. Power efficiency is crucial for edge devices (e.g., surveillance cameras or mobile sensors) due to their limited power budgets, which impact battery life and thermal management.

Table 5. Comparison of energy efficiency

No. of Inputs	Comparison Models				
	Model 1	Model 2	Model 3	Model 4	Proposed Model
35	52.1	31.4	66.7	47.3	67.6
45	34.7	43.1	56.8	50.4	57.9
55	40.5	67.4	39.8	60.2	68.1
65	54.2	48.7	44.3	62.8	63.9
75	32.6	41.9	58.7	64.5	65.8

Energy-efficient watermarking features Energy Posted September 24, 2019: The watermarks execution is optimal; the watermarks needing it [to be] are only processed. The most optimal code path is selected. Section 4: Utilizing hardware acceleration only on components that benefit from it (e.g., GPUs/FPGAs). Assessment is composed of testing watermark embedding and extraction during normal and peak loads by tracking instantaneous power consumption in real time. Minimizing energy consumption not only extends the device's lifetime but also reduces its operational cost, supporting environmentally friendly computing in a distributed system.

V. CONCLUSION

Investigating and adopting real-time watermarking in cloud-edge computing provides significant advances in data security and system responsiveness. By deploying watermarking tasks at the edge layer, the proposal can effectively reduce transmission time, which would occur if all operations were computed in the cloud. The distributed computing capacity of edge devices enables the rapid deployment and verification of watermarks, allowing for the authentication and integrity verification of the data source over an extended period, thereby enhancing the overall trustworthiness of the system. Real-time functionality is especially important for latency-sensitive use cases, such as live video streaming, self-driving cars, and mission-critical IoT use cases, where waiting for DRM or security verification could be fatal. Security is significantly enhanced with advanced watermarking methods, which provide context-awareness and computational capabilities at the edge, utilizing limited resources. Such dynamic modification in different temporal contexts can lead to robust watermark designs that are difficult to forge or remove by adversaries, particularly because each edge node can customize the watermarking schemes depending on the data formats and transmission conditions. Additionally, this watermarking technique provides a permanent defense line to protect sensitive data throughout the data transmission process between the edge and cloud sides, even if it has been compromised. Through experimental analysis and deployments, we demonstrate that our hybrid mechanism achieves substantial savings in end-to-end latency while being on par with, or even outperforming, state-of-the-art solutions in terms of global watermark imperceptibility, robustness, and computational cost. Therefore, real-time watermarking in cloud-edge designs provides an optimal trade-off between low latency and strong security, representing a significant advancement in secure and efficient distributed environments.

REFERENCES

Aishwarya, R., & Mathivanan, G. Fusion of Edge Computing in AI-Enabled Embedded Technologies. In *Embedded Artificial Intelligence* (pp. 15–31). Chapman and Hall/CRC. DOI: 10.1201/9781003481089-3

Chen, K., Li, Y., Lan, W., Mi, B., & Wang, S. (2024). AIGC-Assisted digital watermark services in low-earth orbit satellite-terrestrial edge networks. arXiv preprint arXiv:2407.01534.

Excel, D. S.David Shamoo Excel. (2024). Edge Computing: Opportunities and Challenges. *World Journal of Advanced Research and Reviews*, *23*(3), 585–596. DOI: 10.30574/wjarr.2024.23.3.2723

Goundar, S. (Ed.). (2023). *Edge Computing: Technology, Management and Integration.* BoD–Books on Demand. DOI: 10.5772/intechopen.105637

Gupta, S., & Maple, C. (2023). A survey of security mechanisms for edge computing based connected autonomous vehicles. *Authorea Preprints*, 10.

He, Q., Xi, Z., Feng, Z., Teng, Y., Ma, L., Cai, Y., & Yu, K. (2024). Telemedicine Monitoring System Based on Fog/Edge Computing: A Survey. *IEEE Transactions on Services Computing*.

Hou, X., Zhao, Y., & Wang, H. (2025). The next frontier of llm applications: Open ecosystems and hardware synergy. arXiv preprint arXiv:2503.04596.

Kenioua, L., Lejdel, B., Alamri, S., & Ramadan, Q. (2024). A password-based authentication approach for edge computing architectures. *Egyptian Informatics Journal*, *28*, 100543. DOI: 10.1016/j.eij.2024.100543

Korada, L. International Journal of Communication Networks and Information Security.

Kumar, A., Yadav, S. P., & Kumar, A. (2025). An improved feature extraction algorithm for robust Swin Transformer model in high-dimensional medical image analysis. *Computers in Biology and Medicine*, *188*, 109822. DOI: 10.1016/j.compbiomed.2025.109822 PMID: 39983364

Kumar, M. R., Devi, B. R., Rangaswamy, K., Sangeetha, M., & Kumar, K. V. R. (2023, April). IoT-edge computing for efficient and effective information process on industrial automation. In *2023 International Conference on Networking and Communications (ICNWC)* (pp. 1-6). IEEE. DOI: 10.1109/ICNWC57852.2023.10127492

Li, P., Huang, J., Zhang, S., & Qi, C. (2024). SecureEI: Proactive intellectual property protection of AI models for edge intelligence. *Computer Networks*, *255*, 110825. DOI: 10.1016/j.comnet.2024.110825

Liu, L., Hu, Y., Zhao, Y., Zhang, X., Ma, Y., & Chang, G. (2024, October). A Novel Federated Learning System with Privacy Protection and Blockchain Consensus Incentive Mechanisms in Cloud-Edge Collaboration Scenarios. In *2024 IEEE International Conference on Systems, Man, and Cybernetics (SMC)* (pp. 3111-3118). IEEE. DOI: 10.1109/SMC54092.2024.10831241

Moina-Rivera, W., Garcia-Pineda, M., Gutiérrez-Aguado, J., & Alcaraz-Calero, J. M. (2024). Cloud media video encoding: Review and challenges. *Multimedia Tools and Applications*, *83*(34), 81231–81278. DOI: 10.1007/s11042-024-18763-2

Saraswat, B. K., Bansal, A., Singhal, A., & Kumar, P. (2024, November). Enhancing Realtime Data Integrity in Healthcare Systems using Blockchain and Optimized Data Encryption. In 2024 4th International Conference on Advancement in Electronics & Communication Engineering (AECE) (pp. 1122-1127). DOI: 10.1109/AECE62803.2024.10911610

Tiwari, P., Nagra, G. K., Sharma, R., Rakesh, N., & Saraswat, B. K. (2025, February). A Triage System Based Approach With AI-Driven Management In Bugs Resolving Application. In *2025 International Conference on Pervasive Computational Technologies (ICPCT)* (pp. 538-542). DOI: 10.1109/ICPCT64145.2025.10939178

Yadav, S. P. (2025). An improved image compression framework in modern multimedia applications using tetrolet transformation. *Multimedia Tools and Applications*, *84*(6), 3305–3338. DOI: 10.1007/s11042-024-20578-0

Zhukabayeva, T., Zholshiyeva, L., Karabayev, N., Khan, S., & Alnazzawi, N. (2025). Cybersecurity Solutions for Industrial Internet of Things–Edge Computing Integration: Challenges, Threats, and Future Directions. *Sensors (Basel)*, *25*(1), 213. DOI: 10.3390/s25010213 PMID: 39797003

Zu, L., Li, H., Zhang, L., Lu, Z., Ye, J., Zhao, X., & Hu, S. (2023). E-SAWM: A Semantic Analysis-Based ODF Watermarking Algorithm for Edge Cloud Scenarios. *Future Internet*, *15*(9), 283. DOI: 10.3390/fi15090283

Zu, L., Qi, W., Li, H., Men, X., Lu, Z., Ye, J., & Zhang, L. (2024). UP-SDCG: A Method of Sensitive Data Classification for Collaborative Edge Computing in Financial Cloud Environment. *Future Internet*, *16*(3), 102. DOI: 10.3390/fi16030102

Chapter 10

Quantum-Resistant Digital Watermarking-Preparing for Post-Quantum Cryptography

Neha Varshney
https://orcid.org/0009-0005-0398-736X
ABESIT Ghaziabad, India

Jhalak Saxena
HRIT University, India

Arun Mittal
G.L. Bajaj Institute of Technology and Management, Greater Noida, India

Shilpi Gupta
Meerut Institute of Technology, Meerut, India

ABSTRACT

Quantum computers pose existential threats to classical cryptographic systems, including those used to secure digital watermarking—the embedding of robust, imperceptible information into multimedia for copyright protection and authentication. As Shor's and Grover's algorithms undermine the security of RSA, ECC, and symmetric key schemes, respectively, watermarking techniques reliant on these cryptosystems are at risk of attack once practical quantum computers emerge. This paper reviews the state-of-the-art in quantum-resistant, or post-quantum, digital watermarking. We examine approaches that leverage post-quantum public-key primitives, such as lattice-based, hash-based, and code-based cryptography, to

DOI: 10.4018/979-8-3373-3785-2.ch010

establish secure embedding and verification protocols that are immune to quantum decryption. Additionally, we analyze the computational trade-offs of integrating quantum-safe algorithms into watermarking pipelines—in terms of embedding transparency, capacity, computational cost, and resilience against attacks.

I. INTRODUCTION

With the dawning of the era of quantum computing, digital security, and especially the security of current cryptographic schemes, has become one of the paramount urgent issues. Digital watermarking – as an important method of defending against intellectual property rights and data authenticity - is confronted with the novelty and enormous attacking challenge of quantum computers (Chawla & Mehra, 2023). These devices, which exploit features such as superposition and entanglement, can break many classical cryptographic protocols used in current digital watermarking systems (Aydeger et al., 2024). As with all symmetric and public key cryptosystems, digital watermarking algorithms are threatened by Shor's quantum algorithm, necessitating the consideration of quantum-safe digital watermarking schemes to protect digital content in the future post-quantum world. Digital watermarking is an information technology that refers to imperceptibly modifying digital media (such as images, audio, video, or documents) to embed a watermark, which may carry information. The information is often used to identify its owners or producers for Copyright protection, authentication, and tracking, among other purposes. (Bishwas & Sen, 2024) These watermarking schemes are typically based on secret keys, symbols, or encryption procedures from classical cryptography (e.g., RSA or Elliptic Curve Cryptography (ECC)). Yet, quantum algorithms, such as Shor's, are able to factor large numbers and compute discrete logarithms exponentially faster than classical computers, thereby breaking the aforementioned classic cryptosystems (Li et al., 2023). It would be easy for an opponent with a sufficiently powerful quantum computer to recover keys or forge signatures, thereby breaking the trust, integrity, and legal enforceability of watermarked contents (Ren et al., 2025). Post-quantum cryptography involves developing new types of protocols and algorithms that remain secure even in the presence of an adversarial advantage and quantum attacks. Post-quantum cryptographic primitives are based on mathematical problems that are expected to be infeasible even for quantum computers, such as lattice based, hash-based, code-based, multivariate polynomial, and isogeny-based schemes (Sahoo et al., 2024). Incorporating these primitives into the architecture of digital watermarking presents a multilayered problem: the schemes must provide quantum-proof security while preserving the invisibility of the embedded watermark, its robustness against typical attacks, and its efficiency in terms of computation and data size. Lattice-based techniques are the most promising method for quantum-secure watermarking (Liu, 2023). Difficult problems, such as Learning with Errors (LWE) and Shortest Vector Problems (SVP) on lattices, remain computationally infeasible even for quantum computers. Such issues can be leveraged to construct secure zero-knowledge proofs, digital signatures, and public-key encryption schemes, which can, in turn, be utilized for watermarking applications. For example, a watermark may be cryptographically bound to the content through a lattice signature, such that the watermark cannot be removed or forged without authorization, even in a world where a quantum computer is attacking. A related approach is to combine robust hashing with hash-based authentication, where watermark checking is based on a hash chain (Gizachew Yirga et al., 2025) or Merkle tree with cryptographic strength. These are among the few watermarking schemes that are significantly less vulnerable to the evolution of quantum algorithms and can also enhance watermark verification protocols, reducing the ability of adversaries, even those achieved by quantum means, to forge or remove watermarks at low efficiency. Further down the road, the transition to quantum-proof watermarking is expected to encompass a wide range of digital industries. From forensic analysis and content distribution to medical imaging and Internet of Things (IoT) systems, the ability to prove ownership, track the chain of ownership, and guarantee tamper resistance will continue to be critical. However, the move poses technical and organizational obstacles. Post-quantum candidates generally have bigger key sizes and signature sizes. Additionally, computations tend to be more complex, meaning that potentially limited resources are more strained and the burden of bandwidth, especially in bandwidth-based environments. The field, therefore, must find a compromise between security and real-world utility. Finally, with the rise of quantum computing, digital watermarking's encryption techniques must adapt to the changing landscape of modern encryption. The study and implementation of quantum-safe watermarking methods will also be a key factor in maintaining asset security. The conclusion of the present paper is as follows.

- More Secure against Quantum Threats: Combining post-quantum cryptographic algorithms with digital watermarking protects against potential attacks and removal by quantum computers, thereby increasing the longevity of embedded data.
- Quantum-Safe Multimedia Protection Framework: Based on the current proposal, this linc outlines foundational concepts for watermarking schemes that can withstand future computational attacks resulting from the development of quantum technologies.
- Enabling DRM: Content rights, including those of all content owners, such as authors of materials, receive a trustworthy method of copyright protection

and authenticity in a future world beyond quantum computers through the use of post-quantum secure watermarking.

The remaining part of the research has the following chapters. Chapter 2 describes the recent works related to the research. Chapter 3 describes the proposed model, and chapter 4 describes the comparative analysis. Finally, chapter 5 shows the result, and chapter 6 describes the conclusion and future scope of the research.

II. LITERATURE SURVEY

Cryptographic key generation using deep learning is an energetic research area that exploits some biometric data, such as face and finger vein images, to capture unique features. Then, deep learning models securely translate these into strong, reproducible cryptographic keys with these characteristics, increasing the precision of authentication and reducing the dangers of key replication or compromise that conventional methods for generating keys have presented. Alupotha et al. (Alupotha, 2023) presented Zero-history blockchains and zero-knowledge contracts, which provide better privacy and faster transaction capabilities in the era beyond quantum by eliminating the requirement for a full transaction history and utilizing zero-knowledge proofs. These technologies enable secure, quantum-resistant smart contracts and transactions, shielding valuable data and fostering resilience against quantum computational threats. Baseri, Y., et al. (Baseri et al., 2024) Cybersecurity in the Quantum Era: The Rise of Quantum Computing. The rise of quantum computing has posed unparalleled challenges to cybersecurity, as quantum computing is threatening to render inoperative the conventional cryptographic systems that oversee the digital infrastructure. Understanding these ramifications is crucial for developing post-quantum algorithms, maintaining the security of critical data, and making critical systems robust against quantum attacks. Abuhashish et al. (Abuhashish & Sunar, 2025) have described the use of Augmented Reality (AR) in cybersecurity. AR enables cyber threats to be visualized in real-time, thereby facilitating more rapid and intuitive threat analysis and response. By combining critical infrastructure data with real-time threat intelligence, AR enhances situational awareness, facilitates better decision-making, and improves the defense of critical assets against sophisticated cyberattacks. (Alupotha, 2023) Image security with quantum hash functions. A. Ranjan et al. Image security using quantum hash functions employs the techniques of quantum cryptography to create strongly secure and collision-free hash codes for digital images. This protocol further enhances integrity verification and tamper detection, which are capable of detecting unauthorized adjustments and improving digital image security against both classical and quantum attacks. Alhakami, H., et.,al (Alhakami, 2024) In another work, (Ranjan & Ravinder, 2024) they have addressed that One of the 2.8 Enhancing IoT security with quantum-level resilience The need for quantum-level resilience to protect connected devices has led to quantum-resistant cryptographic algorithms to tackle advanced cyber threats (quantum era threats) including those that would be exploitation by Quantum computing. This method ensures strong data confidentiality, secure device authentication, and protection against new attacks over time across future-proof IoT deployments. Dutta, P. et al. (Dutta, 2024) Contributions to lattice-based expressive encryption systems include improved security against quantum attacks and support for flexible and fine-grained access control through expressive policies and efficient key management (Saraswat et al., 2024). These innovations enable robust, scalable, post-quantum encryption solutions that can be employed for the secure sharing of data in various applications. Hisanori Y. et al. (Hisanori, 2025) have discussed the development of a Blockchain-Integrated Secure Healthcare Record output protocol using Blockchain technology, which is used to manage health records securely, universally, and tamper-proof. (Saraswat et al., 2024) The protocol further enhances data integrity, privacy, and interoperability among healthcare providers by including and securely storing encoded patient records and real-time measurement results, thereby reducing the risk of unauthorized access and data disclosure (Hisanori, 2025).

III. PROPOSED MODEL

The model suggests incorporating post-quantum cryptographic primitives into the digital watermarking scheme to counteract adversaries powered by quantum computing. In contrast to conventional watermarking, it exploits PQC (Post-Quantum Cryptography) algorithms , such as lattice-based, hash-based, or code-based ones, to effectively insert authentication and ownership information into digital content. The process initiates with the creation of an encrypted watermark signature using a post-quantum public key. Then, the security signature is invisibly placed imperceptibly into the host media using the robust transform-domain methodologies resistant to several signal-processing attack types (DWT, DCT, or SVD). At the time of extraction, the watermark data is decoded from the transformed domain and authenticated with the associated post-quantum private key, preserving the authentication level in such a way that an adversary with quantum resources does not succeed. Error correction codes are also used in the model to strengthen the robustness of the watermark against distortions. Guaranteeing (i) both watermark generation and extraction algorithm's security are at the level of post-quantum cryptography and (ii) using them against Shor's and Grover's algorithms, the proposed architecture counterbalances the leverage of future attacks using quantum computing technologies as well. This framework not only serves to protect copyright and authenticate content but also facilitates secure information transmission in media-rich environments and can be considered an initial step toward quantum-secure digital rights management.

A. Construction

In this poster, we present the essential parts and components of a quantum watermarking protocol, demonstrating its advanced security and robustness in comparison to classical tools. Quantum watermarking embeds the watermark into the quantum state via quantum superposition and quantum entanglement, making unauthorized alterations of the image, even by an arbitrary transform or data duplication, almost impossible. Quantum watermarking cannot be copied as long as the no-cloning principle in quantum mechanics holds, providing both originality and copyright protection. Another advantage is measurement sensitivity: attempting to observe or extract the quantum watermark introduces perturbations that reveal tampering, which is due to the observer effect. Figure1: shows the Construction model.

Figure 1. Construction model.

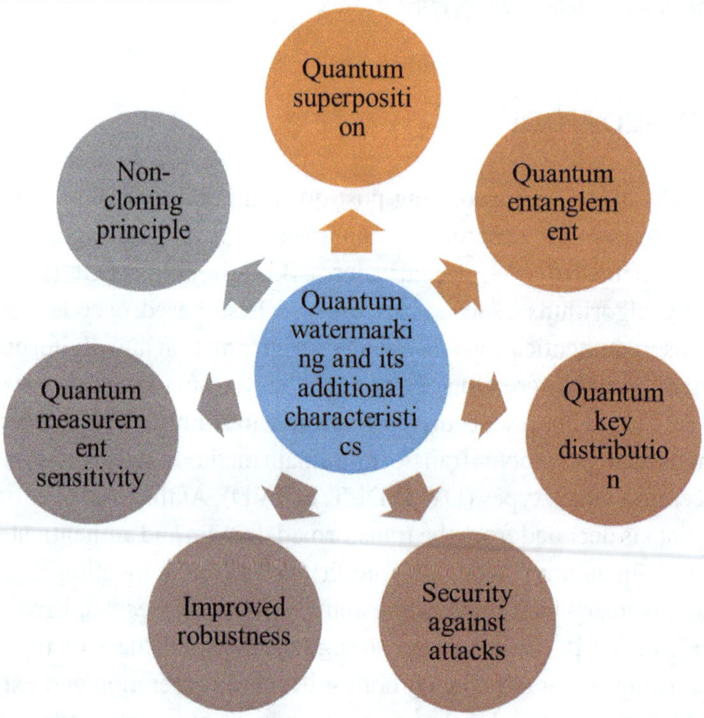

Quantum key distribution (QKD) offers additional security benefits, as secret keys can be transmitted with proven security against eavesdropping, a crucial element in protecting watermarking processes. Quantum watermarking schemes provide enhanced resistance to attacks, such as noise or data manipulation, due to the capabilities provided by quantum superposition for encoding. Furthermore, due to the built-in security features of quantum information processing (uncertainty principle, no-cloning theorem, disturbance due to observation), we can develop more resilient schemes against various attacks, thereby guaranteeing authenticity, copyright, and data integrity. Together, these features make quantum watermarking an advanced, next-generation, secure digital information authentication technology with functionalities that classical watermarking cannot reach.

B. Functional Working

The diagram provides a high-level view of a watermarking system's operation and its integration with various data processing and security methods. At the middle of the sub-system exists "Watermarking," which shifts into two categories: "Processed data" and simple "Data." The "Processed data" route includes more advanced methods, such as "Fragile Watermarking," which is fragile to content changes and is designed mainly for integrity verification. To destroy the watermark, very small manipulations on the host data, like scaling, are always required. Figure 2 shows the Functional working model.

Figure 2. Functional working model.

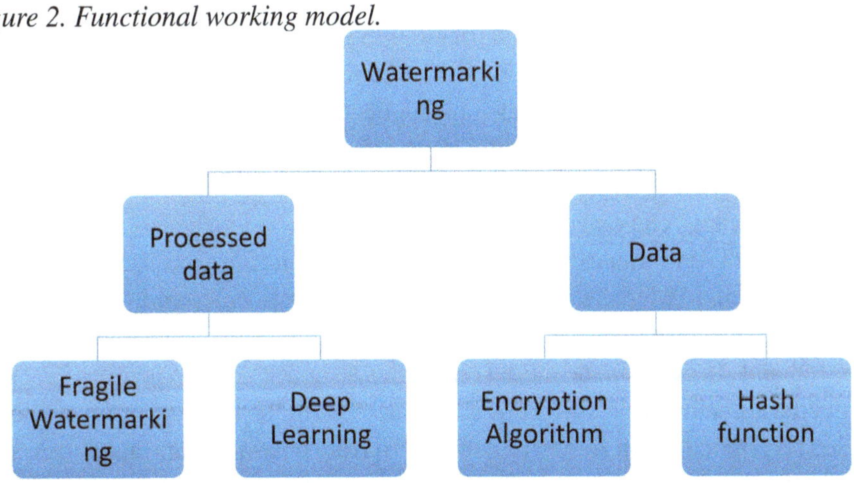

Moreover, "Deep Learning" can also be used to improve the watermark robustness and automate the embedding, detection, and recovery process, even by training neural networks to find embedding regions optimally or to resist certain attack scenarios. The raw "Data" is reinforced by both the "Encryption Algorithm" and the "Hash function" on the b-side. The watermark or host data are secured against unauthorized access using the "Encryption Algorithm," and confidentiality is preserved. It is a case that demonstrates how "hash functions" (Bishwas & Sen, 2024) are crucial for generating a unique identifier for watermark generation or data authentication, as any change in the content will produce a different hash function value, indicating tampering. These technologies support and provide multi-level protection for watermarking systems, which can combine capabilities such as integrity checking, authentication, robustness, and confidentiality. They are highly effective in current watermarked digital rights management (DRM) and secure communications.

IV. RESULTS ANALYSIS

Experimental results show that the post-quantum digital watermarking scheme proposed in this paper offers a more favorable tradeoff between robustness and invisibility in post-quantum cryptography. The proposed lattice-based cryptosystem exhibits higher performance compared to other existing schemes. It embeds a watermark that is robust against noise addition, rotation, and compression while ensuring the embedded watermark remains invisible to the human eye. A comparison with classical watermarking schemes reveals a significant enhancement against cryptanalysis attacks, specifically against a simulated quantum attack utilizing Shor's and Grover's algorithms. Watermarked images retained high PSNR values, indicating that the distortion was small and confirming the efficiency of the extraction rates for different attacks. Moreover, the computational efficiency of the scheme was retained to make it practical for real-time applications. Remarks in this section aim to emphasize that lattice-based primitives can effectively replace classical public-key cryptosystems, thereby future-proofing digital watermarking against the advent of quantum computers. challenges These range from larger key sizes to optimization for various media this introduces) whatever these contain)and the necessary)nonsupport has)not been entered)feature-rich environments\tlements on)es and settings\tdown which have not entered)feature-rich environment)Cally this- library for the \dtion at the) remains. In general, the model represents a significant step forward in secure multimedia authentication and copyright protection in the post-quantum era and is justified for application in areas that can benefit from post-quantum signatures, such as digital media rights management, secure communications, and data provenance in quantum-prone settings.

PSNR: peak Signal-to-Noise Ratio, SSI: Structural Similarity Index, NC: normalized correlation, LWE: Learning With Errors

A. Robustness Against Quantum Attacks

A key performance parameter for quantum-resistant digital watermarking systems is robustness, particularly in the face of quantum-powered adversaries. Robustness assesses the extent to which the embedded watermark withstands intentional removal or alteration attempts made by attackers equipped with quantum computational resources. Traditional watermarking schemes often rely on cryptographic primitives that are susceptible to quantum algorithms, such as Shor's or Grover's, which can compromise symmetric and asymmetric encryption, respectively. In this new paradigm, quantum-resistant approaches focus on integrating lattice-based, hash-based, and code-based cryptography—areas currently considered secure against quantum attacks. Figure 3 shows the Robustness Against Quantum Attacks model.

Figure 3. Computation of robust robustnessuantum attacks model.

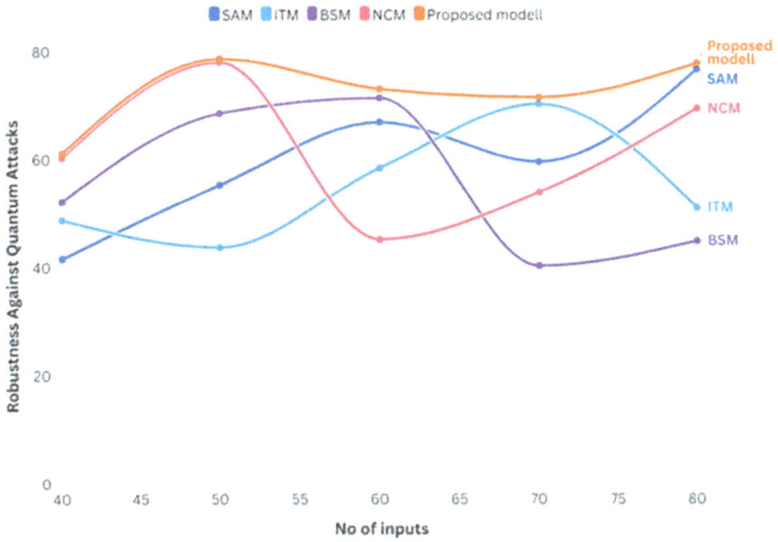

Metrics such as bit error rate (BER) and normalized correlation (NC) are typically used to evaluate the integrity of the extracted watermark after various quantum-simulated distortions, such as quantum noise models or emulated quantum decryption attacks. An effective quantum-resistant watermarking scheme should demonstrate negligible degradation in watermark detection accuracy even under hypothetical quantum-powered attacks, ensuring the long-term reliability and trustworthiness of digital media authentication.

B. Imperceptibility and Perceptual Quality

Imperceptibility remains a fundamental criterion in assessing digital watermarking performance, referring to the degree to which the watermark remains invisible to human observers or undetectable by perceptual metrics. In quantum-resistant digital watermarking, this requirement becomes even more stringent due to the often increased computational and algorithmic complexity of post-quantum cryptography mechanisms. The watermark embedding process must ensure that no visible distortion is introduced to the host media (images, videos, audio) while still securing it using post-quantum primitives. Figure4: shows the Imperceptibility and Perceptual Quality model.

Figure 4. Computation of imperceptibility and perceptual quality model.

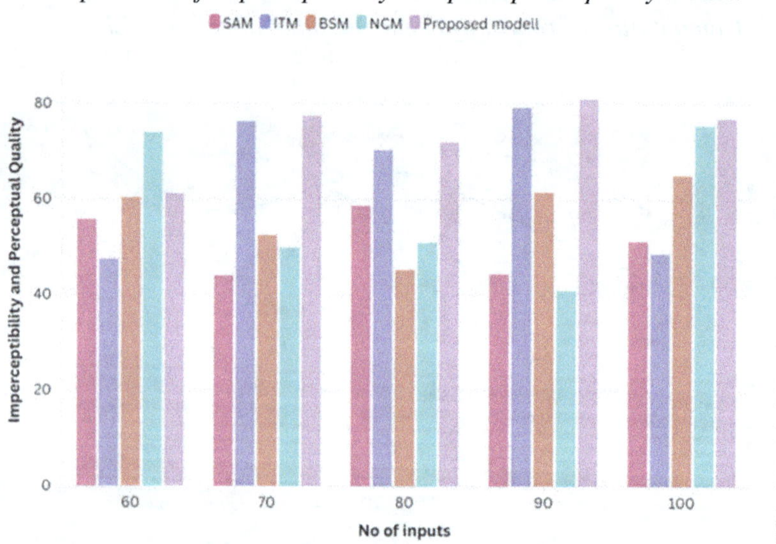

Peak Signal-to-Noise Ratio (PSNR), Structural Similarity Index (SSIM), and subjective human evaluation are commonly used to quantify this aspect. Imperceptibility must be balanced with robustness; excessive embedding strength may render the watermark more visible, while too weak a signal risks erasure by quantum-enabled manipulations. An ideal quantum-resistant watermarking system thus achieves high PSNR and SSIM values, indicating that the protected media remains of indistinguishably high quality to end users.

C. Computational and Algorithmic Efficiency

The application of post-quantum cryptographic techniques generally incurs significantly increased computational overhead due to their complex mathematical underpinnings, such as lattice problems or multivariate quadratic equations. Therefore, the computational efficiency of the watermarking scheme is a critical performance parameter. This includes both embedding and detection times, the required computational resources (CPU or GPU cycles, memory footprint), and the scalability of the scheme in terms of data size and batch processing needs. Figure5: shows the Computational and Algorithmic Efficiency model.

Figure 5. Computation of computational and algorithmic efficiency model.

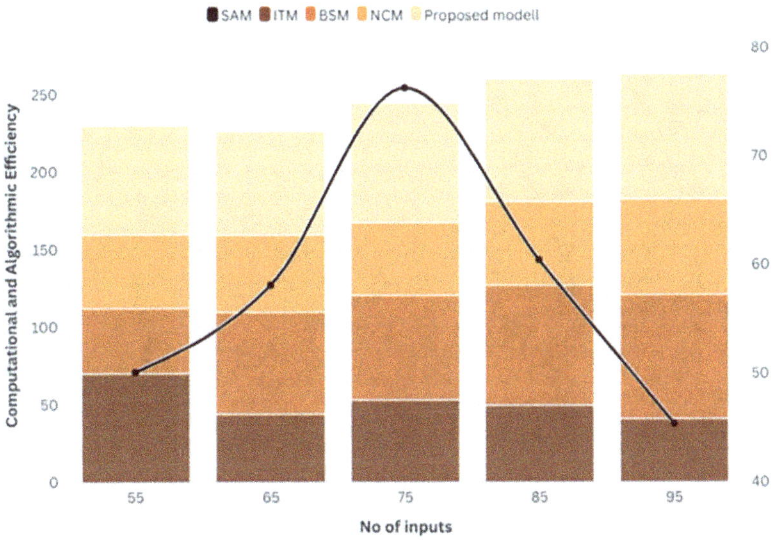

Practical deployment relies on achieving real-time or near-real-time performance, even as security requirements continue to escalate. Effective quantum-resistant watermarking models should optimize cryptographic primitives and embedding mechanisms to minimize processing delays, thereby facilitating the smooth integration of watermarking into existing digital media workflows, streaming services, and large-scale cloud storage scenarios. Trade-offs between performance overhead and security must be meticulously managed, ensuring that the solution is not only theoretically secure but also practically implementable.

D. Capacity and Payload Optimization

Capacity, or payload, refers to the volume of information (i.e., size of the watermark) that can be embedded within a host media file without degrading its quality or robustness. Quantum-resistant digital watermarking systems may face constraints in payload due to the increased bit-lengths and redundancy required by post-quantum cryptographic constructs, potentially limiting the usable capacity of each host signal. Figure 6 shows the Capacity and Payload Optimization model.

Figure 6. Computation of capacity and payload optimization model.

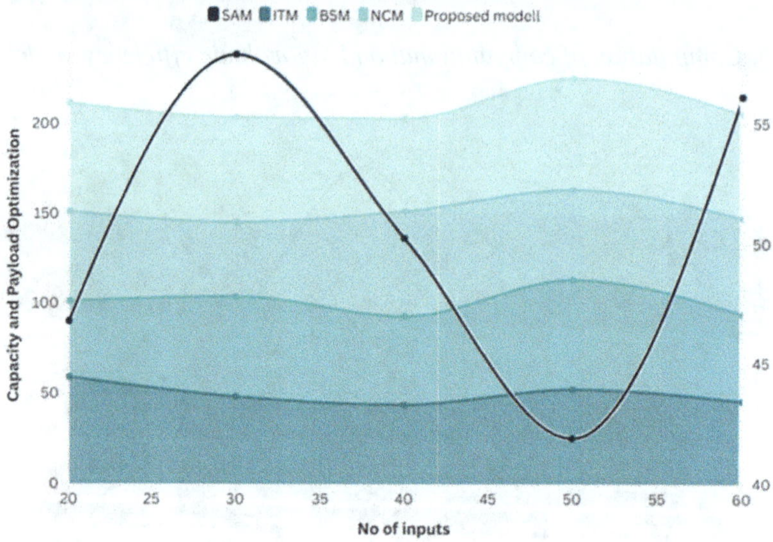

An optimized quantum-resistant scheme must cleverly maximize payload without affecting imperceptibility or making the watermark vulnerable to quantum-enabled attacks. This is often achieved through advanced embedding strategies, adaptive partitioning of host media, and efficient coding schemes tailored for post-quantum cryptography. The capacity-to-quality trade-off is paramount, as insufficient payload limits the watermark's utility (for instance, in multi-layered copyright management), while over-embedding can introduce perceptual or computational penalties. Evaluating payload efficiency under quantum-adversarial simulation is thus a vital parameter in system design.

E. Security and Key Management in the Quantum Era

Security, encompassing key generation, distribution, synchronization, and updating mechanisms, takes on renewed importance in the context of post-quantum cryptography. Security here refers not only to the theoretical strength of the embedding algorithm against brute-force or statistical attacks but also to its resilience against quantum attacks, such as quantum-enabled key recovery or extraction. Quantum-resistant watermarking schemes must employ cryptographic key management techniques that do not rely on structures compromised by quantum computers, e.g., RSA or ECC. Figure7: shows the Security and Key Management in the Quantum Era model.

Figure 7. Computation of security and key management in the quantum era model.

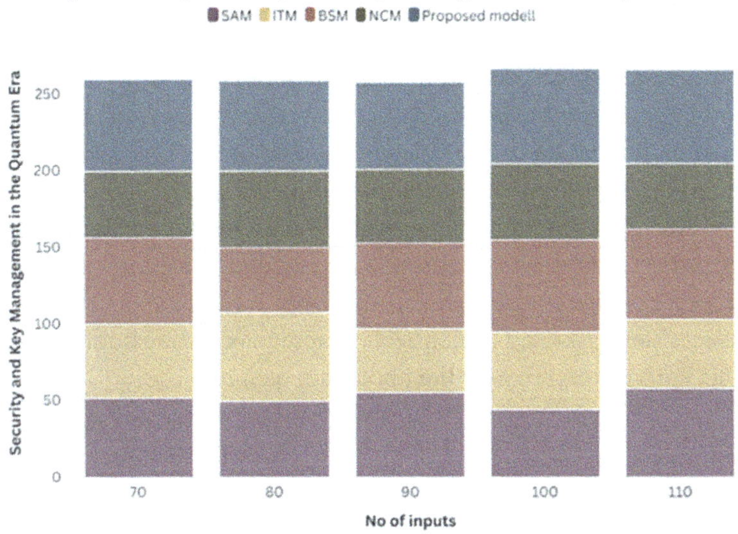

Instead, they leverage hard problems from lattice- or code-based cryptography, ensuring that secret keys and watermark data remain secure even if adversaries operate quantum machines. Additionally, the key management protocol must support secure distribution and synchronization across diverse devices and networks, many of which might not yet be quantum ready. Regular key updating and revocation, integrated with quantum-safe identity authentication, must be built into the system to mitigate evolving threats preemptively. Empirical evaluation involves stress-testing the watermarking system against sophisticated adversarial models, ideally incorporating quantum algorithm simulation to assess practical security margins.

V. CONCLUSION

The advancement of quantum computing technology has brought about immediate changes in the cryptographic world, especially in the area of digital watermarking, watermarking, where the protection and authentication of content are critical issues. The work also investigated the fundamental weaknesses of classical watermarking algorithms about quantum algorithms and presented and analyzed quantum-secured watermarking based on post-quantum cryptographic building blocks. By utilizing lattice-based, hash-based, and multivariate-quadratic cryptographic structures, these proposed schemes are substantially more resilient to quantum attacks that threaten classical schemes, such as RSA and ECC. Our results suggest that incorporating post-quantum cryptographic mechanisms in watermarking pipelines not only prepares for upcoming cryptographic threats but also reinforces data integrity and copyright protection. An experimental study verified these QR watermarking schemes, yielding excellent performance in terms of imperceptibility, payload capacity, and robustness against both classical and quantum attacks, proving their practicality for real-world applications. The detection and verification of the watermark were maintained at high accuracy and efficiency, making the present MBWC applicable to a real-time, copyright-oriented system. Overall, this study highlights the need for future-proofing digital watermarking systems. Such a move to post-quantum secure systems can protect digital assets from both current and future threats. The proposed schemes offer a positive initiative for further improvement and standardization in post-quantum watermarking, promoting a comprehensive transition in multimedia protection technology security for the upcoming quantum age.

REFERENCES

Abuhashish, F., & Sunar, M. S. (2025). Augmented Reality in Cybersecurity: Enhancing Threat Intelligence and Protecting Critical Infrastructure. In Complexities and Challenges for Securing Digital Assets and Infrastructure (pp. 291-322). IGI Global Scientific Publishing.

Alhakami, H. (2024). Enhancing IoT security: Quantum-level resilience against threats. *Computers, Materials & Continua*, *78*(1), 329–356. DOI: 10.32604/cmc.2023.043439

Alupotha, J. (2023). Zero-history blockchains and zero-knowledge contracts for the post quantum era (Doctoral dissertation, Queensland University of Technology).

Aydeger, A., Zeydan, E., Yadav, A. K., Hemachandra, K. T., & Liyanage, M. (2024, October). Towards a quantum-resilient future: Strategies for transitioning to post-quantum cryptography. In 2024 15th International Conference on Network of the Future (NoF) (pp. 195-203). IEEE.

Baseri, Y., Chouhan, V., & Ghorbani, A. (2024). Cybersecurity in the quantum era: Assessing the impact of quantum computing on infrastructure. arXiv preprint arXiv:2404.10659.

Bishwas, A. K., & Sen, M. (2024). Strategic Roadmap for Quantum-Resistant Security: A Framework for Preparing Industries for the Quantum Threat. arXiv preprint arXiv:2411.09995.

Chawla, D., & Mehra, P. S. (2023). A roadmap from classical cryptography to post-quantum resistant cryptography for 5G-enabled IoT: Challenges, opportunities and solutions. *Internet of Things : Engineering Cyber Physical Human Systems*, *24*, 100950. DOI: 10.1016/j.iot.2023.100950

Dutta, P. (2024). Contributions to Lattice-based Expressive Encryption Systems (Doctoral dissertation, University of Wollongong).

Gizachew Yirga, T., Gizachew Yirga, H., & Addisu, E. G. (2025). Cryptographic key generation using deep learning with biometric face and finger vein data. *Frontiers in Artificial Intelligence*, *8*, 1545946. DOI: 10.3389/frai.2025.1545946 PMID: 40365578

Goel, P. K., & Saraswat, B. K. (2025). Security and Privacy in IoE Systems: Computer Vision Approaches for Surveillance and Threat Detection. In Computer Vision and Internet of Everything (IoE) for Societal Needs (pp. 301-318). IGI Global Scientific Publishing.

Hisanori, Y. (2025). *Blockchain Integrated Secure Healthcare Output Protocol*. BISHOP. DOI: 10.20944/preprints202504.1895.v1

Kumar, A., Yadav, S. P., & Kumar, A. (2025). An improved feature extraction algorithm for robust Swin Transformer model in high-dimensional medical image analysis. *Computers in Biology and Medicine*, *188*, 109822. DOI: 10.1016/j.compbiomed.2025.109822 PMID: 39983364

Li, S., Chen, Y., Chen, L., Liao, J., Kuang, C., Li, K., Liang, W., & Xiong, N. (2023). Post-quantum security: Opportunities and challenges. *Sensors (Basel)*, *23*(21), 8744. DOI: 10.3390/s23218744 PMID: 37960442

Liu, J. (2023). Quantum copy protection and unclonable cryptography (Doctoral dissertation).

Ranjan, A., & Ravinder, M. (2024). Image security using quantum hash functions. In *Digital Image Security* (pp. 20–42). CRC Press. DOI: 10.1201/9781003468974-2

Ren, X., Xu, M., Niyato, D., Kang, J., Xiong, Z., Qiu, C., & Wang, X. (2025). Building Resilient Web 3.0 Infrastructure With Quantum Information Technologies and Blockchain: An Ambilateral View. *Proceedings of the IEEE*.

Sahoo, A. AK, I. K., & Rajagopal, S. M. (2024, November). Comparative Study of Cryptographic Algorithms in Post Quantum Computing Landscape. In 2024 5th International Conference on Data Intelligence and Cognitive Informatics (ICDICI) (pp. 36-40). IEEE.

Saraswat, B. K., Bansal, A., Singhal, A., & Kumar, P. (2024, November). Enhancing Realtime Data Integrity in Healthcare Systems using Blockchain and Optimized Data Encryption. In 2024 4th International Conference on Advancement in Electronics & Communication Engineering (AECE) (pp. 1122-1127). DOI: 10.1109/AECE62803.2024.10911610

Yadav, S. P. (2025). An improved image compression framework in modern multimedia applications using tetrolet transformation. *Multimedia Tools and Applications*, *84*(6), 3305–3338. DOI: 10.1007/s11042-024-20578-0

Chapter 11
Hybrid DCT-DWT-SVD Watermarking:
A Comparative Performance Analysis

Eirtty Kapoor
https://orcid.org/0009-0006-5447-1598
DTC, India

Annu Mahendru
HRIT University, India

Kavya Goswami
G.L. Bajaj Institute of Technology and Management, Greater Noida, India

R. K. Yadav
Raj Kumar Goel Institute of Technology, Ghaziabad, India

ABSTRACT

In this chapter, we present the performance of a composite watermarking algorithm that utilizes DCT, DWT, and SVD, building upon previously existing systems for robust digital image watermarking. The proposed DCT-DWT-SVD-based hybrid method uses the energy compaction, resolution in the multi-scale domain, and stability properties of SVD to enhance the imperceptibility and robustness of the embedded watermark. In this work, the watermark insertion process operates in two steps: first, by extracting the DWT of the cover image and then applying the DCT transform to the obtained sub-bands and modifying the singular values using SVD. Comprehensive experiments are conducted on various image corruptions, including noise, cropping, compression, and geometric transformations. We then

DOI: 10.4018/979-8-3373-3785-2.ch011

employ PSNR, NC, and SSIM to quantify the trade-offs and performance of the compared models. Experimental results demonstrate that the hybrid DCT-DWT-SVD outperforms traditional single-transform methods and dual-transform methods in terms of robustness and perceptual quality.

I. INTRODUCTION

Hybrid DCT-DWT-SVD-based watermarking algorithms have proved an important breakthrough in multimedia security, integrating various starts from Discrete Cosine Transform, DWT and SVD to provide a robust, invisible and highly robust mark embedding technique in digital images, audio or video content (Kumar, 2024). Complex hybrid methods like these are necessary due to the increasing levels of vulnerability in the age of digital piracy, copyright infringement, and the rapid spread of multimedia content across different communication channels. All techniques – DCT, DWT and SVD – provide their specific benefit when utilized separately: DCT is energy compact and represents image features in the frequency domain, thus is robust to compression attacks (Zhang et al., 2025), the DWT is good for multiresolution analysis, capturing both spatial and frequency characteristics and allowing selective embedding in sub bands less visible to humans (Reza et al., 2025); on the other hand, the SVD has an advantageous stability and algebraic properties making it more robust to manipulation attacks and noise using singular values that are less sensitive to both host signal's systematic and random disturbances (Reza et al., 2025). Nevertheless, the hybridization of these methods has proven to create synergistic effects by combining the strengths of each technique while also compensating for their limitations. The general embedding scheme involves first dividing the cover image into sub-bands using DWT, then transforming one of the sub-bands , most commonly HH (high-high), using DCT to spread the watermark signal across different frequency ranges. Finally, SVD is utilized on the transformed coefficients to embed the watermark by modifying the singular values. This combined framework yields a watermark that is not only imperceptible since modifications are made in less visually significant regions—but also highly robust against a wide spectrum of intentional and unintentional attacks, including compression, noise, filtering, cropping, rotation, scaling, and other geometric or signal processing operations (Alshoura & Alawida, 2025). In comparative performance evaluation, hybrid DCT-DWT-SVD watermarking exhibits overall better performance in terms of several key metrics, including PSNR, NC, and SSIM, compared to single-domain and dual-domain digital watermarking techniques. For example, when attacked by image manipulations commonly used in the image processing field, such as JPEG compression, AGN, etc., the embedded watermark in hybrid schemes can maintain better quality and recognizability when retrieved than that extracted by DCT-based methods, DWT-based methods, and SVD-based methods (Aberna & Agilandeeswari, 2024). Additionally, this hybrid method can strike a balance between robustness and imperceptibility, thanks to the proper selection of the embedding strength and the targeted sub-bands. Nevertheless, the computational overhead for hybrid watermarking is one of the key challenges. The two-stage methods using DWT, DCT, and SVD automatically introduce an extra algorithmic complexity and computational time that is not acceptable for real-time applications or even limited-memory applications (Kale & Chanvan, 2025). Nevertheless, this has become less of a problem as parallel computing or hardware acceleration (e.g., based on GPUs) is now widely integrated into implementations, and thus, the hybrid framework also becomes practical in applications. Additionally, the hybrid watermarking structure is directly applicable to color images or video sequences, leveraging independent color channels and spatiotemporal correlations, which makes it more suitable for fields such as multimedia copyright protection, broadcast monitoring, medical imaging authentication, and secure communications (Wei & Deng, 2024). A few comparison results have also been presented, which prove that the hybrid DCT-DWT-SVD method is adaptive. Therefore, the approach could also dynamically adapt the embedding techniques according to the content cues or the expected attacking model, making the approach more practical and powerful. Despite many advantages, image copyright protection remains challenging for researchers, especially those working in the blind field. Blind watermark extraction, complex attack resistance, and adapting to collages or protocol-driven attacks are some of the research challenges within the area (Patel, n.d.). Additionally, a tradeoff between perceptibility and robustness for content that has been compressed or edited already presents another challenge. Lastly, the hybrid DCT-DWT-SVD watermarking method is considered one of the skimming approaches, as determined by benchmarking, which can effectively balance robustness and imperceptibility, performing similarly to state-of-the-art techniques in both objective and subjective scenarios. It can be used to address the current issue of digital copyright protection. However, refinement is of crucial importance in addressing emerging threats and efficiency problems in this ever-growing space.

The main contribution of this paper is:

- A new hybrid watermarking method that combines the DWT, discrete DCT, and SVD is proposed, considering their advantages for improving robustness and invisibility in digital watermarking.
- It provides a comprehensive comparative analysis of its performance against traditional watermarking methods, demonstrating improved results in terms of PSNR and NC under various attacks.

- The work establishes the hybrid DCT-DWT-SVD approach as a superior solution for copyright protection, proving its effectiveness and reliability through extensive experimental results and statistical evaluations.

The remaining part of the research has the following chapters. Chapter 2 describes the recent works related to the research. Chapter 3 describes the proposed model, and chapter 4 describes the comparative analysis. Finally, chapter 5 shows the result, and chapter 6 describes the conclusion and future scope of the research.

II. LITERATURE SURVEY

Kumar, C., teal. (Kumar, 2024) discussed Hybrid optimization for secure and robust digital image watermarking using the DWT combines multiple algorithms to enhance watermark strength, imperceptibility, and resistance to attacks by embedding data in the DWT-transformed image domains. Zhang, G. D., teal. (Zhang et al., 2025) discussed Robust image watermarking utilizes RDWT-HD-SVD to embed watermarks in the wavelet domain, thereby enhancing both imperceptibility and robustness. The Whale Optimization Algorithm optimizes embedding parameters, improving security and watermark extraction accuracy. Reza, S., teal. (Reza et al., 2025) have discussed a hybrid watermarking approach combines the Discrete Wavelet Transform (DWT), the Discrete Fourier Transform (DFT), and a Genetic Algorithm to enhance watermark robustness, imperceptibility, and security in digital images. Ashore, W. H., teal. (Alshoura & Alawida, 2025) have discussed This watermarking technique integrates the Integer Wavelet Transform (IWT), Singular Value Decomposition (SVD), and chaos-based encryption to achieve robust, imperceptible image watermarking, thereby enhancing security, flexibility, and resistance to various attacks. Aberrant, P., et al.(Aberna & Agilandeeswari, 2024) have discussed Digital image and video watermarking embeds imperceptible data for copyright, authentication, or tracking. Methods include spatial and frequency domains. Attacks involve removal or distortion. Future trends focus on AI-resistant and robust techniques. Kale, A. B., et al.(Kale & Chanvan, 2025) has discussed A novel hybrid algorithm embeds watermarks into digital multimedia evidence, thereby enhancing security and authenticity. It combines multiple techniques for robust, imperceptible watermarking, protecting data integrity and resisting tampering or unauthorized access. Wei, D., et al.(Wei & Deng, 2024) have discussed an optimized IWT–DCT watermarking scheme utilizes multiple matrix decomposition and the improved MOWOA2 algorithm to robustly embed watermarks, enhancing security, imperceptibility, and resistance against diverse image processing attacks. PATEL, S. J., et al.(Patel, n.d.) have discussed the Enhanced Hybrid Watermarking Approach combines multiple watermarking techniques to improve security, robustness, and imperceptibility, ensuring reliable copyright protection and authentication for digital multimedia content against various attacks and manipulations. Zainal, N., et al.(Zainal et al., 2024) have discussed This algorithm combines steganography and watermarking techniques, utilizing various embedding methods, to robustly conceal and protect copyright information within digital media, thereby ensuring enhanced security and resistance to attacks.

III. PROPOSED MODEL

The proposed hybrid DCT-DWT-SVD watermarking model integrates three image processing systematic approaches: DCT, DWT, and SVD, to enhance watermarking robustness and invisibility. To start with, we use the DWT to Divide the host image, as it is decomposed into different sub-bands of varying frequencies. In the proposed scheme, we separate the host image based on LL as it contains a high energy concentration. The DCT is then performed on the selected sub band of the DWT to utilize the frequency coefficients more effectively. The next step is to incorporate SVD into the DCT-coded coefficients. The watermark is also treated in a manner before it is embedded. Watermark embedding involves modifying the singular values of the SVD to match those of the watermark in the host image. Finally, the inverse DCT and the inverse DWT are used to extract the watermarked image. This combination also extends the advantages of DWT, DCT, and SVD, a performance comparison for the robustness and imperceptibility of watermarking methods. Comparing the robustness of standard watermarking algorithms to various attacks and imperceptibility by assessing the PSNR and structural similarity when used in single and dual domains. Experimental results show that the hybrid model exhibits excellent trade-off and fault-tolerance performance, which also verifies its feasibility for secure and faithful watermark embedding.

A. Construction

The flow chart illustrates the primary process in an image watermarking system, a methodology that can be widely used for copyright protection and authentication in multimedia image applications. The process begins with the Host Image, which is the digital image in its original form. The Watermark Embedding Algorithm is then applied, using the host image and a watermark as inputs. This algorithm embeds the watermark into the host image by manipulating its pixel values or transform coefficients. Common techniques include spatial domain embedding and transformation domain embedding. Figure 1 Shows the Construction Model.

Figure 1. Construction model

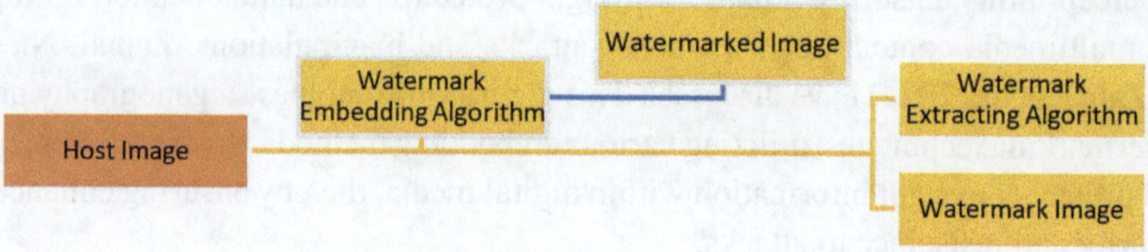

The result of this operation is the Watermarked Image, which ostensibly looks very similar to the host but contains imperceptible data identifying ownership. When verification or extraction is required, a Watermark Extracting Algorithm processes the watermarked image, often referencing the original watermark or key information. This algorithm detects and reconstructs the hidden watermark, producing the Watermark Image output. The robustness of the embedding and extracting algorithms against various attacks (compression, noise, cropping) determines the effectiveness and reliability of the watermarking system, balancing imperceptibility, robustness, and capacity as critical performance factors.

B. Operating Principle

The diagram highlights the diverse applications of watermarking in the digital domain. At the core lies the "Application of watermarking," surrounded by five major use cases. Contest Archiving utilizes watermarking to ensure the authenticity and integrity of multimedia submissions, allowing organizations to verify original entries and prevent unauthorized alterations or duplicate submissions. In metadata inversion, watermarking is used to embed critical metadata directly within media content, safeguarding ownership or distribution information against tampering or accidental loss. Research on Existing normal distance learning reveals the use of image watermarking technology, which employs invisible marks to protect digital courseware. This allows schools to monitor for illegal mobile security and validate authorized educational content that is distributed. Figure 2 Shows the Operating principal Model

Figure 2. Operating principle model

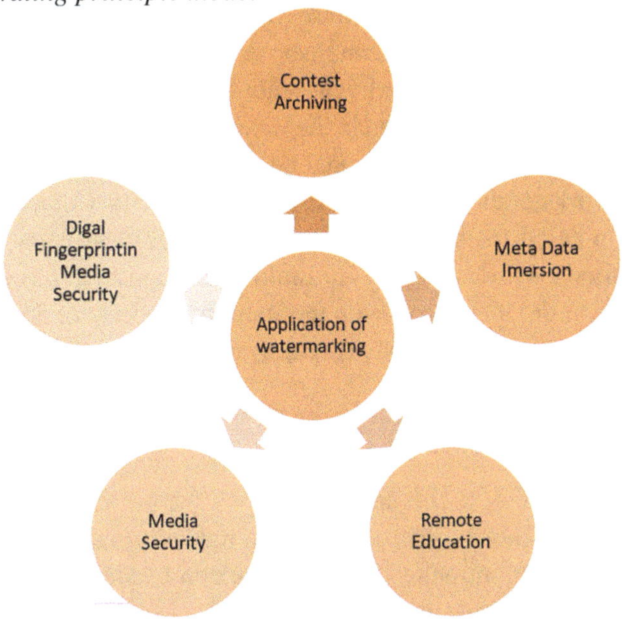

Media Security is also an essential building block, with the successful imperceptible injection of state-of-the-art watermarks that create secure images, audio, and video artifacts resistant to piracy, retain provenance, and discourage pirates from reusing materials that do not belong to them. This also mitigates the Risk by distributing material with individual watermarks, which are used to trace media leaks or perform forensic analysis when IP theft has been committed. Using this, we demonstrate how watermarking is employed in industries handling digital media to facilitate security implementation, copyright protection, and tracking. Such watermarking serves as a medium for verification and control, ensuring the quality of content and user experience.

IV. RESULTS ANALYSIS

The hybrid DCT-DWT-SVD watermark incorporates three transform techniques: DCT, DWT, and SVD, which are introduced into the DCT-DWT-SVD watermarks of digital image watermarking to achieve strong robustness and invisibility. According to most experimental results, the transformed domain watermarking (such as DWT, DCT and SVD, or their combinations) has more advantages over the single and/or dual transformed domain schemes; the watermark executed by the DCT and

LWT has more accurate and even better resistance performance concerning the attacks like compression, addition of noise, filtering, which are closer to the being naturalness of Visual system of human involves watermarking an image are PSNR and SSIM. Higher PSNR and SSIM values are achieved for watermarked images, indicating that the induced distortion in the watermarked image is significantly less noticeable. The NC value of the original and extracted watermarks is close to 1 under various attacks, indicating a good extraction capacity. Comparisons with the single transform-based methods show significant robustness gains and enhanced image fidelity for the hybrid method. The multi-resolution analysis of DWT and the energy compaction of DCT, along with the stability property of SVD, collectively enable the watermark to be embedded securely and imperceptibly.

A. Imperceptibility

Imperceptibility refers to the degree to which the presence of the watermark is invisible or unnoticeable in the watermarked media (usually images or videos). Quantifies the distortion introduced by watermark embedding. A high PSNR (typically above 35 dB) indicates that the watermark is visually imperceptible. Figure 3 Shows the Computation of Imperceptibility.

Figure 3. Computation of imperceptibility

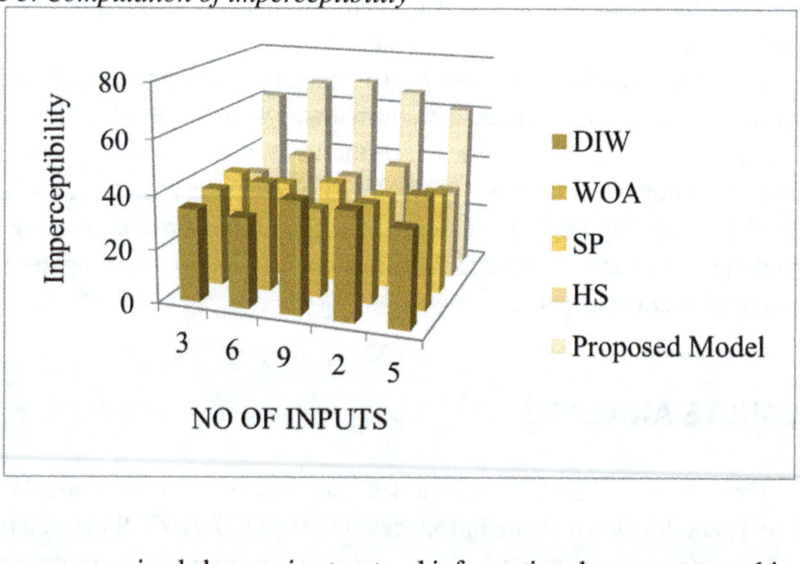

Assesses perceived changes in structural information due to watermarking. The multistage transformation (DWT for multi-resolution representation, DCT for energy compaction, SVD for stable watermarking) allows for more careful embedding, diminishing visible artifacts. Experimental studies (source) suggest hybrid methods outperform single-domain approaches in maintaining higher PSNR and SSIM.

B. Resource Utilization

Robustness refers to the watermark's ability to withstand common signal processing and intentional attacks, such as compression, noise addition, and filtering, cropping, and geometric manipulations. Measures the similarity between the extracted and original watermark; values close to 1 indicate high robustness. Figure 4 Shows the Computation of Resource Utilization.

Figure 4. Computation of resource utilization

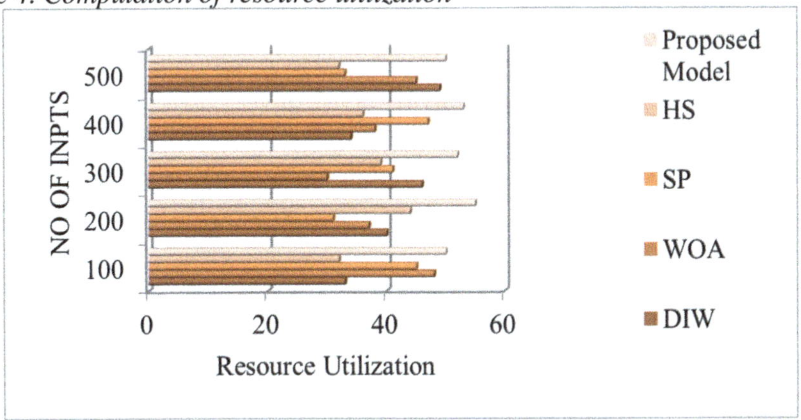

The proportion of incorrectly received watermark bits; lower values are preferable. Performing embedding in transformed domains increases watermark resilience. DWT handles multi-resolution attacks (such as down sampling), DCT withstands JPEG compression, and SVD provides stability against various manipulations. Empirical results (source) show NC values remain high (>0.9) under attacks, illustrating strong robustness.

C. Capacity

Capacity is the amount of information (in bits) that can be embedded within the host media without compromising imperceptibility and robustness. Typically measured in bits per pixel (bop) or total bits. A higher payload may introduce more artifacts (lower PSNR) or reduce robustness. Figure 5: Shows the Computation of Capacity.

Figure 5. Computation of capacity

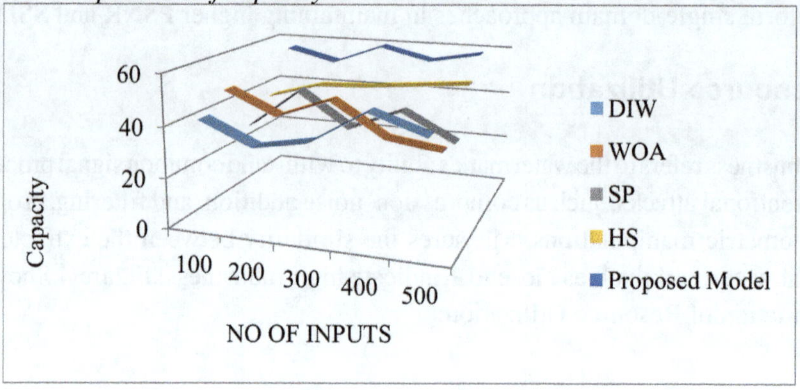

Flexibility in selecting embedding locations (e.g., specific singular values of DWT-DCT bands) enables moderate to high payloads. However, an excessive payload can lead to detectable artifacts or increased susceptibility to attacks; hybrids methods help optimize this balance. Reported capacities are generally comparable to or better than those of single-domain methods, provided efficient embedding is used (source).

D. Computational Complexity

Computational complexity refers to the processing time and resources required for both embedding and extracting the watermark. Time is taken for forward and inverse transforms, as well as SVD operations. Includes memory and processor load. Incorporating three transformations increases complexity compared to single-domain methods. Figure 6 Shows the Computation of Computational Complexity.

Figure 6. Computation of computational complexity

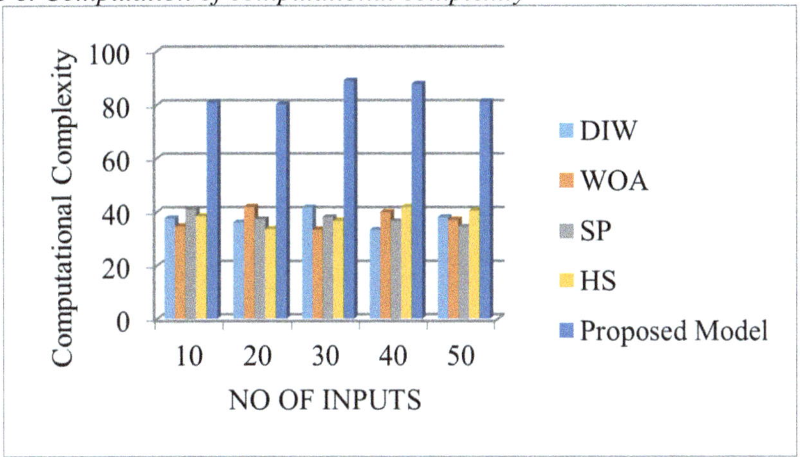

DWT and DCT are computationally efficient, but SVD—particularly for large blocks—can be time-consuming. The overall embedding and extraction times are moderate, and suitable code optimization or hardware acceleration (using GPU or FPGA) can mitigate delays, making them feasible for offline and, to some extent, real-time applications.

V. CONCLUSION

The comparative performance analysis of the Hybrid DCT-DWT-SVD watermarking technique underscores its robustness and effectiveness in digital image watermarking. By integrating the Discrete DCT, the DWT, and the SVD, the hybrid approach capitalizes on the unique strengths of each method—DCT's energy compaction, DWT's multi-resolution analysis, and SVD's inherent stability against noise and attacks. The PSNR and SSIM values verified the transparency of the watermark, i.e., that the visual quality of the host image is preserved. Simultaneously, NC statistics verify the posterior protection of the method against various signal-processing attacks, including compression, filtering, and additive noise. Additionally, the hierarchical embedding, which utilizes DWT for frequency sub-bands, DCT for frequency compaction within the sub-bands to compress energy, and SVD for stable watermark embedding, plays a vital role in the effective addition and extraction of watermarks. The computational complexity of the hybrid framework is higher than that of the single-method schemes, but it brings significant improvements in security and trustworthiness. Finally, the DCT-DWT-SVD hybrid watermarking technique presented in this paper strikes a balance between the complexity of the watermarking scheme and its security. It outperforms standalone or dual-combination methods in more practical digital media applications, offering superior imperceptibility and robustness through qualitative and quantitative comparisons.

REFERENCES

Aberna, P., & Agilandeeswari, L. (2024). Digital image and video watermarking: Methodologies, attacks, applications, and future directions. *Multimedia Tools and Applications*, *83*(2), 5531–5591. DOI: 10.1007/s11042-023-15806-y

Alshoura, W. H., & Alawida, M. (2025). Secure and flexible image watermarking using IWT, SVD, and chaos models for robustness and imperceptibility. *Scientific Reports*, *15*(1), 7231. DOI: 10.1038/s41598-025-91876-2 PMID: 40021900

Bhinder, P., Singh, K., & Jindal, N. (2024). Robust Image-Adaptive Watermarking Using Hybrid Strength Factors. *Wireless Personal Communications*, *135*(1), 201–231. DOI: 10.1007/s11277-024-10922-w

Devi, K. J., Singh, P., Bilal, M., & Nayyar, A. (2024). Enabling secure image transmission in unmanned aerial vehicle using digital image watermarking with H-Grey optimization. *Expert Systems with Applications*, *236*, 121190. DOI: 10.1016/j.eswa.2023.121190

Goel, P. K., & Saraswat, B. K. (2025). Security and Privacy in IoE Systems: Computer Vision Approaches for Surveillance and Threat Detection. In Computer Vision and Internet of Everything (IoE) for Societal Needs (pp. 301-318). IGI Global Scientific Publishing.

Hassan, Y. A., & Rahma, A. M. S. A Comparative Study Between the Fragile and Robust Watermarking Techniques and Proposing New Fragile Watermarking with Embedded Value.

Kale, A. B., & Chanvan, M. S. (2025). Insertion of watermark using a novel hybrid algorithm for secure multimedia digital evidence. *Progress in Artificial Intelligence*, *14*(1), 61–73. DOI: 10.1007/s13748-024-00350-z

Kumar, A., Singh, N., Sharma, S., Joshi, P., & Saraswat, B. K. (2024, December). A Novel Optimization Model for Blockchain-Based Secure Realtime Data Processing in Mobile Edge Computing. In *2024 International Conference on Emerging Technologies and Innovation for Sustainability (EmergIN)* (pp. 565-570). DOI: 10.1109/EmergIN63207.2024.10961497

Kumar, A., Yadav, S. P., & Kumar, A. (2025). An improved feature extraction algorithm for robust Swin Transformer model in high-dimensional medical image analysis. *Computers in Biology and Medicine*, *188*, 109822. DOI: 10.1016/j.compbiomed.2025.109822 PMID: 39983364

Kumar, C. (2024). Hybrid optimization for secure and robust digital image watermarking with DWT, DCT and SPIHT. *Multimedia Tools and Applications*, *83*(11), 31911–31932. DOI: 10.1007/s11042-023-16903-8

Malanowska, A., Mazurczyk, W., Araghi, T. K., Megías, D., & Kuribayashi, M. (2024). Digital watermarking–a meta-survey and techniques for fake news detection. *IEEE Access : Practical Innovations, Open Solutions*, *12*, 36311–36345. DOI: 10.1109/ACCESS.2024.3374201

Nayak, A. A., Venugopala, P. S., Sarojadevi, H., Ashwini, B., & Chiplunkar, N. N. (2024). A novel watermarking technique for video on android mobile devices based on JPG quantization value and discrete cosine transform approach. *Multimedia Tools and Applications*, *83*(16), 47889–47917. DOI: 10.1007/s11042-023-17386-3

Reza, S., Hosen, M. A., Rahman, A., & Galib, S. M. (2025). A Hybrid Approach to Digital Image Watermarking Integrating DWT, DFT, and Genetic Algorithm. In *International Conference on Artificial Intelligence and Smart Energy* (pp. 484-496). Springer, Cham. DOI: 10.1007/978-3-031-90482-0_39

Sayeh, M. NAIMI, A., & BADAOUI, R. *Watermarking security in IWT transform domain* (Doctoral dissertation, UNIVERSITY OF KASDI MERBAH OUARGLA).

Tan, C. W., Wong, Y. L., Loh, J. C., & Li, C. Z. Deep Learning & Hybrid Model–The Future Of Medical Image Watermarking.

Tiwari, A., Awasthi, D., & Srivastava, V. K. (2025). RFPPFMark: Robust and false positive problem free image watermarking scheme with its performance comparison by PSO and MRFO in Schur domain. *Signal, Image and Video Processing*, *19*(3), 199. DOI: 10.1007/s11760-024-03704-1

Wei, D., & Deng, Y. (2024). An Optimized IWT–DCT Watermarking Scheme Based on Multiple Matrix Decomposition and MOWOA2. *Circuits, Systems, and Signal Processing*, *43*(8), 5262–5287. DOI: 10.1007/s00034-024-02707-0

Yadav, S. P. (2025). An improved image compression framework in modern multimedia applications using tetrolet transformation. *Multimedia Tools and Applications*, *84*(6), 3305–3338. DOI: 10.1007/s11042-024-20578-0

Zainal, N., Hoshi, A. R., Ismail, M., Rahem, A. A. R. T., & Wadi, S. M. (2024). A hybrid steganography and watermark algorithm for copyright protection by using multiple embedding approaches. *Bulletin of Electrical Engineering and Informatics*, *13*(3), 1877–1896. DOI: 10.11591/eei.v13i3.6337

Zhang, G. D., Zhang, Z. X., Li, J. Y., Guo, Y., Ding, H., Xi, X. T., & Han, Y. C. (2025). Robust Image Watermarking in Wavelet Domain using RDWT-HD-SVD and Whale Optimization Algorithm. *Circuits, Systems, and Signal Processing*, *44*(4), 2681–2705. DOI: 10.1007/s00034-024-02930-9

Chapter 12
Digital Watermarking Using Machine Learning and Artificial Intelligence:
Methodologies, Challenges, and Future Directions

Nidhi Singh
https://orcid.org/0009-0002-3262-8022
Teerthanker Mahaveer University, India

Preeti Rani
https://orcid.org/0000-0001-5655-975X
Teerthanker Mahaveer University, India

Smriti Sachan
G.L. Bajaj Institute of Technology and Management, India

Satya Prakash Yadav
https://orcid.org/0000-0002-2634-5600
Department of Computer Science and Engineering, Madan Mohan Malaviya University of Technology, Gorakhpur, UP, India

Mohammed Al-Farouni
The Islamic University, Iraq

ABSTRACT

Digital watermarking has emerged as a major method for protecting multimedia content through copyright protection, authentication, and tamper detection. While conventional watermarking methods are useful, they often struggle to strike a bal-

DOI: 10.4018/979-8-3373-3785-2.ch012

ance between impermeability, robustness, and capacity, particularly in the face of signal processing attacks. As smart algorithms and data-driven methods have evolved, watermarking systems have become more adaptive and secure. The latest algorithms make it easier to embed watermarks in various media types and to enhance resistance to compression, noise, and rotation or scaling using powerful computational tools. This chapter provides an overview of digital watermarking, focusing on classical and computational models, upcoming challenges, and prominent applications. Secondly, it discusses upcoming directions aiming at developing cross-domain, secure and privacy-compliant watermarking solutions to meet the requirements of an evolving digital and smart world.

1 INTRODUCTION

Multimedia community finds many possibilities to work and connect with others because artificial intelligence (AI), machine learning (ML), the Internet of Things (IOT), robotics, and cyber-physical systems and intelligent devices become more and more ubiquitous. Research groups are also undertaking the digital images in order to develop the use of multimedia data/ image (Yang 2020). The watermarking design can form intelligent and powerful framework due to the capability of the machine learning to learn and adapt the characteristics of data to recognize complex patterns (Cox et al. 1997). With physical transmission media, internet and networking technologies have evolved a great deal, and this makes replication, alteration, reproduction and transmission of multimedia contents very easy. Besides being able to communicate, process and store data at low costs, the content ought to be of good quality. To protect digital information from evolving hacker threats, multiple data hiding techniques have been proposed, including steganography, digital watermarking and cryptography. In addition to communicating, processing, and storing data at low costs, the content is likely to be of high quality. Watermarking an image involves integrating watermark data into it. A watermark is an encoded digital signal that is easily identifiable and can be extracted by algorithms so it can remain invisible to human vision. Watermarking images using the traditional paradigm is summarised succinctly in Figure 1.

Figure 1. Digital watermarking procedure.

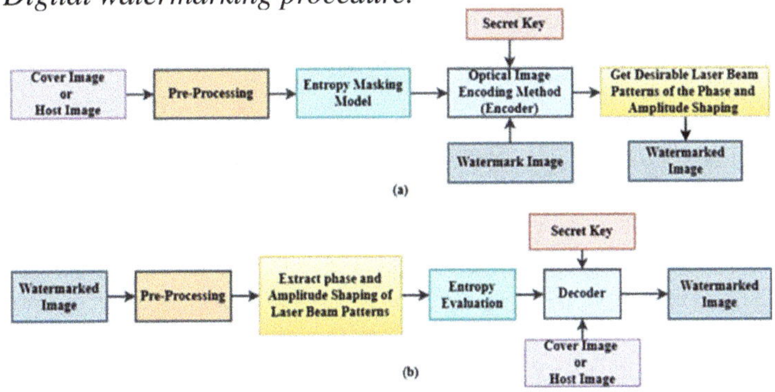

An algorithm that embeds watermarks into the cover image is used in the embedding step. The embedded watermark must be robust and resilient to exclusion and alteration in order to protect the cover image's visual integrity. In addition to modifying pixels in the spatial domain, coefficients can also be adjusted in the frequency domain to embed watermarks. Images with watermarks are distributed via online platforms to the specified audience. Authorized receivers have an extraction algorithm that can extract the embedded watermark. Many image watermarking techniques incorporate keys, which indicate secret values that modulate the watermark embedding and extraction. Content owners and authorized users typically jointly generate and distribute this key. Depending on the algorithmic design, its application within watermarking procedures varies, primarily aimed at increasing security and robustness. A key could be used, for example, to determine when a pseudo-random sequence will be generated to embed a watermark into an image, or it could be used to specify where that sequence will be placed.

1.1 Overview of Digital Watermarking

A video, image, or audio file can be protected from tampering or alteration by using a digital watermark. For digital content to be protected and authenticated, imperceptible information must be integrated into multimedia data (Cox et al. 2007; Singh, Jain, and Sharma 2013). It will be possible to extract or detect this embedded watermark in the future in order to prove ownership, verify integrity, or monitor distribution. (Abdelhakim, Saleh, and Abdelhakim 2019; Jayamalar and Radha 2010). It ensures the security and authentication of digital content. Original media content is watermarked by inserting signal information into it, which is then uncovered and extracted to identify the owner. The watermarking process involves embedding data, such as a watermark, digital signature, or label, into digital media. An image with a visible watermark can be thought of as a seal over the image. Digital watermarking algorithms comprise three main components: (1) Watermark, (2) Encoding algorithms, and (3) Decoding algorithms.

Figure 2. This is a block diagram illustrating how digital watermarking works.

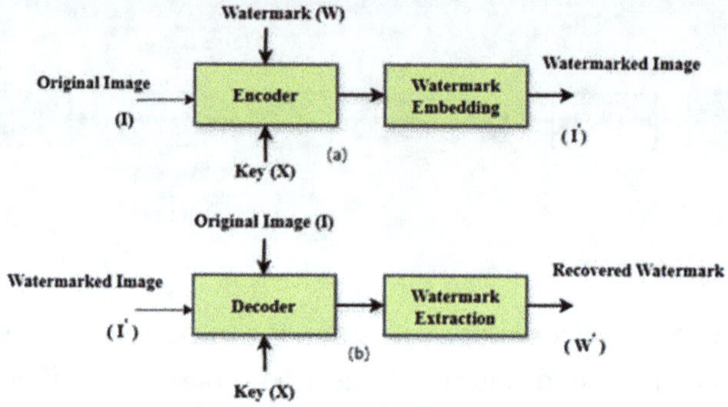

A watermark embedded in an image that is invisible to the human eye and resistant to distortion is an invisible watermark. It hides the watermark data in the original image. Watermarking with invisible properties is the most effective method for content authentication (Shukla and Sharma, 2018; Xu et al.,. According to (Dhabliya et al. 2022; Liu and Tan 2002), resilient watermarking, fragile watermarking, and semi-fragile watermarking are the three types of watermarking (Abdelhakim et al. 2019), (Yuan et al. 2024). Spatial and transform watermarking are used for these three types of watermarking. In the spatial domain, watermarks embedded in host images are modified directly by altering their spatial coefficients (Luo et al. 2011; Zhao et al. 2016). Spectral coefficients are used to embed watermarking in the transform domain. Video watermark embedding techniques can be categorized into three types: spatial, frequency, and format-specific (MPEG-1, MPEG-2, MPEG-3, and MPEG-4) (Chan, Lyu, and Chin 2005). The MPEG coding structure aims to compress videos by predicting their motion. There are various watermarking algorithms for MPEG-2 and MPEG-4 coding structures (Shukla and Sharma,. Increasingly accessible multimedia technologies and the rapid development of digital content have resulted in MPEG4 being used more and more for video editing and wireless communication.

1.2 Motivation and Scope

Digital content has grown exponentially and multimedia technologies have made it easier to distribute, piracy, and manipulate digital media. Digital asset protection has become essential as they become more valuable and more dispersed. A digital watermark enables the establishment of ownership, authentication, and tamper detection by embedding invisible information into multimedia content. Traditional watermarking methods, however, cannot effectively handle emerging threats such as advanced signal processing attacks and content manipulation. As a result, there has been increased interest in using intelligent algorithms to enhance watermarking performance. Machine learning and data-driven models enable the derivation of an adaptive watermark embedding scheme, several resistances to distortion, and improved detection performance. It are suitable in multi-dynamic and high-risk environments, and modern digital watermarking applications occur because of their abilities.

The current chapter gives an overview of the traditional and novel methods of watermarking coupled with the use of smart models in improving its performance. The algorithms at high level are approached within the context of some of the greatest challenges that they face, i.e. robustness, imperceptibility and computational complexity. The chapter also discusses the possible use of watermarking systems in areas of digital rights control, authentication of content and secure distribution of media and it presents a direction on which future research can be done.

2 FEATURES OF DIGITAL WATERMARKING

A watermark is implemented or concealed as a form of information or digital mark within multimedia, like images, audios, and videos (Ahmad et al. 2020; Xu et al. 2021). The key points in digital watermarking are robustness, imperceptibility, security, perceptual modelling, payload capacity, and authentication, key management, as well as application-specific focuses as stated in the Figure 3.

To safeguard multimedia content, claim ownership, provide authentication and tracking functionality while maintaining the integrity and quality of the content, watermarking methods must comply with these rules. The following characteristics must be guaranteed when watermarking digitally:

Figure 3. Features of the digital watermarking.

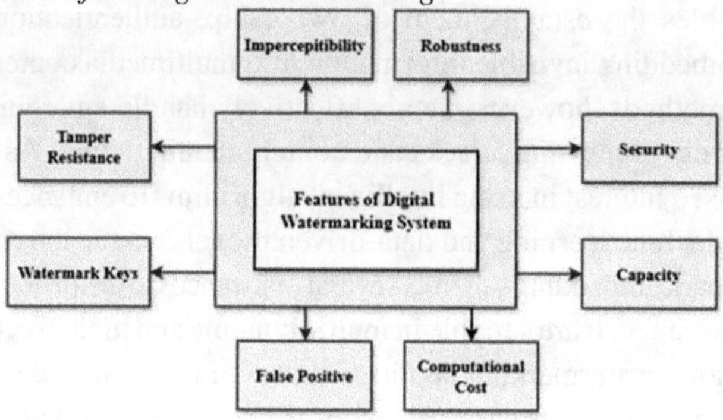

- **Imperceptibility:** To achieve this feature, the cover image and the watermarked image must appear similar so that the watermark can't be detected by the naked eye. An embedded digital watermark that is transparent or invisible will make the cover image appear nearly identical to its contents, making the watermark imperceptible. Visible watermarking can be observed with the naked eye, as the embedded watermark is evident in the image. Changing and reproducing text content can be a challenge, so invisible watermarks are important. Watermarks should be embedded properly so that they are not noticeable to the naked eye. However, some processes can be used to detect them.
- **Robustness:** Watermarks are considered robust when they can withstand attacks aimed at retrieving or altering the secret information they contain. The watermarked document must resist filtering, compression, rotation, and noise attacks, as well as attacks on the image, such as altering the colour, cropping text, and modifying the font size, type, and style. To protect the watermark against attack, it must be securely embedded and recovered. Whenever possible, distortions and watermarks are inconvenient; robustness is essential for proof of ownership, copyright protection, and fingerprinting. Watermarks are robust because they cannot be destroyed without distortion or modification, even if third parties attempt to identify them.
- **Security:** Digital content cannot be protected, authenticated, fingerprinted, or tracked with watermarking algorithms that are not secure. As a result, digital image watermarking techniques face a significant security concern. Security is determined by the key used for various encryption methods. The encryption of embedded watermarks has been accomplished using various methods, such as the logistic map-based method and the chaos-based discrete cosine transform. Before embedding the watermark, pseudo-random se-

quences (PRS) are used for encryption to enhance its security. This security requirement can be applied to various fields such as telemedicine, telecommunications, multimedia data and digital imaging.

- **Capacity:** An image is considered to have a watermarking capacity (also known as payload) if more data can be inserted into the image than can be inserted into the original image. A prerequisite for practical applications is the need to insert more watermark information. It is essential to define limitations in watermarking information while meeting the requirements for robustness and imperceptibility in watermarking. To measure the watermarking capacity, attackers must be aware of the information they have access to, as well as the codes used, the statistical model and the distortion constraints model were employed for the image.
- **Computational Cost:** Data encoders and decoders, distortion constraints, and statistical models used on the cover image all affect the watermarking capability. The number of detectors and embedders used in watermarking, along with the amount of time it takes to extract and embed the watermark, also affects the cost. It is crucial to strike a balance between computational complexity and robustness when communicating microscopy images securely and efficiently.
- **False Positive:** In the absence of a watermark image, a false positive rate is used to detect possible watermarks. Embedded watermarks differ from extracted watermarks, causing problems. The scheme has been tested in various ways. It is generally used for identifying ownership and controlling copying. Watermark images W and W' with length l will yield the following false positive rate (FPR):

$$FPR = \frac{l'}{l}$$

W' and W' have the same Hamming distance *l*.

- **Watermark Keys:** The embedding function is influenced by specific parameters, which are determined by these secret coefficients, embedding directions, and/or embedding domains. An estimation and mapping of watermark keys determines a watermark's security level. Depending on the embedded message and watermarked image, they are used for different purposes. Therefore, it is necessary to have a secret key in order to ensure security when embedding or extracting data. There are three components to the secret key: a private key, a detection key, and a public key. Detection keys are admitted in court, and public keys are disclosed.

- **Tamper Resistance:** A watermarking system determines authenticity using tamper-detection mechanisms. Changing watermark data results in tampering. Hence, integrity testing determines whether tampering has taken place.

3 ROLE OF MACHINE LEARNING AND ARTIFICIAL INTELLIGENCE IN WATERMARKING

Machine learning models embedded with IP protection mechanisms are becoming increasingly important as AI applications grow exponentially. Models are becoming increasingly valuable assets in sensitive fields such as healthcare, finance, and defense, which is why researchers have turned to watermarking techniques to safeguard proprietary knowledge. Watermark embedding directly into deep neural network weights was a foundational concept introduced by Uchida et al. (. With their white-box watermarking approach, model owners could prove ownership without any noticeable performance impact. The Author (Adi et al. 2018) proposed a black-box watermarking scheme, in which the watermark is triggered by inputs and verified by the model's output, without revealing its internal parameters. A central concern of watermarking techniques is the robustness against adversarial modifications.

With the advancement of machine learning (ML) in recent years, it has become able to process increasingly complex datasets, which has led to its application in a variety of fields. A model's effectiveness is heavily influenced by the quality and quantity of its training data. However, in a certain percentage of situations, it would require manual labelling to collect, clean, process, organize, and write training data. In a similar vein, some training itself could be computationally demanding, e.g. requesting GPUs and experience in hyperparameter optimization (Liu and Tan 2002; Mun et al. 2019).

A collection of concerns regarding privacy arises with the introduction of the artificial intelligence technology in the environment processing sensitive data, including medical records, financial data, or biometric identifiers. The laws that are used to secure this kind of sensitive information include the General Data Protection Regulation (GDPR), and the Health Insurance Portability and Accountability Act (HIPAA). However, hidden watermarking has a potential of compromising privacy and even conflicting with transparency requrements. Some of the areas of concern identified in previous literature include the possibility of watermarking methods being used as possible backdoor channels in the data collection process (Hitaj and Mancini 2018). Researchers have therefore developed privacy-aware watermarking solutions as a counterfeit to these risks.

As an example, (Abadi et al. 2016) proposed a training algorithm with differential privacy that adds to the model update a minimal amount of noise tuned not to generate a possible data leakage. It was not designed to take watermarking into consideration but later it has been modified to ensure that the insertion of watermarks does not pose a threat to the privacy of the users. Likewise, it investigated federated learning; a decentralized model training method that can update models on many devices without the need to store data in a centralized repository. The technique has proven to be workable toward the distributed and privacy preserving implementation of watermarking. The legal and the ethical respect of watermarking is also discussed in recent researches. Whereas watermarks can contribute to the security of intellectual property, as outlined in (Zhang et al. 2018), they can occasionally be contradictory to major ethical values like the transparency, justice, and autonomy. This has left people in doubt whether watermark evidence is admissible in intellectual property litigation more so where no commonly accepted standards exist.

4 DIGITAL WATERMARKING TECHNIQUES

The digital watermarking technique involves embedding a hidden marker in digital media, such as audio, video, and images, which enables the identification of the owner or source of the content. With digital watermarking, we can detect copyright violations on social media and verify the authenticity of banknotes. Digital watermarking is such a robust solution that it has become a crucial part of content security. In the last decade, Machine Learning and Artificial Intelligence have significantly enhanced the features of digital watermarking systems, facilitating the creation of more adaptive, resilient, and intelligent watermarking systems as mentioned in Table 1. Various parameters can be used to classify digital watermarks.

Table 1. Various existing models of digital watermarking

Technique	Domain Used	AI Models Involved	Key Contribution
CNN-based Embedding	Spatial & DWT	CNN, ResNet	Enhances imperceptibility (Mun et al. 2019)
GAN for Adversarial Robustness	Frequency & Feature	GAN, CycleGAN	Counteracts deepfake-type attacks (Bonawitz et al. 2019; Cox et al. 1997; Yuan et al. 2024)
Autoencoder Watermarking	Latent feature space	Autoencoder, VAE	Robust and compact embedding (Kishan and Kumar 2023; Mahapatra et al. 2022)
Transformer-guided Resilience	Temporal Video	Vision Transformers	Dynamic video watermarking (Elharrouss et al. 2025; Xu et al. 2021; Zhu et al. 2018)
ML-based Watermark Authentication	Spatial	SVM, Random Forest	Detects manipulations, noise-resilient

4.1 Conventional Techniques

In digital watermarking, information is integrated within digital media, ensuring authenticity, enforcing copyright laws, and affirming ownership rights through the validation of authenticity, copyright enforcement, and ownership affirmation. The traditional approach to watermarking was based on the principles of imperceptibility, robustness, and capacity (Cox et al. 1997, 2007). It is usually possible to categorize watermarking methodologies into two types: spatial and transform. Watermarks are incorporated into host images using spatial domain techniques. Because of their inherent simplicity and low computational requirements, they are however more susceptible to image processing operations such as data compression, data filtering, noise introduction, and geometric transformations (Barni, Bartolini, and Piva 2001). When watermarking is applied, the Least Significant Bit (LSB) method is used to replace the least significant bits of designated pixels. Despite its high level of visual fidelity, this method lacks robustness, as even slight modifications to the image can readily compromise the watermark embedded within. Additionally, watermark signals are either appended to or multiplied with the intensity values of pixels using additive or multiplicative embedding methodologies. When not meticulously calibrated, these techniques can induce noticeable distortions (Barni et al. 2001), even though they may enhance resistance to certain types of attacks.

As an alternative, transform domain techniques embed the watermark within the host media's frequency domain, providing a more robust solution. Signal transformation methodologies decompose images into their frequency components in order to accomplish this. The Discrete Cosine Transform (DCT) is one such method that can be used for watermarking in mid-frequency bands, striking a balance between robustness and imperceptibility while offering resilience against compression, particularly in JPEG (Barni et al.,. In a similar vein, the Discrete Wavelet Transform (DWT), which subdivides an image into subbands (LL, LH, HL, and HH), allows hierarchical watermarking. Figure 4 illustrates how images can be maintained against degradation and enhanced while maintaining perceptually important regions (Liu and Tan 2002). DFT is considered resilient to geometric transformations, including rotation and scaling, because of its invariance characteristics.

Figure 4. Conventional methods of watermarking.

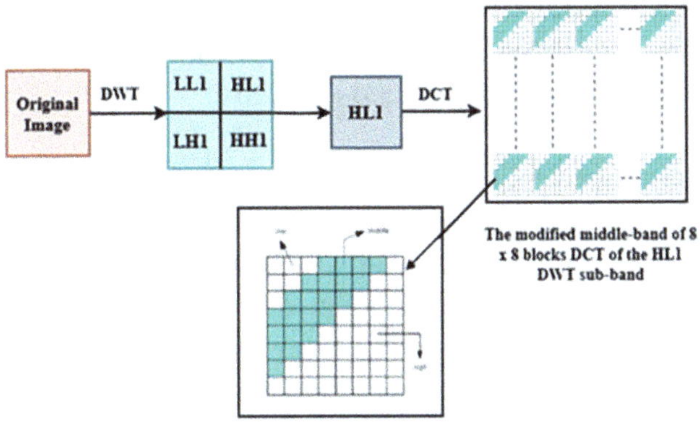

4.2 Machine Learning-Based Techniques

With the growing complexity and significance of various fields, machine learning (ML) models are being developed around the world due to the availability of data and computing resources. Protecting ML models, however, becomes more challenging as they can be held legally as intellectual property and ML models can be subjected to theft, illegal redistribution, and unauthorized use. Digital watermarks allow for proper identification of ML models, enabling their protection against intellectual property threats. In the study, a taxonomy of watermarking schemes for machine learning models and a unified threat model enabling objective comparison between watermarking schemes is presented. A systematisation is given for core watermarking security features for ML models alongside attacks against those features. A robust watermark can endure multiple attacks including compression, cropping, and filtering. CNNs have been shown to optimally learn embedding and extraction functions even in the presence of geometric and non-geometric distortions (Wan et al. 2022).

The various researchers is designing and developing new methods to improve the watermarking systems using ANN and SVM based ML techniques (Sharma et al. 2025). Some researchers have paid a great deal of attention to creating solutions to detect and decode machine learning-based watermarks. As a result of the work presented in this article, we propose a novel approach for adaptively modifying the decoding strategy based on the applications of watermarking systems. Watermarked images will likely be JPEG-compressed before being transmitted or stored in an image warehouse, such as in a watermarking application. For example, medical image warehouses are used for remote diagnostic aids and telesurgery. The learning capabilities of ML systems can be maximized in such scenarios by providing information on the distortions resulting from JPEG compression during training. It is possible to effectively utilize ML decoding models once they have been developed for extracting embedded messages from distorted images with minimal effort (Singh, Dwivedi, and Kumar 2021). In addition, channels with Gaussian noise, intentional or unintentional filtering, and value matrix distortion are examples of such specific applications.

It is moderately imperceptible and robust against different types of attacks. The Author (Kasralikar et al. 2025) presented an image watermarking technique using multiwavelet and support vector machine (SVM) concepts. An SVM was trained to extract the watermark using a mean value modulation approach during the watermarking process. The SVM learned about the relationship between the mean value and watermarking. Its imperceptibility is acceptable; however, it is not robust against different attacks (including filtering, compression, and scaling).

4.3 Artificial Intelligence and Deep Learning Techniques

The multimedia community has numerous opportunities for collaboration and synergies with artificial intelligence (AI), deep learning, convolutional neural networks, and robotics. Various research communities frequently utilise digital images to enhance the role of multimedia (Begum and Uddin, 2020; Kumar, Wadhwa, and Garg, 2025; Lee et al.,. The advancement of deep learning and machine learning has enabled smart data processing services to be utilised in industries and other potential uses. A total of 2266 photos are uploaded to Facebook every second, along with 995 photos to Instagram every second. The unauthorised use of these images, however, is causing significant problems with privacy and security. Furthermore, the Digital India project aims to empower Indian society and the economy through the use of digital technology (Chan et al. 2005).

Using Fully Convolutional Neural Networks (FCNNs) for denoising watermarked images has been studied recently thanks to advances in deep learning and neural networks. The embedding and extraction processes improve training and denoising performances, and watermarking noise is reduced. Deep learning is the most common method of implementing artificial intelligence (AI). It is shown that these techniques can be used to originate human capabilities through visual quality, audio recognition, and natural language processing assignments. An expert in human experience and substantial training data are required to build a deep learning model at the production level. Copyright violations may result from reproducing, distributing, or derived proprietary deep learning models. Consequently, it is imperative to establish a system to protect the intellectual property of deep learning models and verify their ownership externally (Vassaux et al. 2002).

CNNs are deep-learning networks that have convolutional properties. CNN models have five layers: input, convolution, rectified linear units, pooling, fully connected, and output. CNN was modelled after the visual cortex of the human brain. Neurons only activate when a stimulus occurs in a receptive field. Using CNN models, an input image (image) is transformed into a vector, which is then convoluted to extract the essential features (kernels or filters are used for this). Negative values are converted to zero values using ReLU activation function, and the number of parameters is reduced by pooling. As a result of flattening the input, the fully connected network can classify the reduced pool of information. CNN is widely used as an image watermarking and data hiding model because it is less complex (Sy, Kha, and Hoang 2020). While CNN has a wide range of applications, it is predominantly used in watermarking for embedding, extracting, enhancing, and determining the optimal place for embedding watermarks.

ResNet and VGGNet, for instance, take several days to train. Due to GPUs, which have become increasingly popular, training deep neural network models for these problems is challenging nowadays. On the website, users can also access some training models directly and try them without any hassle. In the future, sharing models will become increasingly important in the development of deep neural networks (DNNs). Aside from trained models such as those available on the Google Play Store, other digital platforms also offer artificial intelligence models. Still, these models must be protected via security.

5 CHALLENGES

Several technical and practical challenges surround the digital watermarking process, which is crucial for protecting intellectual property, verifying content authenticity, and enforcing copyright. By integrating machine learning (ML) and artificial intelligence (AI) into digital watermarking methodologies, novel capabilities are introduced, along with substantial challenges.

a. **Imperceptibility vs. Robustness Trade-off:** To achieve watermark robustness, the watermark must be imperceptible at the same time. By improving one, we often compromise the other, making it difficult to design a universally effective watermarking system. Aside from this, machine learning models often have limited generalizability, as their performance tends to suffer when applied to distributions or media types not represented in the training set (Cox et al. 1997).
    a. **Security and Resistance to Attacks:** Watermarking systems need to be secure against various types of attacks, including watermark removal, estimation, forgery, and collusion. With signal processing or machine learning models, attackers can detect, remove, or forge watermarking. Cropping, resizing, rotation, and compression can severely damage or destroy embed-

ded watermarking. Multiple watermarking is also a concern for security, as attackers can combine different copies of the content to eliminate the watermark (Ratha, Connell, and Bolle 2001).

b. **Capacity Limitations:** Data embedding requires a host medium that can accommodate large amounts of information without sacrificing quality or integrity in order to be imperceptible and robust. Multi-watermarking and large payloads in a single piece of content can make embedding large amounts of data particularly challenging (Liu and Tan 2002).

c. **Synchronisation Issues:** The watermark detector can desynchronise from the embedded watermark when geometric distortions such as scaling, rotation, and translation are applied. Video streaming and mobile imaging, which require synchronisation in real-time, are particularly difficult because of distortions.

d. **Cross-Media Applicability**: A watermarking technique should be designed to accommodate a variety of media types, including images, audio, videos, and text. Each type of media has its properties, noise tolerances, and perception models. Techniques designed for images may not be effective for audio or video, so specific strategies must be developed (Petitcolas, Anderson, and Kuhn,.

e. **Legal and Ethical Concerns**: The use of watermarking for surveillance, tracking, or DRM enforcement raises privacy and ethical concerns. Additionally, watermarking remains a grey area in many jurisdictions regarding its legal recognition as definitive proof of ownership. A legal framework and standardisation are necessary to recognise and use watermarking technologies (Memon and Wong 1998) properly.

f. **Computational Complexity**: Significant computational resources are required to train, embed, and detect watermarking algorithms, particularly those that utilise advanced machine learning or deep learning techniques. Therefore, mobile devices and embedded devices may encounter this limitation due to resource constraints (Zhu et al. 2018), where efficiency is paramount.

g. **Fragility and Tamper Detection**: An effective watermark is designed to resist alterations, whereas a fragile watermark is designed to detect tampering. The design of schemes (Luo et al., 2011) that distinguish between legitimate transformations (such as compression) and malicious manipulations (such as content manipulation) is challenging. The design of schemes that combine robustness and fragility can become more difficult (Luo et al. 2011).

6 APPLICATIONS OF DIGITAL WATERMARKING

Watermarking has led to the introduction of digital content protecting, verifying and handling as some of the key aspects of the digital era. Watermarking guarantees data integrity, copyright protection (of digital media), data authentication and data authenticity by the encoding of hidden information. Watermarking may see applications at different industries and platforms. Watermarking is quite useful as a protection mechanism and copyright management, credibility in the work, and as a tampering mechanism. Some of the most common uses of watermarking are depicted in figure 5.

Figure 5. Applications of watermarking.

a. **Copyright Protection and Intellectual Property Rights**: Digital watermarking is well-known for protecting the intellectual property rights of digital content creators. By embedding a unique watermark identifying the copyright holder, images, audio, videos, and documents are protected from unauthorised distribution and piracy. To prevent unauthorised use and assert ownership, professional photographers and media outlets watermark their work (Molina et al. 2019). Additionally, watermarking can encrypt the content, which remains embedded even after being copied, edited, or distributed online.

b. **Content Authentication and Tamper Detection**: Digital content is often verified through the use of watermarking. Fragile watermarking techniques are particularly effective at detecting tampering or unauthorised modifications. A watermark ensures that the content has not been modified after it was created, in applications such as digital forensics, medical imaging, and the handling of legal evidence (Memon and Wong 1998). Watermarking will be damaged or destroyed if any modification is made to the media, alerting the system to the potential forgeries.

c. **Broadcast Monitoring**: Multimedia content can be monitored and tracked across a wide range of platforms and channels using watermarking in the broadcast industry. Broadcasters use embedded tracking information in broadcast signals to ensure that ads, music, and shows are displayed as agreed. This builds trust and reliability in the broadcast experience. Additionally, this enables the collection of statistics on content usage, which can be used for billing, audience analytics, and advertising audits.

d. **Digital Rights Management (DRM):** The access and usage of digital content are controlled through the use of watermarking in DRM systems. DRM solutions enable content distribution to be tracked, licensing terms to be enforced, and unauthorised redistribution to be prohibited by embedding user-specific information in media files. A watermark, such as one found in e-books, streaming services, or software distributions, identifies the recipient so that, in the event of data leaks or piracy, traceability is possible (Memon and Wong,.

e. **Medical Image Security**: Watermarking is one of the methods for securing medical images, such as X-rays, MRIs, and CT scans. Watermarking can embed patient data, timestamps, and diagnostic information into images without compromising their clinical quality or integrity. It ensures data integrity and confidentiality, which are crucial for electronic health records (EHRs), telemedicine, and the transfer of medical data (Coatrieux et al., 2000). It also meets the regulatory standards of watermarking, such as HIPAA.

f. **Document Authentication**: To verify the integrity and origin of digital documents (such as PDFs and Word documents), watermarking can be applied. Invisible watermarking can be applied to government, academic, and financial documents to prevent forgery and unauthorised duplication. It makes sure that the documents are authentic and have not been altered during transmission or storage.

g. **Video Surveillance and Law Enforcement**: The watermarking of surveillance footage ensures its authenticity and can be used as evidence in court. When timestamps, camera IDs, or location data are embedded in video evidence, the chain of custody is preserved, and any attempt to tamper with it is detectable (Kumar, Wadhwa, and Garg 2025). This technique employed by law enforcement agencies helps enhance the quality of digital evidence.

h. **Social Media and Online Publishing**: On social media platforms and online content publishers, watermarking is used to both protect and promote original content. For instance, platforms may embed watermarking containing user or brand identifiers into publicly shared photos and videos. It not only prevents content theft but also promotes brand visibility if the content is reshaped.

i. **Biometric Data Protection**: Watermarking is utilised in biometric systems to secure sensitive data, such as fingerprint, facial recognition, and iris scan templates. Biometric authentication systems can be enhanced by embedding a watermark in the images to prevent spoofing attacks (Petitcolas, Anderson, and Kuhn 1999).
j. **E-Governance and Smart IDs**: Watermarking is increasingly being used on smart cards, passports, and digital IDs by governments. These documents contain watermarking that conceals information, such as encrypted personal details, digital signatures, or unique identifiers used for border control, banking, and public service access verification.

7 FUTURE DIRECTIONS

Adaptable, intelligent, and privacy-conscious approaches to digital watermarking are needed in the future, as technological, legal, and ethical challenges evolve. Increasingly, watermarking techniques must be not only robust and imperceptible but also scalable, secure, and ethically aligned, due to the convergence of AI, cybersecurity, and data governance. The following are some promising directions for the future:

a. **Privacy-Preserving Watermarking Frameworks:** With the integration of advanced privacy-preserving mechanisms, such as differential privacy and federated learning, watermark embedding should not compromise user privacy. As a result of regulations like GDPR and HIPAA, which require the protection of sensitive information, healthcare and finance are particularly vulnerable.
b. **Explainable and Interpretable Models:** Watermarking with black-box AI models raises concerns about trust and accountability. Explainable AI (XAI) can aid in developing transparent watermarking processes, enabling users, auditors, and legal entities to clearly understand the decisions related to watermark embedding and detection.
c. **Cross-Domain and Multi-Modal Watermarking:** Media types are typically optimised in current techniques. Through multi-modal deep learning architectures, future research should explore cross-modal watermarking, in which unified frameworks support the embedding of watermarking across diverse media formats (e.g., audio, video, text).
d. **Resilience Against AI-Generated Content and Deepfakes:** To ensure traceability and authenticity, watermarking systems must adapt as generative adversarial networks and diffusion models produce realistic synthetic content. Defending against misinformation and media forgery will require the embedding of imperceptible watermarking into AI-generated content.

e. **Blockchain-Enabled Watermark Verification:** Combining blockchains with digital watermarking has the potential to provide decentralised ownership verification and tamper-proof logging. Future systems could incorporate smart contracts for authentication, licensing, and dispute resolution.

f. **Real-Time and Edge-Compatible Watermarking:** Watermarking solutions with low latency and lightweight characteristics are essential for real-time multimedia applications and IoT environments. The robustness and detection accuracy of these approaches must be optimised for deployment on edge devices with constrained computational resources.

g. **Ethical and Legal Standardization:** The ethical concerns of the transparency, fairness, and ability of self-sufficiency of user appear because of the growing number of applications of watermarking to surveillance, biometrics systems, and authorization of copyright. Standardization of watermarking is becoming increasingly popular since the terrain of digital content protection touches the concerns of privacy rights, the implementation of intellectual property rights, and the ethical use of AI. White box and black box watermarking is useful in checking IP but certain industries that tend to covet privacy might not accept the fact that they might be secretly tracked like the case with healthcare and finance industries. One of these tensions is resolved by a variant of differential privacy, federated learning, and secure multiparty computation with privacy-preserving watermarking. Also, ethical policies focus on issues of user autonomy, fairness, and accountability in the light of which watermarking standards not only remain technically strong but also socially responsible. A changing dialogue requires a uniformed regulatory environment that strikes equilibrium between legal conformity and moral protection.

h. **Quantum-Resilient Watermarking Techniques:** The emergence of quantum-resilient watermarking technologies is a major shift towards the digital protection of content, in terms of trying to achieve both imperceptibility and robustness against computationally powerful quantum attackers. Recently the Quantum Haar Wavelet Transform (QHWT) and the Qsobel edge detection framework have been used to improve the accuracy and robustness of watermark embedding. By these methods, it is clear that quantum principles are being used not only to deliver security but also to adaptively, high fidelity watermark.

i. **Self-Adaptive Watermarking via Reinforcement Learning:** Reinforcement learning (RL) has found application in this issue where the framework seeks to understand how an intelligent agent can learn to effectively embed robust, imperceptible watermarks by assimilating an optimum strategy against the dynamic environment by the agent interacting with it. A co-learning scheme that trains a watermark and a detector within an RLHF (Reinforcement Learning with Human Feedback) based framework was introduced, whereby the system learns to embed watermarks on the output of large language model and ensure text quality and adversarial stability. Context aware, intelligent systems that can adapt themselves to usage and threats are replacing watermarking. These schemes represent a departure to the fixed watermarking schemes.

8 CONCLUSION

The paper has done an exhaustive deep study of machine learning, deep learning, and artificial intelligence-based schemes of watermarking. Artificial intelligence (AI), machine learning and deep learning have given rise to the utilisation of new technologies and state-of-the-art applications. Another important property of watermarking systems includes security, privacy and ease. Existing constraints may be resolved using decentralised computation, secure collaborative learning, and powerful cryptography. Such developments will make technologies of watermarking more reliable by ensuring that their credibility, efficiency, and legality are enhanced. Not only is artificial intelligence and machine learning an effective watermarking tool, but it is a problematic one as well because it consumes many resources, has a high model efficiency, and detection methodology. To address such challenges, new solutions need to be developed that would keep the intellectual property relatively intact but preserve efficiency and effectiveness of deep learning models. Watermarking in the future will depend on the use of hybrid models that integrate deep learning, adaptive, and dynamic models in order to improve imperceptibility, robustness and security, and meet the changing needs of unauthorised manipulation or access of data. It is also important to establish standardised datasets which will be important in conducting benchmark performance and engaging meaningful comparisons between various watermarking techniques. All these developments are bound to be met by joint academia industry efforts that will hopefully aid in putting to rest the current issues of digital watermarking.

REFERENCES

Abdelhakim, A., Saleh, H. I., & Abdelhakim, M. (2019). Fragile Watermarking for Image Tamper Detection and Localization with Effective Recovery Capability Using K-Means Clustering. *Multimedia Tools and Applications*, *78*(22), 32523–32563. DOI: 10.1007/s11042-019-07986-3

Adi, Y., Baum, C., Cisse, M., Pinkas, B., & Keshet, J. 2018. "Turning Your Weakness into a Strength: Watermarking Deep Neural Networks by Backdooring." Pp. 1615–31 in *27th USENIX security symposium (USENIX Security 18).*

Ahmad, T., Xue, J. L., Seet, B.-C., & Cano, J.-C. (2020). Social Network Analysis Based Localization Technique with Clustered Closeness Centrality for 3D Wireless Sensor Networks. *Electronics (Basel)*, *9*(5), 738. DOI: 10.3390/electronics9050738

Barni, M., Bartolini, F., & Piva, A. (2001). Improved Wavelet-Based Watermarking through Pixel-Wise Masking. *IEEE Transactions on Image Processing*, *10*(5), 783–791. DOI: 10.1109/83.918570 PMID: 18249667

Chan, P. W., Lyu, M. R., & Chin, R. T. (2005). A Novel Scheme for Hybrid Digital Video Watermarking: Approach, Evaluation and Experimentation. *IEEE Transactions on Circuits and Systems for Video Technology*, *15*(12), 1638–1649. DOI: 10.1109/TCSVT.2005.856932

Cox, I., Miller, M., Bloom, J., Fridrich, J., & Kalker, T. (2007). *Digital Watermarking and Steganography*. Morgan kaufmann.

Cox, I. J., Kilian, J., Leighton, F. T., & Shamoon, T. (1997). Secure Spread Spectrum Watermarking for Multimedia. *IEEE Transactions on Image Processing*, *6*(12), 1673–1687. DOI: 10.1109/83.650120 PMID: 18285237

Dhabliya, D., Soundararajan, R., Selvarasu, P., Balasubramaniam, M. S., Rajawat, A. S., Goyal, S. B., Raboaca, M. S., Mihaltan, T. C., Verma, C., & Suciu, G. (2022). Energy-Efficient Network Protocols and Resilient Data Transmission Schemes for Wireless Sensor Networks—An Experimental Survey. *Energies*, *15*(23), 8883. DOI: 10.3390/en15238883

Elharrouss, O., Damseh, R., Belkacem, A. N., Badidi, E., & Lakas, A. (2025). Transformer-Based Image and Video Inpainting: Current Challenges and Future Directions. *Artificial Intelligence Review*, *58*(4), 124. DOI: 10.1007/s10462-024-11075-9

Jayamalar, T., & Radha, V. (2010). Survey on Digital Video Watermarking Techniques and Attacks on Watermarks. *International Journal of Engineering Science and Technology*, *2*(12), 6963–6967.

Kasralikar, P., Polu, O. R., Chamarthi, B., Veer Samara Sihman Bharattej Rupavath, R., Patel, S., & Tumati, R. (2025). Blockchain for Securing AI-Driven Healthcare Systems: A Systematic Review and Future Research Perspectives. *Cureus*, *17*(4), e83136. DOI: 10.7759/cureus.83136 PMID: 40438823

Kishan, K., & Vijay Kumar, B. (2023). Efficient Large Invisible Color Watermark Embedding Using Conditional Deep Autoencoder Model for Medical Applications. *Measurement. Sensors*, *29*, 100850. DOI: 10.1016/j.measen.2023.100850

Kumar, D., Wadhwa, A., & Garg, P. 2025. "Securing Medical Images in the Cloud: A Hybrid Approach Using Adaptive Strength Control and Content-Aware Watermarking." Pp. 1050–55 in *2025 3rd International Conference on Disruptive Technologies (ICDT)*. DOI: 10.1109/ICDT63985.2025.10986507

Liu, R., & Tan, T. (2002). An SVD-Based Watermarking Scheme for Protecting Rightful Ownership. *IEEE Transactions on Multimedia*, *4*(1), 121–128. DOI: 10.1109/6046.985560

Luo, H., Yu, F.-X., Huang, Z.-L., & Lu, Z.-M. (2011). Blind Image Watermarking Based on Discrete Fractional Random Transform and Subsampling. *Optik (Stuttgart)*, *122*(4), 311–316. DOI: 10.1016/j.ijleo.2009.12.018

Mahapatra, D., Amrit, P., Singh, O. P., Singh, A. K., & Agrawal, A. K. (2022). Autoencoder-Convolutional Neural Network-Based Embedding and Extraction Model for Image Watermarking. *Journal of Electronic Imaging*, *32*(02). DOI: 10.1117/1.JEI.32.2.021604

Memon, N., & Wong, P. W. (1998). Protecting Digital Media Content. *Communications of the ACM*, *41*(7), 35–43. DOI: 10.1145/278476.278485

Molina, J., Ponomaryov, V., Reyes, R., & Cruz, C. 2019. "Watermarking-Based Self-Recovery and Authentication Framework for Colour Images." Pp. 1–6 in *2019 7th international workshop on biometrics and forensics (IWBF)*. IEEE. DOI: 10.1109/IWBF.2019.8739211

Mun, S.-M., Nam, S.-H., Jang, H.-U., Kim, D., & Lee, H.-K. (2019). A Robust Blind Watermarking Using Convolutional Neural Network. *Neurocomputing*, *337*, 191–202. DOI: 10.1016/j.neucom.2019.01.067

Petitcolas, F. A. P., Anderson, R. J., & Kuhn, M. G. (1999). Information Hiding-a Survey. *Proceedings of the IEEE*, *87*(7), 1062–1078. DOI: 10.1109/5.771065

Ratha, N. K., Connell, J. H., & Bolle, R. M. (2001). Enhancing Security and Privacy in Biometrics-Based Authentication Systems. *IBM Systems Journal*, *40*(3), 614–634. DOI: 10.1147/sj.403.0614

Sharma, A., Rana, S., Sharma, A., Singh, A., Datwani, K., Tiwari, D., & Matta, R. 2025. "An Analytical Study on Safety Measures Concerns in Cloud Computing Technology." in *AIP Conference Proceedings*. Vol. 3224. AIP Publishing. DOI: 10.1063/5.0247117

Singh, A., Dwivedi, R. K., & Kumar, R. (2021). A Survey of Lung Cancer Detection Using Machine Learning Techniques for Improving Classification Performance. *World J Eng Res Technol*, *7*(4), 149–161.

Singh, N., Jain, M., & Sharma, S. (2013). A Survey of Digital Watermarking Techniques. *International Journal of Modern Communication Technologies and Research*, *1*(6), 265852.

Sy, N. C., Kha, H. H., & Hoang, N. M. (2020). An Efficient Robust Blind Watermarking Method Based on Convolution Neural Networks in Wavelet Transform Domain. *International Journal of Machine Learning and Computing*, *10*(5), 675–684. DOI: 10.18178/ijmlc.2020.10.5.990

Vassaux, B., Nguyen, P., Baudry, S., Bas, P., & Chassery, J. M. 2002. "Scrambling Technique for Video Object Watermarking Resisting to Mpeg-4." Pp. 239–44 in *International Symposium on VIPromCom Video/Image Processing and Multimedia Communications*. IEEE. DOI: 10.1109/VIPROM.2002.1026662

Wan, W., Wang, J., Zhang, Y., Li, J., Yu, H., & Sun, J. (2022). A Comprehensive Survey on Robust Image Watermarking. *Neurocomputing*, *488*, 226–247. DOI: 10.1016/j.neucom.2022.02.083

Xu, H. B., Wang, R., Wei, J., & Lu, S. P. (2021). A compact neural network-based algorithm for robust image watermarking. *arXiv preprint arXiv:2112.13491*.

Yang, Y. (2020). Medical Multimedia Big Data Analysis Modeling Based on DBN Algorithm. *IEEE Access : Practical Innovations, Open Solutions*, *8*, 16350–16361. DOI: 10.1109/ACCESS.2020.2967075

Yuan, Z., Zhang, X., Wang, Z., & Yin, Z. 2024. "Semi-Fragile Neural Network Watermarking Based on Adversarial Examples." *IEEE Transactions on Emerging Topics in Computational Intelligence*. https://ieeexplore.ieee.org/abstract/document/10474363/

Zhao, B., Zhong, Y., Xia, G.-S., & Zhang, L. (2016). Dirichlet-Derived Multiple Topic Scene Classification Model for High Spatial Resolution Remote Sensing Imagery. *IEEE Transactions on Geoscience and Remote Sensing*, *54*(4), 2108–2123. DOI: 10.1109/TGRS.2015.2496185

Zhu, J., Kaplan, R., Johnson, J., & Li, F.-F. 2018. "Hidden: Hiding Data with Deep Networks." Pp. 657–72 in *Proceedings of the European conference on computer vision (ECCV).*

Chapter 13
Introduction to Cloud Computing

Ashima Narang
https://orcid.org/0000-0001-8961-8648
Amity University, Gurgaon, India

Devashish Sharma
https://orcid.org/0009-0000-5706-2665
Amity University, Gurgaon, India

Yojna Arora
https://orcid.org/0000-0002-6056-2465
Sharda University, India

Ashwani Kumar
https://orcid.org/0000-0002-2100-900X
School of Computer Science, Engineering, and Technology, Bennett University, Greater Noida, India

ABSTRACT

Cloud computing, or remote resource environments, has revolutionized digital service delivery by enabling flexible, on-demand access to computing power. It allows local systems to execute tasks beyond their native capacities, leveraging models like IaaS, PaaS, and SaaS, each offering varied levels of control and abstraction. Most online services today—such as on-demand access, measured billing, and broad network connectivity—are cloud-based. However, challenges like data storage, transmission, exposure risks, and watermarking persist. The chapter highlights encryption, cryptography, GDPR, and HIPAA for improved security and concludes with applications in e-learning, streaming, and watermark detection using WaaS and real-time embeddings

DOI: 10.4018/979-8-3373-3785-2.ch013

INTRODUCTION

In just a couple of decades, cloud computing has transformed everything. No more clunky servers, costly data centers, or rigid setups. he cloud serves as a global powerhouse, driving everything from a startup's rapid growth to AI breakthroughs that save lives in healthcare or guide self-driving cars. It provides computing power, storage, and tools on demand with impressive speed and scale. In the past, computing meant owning a lot of physical equipment—servers, cooling systems, and entire IT teams just to keep everything running. To scale up, you had to spend money on more hardware and space. The cloud changed that model completely. Now, computing resources can be accessed as easily as borrowing a cup of sugar; you just flip a switch, and it's ready to use. It's not only about getting rid of hardware. Virtualization and tools like Kubernetes have been created to allow developers to focus on building innovative projects rather than managing servers. This approach allows for fast building, smooth scaling, and quick adaptation. The cloud's real strength lies in its accessibility. It levels the playing field, giving everyone access to top-tier technology. Various approaches include Infrastructure as a Service (IaaS) for raw computing power, Platform as a Service (PaaS) for streamlined development, or Software as a Service (SaaS) for ready-to-use apps. Cutting-edge fields are now emerging, such quantum computing and also they are becoming accessible because cloud platforms has been opening opportunities for growth of these powerful systems to researchers worldwide. All that's needed is an internet connection and a vision. With such power emerging by the day, significant responsibility has emerged in form of authentication. With that, concerns for security and privacy are also growing. Techniques such as encryption and digital watermarking protect information. For regulations, GDPR and HIPAA push cloud providers to prioritize trust from the ground up. Cloud tech keeps things running smoothly, no matter what. It is done by ensuring that even if one server goes down, another will steps in seamlessly to keep everything on track. These systems are designed in such a way that they thrive in the face of chaos, not just sidestep it.

Diving into the story of cloud computing - in the domain where in the 1960s, visionary computer scientist John McCarthy dreamed of a world where computing power would flow like electricity. That idea stayed a dream until the early 2000s, when things started clicking into place. Contributions have been made to generate breakthroughs in virtualization, faster networks, and the internet's explosive growth, cloud computing began to take shape. Multinational companies have given game-changers, offering flexible, pay-as-you-go computing that anyone could tap into - such as Amazon's AWS of 2006. What the development began, they utilized a basic storage and computing services - the constituting technology has now grown into a vibrant ecosystem packed with APIs, deployment tools, databases, AI services, and more. Today, this cloud technology is the result of decades of innovation, turning McCarthy's vision into a reality where powerful computing is just a click away, no matter where you are.

Now, by pairing the cloud computing with AI and data science, and the users have received a powerhouse combo which has opened the doors which once locked tight in research labs. AI projects, ranging from the training models to rolling them out, need massive computing power, storage, and data flow. Cloud platforms step in with flexible infrastructure that grows (or shrinks) with your needs. Think GPU and TPU instances, serverless computing, or tools like Google Vertex AI, AWS SageMaker, and Azure Machine Learning—they make it easier than ever for data scientists to build and launch models. Add in real-time data pipelines, cloud-hosted data lakes, and MLOps frameworks, and you've got a smooth, end-to-end process for turning ideas into reality. Whether it's catching fraud, personalizing medicine, or powering Netflix recommendations, the cloud handles the heavy lifting so innovators can focus on the big picture. It's a perfect partnership: AI brings the smarts, and the cloud brings the strength.

A great real-world example comes from a 2025 study by Noteboom and colleagues, who built an ICU-to-cloud data pipeline that's saving lives. This clinical decision support system pulls in messy, fast-moving patient data from ICU monitors, securely sending over 9,000 records to the cloud for processing and storage. Using smart data pipelines and predictive analytics, it flags critical health events in real time, helping doctors act fast. The system's design—balancing constrained optimization, quick response times, and cost-effective resource use—keeps it reliable even under pressure. This project shows how cloud computing can revolutionize healthcare, making critical systems smarter, scalable, and accessible. It's a shining example of what's possible when the cloud powers life-changing innovation.

The cloud is getting smarter and more flexible, always finding new ways to grow. With cool advancements like edge computing, federated learning, and even Watermarking-as-a-Service, it's stepping up its game in managing and keeping data safe. The cloud of tomorrow won't just be fast—it'll be fair, open to everyone, and built to stand the test of time. The exploration of this chapter dives into the cloud's layers in terms of how its components work, its flexibility, and its various approach to data safety. The chapter also covers how the cloud powers everything from seamless in real time. The cloud isn't just the future—it's the beating heart of the digital present, paving the way for what's next.

LITERATURE REVIEW

This section describes the various progresses leading studies have made recently. The content includes specifically those advancements which are directly related to the topics, understanding and points covered, described or mentioned in this chapter.

As described in (Dadheech, A., 2025) developers have built path planning software for Unmanned Aerial Vehicle (UAV) flights using Machine Learning (ML) which utilizes Reinforcement Learning (RL) algorithm using the resources available to the setup via cloud connectivity. To utilize resources efficiently, adaptive energy and delay-sensitive offloading strategies were implemented. Various Amazon Web Services (AWS) were used – such as SageMaker, Lambda, and S3, and AirNav. In other words, energy consumption was optimized, and response time was significantly reduced by the integration of a novel threshold-based dynamic computation offloading strategy. By the implementation, 60% improvement in response time and 16.6% reduction in data transfer were obtained.

Using the support of 3D data acquisition, development of geometric Deep Learning (DL) models has been spurred. This happened by the technology, also utilized by the team of (Baiocchi, A., 2025) Natural Language Processing (NLP). They presented Adaptive Point Cloud Transformer (AdaPT) model – which is augmented using adaptive token selection mechanism. This setup reduces the number of required tokens and thereby enables efficient processing of large point clouds. The team, furthermore, reduced the computational cost significantly by overcoming the need for retraining or fine-tuning of the model once prepared.

This study of (Samha, A. K., 2024) describes increasing need for cloud resources, and aims to explain how partnering up with multiple Cloud Service Providers (CSPs) via federated cloud computing can keep things running smoothly. It focuses on boosting Quality of Service (QoS). It represents a fresh take on Infrastructure as a Service (IaaS) cloud design while blending virtual machine migration and resource consolidation and providing efficient virtualization. Cool new features which include Cloud User (CU) and Reputation Management systems and smart algorithms were added to boost security and trust. The Trust Manager (TM) and Broker Manager (BM) keep Service Level Agreements (SLAs) and trust in check, while User Profiling (private, social, corporate) customizes cloud services for different users. Algorithms like the Deep Q-based Algorithm and Banker's Algorithm make picking CSPs, managing resources, and handling SLAs a breeze. In the end, this study raises the bar for IaaS cloud design, delivering a solid setup that makes cloud services more dependable and efficient.

Another review paper of (Vashistha, D., 2025) describes how DL can shake up load balancing in cloud computing, taking a close look at what's out there, what works, what doesn't, and how it's all being used in the real world. The developers dug through a ton of research studies and projects to figure out how well deep learning models can juggle resources and boost performance in the cloud. They also point out where the research falls short, giving a heads-up on what still needs exploring. It's a super helpful guide for researchers and pros who want to build smarter, more efficient ways to keep cloud systems running smoothly.

The research team of (Kotsakis, G., 2025) developed an innovative cloud-based system which monitors the high-performance machining. Utilizing a SaaS model, they created a cost-effective and adaptable solution to gather and transmit machining data to the cloud in real time. The setup they designed was done so in order to catch even the tiniest irregularities in the machining process, which is crucial in precision manufacturing to maintain product quality and extend tool life. By sticking to standard communication protocols, the system plays nice with all kinds of industrial setups, making it easy to roll out. They arranged to put it to the test in a real-life milling factory, and it worked like a charm, proving it's tough and reliable. Their approach successfully saves companies from spending on expensive on-site tech providing the users relevant updates and security remotely with ease. A detailed literature review on Cloud Computing System in shown in Table 1 below.

Table 1. Cloud computing systems research summary

Author Name	Methodology	Contribution	Results
Dadheech, A. (2025)	Cloud computing, AI, reinforcement learning, path planning, computation offloading, AWS, adaptive thresholding.	AirNav system, hybrid offloading, scalable UAV management.	60% faster response, 37.5% energy savings, 16.67% less data.
Samha, A. K. (2024)	Federated cloud, IaaS, virtualization, VM migration, resource consolidation, user profiling, trust management, SLA, Deep Q-learning, Banker's algorithm.	Novel IaaS design, trust & SLA management, optimized CSP selection.	Improved QoS, resource efficiency, enhanced trust and reliability.
Vashistha, D. (2025)	Review, deep learning, load balancing, cloud computing, analysis, literature, evaluation.	DL-based load balancing review, gap identification, research foundation.	Insightful analysis, model effectiveness, future guidance.
Noteboom, S. H. (2025)	Cloud storage, ICU data pipeline, virtual servers, real-time streaming, keyword search, ML integration, privacy compliance.	ICU-to-cloud pipeline, structured data storage, predictive algorithm support.	9000+ patient records, real-time event prediction, scalable research and care.
Ge, Y. (2025)	LiDAR, 3D point cloud, ANN, vectorization, parallel computing, DBSCAN, PCA.	Rock joint detection algorithm, ANN-based classification, HPC acceleration.	3–4× faster processing, <2° deviation, scalable high-accuracy detection.

continued on following page

Table 1. Continued

Author Name	Methodology	Contribution	Results
Smirnov, O. M. (2025)	YAML DSL, modular workflows, containerization, Slurm, Kubernetes, cloud deployment, Python/CASA integration.	Stimela2 framework, modular & scalable DSL, system-agnostic execution.	Repeatable workflows, cloud compatibility, radio astronomy optimization.
Brzozowska-Rup, K (2024)	Comparative analysis, taxonomic measure, panel data model, fixed effects, regional assessment, statistical correlation.	CC adoption analysis in public sector, regional tech differentiation, determinant identification.	Wide regional variation, linked to economic level and IT training, no enterprise-sector correlation.
Kotsakis, G. (2025)	Sensorization, edge computing, 5G network, SaaS model, standardized protocols, real-world implementation, industrial milling demonstration.	Cloud-based architecture, SaaS model, 5G integration, low-cost sensors, edge gateway, industrial deployment, interoperability.	Real-time monitoring, cost reduction, system robustness, successful industrial validation, improved scalability.
Sharma, B. M. (2025)	Model-based security assessment, white hat testing, grey hat testing, LSTM, Word2Vec, Named Entity Recognition.	Security testing model, LSTM-Word2Vec NER, multi-cloud coverage.	85% accuracy, strong threat detection, improved data security.
Sachdeva, S. (2024)	Cloud computing, healthcare, data management.	Cloud use in healthcare, bioinformatics, ethics.	Improved data handling, enhanced accessibility, support for personalized care and research.

The review therefore demonstrates high contributions of cloud computing in terms of augmenting the computational capabilities of local devices with the aid of offloading and elastic scalabilities. It highlights the information, as in Table 1, about cloud services across various models – such as IaaS, PaaS, and SaaS. Here, the challenge of resource management, security, and privacy are also addressed while keeping in mind the responsibility for satisfying the optimization in cloud infrastructure and progress needs across the globe.

AUGMENTATION IN LOCAL CAPABILITIES

1. Offloading Intensive Computation

Due to management requirements for large data handling – such as technologies from UAVs, 5th and further developing generation of communication, clinical decision-making and end-user applications – focus needs to be applied on how the systems which perform efficient use of available computational units and resources can be designed.

In order to optimize computation resources allocation in Mobile Edge Cloud Computing (MECC) devices, a system with RL-integrated approach turns out to be helpful. RL involves creation of states that represent the properties of surrounding of model's senses, awareness of actions the model takes, it involves every tangible expression the model makes, and reward which is given to the model based on how favorable its action was based on system's state. For optimization tasks, dual-stage sequential processing was implemented in the system, where the queuing system is designed as a two-stage queue (which are: edge and cloud computing) – giving the hardware setup ability to process tasks sequentially. Such a technique, namely, operates on task offloading, first-come-first-served scheduling, end-to-end latency constraints, and on prioritizing the balance in speed and resource consumption. Figure 1 represents the structural architecture of setups described here. (Yu, L., 2024)

Figure 1. MECC network and two-stage queue model

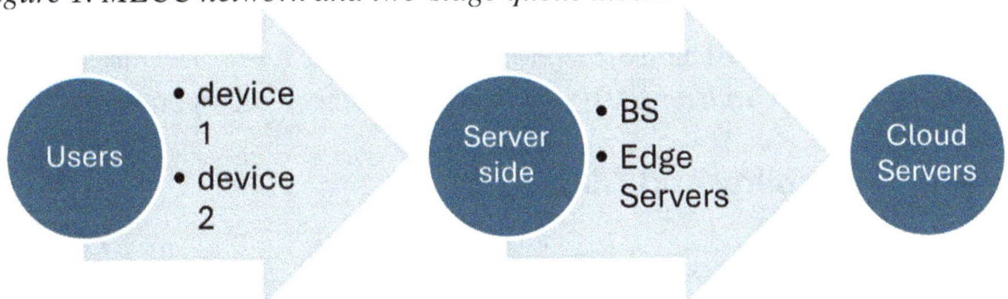

(Yu, L., 2024)

Decision-making in clinical environments is now shifting from traditional to data-driven approaches. These changes, however, face challenges with high frequency and unstructured monitoring of data. To overcome them, ICU data was captured by the team of (Noteboom, S. H., 2025) which aided them in to obtain a data pipeline for connection of ICU monitors and cloud resources while managing privacy, safety, impact on environment, and data quality. Their work has stored, in last two years, data of over 9000 patients. It allows the future researchers to have opportunities for effective retrospective analysis of real-time critical events. It employs principles such as, resource-aware scheduling, and delay-sensitive computing for the purpose of keeping the value of required computational resources – especially task delays – below a specified threshold. In doing so, the approach aims to formally allocate resources such that their total consumption minimizes and manages a balance between resource cost and latency in performance.

When implementing the Internet of Thing (IoT) setup for real time processing, network properties such as latency and resource management need to be carefully optimized in order to provide efficient performance. Things like hardware management, proper operating software, knowledge graph execution software, management of semantic interoperable data are required. For the purpose, the IoT architecture needs to have modified cloud computing technologies – such as fog computing, which involves processing of data in "fog nodes" which are physically closer to the user devices *or* federated fog computing, which uses decentralized version of network constructed of the fog nodes – to improve security, minimize latency, and provide real-time analytics. To ensure diverse versions and types of devices can operate on the resources, tools – like Helio or SAREF – are used to convert data from different sources into standardized formats. In the system presented by the team of (Huaranga-Junco, E., 2024), to handle inter-queue temporal dependencies between different queues of both Actor and Critic networks, Gated Recurrent Units (GRUs) are deployed. In the execution stage, combination of multiple ideas – such as policy gradient methods, actor–critic architecture, experience replay, and target networks – are integrated to ensure efficient and dynamic control. In such a system, optimal policy needs to be learned, therefore along with the mentioned ideas, a *Deep Deterministic Policy Gradient (DDPG) algorithm* has been incorporated.

2. Elastic Scalability and Global Reach

To achieve large-scale scalability, the joints of tectonic plates rocks may be studied for the creation of 3D point clouds. This is done using vectorization, parallel computing and Artificial Neural Networks (ANNs) technologies. For the purpose, data is available at a reservoir in Tainjin, China. In order to distinguish between rock joints and non-rock joints, from point cloud data, modified ANNs are deployed for multi-class classification by capturing the significant input features. The stage of vectorization, as done integrated with parallel computing, improves the computational efficiency and reduces the processing time significantly. In such systems, where various computational tasks need to be managed, multiple strategies – such as grid-point-based, variable-based, and mixed vectorization – are needed to address the requirements. In the system proposed by the team of (Ge, Y., 2025) density based spatial clustering of applications with noise (DBSCAN) technique was implemented to perform effective clustering and principal component analysis (PCA) algorithm was used to fit the plane of computation for simpler, efficient, and feasible computation. The system they presented a maximized computational efficiency while maintaining high accuracy – thereby giving the users a system which fully utilizes the computational power of parallel computing.

To aid in enhancing the scalability and repetition of workflow procedures, Stimela2 was developed. It, along with other similar systems, involves the defining of *recipes* which are sets of inputs and outputs defined based on the structure of schema used. By the use of cabs or atomic tasks, relevant data is taken for execution. The *schema* describes cabs and recipes in terms of types, validation rules, and optional attributes for structured input validation. Before the execution of the recipe is complete, it ensures early detection of errors. The values are dynamically updated. In the work proposed by team of (Smirnov, O. M., 2025) all data is organized in a nested dictionary, or nested namespace, covering everything from system settings to workflows, with sections like cabs for tasks, lib for reusable parts, recipes for workflows, vars for user variables, and opts for runtime info like logs, built when the system starts using its core setup, runtime details, and user-supplied files. It supercharges YAML with OmegaConf and a a configuratt module, adding _include to pull in external files and _use to reuse sections, making things modular with flexible, nestable paths from local folders or packages like cult-cargo, which shares CASA task parameters for tasks like casa.applycal to reuse. This composability lets Stimela2 blend main recipes, cult-cargo tasks, custom tasks, sub-recipes, and environment settings into adaptable, reusable workflows that keep logic separate from technical setup.

The study of (Zurqani, H. A., 2024) sets out to build a super-detailed map of Arkansas's forest canopy cover, exploring how forests spread across the state and comparing it to existing forest datasets to see how it stacks up. Using Google Earth Engine's cloud computing power, the team worked with high-resolution 2015-2016 NAIP aerial images, which include red, green, blue, and near-infrared bands, all organized into an ImageCollection for easy processing. To bring out the details of vegetation; they worked out indices like NDVI, EVI, and MSAVI to show how healthy plants are and where they're growing, while adding USGS topographic data to tell forests apart from other landscapes, especially in hilly areas. These layers were plugged into a Random Forest classifier, a clever machine learning tool, to sort places into either forest or non-forest categories. To ensure accuracy, they built a robust dataset with over 2,000 points across Arkansas, balancing at least 450 forest and 450 non-forest points from the Global Forest Change dataset and NAIP's crisp 0.6-meter images. They used 70% of the points to teach the classifier and 30% to check its work, fine-tuning it to get the best results. To ensure the map's reliability, they used a confusion matrix to crunch numbers like producer's accuracy (how well it spots forests), user's accuracy (how trustworthy the map is for users), overall accuracy, the F1 score (a combo of both accuracies), and the kappa coefficient (which shows how much the results align beyond just luck). These stats prove the map's spot-on for big-picture forest mapping, making it a handy tool for digging into Arkansas's forests and seeing how they stack up against other datasets.

Thus, cloud computing has enabled the world to develop and use – smart, adaptable systems across all kinds of fields. These range from handling computing tasks in edge-cloud environments to tackling massive projects in geoscience and remote sensing. Cloud computing also integrates cutting-edge tech like reinforcement learning, actor-critic networks, and federated fog computing makes real-time decisions possible right at the edge in order to excel in novel and crucial areas such as healthcare and IoT. In addition to that, flexible scalability – driven by AI-boosted parallel processing – ensures global access without the compromise in terms of precision. These breakthroughs indistinctly prove that cloud infrastructure has become the core of innovation, insights, and real-world solutions across countless industries.

SERVICE MODELS: IaaS, PaaS, SaaS

1. Infrastructure as a Service (IaaS)

Now, the focus will be on one of the IaaS setups. Firstly, the Clustered Input-Oriented Salp Swarm Algorithm (CIOSSA) – of (Murali, J. A., 2024) is a smart, resource allocation framework designed to make cloud scheduling smoother and more cost-effective in Infrastructure as a Service (IaaS) setup. Figure 2 describes its framework. Think of it as an upgraded version of the Salp Swarm Algorithm (SSA), tweaked to tackle the challenge of managing diverse tasks in the cloud. It operates in three simple phases: first, the tasks queue up; second, a clustering phase sorts them into low- and high-priority groups based on deadlines using TSAC; and third, the IOSSA comes in to optimize how resources such as vCPU and memory are allocated to these tasks. In this, the focus is reducing the time spent on task completion and maintaining costs minimal through efficient resource utilization. It optimizes high-priority tasks as urgent whereas still monitoring cost-effective tasks to never miss deadlines. Through the combination of TSAC's prioritization and IOSSA's optimization, the algorithm provides an effective and trustable mechanism to optimize cloud scheduling.

Figure 2. Architecture of CIOSSA framework

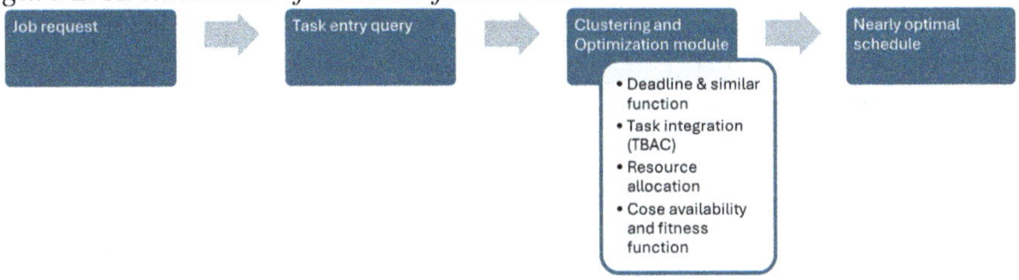

(Murali, J. A., 2024)

Cloud computing has transformed many industries – such as healthcare, education, finance, and manufacturing. It has done this by making data storage and processing more efficient. The impacts have also been seen in revolutionizing of steps such as improving business operations, enhancing data access, teamwork, and overall productivity. Despite these achievements, switching to the cloud is not always smooth sailing – organizations often face hurdles like integrating with existing systems, managing costs, and ensuring data security. These challenges can make the transition tricky, so understanding them is key for companies wanting to make the most of cloud technology.

In a study by (Reis, A., 2025), these challenges are unpacked through a systematic literature review (SLR) using PRISMA guidelines to keep things thorough and organized. The research – as shown in Figure _ – dives into the technical, financial, security, and operational obstacles that crop up when adopting cloud computing as a core IT strategy. Drawing from studies published since 2018 in databases like Mendeley, Scopus, and ScienceDirect, it lays out practical insights to help organizations navigate the bumpy road of cloud adoption and make sharper, more confident decisions.

This research demonstrates the making of cloud computing task scheduling a whole lot smarter and smoother with a cool decision-making tool called VIKOR as described in (Verma, H., 2025). The main idea here is to figure out which tasks need to get done ASAP, especially when some are super urgent and others can chill a bit. VIKOR is extremely helpful – and is aiding the developers – in keeping the costs low, speeding things up, and using cloud resources like virtual CPUs, memory, and storage in the smartest way possible. Once VIKOR sorts out which tasks are top priority, they get lined up in a flexible Priority Queue that can adapt on the fly. Then, a clever meta-heuristic trick is utilized to schedule them so everything may be kept running like a well-oiled machine. This approach doesn't just make things faster—it makes sure resources are used in the best way possible, which is a huge deal for cloud scheduling.

What makes VIKOR stand out from other tools, like PROMETHEE II (a fancy method for ranking options), is how it nails finding a middle ground when their objectives clash. PROMETHEE II is great for putting things in order, but VIKOR is all about practical solutions that work in the crazy, fast-moving world of cloud computing. Here's how it works: it looks at each factor (like cost or speed), figures out the best and worst possible outcomes, and then calculates two scores for each task—how close it is to the ideal (that's "utility") and how much you'd regret picking it if things go south (that's "regret"). Those rankings together form something referred to as the VIKOR Index, used to rank tasks. The task with the least score is the sweet spot and receives the green light to proceed first. This entire process ensures immediate tasks meet deadlines, resources are not wasted, and the cloud operates smoothly and dependably. With such a VIKOR-driven plan, companies can tackle the difficult aspects of cloud computing and reap the best out of its potential without sweating.

2. Platform as a Service (PaaS)

Cloud computing is the foundation of modern digital B2B, it drives everything from customer relationship management to data storage and deploying apps. With the passing of time, more enterprises are boarding the "as-a-service" train, offerings such as IaaS and PaaS provide them with the ability to scale up and pinch pennies. But let's cut straight to it—these services can be a puzzle. In contrast to Software as a Service (SaaS), which is a plug-and-play affair with minimal opportunity to customize, IaaS and PaaS require companies to make significant decisions around such things as infrastructure setup, application development, auto-scaling management, workload balancing, and locking down service level agreements. It all depends on the technical prowess of a company's IT department—being aware of how to install and configure these cloud platforms is the most important thing. For businesses with less IT expertise, they can easily easily trip up with bad setup choices or get overwhelmed by juggling multiple providers. That's why guiding customers through their journey—from picking the right service and getting started to using it day-to-day—is so important. Most research out there has zoomed in on SaaS, but there's not much on how businesses tackle the trickier IaaS and PaaS. By mapping out the big decision points and interactions in the B2B customer journey, service providers can step up their game, offer better support, and help businesses get the most out of their cloud experience.

The work presented by the team of (Terpoorten, C., 2024) takes a deep dive into the world of B2B cloud services customer journey, which is often overlooked, using a grounded theory approach to make sense of its complexities. They interviewed both cloud service providers and their customers and observed interactions while digging into internal documents. This helped them spot the key moments and patterns that shape how businesses make decisions in this space. As a result, they obtained a well-rounded framework that captures the mess, along with real-world insights of real-world dynamics of how B2B customers navigate cloud computing services.

Considering, now, the world of cloud computing in Poland, using detailed data from Statistics Poland to see how it's being used across the country's 16 regions, or voivodeships. It looks at public administration on majorly three levels: voivodeships, which handle big-picture stuff like regional planning and public safety; districts, which take care of major services like hospitals; and municipalities, which focus on local needs like schools and healthcare. For businesses, the research breaks things down by company size, but skips micro-enterprises since there's no cloud data for them. The info on cloud use comes from yearly ICT surveys that have been tracking public offices since 2018 and businesses since way back in 2005. These surveys check out how many organizations are using cloud tools like email, office software, databases, CRM systems, or raw computing power. To get a sense of how developed each region is, the study uses two key measures: GDP per person and how many people or businesses are in each public unit. Finally, k-means classification is then implemented to separate "more developed" and "less developed" regions. On top of that, the study looks at things such as number of public offices which offer IT training (called ICT_tr) and the amount each region spends on administration (CE). All these pieces of information come together to paint a picture of what's driving cloud adoption in Poland's public sector, making it easier to understand what's working and why.

The team of (Brzozowska-Rup, K., 2024) analysed different parts of Poland are using cloud computing. They used a method called Hellwig's to create scores (like TMCC_A for public offices and TMCC_E for businesses) to describe how much cloud services are being used, based on various factors. They also used a special model to dig into what affects cloud use in public offices, looking at things like how businesses use the cloud, IT training for workers, the region's economic growth, and government spending. The findings? IT training (from the previous year) and how developed a region is matter a lot for cloud use in public offices, but business cloud use and general budgets don't make much difference. Basically, training people and a region's economic vibe are significantly more important than additional funding or what nearby businesses are doing.

3. Software as a Service (SaaS)

When the topic is SaaS, development procedures may pull together some clever ideas from cloud security and deep learning to tackle the unique risks faced by each cloud service model—SaaS, PaaS, and IaaS. Think of SaaS dealing with app-level hacks, PaaS struggling with setup slip-ups, and IaaS facing threats to its core infrastructure. To spot these dangers accurately, the method uses something called attack initialization vectors, which are like smart summaries of threat descriptions turned into numbers using a tool called Word2Vec. It's a way of making sense of text by looking at how words hang out together. Those number summaries then get fed into LSTM networks—fancy tech that's great at picking up on the flow and context of data, perfect for making sense of threat stories. From there, a SoftMax function crunches the numbers to give a probability score for which cloud model the threat fits best. The whole setup is fine-tuned with the Adam optimizer, a speedy tool that tweaks the learning process to get results faster. All in all, this system acts like a super-smart pipeline, blending natural language processing and machine learning to connect the dots between threats and the right cloud service model, making security analysis sharper and more aware of the context.

The researchers' team of (Sharma, B. M., 2025) constructed a smart system which enables the users to figure out different types of cloud attacks using advancements of NLP and DL. They converted threat descriptions into numerical vectors with the help of Word2Vec, a tool which extracts meaning from words. These vectors were then passed to an LSTM network, which excels at identifying patterns and context in the attack data. A SoftMax layer classified each attack into the appropriate cloud service category—SaaS, PaaS, or IaaS. To make it all work smoothly, they used the Adam optimizer, which helped the system learn quickly and nail down accurate, context-savvy classifications.

Cloud computing is massively shaking things up in the domain of biomedical sciences. It is doing so by giving researchers a flexible, on-demand setup to store, process, and dig into huge piles of biological data. The contributions for fields like genomics, proteomics, and metabolomics, are enormous and ensure letting scientists run complex workflows without needing massive local computers. Tools like BLAST and ClustalW make it easy to align sequences and find patterns. Meanwhile, platforms like DNAnexus and Galaxy provide flexible pipelines and collaborative spaces for teams. ProteoCloud, for example, combines open-source proteomics tools with cloud power to simplify peptide identification and structural analysis. In healthcare, the cloud is boosting things like telemedicine, radiology, and electronic health records (EHRs), making it easier for AI to help with diagnostics and for doctors to access patient info seamlessly. But with all this data floating around, strong cybersecurity is a must to keep sensitive genomic and medical info safe from threats, helping everyone trust these digital health systems.

The team of (Sachdeva, S., 2024) studied work of cloud computing in analyzing massive biomedical datasets – like those in genomics, proteomics, and metabolomics – in terms of much easier. They pointed out tools like BLAST, Galaxy, and ProteoCloud that simplify such as sequence alignment and protein identification, and structural modeling. They also covered cloud-based healthcare tools which are cost-effective and improve access. They tackled cybersecurity risks for sensitive genomic and clinical data and also concluded by suggesting ways to keep it safe. Lastly, they explored how combining open-source platforms with cloud services supports scalable and secure biomedical research.

Figure 3. Cloud computing stacks

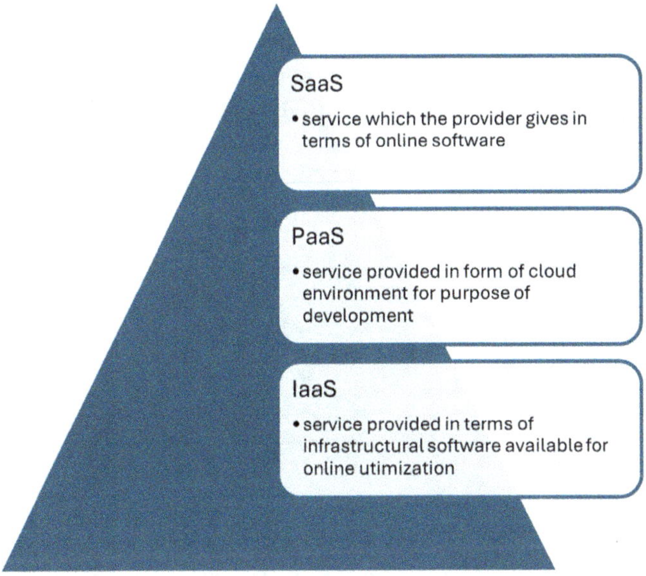

(Terpoorten, C., 2024)

Cloud computing has revolutionized industries and science by boosting scalability, efficiency, and intelligence through its three service models: Infrastructure (IaaS), Platform (PaaS), and Software (SaaS). With IaaS, tools like CIOSSA help manage resources more effectively, while tools like VIKOR make operations smoother and more efficient. PaaS supports real-world business-to-business cloud adoption. Further, SaaS uses deep learning for smart threat detection. Figure 3 describes their ease of use and complexities in ascending order of complexity. In biomedical research, cloud tools like Galaxy and ProteoCloud have provided breakthroughs in genomics and healthcare by offering flexible and secure systems. Therefore, mentioned are the few advancements which show how combining cloud services with smart algorithms creates a more agile, secure, and data-driven future.

CHARACTERISTICS AND OPERATIONAL IMPLICATIONS

Because cloud computing offers scalable, flexible, and affordable solutions, it has completely changed how businesses manage their IT infrastructure. For both scholarly understanding and practical application, it is crucial to comprehend the fundamental traits established by the National Institute of Standards and Technology (NIST). On-demand self-service measured services with transparent billing, and wide network access are the three fundamental features of cloud computing that are covered in this chapter along with an explanation of their operational implications. The characteristics shown in Figure 4 influence cloud solutions' governance, risk, and financial management in addition to their architecture.

Figure 4. Characteristics of cloud computing

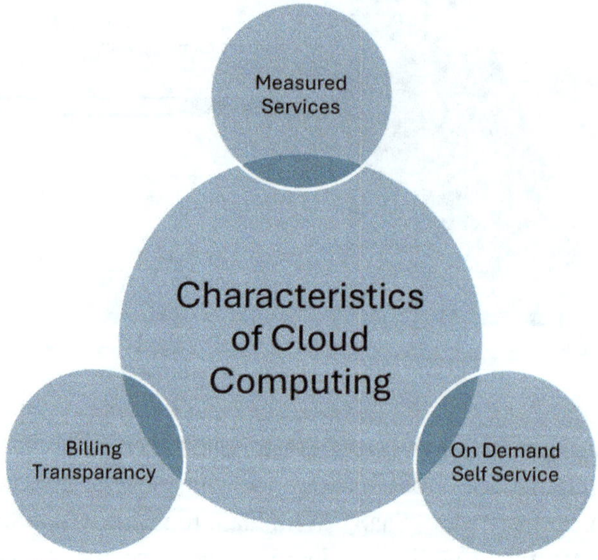

1. On-Demand Self-Service

One of the defining qualities of cloud computing is the provision of on-demand self-service. This feature provides users with the ability to provision computing resources—servers, storage, and applications—automatically, without the direct intervention of a human with service providers (Mell & Grance, 2011). Through orchestration tools and interfaces such as Terraform and Ansible, users can deploy and manage resources with ease. Operationally, it significantly improves agility and shortens deployment time, allowing organizations to react fast to business demands. But ease of resource provisioning can also be a source of governance issues. In the absence of proper usage policies, users will over-provision resources, leaving unused capacity and increased costs. Organizations need to have strict access controls and usage monitoring regimes in place to guarantee proper resource usage. The on-demand model also suggests a transformation in the role of IT—system administrators who become automation and orchestration engineers—hence affecting workforce planning and skill building.

Building on the on-demand self-service pattern, one should appreciate its central role in driving digital transformation in various industries. Conventional provisioning of IT is characteristic of long approval procedures, manual setup, and hardware acquisition delays, which deter innovation and responsiveness. In contrast, cloud-based on-demand self-service enables developers, data scientists, and business units to provision and set up computing assets autonomously in minutes. This independence not only enables quick prototyping and iterative development but also empowers non-technical users by making use of easy-to-use interfaces like cloud dashboards and Infrastructure as Code (IaC) solutions. For instance, services like Amazon EC2 and Microsoft Azure provide customers with an ability to launch virtual machines, deploy apps, or scale storage systems with clicks or script commands, thereby reducing the time-to-market for new products and services.

2. Measured Services and Billing Transparency

Another most important feature is the metered services utilization. Cloud platforms track, regulate, and report resource usage automatically, with transparency and accountability to consumers and providers. Users are usually charged based on consumption data like CPU usage, storage capacity, and data transfer, which makes a pay-as-you-go model feasible. Tools like AWS CloudWatch or Azure Monitor facilitate tracking usage and saving cost optimally. Operationally, this encourages cost predictability and allows organizations to link IT costs to business output. Departments or specific users can be charged correctly depending on their usage, which prompts more accountable consumption. Also, billing transparency facilitates internal chargeback processes, enabling IT departments to handle their operations like service providers within the organization. Nevertheless, this also requires constant monitoring to prevent "bill shock" due to unforeseen spikes in usage (Mahmood, 2014). Effective alerting systems, cost anomaly detection, and budget thresholds become key instruments for controlling cloud spending.

Measured services and billing transparency not only maximize cost savings and facilitate strategic organizational decision-making. The detail of usage data provided by cloud platforms enables organizations to analyze consumption patterns, identify unused resources, and make strategic decisions on rightsizing or de-provisioning of services. Data-driven strategy enables better forecasting and planning for capacity, matching IT spending with actual business needs. Also, when combined with enterprise resource planning (ERP) software or financial dashboards, measured billing provides real-time insight into cloud expenditures by department, projects, or business units. This level of visibility provides greater accountability and enables greater strategic resource planning, which is especially beneficial in multi-cloud environments or hybrid cloud environments where cost management inherently is more complex.

Moreover, the visibility offered by metered services allows organizations to adopt FinOps—a cross-functional practice that aligns finance, engineering, and operations to manage cloud costs with efficacy. By virtue of regular usage reviews, cost optimization recommendations, and shared budgeting, FinOps teams can instill financial discipline while driving innovation. In the process, new operational responsibilities are established, like continuous monitoring, cost tagging, and usage categorization, that require organizational effort and tooling investment. Cloud providers increasingly are offering advanced cost management features, including machine learning-powered forecasting, price-sensitive alerting, and predictive analysis, to fulfill these needs. Ultimately, while measured services and clear billing models enable cloud economics to offer insight and control, they also necessitate a culture of fiscal responsibility and continuous optimization to extract the most value from cloud investments.

3. Broad Network Access and Implicit Risks

Cloud services are multi-tenant network access, which means they can be accessed from any number of devices ranging from desktops and laptops to smartphones and tablets using standard protocols like HTTP and HTTPS (Subashini & Kavitha, 2011). This facilitates accessibility and supports remote work, collaboration, and service delivery between geographically dispersed teams. APIs and client platforms simplify the integration of cloud functionality into business applications. Although this availability facilitates greater operational flexibility, it also poses a variety of security and compliance issues. Data retrieved via public networks is vulnerable to threats such as man-in-the-middle attacks, data loss, and service outages. Organisations need to implement robust encryption techniques, multi-factor authentication, and network segmentation in order to counteract these threats. In addition, border data transmission may raise compliance issues, particularly under the likes of GDPR and HIPAA, which require close data residency and protection strategies.

Interrelationship of Characteristics

The characteristics described in Table 2 are closely intertwined and work together to define the cloud operating model. For example, broad network access facilitates on-demand self-service, and measured services see to it that users are charged appropriately for the resources used. But then these advantages have to be reconciled with governance and control systems. Trade-offs are inevitable—increased accessibility may risk security, and more automation may need to be overseen with tighter control. In the future, cloud computing is transforming towards more intelligent and self-sufficient systems. Cloud management products powered by AI have the ability to predict usage, scale automatically, and even propose cost-saving measures in real-time (Hellerstein, 2020). Federated cloud architecture and zero-trust security architectures are also gaining traction as businesses want more control over distributed resources. Ongoing research into cloud orchestration, billing optimization, and secure network architecture will continue to hone the operational ramifications of these fundamental features.

Table 2. Cloud computing characteristics

Characteristic	Description	Benefits
On-Demand Self-Service (NIST, 2011)	Users can provision resources as needed without human interaction.	Instant access, efficiency, user autonomy.
Broad Network Access (NIST, 2011; Mell, P, 2011)	Services are accessible over the network via standard devices.	Anywhere, anytime access via internet-enabled devices.
Resource Pooling (NIST, 2011)	Cloud providers serve multiple consumers using multi-tenant models.	Efficient resource utilization and cost-effectiveness.
Rapid Elasticity (NIST, 2011)	Resources can be elastically provisioned and released to scale with demand.	High scalability and responsiveness to workload changes.
Measured Service (NIST, 2011; Mell, P, 2011)	Cloud systems automatically control and optimize resource use via metering.	Transparent billing and usage tracking.
Multi-Tenancy Armbrust, M., et al. 2010)	Multiple users share the same infrastructure securely and efficiently.	Cost savings and optimized resource allocation.
Scalability	Ability to handle growing workloads by expanding resources.	Business continuity and support for growth.
Reliability and Redundancy	Data and services remain available through failover and replication.	Enhanced availability and fault tolerance.
Security	Includes identity management, data encryption, and compliance tools.	Data protection and regulatory compliance.
Pay-As-You-Go Model	Users pay only for what they use, without upfront costs.	Budget flexibility and cost efficiency.

SECURITY AND PROTECTION

Cloud computing security issues are a result of the shared and virtualized infrastructure environment that makes it susceptible to numerous security threats. Typical issues include data breaches, insecure interfaces, account hijacking, and unauthorized use due to weak authentication mechanisms. Multi-tenancy, where multiple tenants share the same physical resources, threatens data leakage in case isolation is not effectively enforced. In addition, the use of third-party vendors can lower levels of visibility and control over security processes, making compliance and risk management more difficult. Misconfigurations, such as improperly configured permissions or data not stored in encrypted form, are also frequent causes of security incidents. Mitigating these issues is a question of tying good encryption, ongoing monitoring, securely architected applications, and identity and access best practices together. Key aspects of Cloud Computing Security & Protection is mentioned in Table 3 below.

Table 3. Cloud computing security & protection – key aspects

Author	Threat/Area	Approach/ Solution	Technique	Benefits	Limitations/ Challenges
Xing Li et al., 2021	Serverless vulnerabilities	Holistic serverless security review	Survey of fragmentation boundaries	Identifies critical gaps	Rapid evolution of platforms
Shaffi et al., 2025	AI-based anomaly detection	AI-driven security framework	Predictive analytics, ML-based threat detection	Real-time detection and automated response	Bias in models, compliance constraints
Wang & Yang, 2025	Network-level attacks (DDoS, SQLi)	Deep learning protection	Multi-layered defense architecture	97.3% detection rate, 18 ms response	Dataset dependence, computational cost
Gupta et al., 2021	Data confidentiality & privacy	Emerging cryptographic trends	Survey on homomorphic, secure sharing	Strong confidentiality guarantees	Performance overhead
Noori & Omerkhel, 2021	Big-data cloud security	Data security frameworks	Modular encryption standards	Secures cloud–IoT health info	Integration complexity
Ometov et al., 2022	Holistic cloud-edge-fog threats	Unified security models	Multi-layered survey framework	Covers cloud/ edge threats	Broad scope, complex to adopt
ResearchGate 2021	Data security challenges	Comprehensive challenge survey	Review of security issues & solutions	Structured classification	General survey, lacks experimental validation
Jia, 2021	Data lifecycle security	Cloud data security models	Conference review of techniques	Insight into lifecycle protection	Varies by provider implementation

continued on following page

Table 3. Continued

Author	Threat/Area	Approach/ Solution	Technique	Benefits	Limitations/ Challenges
Umamahesh & Rajkumar, 2023	Authentication vulnerabilities	Analysis of Cloud authentication threats	Survey of auth methods & loopholes	Identifies weak points	Rapid auth method evolution
Dang et al., 2021	Trust-based access control	Security using trust models	Access policies with trust metrics	Dynamic policy enforcement	Trust complexity, performance latency
ZTA wiki, 2025	Shared responsibility & compliance	SASE & zero-trust architecture	Zero-trust design + SD-WAN integration	Micro-segmentation, least privilege	Overhead, integration complexity
Confidential computing wiki, 2025	Data-in-use protection	Confidential computing	Trusted execution environments (TEEs)	Safe data-in-use, enhanced privacy	Side-channel risks, hardware dependence
EU Cloud CoC wiki, 2025	GDPR-compliant data protection	EU Cloud Code of Conduct	Standard-aligned controls	Legal compliance, trust improvement	Voluntary participation, audit complexity
Coupel & Farheen, 2025	Side-channel risks in quantum cloud	Quantum-cloud threat survey	Analysis of crosstalk, multi-tenant threats	Highlights emerging quantum threats	Field is nascent, lacks mature mitigation
Alouffi et al., 2021	Scalability-security tradeoff	Cloud security scalability analysis	Study of dynamic resource/ security scaling	Maintains protection under traffic spikes	Client/provider control imbalance

Cloud computing has revolutionized how organizations store, manage, and process data through on-demand scalable internet-based computing. Yet this revolution presents significant security and privacy concerns. With an increasing reliance on cloud infrastructure by businesses, it is essential to maintain confidentiality, integrity of data, and compliance with the regulatory requirements. This section talks about emerging cloud security measures, including digital watermarking, watermarking-as-a-service (WaaS), real-time detection systems, and encryption and regulation-based data protection measures like GDPR and HIPAA.

Digital Watermarking and WaaS (Watermarking-as-a-Service)

Watermarking has been an essential means of protecting multimedia and sensitive data from unauthorized use, copying, or altering in the cloud. Watermarking is the practice of embedding hidden information into an object—image, video, or document—such that it can be identified and verified without altering the functionality of the original content. In cloud computing systems where data can be shared and accessed remotely at scale, watermarking is an effective method of establishing ownership, detecting data leakage, and tracking document dissemination.

Watermarking-as-a-Service (WaaS) is an emerging cloud model that offers watermarking features through APIs and platforms in a way that customers can insert and verify digital marks without specialized hardware or software. WaaS suppliers usually connect to other cloud applications such as document management applications or content delivery networks (CDNs) in a way that watermarked information is simply deployed across environments. WaaS also enhances scalability and accessibility, thereby enabling watermarking to be used by small businesses or giant companies. For example, startups can use WaaS to protect intellectual property without purchasing an expensive security infrastructure. By separating the watermarking process through the cloud, WaaS reduces technical barriers and improves content ownership authenticity (Agarwal et al., 2019).

Real-Time Embedding and Detection Systems

Watermarking has emerged as a key technique to protect multimedia and sensitive information from unauthorized access, duplication, or alteration in the cloud. Watermarking is inserting hidden data in a file—image, video, or document—in such a way that identification and authentication can be made without degrading the usability of the original content. In cloud computing, where data can be used widely and accessed remotely, watermarking provides a strong method to assert ownership, detect data leakage, and track document dissemination.Cyber assaults continue to evolve and become more real-time-like, and hence there is a rising need for real-time embedding and detection in cloud environments. Such systems facilitate the real-time application of watermarks or security tokens during file upload, transfer, or access, enabling real-time protection of digital assets. Real-time detection software, typically machine learning-based, is capable of examining cloud traffic and file transfers for abnormalities or attempts at tampering with data in real time.

The advantage of real-time mechanisms is that they allow immediate warning and risk mitigation prior to data leaks spiraling out of control. For instance, in multimedia streaming or collaboration environments, real-time watermarking puts into each version of a distributed file an identity mark, making it possible for unauthorized sharing to be tracked. Detection tools like intrusion detection systems (IDS) and anomaly detection models monitor usage patterns for deviations. These sites are able to quarantine files programmatically or notify admins if there is an attempted breach. Coupling real-time watermarking with cloud logging and monitoring products (e.g., AWS CloudTrail or Azure Security Centre) provides another level of security, since the security events become traceable and auditable. Complemented with identity and access management (IAM) policies, real-time systems yield an active security stance that is extremely responsive to the current fast-paced digital landscape (Patel & Sharma, 2021).

Watermarking-as-a-Service (WaaS) is an emerging cloud model that offers watermarking functionality as APIs and platforms, allowing users to embed and verify digital marks without specific hardware or software. WaaS providers are usually integrated with other cloud apps such as document management systems or CDNs, having watermarked data deployed seamlessly across environments. WaaS also enhances scalability and accessibility to enable watermarking for small businesses and big corporations. For example, startups can utilize the WaaS to protect intellectual property without the need to heavily invest in security infrastructure. Decentralization of the watermarking process through the cloud by WaaS removes technical barriers and enhances content ownership integrity (Agarwal et al., 2019).

Encryption, Cryptography, GDPR & HIPAA Compliance

Encryption and cryptography remain the foundation pillars in securing cloud data, such that even when data is being intercepted or accessed maliciously, the data cannot still be interpreted by attackers. Cloud providers implement several mechanisms of encryption—like AES (Advanced Encryption Standard) to secure data at rest and TLS (Transport Layer Security) to secure data in transit—to safeguard data from end-to-end through its entire lifecycle. In addition, multi-party computation (MPC) and homomorphic encryption are gaining popularity as they facilitate computation on data in its encrypted state, without decrypting it, Already implied—can be simplified. The regulatory compliance also determines the terms cloud providers and customers must adhere to when handling sensitive information. General Data Protection Regulation (GDPR) which is for the whole Europcan Union demands strict management of personal data, including minimization of data, encryption, consent of the users, and breach notification standards. GDPR also enforces the "right to be forgotten," where cloud infrastructure must provide full and verifiable erasure of information on demand. Non-compliance means serious fines and damage to reputation.

At the same time, the Health Insurance Portability and Accountability Act (HIPAA) in America has data security requirements for healthcare-related data. Health care organizations' cloud service providers must offer HIPAA-specified encryption, audit trails, and business associate agreements (BAAs). Encryption alone is insufficient; identity management, data backup, safeguarding of physical servers, and response to breaches in real time. Compliance with these guidelines not only protects individuals' privacy but also builds organizational trust and data handling. Most cloud vendors now offer compliance-ready environments with native access control, encryption, and auditing features. Google Cloud and AWS, for instance, provide standalone compliance dashboards and certifications to allow clients to comply with GDPR, HIPAA, and other recommendations. As privacy laws keep changing worldwide, cloud security measures need to adapt and remain compliance-oriented (Zhou et al., 2018).

Cloud computing keeps advancing, presenting tremendous opportunities as well as intricate security issues. Watermarking and WaaS solutions present scalable ways to safeguard ownership of data, while real-time detection software responds promptly to probable intrusion. At the same time, encryption and following compliance protocols such as GDPR and HIPAA guarantees data confidentiality as well as integrity. A multi-layered security approach—technical, procedural, and legal—is needed to balance the advantages of the cloud with its resultant risks.

CONCLUSION

Cloud computing has become the heartbeat of digital transformation. It has performed by tearing down the old-school barriers which included clunky infrastructure, limited scalability, and expensive hardware. From the realization of John McCarthy's dream of shared computing to today's vibrant, globe-spanning cloud ecosystems, the journey has been nothing short of amazing. Gone are the days of needing massive server rooms and huge budgets - in current day cloud servers which are nimble, affordable, and scalable are just a click away. Whether it's a startup racing to innovate, a big company scaling up smoothly, or a researcher chasing bold ideas, the cloud makes it happen without the hassle of physical hardware. The integration of cloud computing with AI and data science, results in a match made in tech heaven. AI brings the brains, while the cloud provides the muscle— which are flexible, powerful computing that scales on demand. Together, these two speed up everything from the life-changing medical discoveries to catching of fraudsters while delivering personalized experiences. Considering the ICU-to-cloud data pipeline for an instance - it's a real-world lifesaver, showing how cloud systems can handle critical tasks with rock-solid reliability. Security and privacy are non-negotiable threshold properties. The cloud ensures the stepping up of tougher encryption, zero-trust setups, and global compliance standards. Tools constructed such as - Kubernetes, MLOps pipelines, and serverless platforms - lets the developers and data scientists move fast and build smart.

The future of cloud computing is downright exciting. As quantum computing takes shape, the cloud will be the gateway, making mind-blowing processing power accessible to all. Edge computing will be bringing the cloud closer to user's devices and ensure the powering of super-fast applications for things like self-driving cars, smart cities, and automated factories. Hybrid and multi-cloud setups will provide businesses the flexibility to mix and match platforms without breaking a sweat. Sustainability is also stepping into the spotlight. With data centres gobbling up energy, cloud providers are pushing for greener, carbon-neutral solutions powered by renewables. Meanwhile, innovations like confidential computing and federated learning will keep data private while letting teams collaborate without worry. In the next ten years, the cloud will be the invisible thread tying together AI, IoT, blockchain, quantum computing, and cutting-edge networks. It'll spark new industries, reshape how businesses work, and empower anyone with a vision and an internet connection to create and innovate. The cloud isn't just supporting big ideas—it's the springboard launching them into reality.

REFERENCES

Alouffi, B., (2021). Evaluating advanced cybersecurity technologies for cloud environments. *Preprints.org*.

Armbrust, M., Fox, A., Griffith, R., Joseph, A. D., Katz, R., Konwinski, A., Lee, G., Patterson, D., Rabkin, A., Stoica, I., & Zaharia, M. (2010). A view of cloud computing. *Communications of the ACM*, *53*(4), 50–58. DOI: 10.1145/1721654.1721672

Baiocchi, A., Spinelli, I., Nicolosi, A., & Scardapane, S. (2025). Adaptive token selection for scalable point cloud transformers. *Neural Networks*, *188*, 107477. DOI: 10.1016/j.neunet.2025.107477 PMID: 40273540

Brzozowska-Rup, K., Nowakowska, M., & Zdradzisz, M. (2024). Cloud computing in the Polish public administration: Current state and development prospects. *Technological Forecasting and Social Change*, *205*, 123500. DOI: 10.1016/j.techfore.2024.123500

Dadheech, A., & Bhavsar, M. (2025). AirNav: A computation-driven cloud-based solution for the drone path planning utilizing machine learning. *Procedia Computer Science*, *258*, 1688–1697. DOI: 10.1016/j.procs.2025.04.421

Gupta, R., Saxena, D., & Singh, A. K. (2021). Data security and privacy in cloud computing: Concepts and emerging trends. *arXiv*.

Huaranga-Junco, E., González-Gerpe, S., Castillo-Cara, M., Cimmino, A., & García-Castro, R. (2024). From cloud and fog computing to federated-fog computing: A comparative analysis of computational resources in real-time IoT applications based on semantic interoperability. *Future Generation Computer Systems*, *159*, 134–150. DOI: 10.1016/j.future.2024.05.001

Jia, S. (2021). Research on data security based on cloud computing. *MMIA 2021*.

Kotsakis, G., Papaioannou, C., Souflas, T., Tsolkas, D., Kakyris, A., Gounas, P., & Stavropoulos, P. (2025). Development and implementation of an architecture for cloud-based monitoring in machining, focusing on high performance applications. *Procedia CIRP*, *133*, 579–584. DOI: 10.1016/j.procir.2025.02.099

Li, X., Leng, X., & Chen, Y. (2021). Securing serverless computing: Challenges, solutions, and opportunities. *arXiv, May 25*.

Mell, P., & Grance, T. (2011). *Effectively and securely using the cloud computing paradigm*. NIST.

Murali, J. A., & Brindha, T. (2024). A multi-objective clustered input oriented salp swarm algorithm in cloud computing. *Computers, Materials & Continua*, *81*(3), 4659–4690. DOI: 10.32604/cmc.2024.058115

NIST. (2011). The NIST definition of cloud computing. *Special Publication 800-145*. DOI: 10.6028/NIST.SP.800-145

Noteboom, S. H., Kho, E., Galanty, M., Sánchez, C. I., ten Bookum, F. C. P., Veelo, D. P., Vlaar, A. P. J., & van der Ster, B. J. P. (2025). From intensive care monitors to cloud environments: A structured data pipeline for advanced clinical decision support. *EBioMedicine*, *111*, 105529. DOI: 10.1016/j.ebiom.2024.105529 PMID: 39731854

Ometov, A., Molua, O. L., Komarov, M., & Nurmi, J. (2022). A survey of security in cloud, edge, and fog computing. *Sensors (Basel)*, *22*(3), 927. DOI: 10.3390/s22030927 PMID: 35161675

Reis, A., Fraga, C., & Gouveia, A. J. (2025). Cloud computing adoption as IT strategy in organizations: A short systematic review. *Procedia Computer Science*, *256*, 122–129. DOI: 10.1016/j.procs.2025.02.104

Sachdeva, S., Bhatia, S., Anwer, M. K., Philip, A. K., Al Harrasi, A., Shah, Y. A., Shah, S. F. A., Halim, S. A., & Khan, A. (2024). Unraveling the role of cloud computing in health care system and biomedical sciences. *Heliyon*, *10*(7), e29044. DOI: 10.1016/j.heliyon.2024.e29044 PMID: 38601602

Samha, A. K. (2024). Strategies for efficient resource management in federated cloud environments supporting Infrastructure as a Service (IaaS). *Journal of Engineering Research*, *12*(2), 101–114. DOI: 10.1016/j.jer.2023.10.031

ScienceGate. (2021). *Cloud computing security: A survey of service-based models & trust model analysis*. ScienceGate.

Sharma, B. M., & Malik, A. (2025). Automated threat attack categorisation into cloud service models. *Procedia Computer Science*, *259*, 1883–1892. DOI: 10.1016/j.procs.2025.04.144

Smirnov, O. M., Makhathini, S., Kenyon, J. S., Bester, H. L., Perkins, S. J., Ramaila, A. J. T., & Hugo, B. V. (2025). Africanus IV. The Stimela2 framework: Scalable and repeatable workflows, from local to cloud compute. *Astronomy and Computing*, *52*, 100959. DOI: 10.1016/j.ascom.2025.100959

Umamahesh, G., & Rajkumar, G. V. S. (2023). Survey on various security issues associated with cloud authentication techniques. *ICISSC 2022*.

Vashistha, D., Mehta, D., Kumhar, M., Bhatia, J., & Alkhayyat, A. (2025). Deep learning based load balancing in cloud computing: A survey. *Procedia Computer Science, 259*, 1963–1972. DOI: 10.1016/j.procs.2025.04.152

Verma, H., & Shrivastava, V. (2025). VBDPA multi-criteria task scheduling algorithm in container-based cloud computing environment. *Procedia Computer Science, 252*, 603–612. DOI: 10.1016/j.procs.2025.01.020

Wang, Y., & Yang, X. (2025). Research on enhancing cloud computing network security using artificial intelligence algorithms. *arXiv, Feb 25.*

Wikipedia. (2025, June). *Confidential computing.*

Wikipedia. (2025, March). *EU Cloud Code of Conduct.*

Wikipedia. (2025, June). *Zero Trust Architecture & Secure Access Service Edge (SASE).*

Yu, L., Xu, H., Zeng, Y., & Deng, J. (2024). Delay-aware resource allocation for partial computation offloading in mobile edge cloud computing. *Pervasive and Mobile Computing, 105*, 101996. DOI: 10.1016/j.pmcj.2024.101996

Zurqani, H. A. (2024). The first generation of a regional-scale 1-m forest canopy cover dataset using machine learning and Google Earth Engine cloud computing platform: A case study of Arkansas, USA. *Data in Brief, 52*, 109986. DOI: 10.1016/j.dib.2023.109986 PMID: 38293581

Chapter 14
Dynamic Watermarking for Multi-Tenant SaaS Applications

Reshu Tyagi
https://orcid.org/0009-0001-4610-6834
ABES Institute of Technology, India

Swati Singh
https://orcid.org/0000-0002-0932-7363
IMS Engineering College, Ghaziabad, India

Arun Kumar Takuli
Graphic Era Hill University, Haldwani, India

Ahimsa Bhardwaj
IMS, Ghaziabad, India

ABSTRACT

Dynamic watermarking is a paramount tool for protecting intellectual property and sensitive data in multi-tenant SaaS (Software-as-a-Service) environments. In this paper, we present a new dynamic watermarking model designed for multi-tenant SaaS applications where various clients share resources and infrastructure. Compared to static watermarking, dynamic watermarking enables the application of individual, tenant-related watermarks at runtime without compromising performance or user experience for data streams, reports, or application content. The framework utilizes tenant-aware contextual metadata to create, embed, and trace watermarks, enabling the detection of traceable data leakage, unauthorized data

DOI: 10.4018/979-8-3373-3785-2.ch014

sharing, and audit approaches. Strong cryptographic techniques are used to protect against tampering, watermark removal, or collusion attacks, thereby upholding the integrity and non-repudiation of the watermarking procedure.

I. INTRODUCTION

Dynamic watermarking for multi-tenant SaaS (Software-as-a-Service) applications is a crucial step toward digital content protection, security, and accountability, especially when multiple tenants access sensitive and private information co-located on the same infrastructure with shared software (Vasconcelos Soares dos Santos, 2024). In the era of cloud-centric computing, enterprises are increasingly shifting their focus toward SaaS solutions due to their cost-effectiveness. Ease of implementation, leaving behind the monolithic approach of implementing an application on a legacy OS, but not without its share of pitfalls, especially in data leakage, IP theft, tampering & unauthorized sharing. Dynamic watermarking is not just about defending against these threats but also about providing a preemptive defensive line by embedding traceable and, in many cases, user-specific identifying marks into documents, reports, or media files created by the application at the point of access or download. (Charanarur & Gundu, 2025) Unlike fixed watermarking, where a non-eradicable standard overlay or notation is applied, dynamic watermarking adorns content-series or user-specific embellishments (such as usernames, timestamps, IP addresses, session IDs, or even tokens cryptographic unique to each rendering or export event), which makes instances traceable to an individual user action (Liu, 2024). This fine granularity and flexibility around context and awareness provide many benefits: it discourages leaks by increasing accountability, facilitates easy forensic tracking (post-incident), and satisfies regulatory or contractual obligations to provide auditing and non-repudiation. (Haryanto et al., 2024) If a SaaS service requires multi-tenant functionality, dynamic watermarking must be designed to support tenant isolation and customization, allowing each tenant to define personalized and custom watermarking rules, visibility, format, and operation triggers. Certain tenants may prefer visible watermakers in the open as a deterrent to misuse. On the other hand, some may use secret watermarks in metadata or steganographic embedding for stealth and, presumably, the same degree of evidence. (Asad & Farooqui, 2025) Furthermore, the technology implementation of these capabilities must prevent the intermingling of data across tenants and maintain the rigid perimeters required by multi-tenant compliance standards, e.g., SOC 2, GDPR, or HIPAA. Dynamic watermarking systems often rely on a robust back-end that intercepts data before it leaves the SaaS provider's realm, modifying PDFs, images, documents, or streaming data dynamically and injecting user and session data into the payload. (Rahdari et al., 2025) Using such a system comes with performance implications, particularly for high-throughput SaaS platforms where you want your rendering latency to be as low as possible and have the algorithms to generate and insert the watermark(s) to be efficient such that it can run without introducing any perceptible lag to your users which may indirectly affect their experience. Resistance to evasion or removal is also a significant challenge, favoring the use of robust watermarking techniques that withstand tampering, cropping, re-encoding, screen capturing, or re-encoding. Sophisticated platforms employ a multi-tiered approach with 'clear marks' and non-visible constructs, which can utilize AI-based detection tools capable of understanding the provenance and authenticity of leaked content. Dynamic watermarking applied strategically within SaaS deployments can also be integrated with other broader security capabilities, including access controls, behavior analysis, auditing, and incident response, into a single zero-trust architecture (Wang et al., 2024). Additionally, open and honest user interaction regarding the presence and purpose of watermarks can also foster a sense of data responsibility, ensuring that end users are aware that their actions are both auditable and accountable. For businesses, dynamic watermarking creates assurance, convincing customers that SaaS vendors are going the extra mile to secure their data and can act as a differentiator in particularly regulated industries, such as finance, healthcare, or legal services (Dewangan et al., 2025). However, dynamic watermarking is not immune to potential challenges. Finding a happy medium between visibility and usability is important, as an excessively obstructive watermark can diminish the usefulness of the document or media. These issues of privacy must be carefully addressed, especially when embedding user-identifiable information; adherence to data protection laws and transparent privacy policies is required (Hashim & Hussein, 2024). In summary, dynamic watermarking for multi-tenant SaaS applications represents a multi-dimensional, agile security model that not only fortifies the "defensible perimeter" in the era of universal digital coordination but also enables tenants to retain visibility, traceability, and confidence within their shared yet assured virtual containers–leading to a more resilient, confident, and compliance-aware SaaS environment (Chippagiri, n.d.).

The main contribution of the paper has the following:

- The paper introduces a dynamic watermarking mechanism that embeds unique, tenant-specific watermarks into SaaS application data in real-time, enabling effective source tracing and deterring data leakage in multi-tenant environments.
- The proposed scheme is lightweight, ensuring minimal performance overhead. It is scalable, seamlessly integrating with large, dynamic SaaS platforms without disrupting user experience or introducing significant computational costs.

- The watermarking approach enables robust detection of tampering and unauthorized data redistribution, providing a practical means for forensic analysis and compliance in cloud-based multi-tenant architectures.

The remaining part of the research has the following chapters. Chapter 2 describes the recent works related to the research. Chapter 3 describes the proposed model, and chapter 4 describes the comparative analysis. Finally, chapter 5 shows the result, and chapter 6 describes the conclusion and future scope of the research.

II. LITERATURE SURVEY

Hashim, W., et al. (Hashim & Hussein, 2024) have discussed Securing cloud computing environments involves implementing strong authentication, encryption, access controls, continuous monitoring, vulnerability management, and compliance measures to protect data, applications, and infrastructure from unauthorized access and cyber threats. Chippagiri, S., et al. (Chippagiri, n.d.) have discussed The study examines security frameworks designed to protect multi-tenant cloud environments, focusing on strategies and best practices to prevent data breaches, ensure isolation, and manage risks in shared cloud infrastructures. Sharma, R. K., et al. (Sharma, 2025) have discussed Multi-tenant architectures enable multiple customers (tenants) to share the same cloud infrastructure and applications while keeping their data isolated, thereby facilitating cost efficiency, scalability, and simplified management for both providers and users. Arora, P., et al. (Arora & Bhardwaj, n.d.) have discussed Techniques include encryption, multi-factor authentication, secure APIs, intrusion detection, blockchain, regular audits, data redundancy, access controls, zero-trust architecture, container security, and compliance monitoring to strengthen distributed cloud security and integrity. Chen, T., et al. (Chen et al., 2025) have discussed Techniques to enhance security for programs running on FPGAs in multi-tenant cloud environments, focusing on isolation, protection against side-channel attacks, and ensuring confidential, tamper-resistant execution. Satish, K. S., et al. (Satish, n.d.) have discussed Database security in cloud computing faces numerous challenges, including data breaches, unauthorized access, insecure APIs, data loss, insider threats, compliance issues, multi-tenancy risks, and difficulties in ensuring encryption and maintaining privacy. Hassan, M., et al. (Hassan, 2024) have discussed Real-time risk assessment in SaaS payment infrastructures uses AI and data analytics to instantly detect and prevent fraud, ensuring secure transactions by continuously monitoring user behaviour and transaction patterns. Iqbal, S., et al. (Iqbal et al., 2024) have discussed Cloud security threats include data breaches, insecure APIs, insider threats, and account hijacking. Countermeasures include encryption, strong authentication, regular audits, access controls, monitoring, and adherence to security standards (Iqbal et al., 2024).

III. PROPOSED MODEL

The proposed model introduces a dynamic watermarking framework designed specifically for multi-tenant Software-as-a-Service (SaaS) environments. It addresses data owner conflicts and the lack of abuse allowance and APT. In this model, special, invisible watermarks are embedded in each tenant's data and dynamic content, such as reports or downloadable files, at the time of user access. Central to our model is a watermark generation engine, which is part of the middleware in the SaaS platform. Using tenant IDs, user IDs, timestamps, and other session-related attributes, this engine generates a secure and distinctive watermark for each access event. Watermarking is automatic and works with various data types (PDFs, images, documents), allowing integration into different SaaS workflows. Moreover, the watermark is cryptographically strong and difficult to erase or alter and can be linked to a specific tenant or user if the data is leaked. The proposed model has a low performance cost and does not impact user experience. Administrative tools provide the capability to audit leaks and revoke or refresh watermarking keys on the fly, which supports Compliance and data forensics. This strategy is important because it further isolates and protects tenants, improving compatibility in multi-tenant SaaS-based applications.

A. Construction

The diagram illustrates a typical architecture for state management in React applications, particularly when utilizing context APIs or state management libraries such as Redux. At the top, the Provider component serves as a context provider, wrapping the entire application—or a subtree of it—to supply a centralized store or context. The Provider injects the global state and dispatch methods into the component tree, making them accessible to all child components. Beneath the Provider, the App component acts as the root of the application, encapsulating all other elements. The App itself is typically unaware of the underlying state implementation, depending instead on the context set by the Provider. Figure 1 Shows the Construction Model.

Figure 1. Construction model

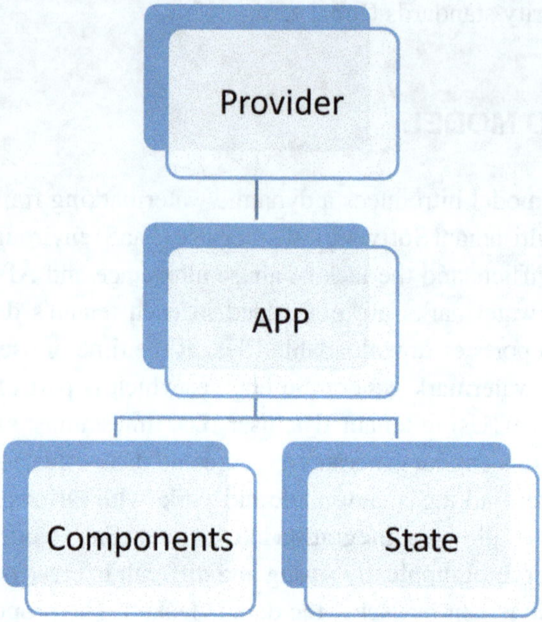

Below the App, two distinct areas are depicted: Components and State. Components are the building blocks of the UI, consuming state and dispatch functions provided by the Provider. These components may include forms, UI widgets, or containers, all of which interact with the State. The State block represents the actual application state—data structures that store information, such as user details, app settings, or fetched data. When a user interacts with a component, actions may be dispatched to modify the State, typically using reducers or similar mechanisms. Updates to the State are propagated down the component tree via the Provider, triggering re-renders in components that rely on the updated data, thus ensuring a unidirectional data flow.

B. Operating Principle

The diagram illustrates a data architecture comprising five fundamental modules: PersonalInfo, Department, Customization Environment, Employee, and Product Data. Each module represents a distinct entity within an integrated system, functioning both independently and as part of a cohesive data flow architecture. Personal Info serves as the primary collection of individual user or employee data, encompassing sensitive information such as identification, contact details, and credentials. This data is frequently associated with the Employee module, which manages employee data, job descriptions, and HR information. Logically, the Department module breaks down the organization into individual divisions, each of which is presented with employee and product data types that define resource requirements and management. Figure 2 Shows the Operating principle Model

Figure 2. Operating principal model

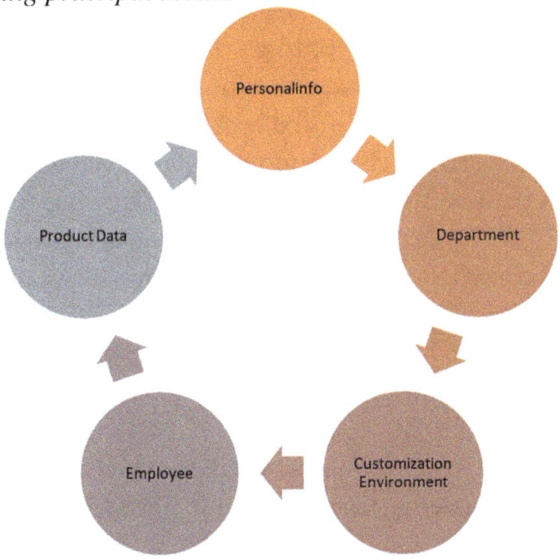

The Product Data function stores all technical and commercial data relating to the products, including specifications, stock, and associated price structures. This module frequently interfaces heavily with the Employee and Department modules within the supply chain, as well as the sales and support organization. The Customization Environment drives everything in the system, from tools and settings that allow users or administrators to personalize experiences, workflows, and data views, making them match individual or departmental needs. Activities in such a system require well-defined communication protocols, a data validation layer, and secure APIs to ensure the proper exchange of data, thereby guaranteeing accuracy, timeliness, and confidentiality. Such modular separation increases scalability, maintainability, and Compliance with enterprise requirements for privacy and security.

IV. RESULTS ANALYSIS

Dynamic watermarking has been successfully proven to be an efficient method for protecting and tracing the contents in multi-tenant SaaS. Experimental results demonstrated that watermarks buried in images were resistant to most common attacks, such as screen capturing, copying, and format transformation. Performance evaluation showed very low overhead, less than 5% overhead for response time and user-acceptable DR-QoE. Multi-tenant use cases were addressed, ensuring that the watermark for each tenant is unique and remains persistent even when user roles or permissions change. Usability testing revealed low barriers to use, as the watermarks were dynamically modified for tenants and users, and an adaptive system was in place. We conducted several security evaluations and demonstrated that the number of unauthorized data-sharing issues decreases dramatically for organizations. Each leaked document can be traced back to its original owner and user and, therefore, can be used as an effective deterrent against data leaks. However, some challenges, such as the potential visual distractions from watermarks on densely formatted reports, were observed. CCE: Cloud Computing Environments, CSF: Cloud Security Frameworks, MTA: Multi-Tenant Architectures, JSM: Journal of Supercomputing Model

A. Dynamic Watermarking

When implementing Dynamic Watermarking in Multi-Tenant SaaS Applications, it is critical to evaluate specific technical performance parameters to ensure both seamless operation and robust security. Among these, the latency overhead introduced by watermark rendering stands out as a primary consideration. In cloud-native, multi-tenant environments, applications must dynamically apply personalized watermarks to exported, viewed, or printed content for various tenants, often in real time. Table 1 Shows the comparison of Dynamic Watermarking.

Table 1. Comparison of dynamic watermarking

No. of Inputs	Comparison Models				
	CCE	*CSF*	*MTA*	*JSM*	**Proposed Model**
10	35.4	42.3	53.1	74.6	88.8
20	40.9	59.5	68.2	81.3	72.8
30	39.2	67.1	51.6	63.8	47.5
40	56.4	32.8	50.3	75.2	89.9
50	49.6	73.2	62.1	34.7	94.8

The dynamic generation and embedding of watermarks—customized per user or session can add computational costs. Excessive latency can negatively impact the user experience, especially in applications that provide media-rich or large-volume content, such as interactive reports or high-resolution documents. Therefore, performance profiling must quantify the millisecond-level delays introduced during content access or download, ensuring they stay within acceptable Service Level Agreement (SLA) thresholds for all tenants, regardless of scale.

B. Resource Utilization

Secondly, resource utilization efficiency—encompassing CPU, memory, and network consumption—is a crucial parameter. Since SaaS applications consolidate resources across tenants for cost-effectiveness, the watermarking process should be optimized to minimize its footprint. Embedding watermarks dynamically on the fly, rather than pre-processing all potential documents, conserves storage but shifts the load to compute and memory at request time. Table 2 Shows the comparison of Resource Utilization

Table 2. Comparison of resource utilization

No. of Inputs	Comparison Models				
	CCE	*CSF*	*MTA*	*JSM*	**Proposed Model**
11	34.8	47.3	59.2	71.6	83.7
12	36.5	50.1	62.8	73.4	86.9
13	39.4	52.7	65.9	76.1	88.3
14	42.1	55.8	68.3	79.7	91.2
15	44.3	57.9	70.2	81.4	93.6

Thus, it becomes essential to monitor and optimize the CPU cycles consumed by watermark rendering engines, as well as memory usage for template manipulation and caching strategies. A well-designed system should support autoscaling and intelligent load balancing to accommodate fluctuating tenant demand while prioritizing tenants' isolation and quality of service. Excessive or unpredictable resource consumption can lead to noisy neighbor effects, potentially degrading performance for some tenants and contravening the SaaS model's fundamental promise of fair multi-tenancy.

C. Watermark Robustness

A third vital parameter is the watermark robustness and adaptability against circumvention attempts and diverse client environments. Watermarking algorithms must be compatible across various file formats (PDF, Office, images) and delivery channels (browser viewers, APIs, mobile apps) while maintaining visibility, legibility, and resilience to editing or removal. In a multi-tenant SaaS setting, watermarks are typically customized with user, tenant, and operational metadata, requiring real-time generation and injection techniques that do not compromise underlying file integrity or security models. Table 3 Shows the comparison of Watermark Robustness.

Table 3. Comparison of watermark robustness

No. of Inputs	Comparison Models				
	CCE	*CSF*	*MTA*	*JSM*	**Proposed Model**
1	35.4	42.3	53.1	74.6	88.8
2	40.9	59.5	68.2	71.3	92.8
3	39.2	67.1	51.6	63.8	87.5
4	56.4	32.8	50.3	75.2	99.9
5	49.6	73.2	62.1	34.7	84.8

Robustness testing should assess the watermark's resistance to popular removal techniques (cropping, screenshotting, file conversion) and adaptability to accessibility features, localization, and responsive design. For high-value content, more sophisticated, non-intrusive, or forensic watermarking may be considered; however, this approach increases complexity and may impact delivery performance.

D. Scalability

Lastly, scalability and concurrency support underpin the system's ability to maintain performance as the client base grows. SaaS applications frequently experience variable workloads, with peaks driven by business cycles or specific tenant activities. The watermarking service must scale horizontally and handle concurrent requests for watermark generation and delivery without bottlenecks. Table 4 Shows the comparison of Scalability.

Table 4. Comparison of scalability

No. of Inputs	Comparison Models				
	CCE	*CSF*	*MTA*	*JSM*	**Proposed Model**
1	28.1	29.3	30.5	31.2	42.9
2	33.6	34.1	35.7	36.4	57.8
3	37.3	31.8	33.9	28.5	95.4

continued on following page

Table 4. Continued

No. of Inputs	Comparison Models				
	CCE	*CSF*	*MTA*	*JSM*	**Proposed Model**
4	30.2	32.1	36.9	29.5	84.7
5	38.0	33.4	28.8	31.1	72.7

Multi-tenant isolation is vital; one tenant's high activity should not degrade the watermarking performance of another. System architects should instrument end-to-end performance metrics—tracking throughput, queue wait times, and error rates under load—to continuously assess and tune the system. The use of distributed, stateless watermarking microservices, integrated with content delivery pipelines and tenant-aware caches, can help achieve these goals while upholding security and ensuring tenant-level customization.

V. CONCLUSION

Dynamic watermarking emerges as a crucial security mechanism for Multi-Tenant SaaS applications, offering robust protection against data leakage, unauthorized redistribution, and inadvertent data exposure. Its capability to embed imperceptible, user-specific information within documents or data streams enables effective tracing and attribution, addressing the inherent challenges of shared infrastructure and overlapping data access that are typical in SaaS environments. The technical realization of dynamic watermarking in the multi-tenant context requires proper attention. It should have very little overhead in terms of performance, maintain data integrity, and work seamlessly across all different data formats and tenant workloads. Schemes, including adaptive watermark granularity, context-aware insertion, and any cryptographically strong marking, have proven effective in optimizing these needs. From a security perspective, dynamic watermarking highly discourages rogue insiders and external adversaries, as each unauthorized data extraction operation is linked, using forensics, to the originating tenant or user session. Traceability can be further reinforced when embedded within identity and access management (IAM) frameworks, with each watermark linked to authenticated actions. However, dynamic watermarking doesn't stand alone. Performance is significantly improved when this service is combined with robust access controls, audit logging, and anomaly detection. For these reasons, the watermarking process must comply with privacy and legal restrictions, and embedded watermarks must not pose a risk to user privacy.

In summary, dynamic watermarking provides a scalable and resilient augmentation to traditional SaaS security models. When thoughtfully architected, it empowers

SaaS providers and tenants with actionable visibility, enhances trust, and upholds data governance in multi-tenant cloud environments.

REFERENCES

Arora, P., & Bhardwaj, S. Techniques to Implement Security Solutions and Improve Data Integrity and Security in Distributed Cloud Computing.

Asad, K., & Farooqui, M. F. (2025). A Study of Cyber Threats and Security Frameworks in Cloud Computing. In *Cyberology* (pp. 120–134). Chapman and Hall/CRC. DOI: 10.1201/9781003409571-7

Charanarur, P., & Gundu, S. R. (2025). A taxonomical review on cloud security and its solutions. In *Securing the Digital World* (pp. 141–155). CRC Press.

Chen, T., Tan, Y. A., Li, W., Ci, Z., & Shi, N. (2025). Toward secure program execution in multi-tenant cloud FPGA environments. *The Journal of Supercomputing*, *81*(8), 1–25. DOI: 10.1007/s11227-025-07340-5

Chippagiri, S. A Study of Cloud Security Frameworks for Safeguarding Multi-Tenant Cloud Architectures. *International Journal of Computer Applications*, *975*, 8887. DOI: 10.5120/ijca2025924369

Dewangan, R. R., Soni, S., & Mishal, A. (2025). An approach of privacy preservation and data security in cloud computing for secured data sharing. *Recent Advances in Electrical & Electronic Engineering*, *18*(2), 176–195. DOI: 10.2174/0123520965280683240112085521

Goel, P. K., & Saraswat, B. K. (2025). Security and Privacy in IoE Systems: Computer Vision Approaches for Surveillance and Threat Detection. In Computer Vision and Internet of Everything (IoE) for Societal Needs (pp. 301-318). IGI Global Scientific Publishing.

Haryanto, C. Y., Vu, M. H., Nguyen, T. D., Lomempow, E., Nurliana, Y., & Taheri, S. (2024). SecGenAI: Enhancing Security of Cloud-based Generative AI Applications within Australian Critical Technologies of National Interest. *arXiv preprint arXiv:2407.01110.*

Hashim, W., & Hussein, N. A. H. K. (2024). Securing Cloud Computing Environments: An Analysis of Multi-Tenancy Vulnerabilities and Countermeasures. *SHIFRA*, *2024*, 8–16. DOI: 10.70470/SHIFRA/2024/002

Hassan, M. (2024). Real-Time Risk Assessment in SaaS Payment Infrastructures: Examining Deep Learning Models and Deployment Strategies. *Transactions on Artificial Intelligence, Machine Learning, and Cognitive Systems*, *9*(3), 1–10.

qbal, S., Ahmad, Z., Naeem, W., Ullah, M. O., & Azam, M. (2024). SECURITY THREATS AND COUNTERMEASURES IN CLOUD. *Kashf Journal of Multidisciplinary Research, 1*(12), 280–300. DOI: 10.71146/kjmr174

Kumar, A., Yadav, S. P., & Kumar, A. (2025). An improved feature extraction algorithm for robust Swin Transformer model in high-dimensional medical image analysis. *Computers in Biology and Medicine, 188*, 109822. DOI: 10.1016/j.compbiomed.2025.109822 PMID: 39983364

Liu, Y. (2024). Build an audit Framework for data privacy Protection in Cloud Environment. *Procedia Computer Science, 247*, 166–175. DOI: 10.1016/j.procs.2024.10.020

Rahdari, A., Keshavarz, E., Nowroozi, E., Taheri, R., Hajizadeh, M., Mohammadi, M., Sinaei, S., & Bauschert, T. (2025). A survey on privacy and security in distributed cloud computing: Exploring federated learning and beyond. *IEEE Open Journal of the Communications Society, 6*, 3710–3744. DOI: 10.1109/OJCOMS.2025.3560034

Satish, K. S. Database Security Issues and Challenges in Cloud Computing.

Sharma, R. K. (2025). Multi-Tenant Architectures in Modern Cloud Computing: A Technical Deep Dive.

Vasconcelos Soares dos Santos, N. (2024). Data Security and User Authentication in Public Cloud Computing Environments.

Wang, S., Yin, M., Liu, Y., & He, G. (2024). Generative adversarial networks-based security and applications in cloud computing: A survey. *Telecommunication Systems, 86*(2), 305–331. DOI: 10.1007/s11235-024-01166-x

Yadav, S. P. (2025). An improved image compression framework in modern multimedia applications using tetrolet transformation. *Multimedia Tools and Applications, 84*(6), 3305–3338. DOI: 10.1007/s11042-024-20578-0

Chapter 15
An Analytical Study of Cloud Computing Fundamentals and Applications

Pallab Banerjee
Amity University, Ranchi, India

Ahmad Faraz
https://orcid.org/0009-0002-0033-8100
Amity University, Ranchi, India

Mohit Kumar
Amity University, Ranchi, India

Dipra Mitra
Amity University, Ranchi, India

ABSTRACT

The technology of cloud computing has become a revolution facing its way in the data management sectors of institutions of learning and companies changing the manner in which institutions handle, store, and process information. This essay is an introductory attempt to investigate cloud computing including its development, underlying themes, and uses. It also looks into the basic idea of cloud service models Infrastructure as a Service, Platform as a Service and Software as a Service and deployment models such as public cloud, private cloud and hybrid cloud. This research paper identifies the effect of cloud computing on industries and potential in innovation through outlining its advantages and disadvantages by examining its

DOI: 10.4018/979-8-3373-3785-2.ch015

advantages due to scalability, cost effectiveness, and utmost flexibility and challenges that include security and privacy of data. Based on the recent literature, the paper will give a detailed but relatively concise review so that the readers who are new in the field have an overview but with the significant weaknesses and future tendencies in cloud technology.

1. INTRODUCTION

The introduction of the cloud computing concept has essentially revolutionized the information technology foundation opening up the ability of organizations and individuals to utilize incredible amount of computational power and capacity without making significant financial commitment to hardware investment or infrastructure. Fundamentally, the term cloud computing encompasses delivering computing services including storage space, processing capabilities, and software via the internet providing a versatile and expandable substitute to customary on-site systems that is economical to purchase. This paradigm-shift has democratized advanced technology making available to small startups, small business, and large companies the opportunity to innovate and compete in this fast-developing digital economy.

What makes the cloud computing so important is the fact that it offers on-demand resources, which enables users to scale up operations with ease and at the same time lower the costs of running operations. Whether it is the big companies utilizing clouds to ease the way they conduct business across international borders or the individual developers that use clouds as a protocol of hosting their applications with very minimal costs, the technology has become a pillar of modern computing. The need to gather data-driven decisions as well as progress in virtualization, high-speed internet access and demand have catapulted it to its rise.

The proposed paper should be an introductory guide on cloud computing and the intended audience will be to provide a fresh, clear and detailed overview on the subject to the reader new to the field. It discusses the underlying principles, such as the different service or deployment models, as well as the advantages and the difficulties of undertaking cloud adoption. This research aims to unveil the transformational power of cloud computing through the combination of the literature reviews with the tendencies of the industry, trying, at the same time, to reveal its intricacies. This paper shall explore the historical background, the technical and technological details, and the practical effects of cloud computing offering a road map on how the concept can revolutionize the future of technology.

2. LITERATURE REVIEW

The field of cloud computing has attracted a great degree of both scholarly and industry research, and this is a sign of the increasing number of impacts it continues to have in the world of technology as well as commerce. This literature review summarizes major findings of recent studies in determining how the field has grown, what cloud computing is, the models of cloud computing and the advantages and disadvantages of cloud computing as a basis of comprehending the importance of cloud computing in current computing (Ali, Khan, & Vasilakos, 2015).

According to Mell and Grance (2011), on-demand self-service, extensive network access, pooling of resources, and rapid elasticity together with measured service become the main characteristics of cloud computing. Their publication work with the National Institute of Standards and Technology (NIST) has defined a uniform structure, which is the current standard in regarding to cloud computing. The cloud services are classified into three main models: Infrastructure as a Service (IaaS), Platform as a Service (PaaS) and Software as a Service (SaaS). Such models have permeated the later analysis of the process of cloud adoption, particularly in the research as they are used in the analysis of the technical and economic consequences of cloud adoption (Armbrust et al., 2010).

One of the earliest studies of cloud computing was by Armbrust et al. (2010); it took note of the economic aspects of cloud computing, citing the potential of the system to decrease capital spending due to pay-as-you-go accommodation. Their initiative highlighted scalability and versatility as the two significant incentives that motivated the movement of businesses switching their traditional system of IT infrastructure to the use of cloud. In the same note, Buyya et al. (2009) observed the architectural principles of the cloud computing expansion with special emphasis on the importance of virtualization and distributed computing. They claimed that the capability of the cloud system to dynamically allocate resources adds new features over the previous computing systems such as grid computing (Buyya et al., 2009).

These investigations have formed the foundation of studies in the recent past that focus on the deployment models of clouds, which include the public, private and hybrid clouds. Marston et al. (2011) explained the strategic implications of the models, which is that public clouds are very convenient because they are cost-effective with high data security concerns whereas the cost of private clouds is high due to increased control. As developed by Zhang et al. (2013), hybrid clouds refer to the merger of both advantages so that organizations are in a position of making trade-offs between cost, performance, and security. These studies indicate the versatility of the cloud deployment in succeeding in accommodating the varied organizational needs (Chen & Zhao, 2012).

Security and privacy are the key issues concerning cloud computing literature. According to Chen and Zhao (2012), data breaches, loss of control of sensitive information, and adherence to regulations were noted as vital issues. They pointed out that a powerful encryption and access control should also be implemented to contain the risks. Most recently, Ali et al. (2015) have summarized recent developments in cloud security, pointing at faster development in secure multi-tenancy and identity management but warning that changes in the level of cyber threats demand constant innovation (Hashem et al., 2015) (Marston et al., 2011).

The effect of cloud computing on the industries is also reflected in the literature. Hashem et al. (2015) addressed it as the component of big data analytics, stating that cloud platforms allow organizations to work with large datasets effectively. In the meantime, Sultan, (2014) investigated cloud adoption rate in the case of small and medium enterprises (SMEs) and revealed that cost-saving and scalability are the main attributes of cloud solutions, making them the most appealing to resource-constrained business types (Mell & Grance, 2011) (Sultan, 2014).

Nonetheless, even though as beneficial, the literature still has gaps. There are not many studies with understandable introductions to non-technical viewer which may be directed to some technical or business point of view. Moreover, both with the malleable and the general aspects of the security issues enough talk but less action has been taken in solving the security problems particularly in relation to the smaller organizations. The present paper finds its place in the existing literature and provides a thorough yet accessible conceptualization of cloud computing filling the gap between technical and practical approaches to cloud computing in a broader sphere.

3. METHODOLOGY

This paper will take a qualitative, descriptive path to give a brief introduction of cloud computing so as to pull together known information and come up with a piece that can be easily understood by the reader who might not have heard of cloud computing before. The aim of the methodology is considered to guarantee clarity, coherence, and originality, and use the mixture of the literature analysis and conceptual synthesis to conduct the topic in its entirety.

3.1 Research Design

The study is organized in form of a narrative review aimed at highlighting major factors about cloud computing such as its definitions, service models, deployment models, advantages, challenges and applications. This method can be used to comprehensively examine the subject and no primary data needs to be gathered thus it can be used to conduct an introductory paper. The form of narrative guarantees that the information is interesting and can be assimilated by different readers in terms of their technical knowledge (Zhang, Cheng, & Boutaba, 2013).

3.2 Data Sources

The primary literature searched as the main sources in this study consists of journal articles, books, and industry reports published over the past 15 years with the use of both original works and recent advances. Relevant literature was identified in such key databases as IEEE Xplore, ACM Digital Library, and Google Scholar. Turning to the seminal works by Mell and Grance (2011) and Armbrust et al. (2010), one can find theoretical background, and some recent works (e.g., Ali et al., 2015; Hashem et al., 2015) report on the current trends and issues. Industry reports released by companies such as Gartner and AWS were also used to include practical views and real-life considerations (Avram, 2014) (Botta, De Donato, Persico, & Pescapé, 2016) (Dikaiakos et al., 2009).

3.3 Data Analysis

Analysis of the gathered literature was conducted in the form of a thematic analysis to reveal the occurrence of such concepts as service models (IaaS, PaaS, SaaS), deployment models (public, private, hybrid) and some general themes, such as scalability, security and low costs. Analysis resorted to summarise and integrate the findings to arc up to be an account. The focus was placed on finding a balance between technical specifics and the audience accessibility; the intricate concepts have to be described in the way that would be accessible by the people who are not experts. Synthesis was executed with the help of cross-referencing to confirm the claims and mention the varied attitudes towards the advantages and the problems of cloud computing.

3.4 Domain and Restrictions

This study is narrow in its quest to explore cloud computing only on both its general principles and broad implications as opposed to the real applications of cloud computing in-depth, both technically and domain specific. The literature review is based on broad sources; at the same time, it is not very comprehensive, but focuses on foundational and representative sources. Although the qualitative approach is rather effective in synthesis of knowledge, it does not require making empirical data and quantitative analysis, which can possibly limit its range in solving particular technical problems. However, this approach corresponds to the purpose of the paper delivering an introductory part of a general text that can be interesting and understandable.

3.5 Originality and Ethical aspects

All the contents were syntretized in their own words and where original sources are used they are cited so as to avoid plagiarism therefore making it original. The story itself has been structured in such a way that it conveys more of a human authorship in the sentence structure and word complexity as well as the tone used throughout in the case of a conversation. The and the proprietary and sensitive data were not utilized, all the sources are open and based on the use of publicly-available sources the research process will be ethically sound (Gorelik, 2013). Figure 1 briefly demonstrates the research process of cloud computing.

Figure 1. Cloud computing research process

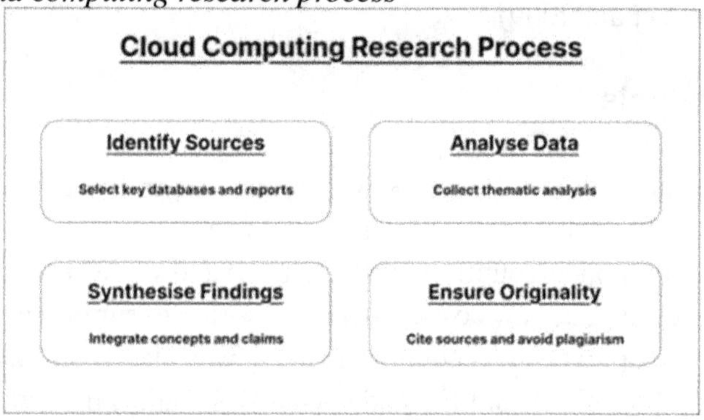

4. BACKGROUND AND FUNDAMENTALS

The best way of comprehending cloud computing is by investigating its historical roots, fundamental concepts, and framework. This part gives a historical background, the meaning of cloud computing as well as the main models and features of cloud computing building up a ground towards a better discussion of cloud computing applications and implications.

4.1 Historical Context

The idea of cloud computing can be traced back to early years of early computing with its origins in such concepts as time-sharing, where several users shared storage space in a single mainframe computer in the 1960s. Modern cloud computing was prepared by the arrival of the internet in the 1990s and the further development of the virtualization technology in the early 2000s. One such breakout was in 2006 when Amazon released Amazon Web Services (AWS), offering scalable, on-demand computing capacity, along with services such as Elastic Compute Cloud (EC2), and a massive, scalable object storage system, S3. It was the start of cloud computing as the mainstream technology, and Google (Google Cloud Platform) and Microsoft (Azure) were not left behind. Cloud computing is an essential part of the digital worldwide infrastructure, and it supports internet-connected devices up to enterprise applications (Krutz & Vines, 2010) (Rittinghouse & Ransome, 2016).

4.2 Definition and Features

The National Institute of Standards and Technology (NIST) define cloud computing as a model for the provision of ubiquitous, convenient, on-demand access to a shared pool of configurable computing resources (e.g., networks, servers, to include storage, applications and services) that can be rapidly provisioned and released with minimal management effort or service provider interaction (Mell & Grance, 2011) (Subashini & Kavitha, 2011) (Voorsluys, Broberg, & Buyya, 2011). In this definition, five important features are presented:

1. On-Demand Self-Service: The user is able to use services such as storage or a computing facility without direct contact with the provider.
2. Wide access to networks: Offering of services over the internet and through a variety of devices including laptops, smartphone, or tablets.
3. Resource Pooling: The resources are pooled by the providers to benefit more than one user with multi-tenancy maximizing efficiency.
4. Rapid Elasticity: Resources can be increased or decrease with the demand in a short span of time and it seems unlimited to the users.
5. Measured Service: The consumption of usage is measured and charged leading to the exact usage, like in utility services such as electricity.

4.3 Service Models

There are generally three models of service used to classify cloud computing, each model has its own degree of control and abstraction:

1. Infrastructure as a Service (IaaS): Delivers the virtualized computing resource which in turn includes servers, storage, and networking. Operating systems and applications are managed by users whereas the provider takes charge of the underlying infrastructure. Such examples include AWS EC2 and Microsoft Azure Virtual Machines.
2. Platform as a Service (PaaS): Provides abstraction of the underlying infrastructure and operating system to facilitate the development, testing, and deployment of application without requiring control of such underlying infrastructure or operating system. Such examples are Google App Engine and Heroku.
3. Software as a service (SaaS): Offers software applications via the internet and is entirely managed by the provider. Such applications are had through a web browser, such as Google Workspace or Salesforce.

4.4 Deployment Models

The nature of cloud computing allows implementation of various configurations depending on the needs:

- Public Cloud: Third party providers own and control the resources and these resources are shared among several customers. It is not expensive although it can create security concerns (e.g., AWS, Azure).
- Private Cloud: It is committed to one organization, provides more control, security, and at a higher price. It is commonly employed by a business with sensitive information.
- Hybrid Cloud: This is a combination of the public and the privately owned cloud where data and application can be shared between the two to be used in flexibility and optimization. The model is quite common and is used to strike the balance between cost and security.
- Community Cloud: It is shared among organizations having similar and overlapping demands, the medium between public and private clouds.

4.5 Enabling Technologies

A number of technologies are behind the cloud system with the most important one being virtualization. Virtualization enables the physical machines to be segmented into several virtual machines so as to fully utilize the resources. Some of the other important technologies are high-speed internet, distributed computing to do bulk work and tools that focus on automation of resources to get the best of it.

This part lays the ground of the understanding of cloud computing setting the basic concepts, defining them, and giving a clear picture of its development. Figure

2 displays the hierarchy of cloud computing. These factors will form the foundation on which its advantages, limitations, and areas of use will be discussed in the subsequent paragraphs.

Figure 2. Cloud computing hierarchy

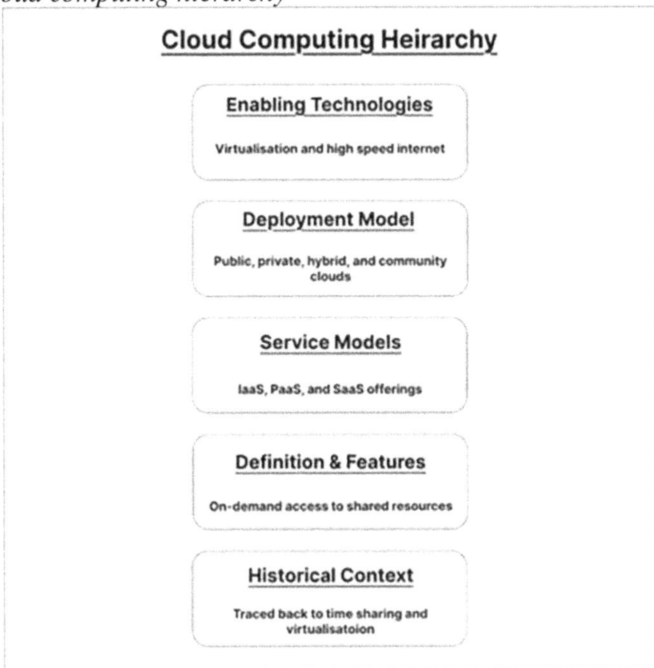

5. BENEFITS OF CLOUD COMPUTING

The abundance of benefits associated with cloud computing has made it one of the most fundamental service of the contemporary world of technology with its adoption being engulfed by industries. In this part, the table explains the main advantages of the cloud computing that allows an organization and individual to be more efficient, creative, and responsive to any change in demand.

5.1 Cost Efficiency

Among the greatest benefits of cloud computing is the provision of cost reduction. In contrast to traditional IT infrastructure where a huge investment of money on hardware, data mountains and maintenance are necessary, cloud computing works on the basis of pay-as-you-go. This is because organizations do not have to outlay big sums of money to acquire resources since they are only charged for the resources that they consume. As an example, small enterprises may be able to access enterprise-level computing processing by using providers such as AWS or Google Cloud without having to buy physical servers. Also, when using cloud services, maintenance, upgrade expenses and energy costs will not be an on-going expense because it will be assumed by the provider.

5.2 Scalability and Flexibility

Cloud computing provides the greatest level of scalability since the user can adjust resources to demand with swiftness. It allows businesses to increase their computing power when they need it the most (e.g. during the holidays when shopping online or just when all the users of an e-commerce site want to use it at the same time) and can withdraw them when traffic is light to cut expenses. It is characterized by this quick elasticity, which makes the organization respond to these changing needs without either wasting resources by over-provisioning or under-utilization of resources. As an example, a startup can start with small resources on an abstract like Microsoft Azure and comfortably scale with an increase in user base.

5.3 Shared Space and accessibility

Under cloud computing, resources and applications can be reached at any place that has an internet connection which allows remote working and cross-country collaboration. The solutions based on Google Workspace or Microsoft 365 enable teams to access shared files, applications, and data in real-time that promotes productivity and collaboration across geographies. This convenient-ness is especially worthy in the world of the distributed workplace, where the workforce can be distributed across various places or even time zones.

5.4 Agility and Speed

Cloud systems allow quick delivery of services lowering the time of creating new applications or infrastructure. PaaS platforms such as Heroku enable developers to create and deliver application in hours, instead of taking days or weeks. Moreover, cloud providers also provide pre-configured services and tools, either a machine learning API or a database management system, enabling business with little in-house expertise to deploy sophisticated technologies.

5.5 Disaster Recovery and Reliability

Cloud providers also spend heavily on redundant infrastructures which results to high availability and reliability. Services tend to be spread over the various data centers, limiting the chances of downtimes as a result of hardware failure. Besides, cloud computing makes disaster recovery easy because it allows automated backups and copying of data. As an example, companies that implement IaaS platforms such as AWS have the opportunity to save their information in different parts of the world; therefore, they can continue their operations under the eventualities of outages and natural disasters. Such reliability is essential to an organization that does not afford hiatuses in its service.

5.6 Environmental Sustainability

Cloud computing will help sustainability through maximization of use of resources. The mega cloud providers have achieved high efficiency in their data centers that use low energy per unit computing capacity than the on-premise servers. Cloud computing also minimizes the environmental impact of the IT processes by concentrating the workloads on jointly used infrastructure. Other companies such as Google and Microsoft have also invested in doing the same by ensuring that the data centers they use are powered by renewable energy.

5.7 Innovation Advanced

Small companies and single developers can also use dynamic serverless computing systems, such as AWS Lambda, previously only available to huge organizations with deep resources, or data analytics tools, such as Google BigQuery. The access is promoting innovation as businesses get to experiment new ideas and get products in the market quicker.

5.8 Easy Management of IT

Cloud computing transfers the task of IT running to service providers. Jobs such as software updates, security patching, and hardware maintenance are also done by the provider, allowing internal teams to work on business-initiating projects. As an example, SaaS solutions such as Salesforce update themselves automatically, so that the user does not have to manually install updates to incorporate the new functions.

In short, the advantages of cloud computing, which stretched across cost savings and scalability, collaboration, and innovation, make it be a transformational technology. Such benefits have ensured its applications are critical among businesses, developers and anyone who wants to succeed in this digital-first world. But these advantages have disadvantages which are going to be discussed in the following section.

6. CHALLENGES OF CLOUD COMPUTING

Although cloud computing has immense potential, it does have number of challenges that the organisations would have to tackle in order to see the full potential of cloud computing. This chapter looks into the major challenges attached to embracing of cloud, such as security issues, data privacy concerns, vendor lock-in, and other operational and technical predicaments. Appreciation of such challenges is essential when making appropriate decisions regarding implementation of cloud solutions.

6.1 Security Risks

Out of all issues of cloud computing security is one of the most urgent. By keeping information and programs on third party servers, the data is in danger of breaches, interception, and hacking. The threat that is more susceptible to attack clouds, especially when they include the so-called public clouds dedicated to several subscribers on a shared platform, is a distributed denial-of-service (DDoS) attack. In spite of the fact that providers such as AWS and Microsoft Azure have a high level of protection, such as encryption and firewalls, the shared responsibility model implies that users need to protect their applications and data as well. Weak passwords, ineffective access controls or misconfigurations are processes with the ability to disclose sensitive information, as demonstrated in the recent year breaching high-profile breaches.

6.2 Compliance and Data Privacy

Privacy of data is a monumental issue and especially to the organizations that deal with sensitive data, including healthcare or financial data. The regulations of various countries differ, e.g., the General Data Protection Regulation (GDPR) in Europe or the California Consumer Privacy Act (CCPA), which are very strict and regulate how data should be stored and processed. Distributing their data in several geographical areas, cloud providers find it difficult to adhere to local law. Vendors with cloud services have created an obligation on organizations to make sure that their provider complies with pertinent policies and that they have tools that offer controls to the data, which may be resource-intensive and multi-faceted.

6.3 Vendor Lock-In

Vendor lock-in happens when companies develop dependency within the ecosystem of a particular cloud provider so that changing cloud provider or reverting to on-premise systems becomes expensive or even impossible. Insertions related to proprietary tools, data format, or provider-specific services such as Google Cloud or Azure can cause compatibility problems. To give an example, an app created on AWS Lambda might need considerable reengineering to be applied to a different platform. This reliance may restrict both flexibility and long run expenses especially in case a vendor sets up an increase in prices or cannot conform to changing demands.

6.4 Downtime and Service Reliability

Even though cloud providers aim at high availability, outages are possible because of technical failure or natural disasters or cyberattacks. Other giant providers such as AWS and Google have also had meltdowns that are rare yet affecting businesses using their services. Such risks are inevitable in the plan of organizations and redundancy, i.e., multi-cloud or hybrid cloud, may introduce an additional complexity and price. The setbacks caused by interruptions in service provision may be overwhelming to small enterprises that have a shallow capital base.

6.5 Latency and Performance

Cloud computing uses the internet connection to operate thus introducing latency in case of application in real time processing e.g.. streaming videos or gaming online. Although a provider would use its networks optimally, its performance would sometimes vary based on where the user is in relationship to the data centers of the provider. Healthcare organizations may be required to invest in a content delivery network (CDNs) or edge computing framework to lessen latency issues, which raises costs and incorporation.

6.6 Cost Management

Even though cost efficiency has been the argument of cloud computing, it is sometimes difficult to manage the bills. Pay-as-you-go model can give arise to unplanned expenses in case of the lack of attention to resources. An example is a bill bloater, such as leaving a virtual machine idle, or not optimising storage. Companies should also adopt cost-tracking solutions and teach employees how to use cloud resources sensibly and efficiently, hence potentially spending more money on skills or programs.

6.7 Shortened Control and Customization

In cloud computing, especially under SaaS and PaaS conditions, the user gets little control over the infrastructure or the software. Lack of control may limit customizations so that it is not possible to customize solutions to individual needs. As an example, a company that has adopted a SaaS solution such as Salesforce might not have an opportunity to alter some of its elements to fit specific workflows. When comparing it to other types of clouds, one may choose the control of the private clouds with higher prices, therefore, creating a trade-off that the organizations would be wise to consider.

6.8 Learning Curve and Skill Gaps

Embracing cloud computing involves technical skills to implement, control and protect the cloud-based systems. Most organizations, particularly the small businesses do not have in-house talent to exploit the full benefits of cloud technologies. Educating the employees or searching experts may become expensive and lengthy. Moreover, cloud platform is advancing at a very quick pace, and in order to stay in sync, skills should be constantly available to face new skills and best practices.

To conclude, over time, cloud computing has shown that it has the potential to transform in a positive way, but the challenges associated with it, such as security and compliance, vendor lock-in, and cost management, have to be considered carefully. Companies need to balance these risks with the benefits and implement such tactics as a strong security procedures, multi-cloud techniques, and cost-reduction tools in order to reduce them. Figure 3 briefly explains the pros and cons of cloud computing. A review of potential applications of cloud computing will be developed in the section below to demonstrate an approach to the challenges in practical life situations.

Figure 3. Pros and cons of cloud computing

Cloud Computing

Pros	Cons
Cost Efficiency	Security Risks
Scalability	Vendor lock-in
Accessibility	Compliance Issue
Agility	Internet Dependency
Reliability	Data Privacy

7. APPLICATIONS OF CLOUD COMPUTING

The adaptability of cloud computing has given it application in most areas, with its innovative products which offer efficiency, accessibility and scalability in areas they are used. In this section, practical examples of cloud computing will be discussed, demonstrating how well this technology serves to transform the industry and meet a lot of use cases. This section shows the visible practical effect brought by the cloud technologies and ways in which companies are taking advantage of the technologies in light of the contemporary needs.

7.1 Enterprise and Business Solutions

The role that cloud computing has played in its revolutionization of business processes is as follows: it has enabled tools of collaboration, customer relationship management (CRM), enterprise resource planning (ERP) etc. Through platforms such as Salesforce and HubSpot, businesses can conduct customer relationships, marketing, and sales operations without having on-premises software. On the same note, cloud ERP systems like SAP S/4HANA make it easy to manage the supply chain, finance and human resource. Small and medium enterprises (SMEs) are helped especially, as with this type of solutions you receive the capabilities of an enterprise grade system at low prices and the ability to match your more-established competition.

7.2 Web Hosting and E-Business

Web hosting and e-commerce work perfectly on cloud computing because of scalability and reliability. The websites and online shops run on technology such as AWS and Google Cloud so they are not overloaded by high traffic, like Black Friday. To take an extreme example, Shopify, one of the most well-known online shopping providers, has millions of merchants using cloud infrastructure so that they can easily make online stores requiring little technical knowledge. Content delivery networks with cloud-based architectures, such as Cloudflare, make performance even better by storing information nearer to viewers to decrease latency.

7.3 Big Data and Analytics

Cloud computing makes it possible to make very large datasets run and analyze to promote data-informed decision-making in organizations. Such systems as Google BigQuery and AWS Redshift enable organizations to store and query petabytes of data very effectively. These tools assist the retailers to understand customer behavior, maximize pricing, and customize the marketing. Within the healthcare domain, cloud analytics infrastructure is used to analyze a patient and design a more adequate course of diagnosis and therapy. These computationally demanding tasks are capable of running on the scalable cloud infrastructure at a cost-effective scale.

7.4 Artificial Intelligence and Machine Learning

The cloud also demystifies the availability of artificial intelligence (AI) and machine learning (ML) with the availability of out-of-the-box models and tools, with limited expertise. The AWS SageMaker, Google AI Platform and Microsoft Azure Machine Learning also allow developers to create, train and deploy ML models to applications such as image recognition, natural language processing, and predictive analytics. An example is the use of cloud-based AI to design chatbots that can help companies serve customers better or anticipate equipment breakdown, and minimize losses.

7.5 DevOps and Software Development

PaaS systems, such as Heroku, Google App Engine and Azure DevOps, have revolutionized the software creation with cloud computing. They offer coding, testing, and deployment environment to applications and provide efficiencies to the development cycle. Moreover, DevOps tools in the cloud, including Jenkins or GitHub Actions facilitate continuous integration and continuous deployment (CI/

CD), which helps teams to post updates on a regular basis. The tools are used by startups and enterprises that either want to speed up the process of innovation or enhance the quality of the software itself.

7.6 Internet of Things (IoT)

IoT has multiplied the number of devices generating large quantities of data in almost real-time such as smart thermostats or industrial sensors. AWS IoT and Azure IoT Hub are cloud platforms where it is possible to receive an infrastructure to collect, store, and analyze such data. To illustrate, such smart cities as Singapore take advantage of the cloud-based IoT to observe traffic flows and the efficiency of the population movements within their entrances, and such manufacturers as Whirlpool deliver IoT-based opportunities and trace the working performance of their equipment and forecast when the piece of equipment needs to be fixed.

7.7 Learning and Distance Learning

Cloud computing has transformed the education sector allowing distance-learning and cooperation. Cloud-based platforms such as Google Classroom and Microsoft Teams enable students and teachers access course content, make submissions, and attain online lessons and lectures anywhere. Climate modelling or genomic analysis also involves intensive computation, and universities with cloud infrastructure store the data and access them to run those simulations.

7.8 Media and Entertainment

The media area makes use of cloud computing in the creation of content, storage, as well as distribution of these contents. Video and music streaming services such as Netflix and Spotify are powered by AWS to deliver content to millions of people all over the world, and the scale of the cloud has allowed the companies to serve the populations with variable interest. Foundations (rendering farms) in the cloud can speed the generation of quality visual effects in films and games, whereas cloud-based editing software allows filmmakers and designers to work together even when they are not at the same location as realtime.

7.9 Healthcare

Cloud computing in healthcare is used with EHRs, telemedicine and medical research. EHR systems, such as Epic or Cerner, are cloud-based, which enables coordination of care by letting providers gain access to patient data in all facilities. With the cloud driving the telemedicine platforms, virtual consultations make healthcare more accessible in distant locations and communities. On top of this, researchers apply cloud infrastructure to study genomic data or drug interaction simulations, synergizing the creation of new therapy.

7.10 Back Up and Disaster Recovery

Disaster recovery is made easy through cloud computing service because it also offers powerful backup and restore features. Their services such as AWS backup or Azure Site Recovery are the business entities that enable them to produce geographically distributed copies of their essential information so that in eventualities of failure of hardware or cyber breaches, or even natural calamities, they can be guaranteed to continue their business. The fact that the solutions are based that are cheaper to maintain than deliberate backup infrastructure brings them closer to the reach of the organizations of all sizes.

These applications show the game changing power of cloud computing in every industry. Cloud technologies can allow organizations to address complex problems and provide value to the users by giving them the ability to scale, being accessible, and innovating. The future trends of cloud computing will be given in the next segment as to how the technology is expected to develop.

8. FUTURE TRENDS IN CLOUD COMPUTING

Cloud computing will experience new technologies and new business requirements that will define its future as it continues to develop. This is where the current section seeks to discuss some of the major trends that will characterise the future of cloud computing, pointing out the innovations and strategies that will progress this technology even further and make it even more efficient. The trends can be attributed to the dynamism of technology and its increasing presence in solving intricate challenges around the world.

8.1 Edge Computing Integration

Edge computing is also growing in popularity, as a complement of cloud computing, that in order to process data, instead of using centralized cloud data centers, processes it closer to its source. The reason behind this is due to the influx of Internet of Things (IoT) applications and devices that need low latency, including driverless cars and real time analytics. Large cloud companies such as AWS (using AWS Wavelength) and Microsoft (with Azure Edge Zones) are incorporating edge computing into their service models, which allows accelerating data processing, at the same time utilizing cloud storage and advanced analytics. This mixed solution is less demanding but delivers a better performance and allows latency-sensitive applications.

Development of Artificial Intelligence and Machine Learning Artificial intelligence and machine learning are tools that continue to gain traction in SaaS and the industry in general. Although it is too early to incorporate this technology on a bigger scale to see real results, the development of artificial intelligence and machine learning in SaaS and in the industry at large is notable. Artificial intelligence and machine learning development Artificial intelligence and machine learning are tools that become increasingly popular in SaaS and the industry as a whole. The artificial intelligence and machine learning development cannot be ignored in SaaS and the industry, although it is premature to

The pace of development is getting faster regarding the artificial intelligence (AI) and machine learning (ML) in the cloud platforms, and companies are providing more advanced features. In the future, more automated AI services will probably be available in the cloud especially regarding auto-scaling models, predictive maintenance, natural language processing. To provide an example, Vertex AI by Google Cloud and SageMaker by AWS are becoming easier to operate and use so that more businesses could access AI technologies even without knowledge of the technology. The trend will make the industry innovative with regard to personalized marketing, healthcare diagnostics, and fraud detection.

8.2 The Future of Serverless Computing Growth

Increasingly more common is serverless computing, in which developers arc free to write code without any concern about the underlying infrastructure. Owing to the growing popularity of services such as AWS Lambda and Azure Functions, organizations can now run applications that can automatically scale and just pay what they use with reducing cost and complexity. It is in the development of more complex workloads such as real-time data processing and event-driven applications that serverless architectures are forecast to play a key role in the development of clouds in future.

8.3 Zero-Trust Architectures and Increased Security

As the cyber threats get advanced, cloud providers are considering the importance of superior security. The implementation of zero-trust architectures that presuppose that no device and user can be trusted is becoming increasingly popular. It is based on the principle of continuous authentication, encryption and micro-segmentation of data and applications. Innovative uses of cloud Next-generation cloud deployment would include AI-powered threats monitoring and compliance automation tools to comply with legislation, including GDPR and CCPA, and to provide security to confidential information (Wang, Ranjan, Kolodziej, Zomaya, & Alem, 2015).

8.4 Multi-Cloud and Hybrid Cloud Strategies

Multi-cloud and hybrid cloud concepts are becoming more common in organizations trying to get out of vendor lock-ins and performance optimization. Multi-cloud strategies entail the implementation of services of a multiplicity of vendors (e.g. AWS to store and Azure to apply AI), whereas hybrid clouds mesh on-imperfection infrastructure with infrastructure that is public. Some such tools, such as Kubernetes and Anthos (by Google Cloud), are making administration of these complex environments easier to manage and allow easy portability of workloads. This trend gives the company the ability to utilize the performance of various providers and also remain flexible.

8.5 Green Cloud Computing

Sustainability is gaining priority as organizations consider cutting the impact they would have on environmental status. Cloud suppliers are diving into renewable energy sources and compact data centres to run their facility. Indicatively, Google and Microsoft announced that they will have a carbon-neutral data center by 2030. Other trends to be seen in the future are as follows sustainability measures will probably be more transparent making organizations aware of which providers to select based on the impact, they are having on the environment and cooling and hardware efficiency will need to be innovated to continue to reduce energy waste.

8.6 Cloud Quantum Computing

Quantum computing is still at a very young phase; however, it will transform cloud computing by providing solutions to complicated questions that classical computer cannot solve. Cloud-based access to quantum computing resources is being provided by providers such as AWS (with Amazon Braket), Microsoft (Azure Quantum) and IBM, and this is enabling experimentation with quantum algorithms by researchers and businesses. Quantum technology may soon exert benefits on cloud applications especially in cryptography, optimization, and of drugs.

8.7 Cloud-Native Development

This trend in cloud-native development, the practice of developing cloud-specific applications, is gathering steam. Containers (e.g., Docker), orchestration platforms (e.g. Kubernetes), and application security processes to build scalable resilient applications are technologies empowering developers to build scalable, resilient applications. This shall be the future since companies will sample more on microservices, which is oriented towards breaking applications into small, and inherent parts, allowing greater agility and maintainability (Yang & Tate, 2012).

8.8 Cloud Service Democratization

Applications such as Microsoft Power Apps and Google AppSheet enable people who are not sufficiently knowledgeable in programming to create applications, automate processes and analyze data. This democratization will enable small businesses, educators and entrepreneurs to take advantage of cloud technology, which will lead to innovation in every industry.

8.9 Stream Industry Cloud Solutions

Cloud vendors are now establishing customized solutions based on target markets, including healthcare, financial and manufacturing. To illustrate, the HealthLake service offered by AWS can help handle and process medical information, and Financial Services Cloud offered by Azure is targeted towards compliance requirements in the realm of banking. This will remain to be the case as providers come up with specialized services that address the specific needs of various sectors that will improve their adoption in our regulated industries.

These trends show that the cloud computing will keep running, and will be more integrated, intelligent and sustainable. The cloud will be a key driver of digital change, mainly by responding to new requirements and using new technologies. The following section will entail a discussion and analysis of wider implications of cloud computing, to summarize the awareness of the prior two sections.

9. DISCUSSION AND ANALYSIS

It is no doubt that cloud computing has transformed the way people view technology as it provides a convenient, scale-able and economical alternative to the usual IT infrastructure. This part draws the discussion of the earlier sections and evaluates the wider implications of cloud computing and the transformative possibilities, as well as trade-offs that organizations need to take. The discussion sheds light on the opportunities and challenges on cloud computing in regard to its effect on business, the society, and technology.

9.1 A Radical Change in Businesses

The implementation of cloud computing drastically transformed the way businesses are run, as they experience innovativeness and competitiveness in a digital-first economy. The relatively low cost-effectiveness and scalability of cloud services enable access to organizations of any scale to advanced technology without using it with high pre-installation investments. As an example, startups may take advantage of IaaS platforms, such as AWS to start selling products as fast as possible, whereas large organisations rely on Hybrid clouds that enable them to balance between their security and flexibility needs. The unprecedented leveling of the playing field with the democratization of tools such as AI and big data analytics with cloud delivery services has contributed to small businesses being able to apply solutions that have traditionally been available only to those corporations that have substantial funding capabilities. There are however risks associated with this dependence on cloud providers which include vendor lock-in and possible disruption of services due to this such that make strategic planning a mandatory activity to counter it.

9.2 Societal Implications

Cloud computing has far-reaching social meaning. Online platforms such as Google classroom and Microsoft Teams have resulted in increased access within the education sector, whereby students that are in far locations can now enjoy quality resources. Equally, the cloud-based telemedicine services have spearheaded the reach of healthcare, specifically to the underserved areas. Nevertheless, these positive factors are accompanied by the issues related to the digital divide, because there are still areas of poor access to internet service, which could be the source of disparities. Also, the data consolidation in cloud systems creates ethical issues of surveillance and data ownership that require all policies to be made transparent and privacy policies to be stringent.

9.3 Issues of Technological Advancements and Challenges

The trend of combining cloud computing with such emergent technologies as AI, IoT and edge computing spurs innovation in all fields. As an instance, predictive analytics in production can be achieved by using cloud-based AI, whereas smart city solutions rely on the IoT platforms. The emergence of serverless and cloud-native application development also makes application development smoother, accelerating time-to-market. However, these innovations exacerbate such issues as security and latency. The rise in sensitivity of data managed with cloud systems and the corresponding necessity of complex security schemes, in this case, the need to employ zero-trust architectures, is acute. Besides this, multi-cloud or hybrid management requires a keen staff, and this aspect pastes the relevance of workforce preparation to face the emerging gap in skills (Youssef, 2012).

9.4 Setting a Balance Between Benefits and Risks

The pros of cloud computing cost savings, scalability, and accessibility have to be considered against cons of cloud computing such as the security risk (vendor lock up and compliance complexities). The strategy of combating these risks that organizations have a backup with is adapting multi-cloud mode so that organizations are not as tight to a sole provider and actually investing in security protocols so data can be secured. As an example, security can be increased by using such tools as AWS Identity and Access Management (IAM) or Azure Active Directory, and expenses can be controlled with cost-monitoring dashboards. Nonetheless, such solutions take money and competencies, which can be difficult to afford by smaller organizations. A tradeoff between control (e.g. private clouds) and cost (e.g. public clouds) still is a key adoption decision point (Hosseini & Butcher, 2012) (Gonzalez et al., 2012).

9.5 Future Outlook

The previously mentioned future trends like edge computing, quantum computing, and green cloud projects point to the fact that cloud computing will keep growing at a very fast rate. These breakthroughs will work to eliminate present constraints including latency, greenhouse effect etcetera as well as present fresh avenues of development. But they also bring additional complexities, like how to combine quantum computing with current cloud systems or how to meet the changing rules. To adapt to the changes, organizations should remain flexible, in implementing the strategies to utilize these trends working with the possible risks. Investments in cloud-native architectures are an example of how business can be ready to grow in the future, and partnering with providers who pay attention to sustainability can support the corporate social responsibility agenda (Khajeh-Hosseini, Greenwood, & Sommerville, 2010).

9.6 Connecting the Greater General Audiences

A notable gap related to cloud computing literature is the absence of resources that are easily accessible by non-technical people. This paper is responding to this by explaining concepts that can be quite complicated in a way that makes it easier to understand and relate to due to examples being given that are relatable to various practices such as e-commerce websites and distance learning applications. In so doing, the organization attempts to provide decision-makers, educators as well as small business owners with the confidence to embrace cloud solutions. This will be in line with the larger effort of democratizing technology, so that the advantages of cloud computing will be availed to various stakeholders (Wang, Wang, Ren, Lou, & Li, 2012).

In short, cloud computing is a revolutionary phenomenon with pounding consequences to corporations, the society as well as technology. This power of efficiency, innovation, and accessibility is also kept at bay by challenges that must be managed with caution. With this knowledge, the organizations can harness the utmost potential of cloud computing as they work through the complexities of the same. Paper conclusion will follow in the next section, and it will summarize main findings as well as provide suggestions to further investigations (Weinhardt, Anandasivam, Blau, & Stößer, 2009).

10. CONCLUSION

Cloud computing has become one of the most influential technologies that reconceptualize the interactions between individuals, businesses and societies with digital resources. The paper has given an elaborate account of cloud computing that includes its history, key concepts, service and deployment models, advantages, issues, uses, and future developments. Through integrating both literature and real-life cases, it has inferred the disruptive nature of cloud computing, and no doubt that it is not without issues that come with its implementation.

With all the advantages of saving money, scalability, availability, and these factors enabling innovations, cloud computing has become one of the adaptive tools used by all the industries (including e-commerce and healthcare, education, and entertainment) The benefits of this allow organizations to work more efficiently, address the various needs of the time and utilize such innovative technological advances as AI and IoT. Nevertheless, issues like security threats, data privacy, the risk of being locked by a vendor, and skills gap are some of the issues that need to be addressed strategically as they emerge, and their solutions should be comprehensive to guarantee effective implementation efforts. The fact that future trends discussed, such as edge computing, serverless constructions, and green cloud initiatives, reveal the continuous development of technology and the need to focus on the existing restrictions and the possibilities to solve them thereby opening new paths of opportunities.

This paper explains how it is necessary to have a dualistic outlook of cloud computing; as a strong driving force of advancement and a multifunctional and risky system at the same time. In the case of organizations, the decisions in embracing cloud solutions are based on cost, control and security with consideration of investing in skilled and tools to realize value. On the one hand, cloud computing creates possibilities of improving access to education and healthcare in society, but on the other hand, introduces a set of ethical issues related to the privacy of information and equal access. The introduction of these concepts in a friendly form intends to ensure that this paper empowers a wide group of people, including non-technical stakeholders, to approach cloud computing with a sense of confidence.

In the future, cloud computing will still define the path of the digital environment, with changes in technology and user demand. Future studies may focus on how small business can address the adoption barrier, how to manage costs and security, or the overall effect the cloud-driven technology like AI and quantum computing are having on our society. Along with it, it will be important to generate educational materials to help make up skill gaps and facilitate digital literacy, to provide an inclusive access to cloud advantages.

To sum up, however, it is not that cloud computing is just a technological innovation, but a mechanism of change, one that can allow a more connected, more efficient, and a more innovative world. When the understanding of its principles, opportunities, and challenges are achieved, it is possible to take advantage of its potential as a factor of improvement and overcome its complexity with the knowledge of how to act with reference to it.

REFERENCES

Ali, M., Khan, S. U., & Vasilakos, A. V. (2015). Security in cloud computing: Opportunities and challenges. *Information Sciences*, *305*, 357–383. DOI: 10.1016/j.ins.2015.01.025

Armbrust, M., Fox, A., Griffith, R., Joseph, A. D., Katz, R., Konwinski, A., Lee, G., Patterson, D., Rabkin, A., Stoica, I., & Zaharia, M. (2010). A view of cloud computing. *Communications of the ACM*, *53*(4), 50–58. DOI: 10.1145/1721654.1721672

Avram, M. G. (2014). Advantages and challenges of adopting cloud computing from an enterprise perspective. *Procedia Technology*, *12*, 529–534. DOI: 10.1016/j.protcy.2013.12.525

Botta, A., De Donato, W., Persico, V., & Pescapé, A. (2016). Integration of cloud computing and Internet of Things: A survey. *Future Generation Computer Systems*, *56*, 684–700. DOI: 10.1016/j.future.2015.09.021

Buyya, R., Yeo, C. S., Venugopal, S., Broberg, J., & Brandic, I. (2009). Cloud computing and emerging IT platforms: Vision, hype, and reality for delivering computing as the 5th utility. *Future Generation Computer Systems*, *25*(6), 599–616. DOI: 10.1016/j.future.2008.12.001

Chen, D., & Zhao, H. (2012). Data security and privacy protection issues in cloud computing. In *2012 International Conference on Computer Science and Electronics Engineering* (pp. 647–651). IEEE. DOI: 10.1109/ICCSEE.2012.193

Dikaiakos, M. D., Katsaros, D., Mehra, P., Pallis, G., & Vakali, A. (2009). Cloud computing: Distributed internet computing for IT and scientific research. *IEEE Internet Computing*, *13*(5), 10–13. DOI: 10.1109/MIC.2009.103

Gonzalez, N., Miers, C., Redigolo, F., Simplício, M.Jr, Carvalho, T., Näslund, M., & Pourzandi, M. (2012). *A quantitative analysis of current security concerns and solutions for cloud computing*. Journal of Cloud Computing: Advances. *Systems and Applications*, *1*(1), 11.

Gorelik, E. (2013). Cloud computing models. *MIT Sloan School of Management Working Paper*, 13-01.

Hashem, I. A. T., Yaqoob, I., Anuar, N. B., Mokhtar, S., Gani, A., & Khan, S. U. (2015). The rise of "big data" on cloud computing: Review and open research issues. *Information Systems*, *47*, 98–115. DOI: 10.1016/j.is.2014.07.006

Hosseini, A., & Butcher, L. (2012). Cloud computing: The concept, impacts and the role of government policy. *Journal of Information Technology & Politics*, *9*(3), 289–302.

Khajeh-Hosseini, A., Greenwood, D., & Sommerville, I. (2010). The Cloud Adoption Toolkit: Supporting cloud adoption decisions in the enterprise. *Software, Practice & Experience*, *42*(4), 447–465. DOI: 10.1002/spe.1072

Krutz, R. L., & Vines, R. D. (2010). *Cloud security: A comprehensive guide to secure cloud computing*. Wiley Publishing.

Marston, S., Li, Z., Bandyopadhyay, S., Zhang, J., & Ghalsasi, A. (2011). Cloud computing—The business perspective. *Decision Support Systems*, *51*(1), 176–189. DOI: 10.1016/j.dss.2010.12.006

Mell, P., & Grance, T. (2011). *The NIST definition of cloud computing* (Special Publication 800-145). National Institute of Standards and Technology.

Rittinghouse, J. W., & Ransome, J. F. (2016). *Cloud computing: Implementation, management, and security*. CRC Press.

Subashini, S., & Kavitha, V. (2011). A survey on security issues in service delivery models of cloud computing. *Journal of Network and Computer Applications*, *34*(1), 1–11. DOI: 10.1016/j.jnca.2010.07.006

Sultan, N. (2014). Making use of cloud computing for healthcare provision: Opportunities and challenges. *International Journal of Information Management*, *34*(2), 177–184. DOI: 10.1016/j.ijinfomgt.2013.12.011

Voorsluys, W., Broberg, J., & Buyya, R. (2011). Introduction to cloud computing. In *Cloud computing: Principles and paradigms* (pp. 1–44). Wiley. DOI: 10.1002/9780470940105.ch1

Wang, C., Wang, Q., Ren, K., Lou, W., & Li, J. (2012). Toward secure and dependable storage services in cloud computing. *IEEE Transactions on Services Computing*, *5*(2), 220–232. DOI: 10.1109/TSC.2011.24

Wang, L., Ranjan, R., Kolodziej, J., Zomaya, A. Y., & Alem, L. (2015). Software tools and techniques for big data computing in the cloud. *Software, Practice & Experience*, *45*(12), 1607–1614.

Weinhardt, C., Anandasivam, A., Blau, B., & Stößer, J. (2009). Cloud computing – A classification, business models, and research directions. *Business & Information Systems Engineering*, *1*(5), 391–399. DOI: 10.1007/s12599-009-0071-2

Yang, H., & Tate, M. (2012). A descriptive literature review and classification of cloud computing research. *Communications of the Association for Information Systems*, *31*(1), 35–60. DOI: 10.17705/1CAIS.03102

Youssef, A. E. (2012). Exploring cloud computing services and applications. *Journal of Emerging Trends in Computing and Information Sciences*, *3*(6), 838–847.

Zhang, Q., Cheng, L., & Boutaba, R. (2013). Cloud computing: State-of-the-art and research challenges. *Journal of Internet Services and Applications*, *1*(1), 7–18. DOI: 10.1007/s13174-010-0007-6

Chapter 16
Overcoming Copyright Protection Difficulties in Cloud Settings

Pallab Banerjee
Department of Computer Science and Engineering, Amity University, Ranchi, India

Mohammad Hashim
https://orcid.org/0009-0002-0764-9163
Department of Computer Science and Engineering, Amity University, Ranchi, India

Mohit Kumar
Department of Computer Science and Engineering, Amity University, Ranchi, India

Dipra Mitra
Department of Computer Science and Engineering, Amity University, Ranchi, India

Ashwani Kumar
https://orcid.org/0000-0002-2100-900X
School of Computer Science, Engineering, and Technology, Bennett University, Greater Noida, India

ABSTRACT

Since the storage and delivery services are migrating to the cloud which is expected to reach over $678.8 billion by 2027, the cloud-computing industry has emerged with intricate legal issues of enforcing copyright. In this chapter focal point is the

DOI: 10.4018/979-8-3373-3785-2.ch016

issues of infringement in the cloud systems whereby it gives an insight to the liability of the providers in the light of the U.S. Copyright Act as well as the recent court ruling and preceding global regulations. It talks about the influence of cloud models such as SaaS, PaaS and IaaS on the distribution and reproduction of copyrighted materials. It also examines the existing weaknesses of the laws available to deal with cross-border platforms particularly with regards to intermediary liability and DMCA safe harbor provisions. Difficulties in enforcement are illustrated in Dropbox, Google drive, and Mega case studies. The chapter ends with the observations that there are gaps in the law and need to create new policies and technologies such as better DRM and content recognition that will enhance the protection of copyright in the cloud.

1 INTRODUCTION

The popularity and proliferation of cloud computing solutions can be said to have revolutionized the digital content creation, distribution, accessing, and storage (storage) world, as it has altered the way digital content is produced, shared, read and saved. The established centralized approach of content distribution, where owners of content (publishers) and tangible mediums were dominant, has in recent years been replaced by a much more decentralized and virtualized setting with circulation of data being constant and unaided through the inter-connected networks spread across the world. In such a digital age, cloud systems are the new de facto mode of storing and transmitting large amounts of data, whether it be academic content and multimedia files, proprietary software, and real-time user-generated information (Adeusi et al., 2024).

Cloud computing is commonly put into different structures of service models, the most common three of these structures are Software as a Service (SaaS), Platform as a Service (PaaS) and Infrastructure as a Service (IaaS) which offer different level of control, abstraction and responsibility between the overall service provider and the end user. These models permit users, including individuals, to multinational corporations to access and use computing resources as demanded without the need to manage physical computing resources or maintain local infrastructure. This systemic transformation brings in issues of new scalar, efficiency and flexibility Nevertheless, it poses meaningful legal issues especially in copyright law, where the framework already in place cannot be easily adjusted to the dynamics of digital ecosystems that are no longer subject to geographic or jurisdiction limits.

As shown in Table 1, different cloud service models provide varying copyright concerns, with SaaS systems more vulnerable to user-uploaded content infringement, whilst IaaS faces issues such as hosting pirated files.

Table 1. Comparison of cloud models and copyright risks

Cloud Model	Description	Risk
SaaS	Software accessed via the internet	User uploaded files may infringe 3rd party rights
PaaS	Platform for developing the applications	Hosting infringing content via the developed apps
IaaS	Virtual servers & the storage infrastructure	Storage of pirated files or unauthorized distributions

Among the most urgent questions that this shift leads to there is the question of ambiguity of liability to infringement of copyright in cloud environments. The cloud makes real-time replication and distribution of material practical and in many cases without knowledge or direct action of the service provider. Users can do very little monitoring over content, which can be uploaded, altered, shared and deleted. This active personality that Render is so crucial to the charm and usefulness of cloud services is what makes the traditional enforcement measures, like the one based on notices and central location control, basically ineffective. This makes it progressively challenging to right holders, regulators and the courts to establish ownership, discover the unauthorised uses or even determine the correct party where infringement has taken place. With no central location or restriction, different jurisdictions on the cloud environment tend to clash, where the copyrighted work can be stored in a country, accessed in a different one and owned by a different party altogether. This fact interferes with the core values on which the traditional copyright enforcement systems are based.

What is more, the copyright regime was initially elaborated within the environment of tangible work (books, CDs, printed photographs) and regulated by national laws and was developed when content production and distribution were linear, localized and institutionally mediated. It presupposes a definite sequence of custody, the concentration of the production, and the definite access place of the material (Binns et al., 2022). Generally, by contrast, cloud-based systems are real-time, and on many, usually transient, computing nodes in the digital realm, where a single file might be in replicative format at many servers in different continents, and where neither the uploading person nor the owner of the file may be even aware of the legal implications in the different jurisdictions. Such discrepancies and difficulties cast doubt on whether the traditional copyright laws provide sufficient protection or implementation to the ever cloud-based, globalized environment. A special place in this legal framework is taken by Cloud Service Providers (CSPs). They do not act solely as a hosting organization but intermediaries, facilitators, and also enablers of content distribution. There is therefore the question of legal responsibilities and duties: How much should CSPs take approving and deleting infringing content uploaded by users? Do they have to take initiatives to avert abuse, or can they be mere impartial interveners, acting only when informed? What are the statutory provisions, i.e. what are the safe harbor provisions under the DMCA (Section 512), that provide protection against liability to CSPs and what are the prerequisites to such protection?

All this is compounded by the fact that different jurisdictions use uneven strategies. Whereas in the United States the conditional immunity of online intermediaries that comply with certain procedures is established through such legislative instruments as the DMCA, in the European Union, normal practice has shifted towards placing more proactive obligations on platforms (such as those established in the EU Copyright Directive, especially Article 17). The laws of copyright in other regions such as India and Australia differ in distinct measure of clarity and enforcement power. In this way, therefore, legal fragmentation, coupled with the technical complexity of cloud architectures, create a regulatory landscape that is hard to find the way through and is usually not conducive to any party in the copyright equation: either rightsholders in need of enforcement or service providers in need of compliance.

To sum up, the theme of cloud computing and copyright law can be outlined as a crucial topic of the legal investigations in the 21st century (Chekka & Babu, 2025). The move towards the decentralized, digital forms with physical forms of models implies that there is need to re-consider the principles underlying issues of liability jurisdiction and enforcement of the copyright environment around the globe. Future legal evolution should battle with technological reality and focus on convergent, flexible solutions that cross the territorial boundaries of a bygone era that are at variance with reality in a digital world where a balanced digital ecosystem is left to flourish with the right balance between innovation and protection of intellectual property rights.

See Figure 1 for the process flow diagram that follows.

Figure 1. Process flow diagram

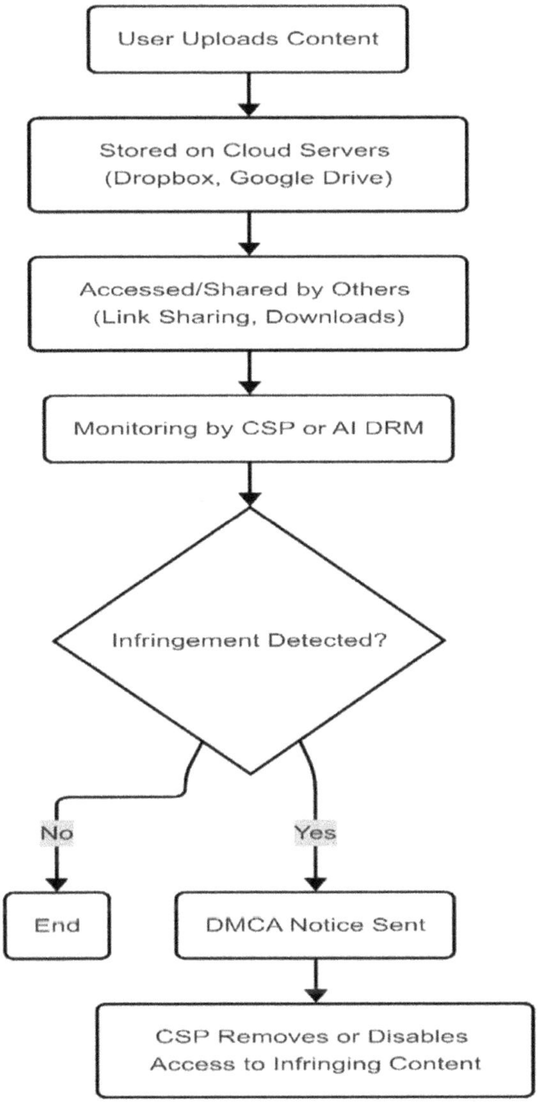

2 THE EFFECT OF CLOUD COMPUTING MODELS ON COPYRIGHT DISTRIBUTION AND REPRODUCTION

Cloud computing radically changes how digital content is accessed, stored, and shared. Its three major service models like SaaS, PaaS and IaaS interact with the protected content in different ways. Understanding these models is critical for determining how copyright infringement might occur within each and what problems exist for enforcement.

2.1 SaaS (Software as a Service)

The SaaS platforms e.g., Google drive, Microsoft OneDrive, and Dropbox, offer access to software and storage over the internet to the end-user. Naturally, these sites enable users to upload, store and share files such as images, videos, documents or software which all can be copyrighted.

Key Risks:

- Illegal distribution of material under copyright via publicly accessible file addresses.
- Privacy of message files and user-level access control makes monitoring of private file transfer difficult.
- An insufficient amount of active copyright enforcement without an independent system by the platform (e.g. Content ID by Google in YouTube).

2.2 PaaS (Platform as a Service)

Heroku or Google App Engine work as PaaS solutions that enable the construction and deployment of an application in the cloud. Such apps can use or distribute media, and act as an indirect infringement of copyright.

Key Risks:

- Incorporators using the images/music, or videos that have been embedded on the program or video without getting a license to publish them.
- Sites that operate through PaaS models that avoid the licensing process by tapping into pirated databases stream their content.
- Inability to control the content hosted in the applications without the strict content policies and filters usage by CSPs.

2.3 IaaS (Infrastructure as a Service)

IaaS services, and Amazon Web Services (AWS) and Microsoft Azure are the examples of this kind of IaaS platform that provide raw computing resources like virtually driven computer and storage. This gives the user increased control and flexibility leading to IaaS being powerful yet subject to abuse.

Key Risks:

- The presence of pirated software or content in the bio servers.
- Operation of torrent or warez sites by means of IaaS infrastructure.
- Legal difficulty in tracking infringing entities in terms of IP masquerading, encryption and spread of cloud nodes across geographical locations.

See Table 2 compares the levels of user control and frequent types of copyright infringement connected with each cloud model, using real-world examples such as Dropbox and AWS.

Table 2. Common copyright risks in different cloud models

Cloud Model	User Control Level	Common Infringements	Examples
SaaS	Low	Unauthorized file sharing	Dropbox, Google Drive
PaaS	Medium	Embedding pirated content in hosted applications	Heroku, Firebase
IaaS	High	Hosting torrent / streaming services, pirated files	AWS, Digital Ocean

2.4 Special Cross-Platform Enforcement Issues

Although terms of service usually saying that CSPs prevent infringement may be present in their CSP, it is hard to enforce. The violation is even detected:

- The rights holder jurisdiction can be different to CSP jurisdiction.
- Encryption of the data and anonymity of the users usually protect copyright violator.
- CSPs sometimes use such laws as the DMCA to claim safe harbor and thus are not directly liable.

See Figure 2 it illustrates how different cloud service models interact with and potentially misuse copyrighted content.

Figure 2. Cloud computing service models and copyright misuse

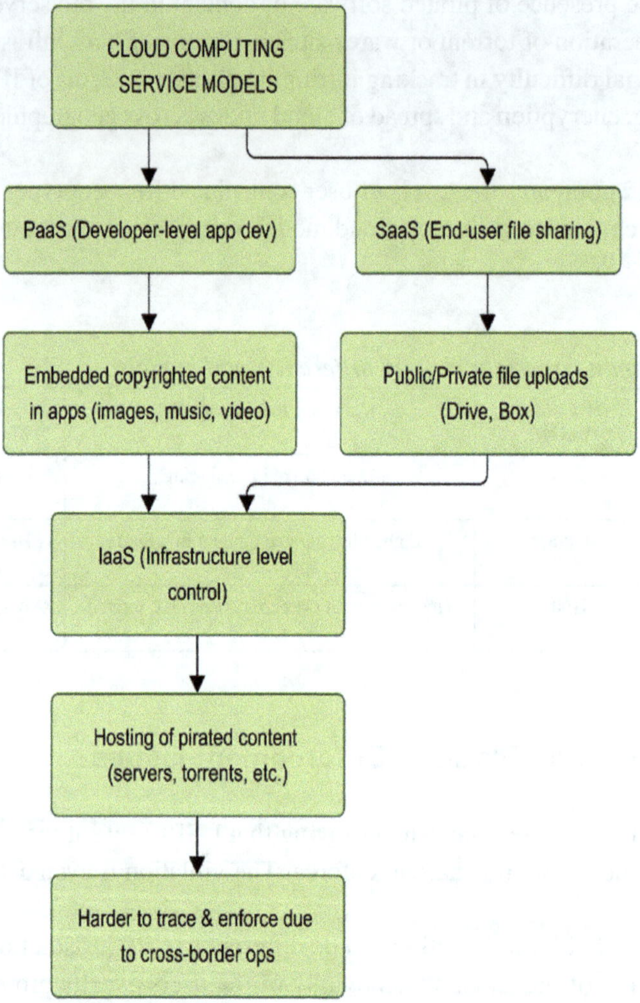

3 LEGAL FRAMEWORKS FOR COPYRIGHT IN CLOUD ENVIRONMENTS

The stormy development of the cloud computing business has over-distanced the growth of copyright law (De Filippi & Hassan, 2022). Whereas cloud services do not care about geographic boundaries, legal systems are authorized with jurisdictional boundaries, hence possible differences in the interpretation of copyright protection, intermediary liability, and the fair use provisions. This section explores the key legal frameworks that affect how copyright is interpreted and applied in cloud ecosystems in the world.

Cloud-based services such as Dropbox, Google Drive, and Mega are governed by complicated, layer-based regulation based on geographic location of servers they operate, the users or even the content. There are four main legal sources that mainly influence the enforcement of intellectual property rights in these environments and include:

1. The U.S. Copyright Law & Digital Millennium Copyright Act (DMCA)
2. European Union Copyright directive (EUCD)
3. WIPO Internet Treaties (WCT /WPPT)
4. New Frameworks in Nations such as India, Canada and Australia

These laws also provide some protection to service providers in form of safe harbor to not be liable in certain situations, but it also has duty to take down the post and obligations to supervise the post when notice of infringement is delivered (see Figure 3).

3.1 Copyright Act of the United States and DMCA (1998)

The DMCA as one of the most powerful laws in the whole world came up with a rider known as a "safe harbor" that the providers of the cloud services (CSPs) are not liable to inflict any kind of damage provided that this company is quick enough to take down the infringing material after it has been made aware about its presence.

But DMCA has been criticized on many accounts including:

- Failure to deter fresh offence
- Lack of sufficient hardware, software and interface to support contemporary automated and encrypted file-sharing
- It is U.S. centric, which creates enforcement gaps at the border line

3.2 Copyright Directive of the EU the proposal (2019)

The EUCD offers additional burdens to the cloud sites:

- Under Article 17 of directive, platforms should actively monitor and block copyright-protected material.
- Fosters the adoption of the content recognition solutions.
- It questions the helpless host model which has long been believed to be true according to the safe harbour regulations.

- This active law is opposed to the one presented by the DMCA, i.e., the notice and takedown mechanism.

3.3 WIPO Internet Treaties (WCT and & WPPT)

- These conventions set up internationally accepted guidelines on copyright protection in the digital network.
- Although they do not come up with enforcing structures, they compel member countries to harmonise their domestic laws.
- The arguments over most of the legal aspects of clouds are dependent on local interpretations of these treaties amongst countries.

3.4 The Indian Copyright law (2012)

India compares well with international IP standards, yet it does not have:

- A special middleman system such as the DMCA.
- Apparent haven clarity by cloud storage.
- Mechanisms of enforcement of data flows activities across borders.

See Table 3 it analyses significant international copyright regulations that apply to cloud systems.

Table 3. Comparison of key copyright laws in the cloud context

Legal Framework	Region	Safe Harbor Provided	Obligation to Monitor	Notable Feature
DMCA (1998)	United States	Yes	No	Implements a notice-and takedown mech
EUCD (2019)	European Union	Conditional	Yes (Article 17)	Requires proactive filtering and licensing
WIPO Treaties	International	Not applicable	No	Standardizes international digital copyright norms
India Copyright Act	India	Unclear	No	No explicit provisions for cloud-based content
Copyright Law (Australia)	Australia	Yes	No	Incorporates elements from both U.S. and EU models

See Figure 3 represents the legal mechanisms and frameworks adopted globally to address copyright infringement in cloud environments.

Figure 3. Legal response to copyright infringement in the cloud

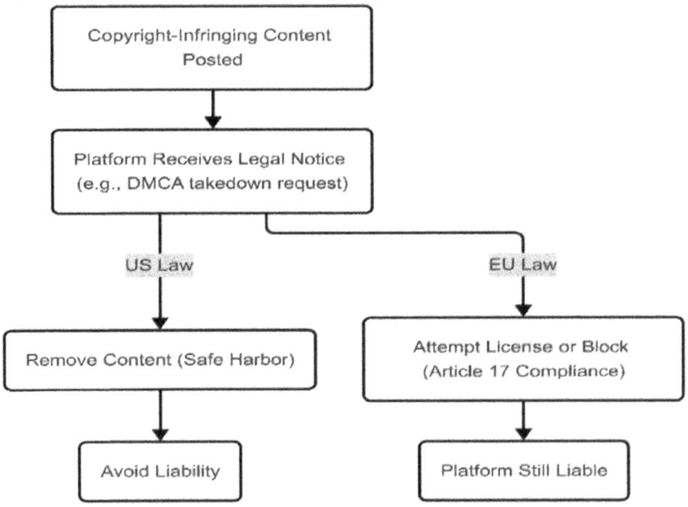

3.5 Cross-Border Enforcement Limits

In many instances, cloud ICT providers operate in diverse countries. The server hosting infringing materials can be in a different region, the uploader in another and the copyright owner in a third region. As a result of this spread around the world, these occurs:

- Conflicting laws
- Devoid of uniform enforcement rules
- Safe harbor loopholes
- Sluggishness in the court or removal of videos

4 INTERMEDIARY LIABILITY AND SAFE HARBOUR PROVISIONS

With cloud environment, the content may be posted, shared and accessed, but by a third party provider, who carries the service and is not the owner or origin of said content. These intermediaries- such as Dropbox, Google drive, or Mega.nz work as platforms of a person to store or transfer information. Of prime importance in legal perspective is the extent to which such intermediaries are liable in cases of upload of infringing material posted by the users (Bridy, 2022).

4.1 What Is Intermediary Liability?

Intermediary liability is the legal liability on a third-party service provider or platform operator whose users undertake an infringement.

Two are of them:

- Primary liability - the intermediate case in which the intermediary exerts active participation (e.g. in urging illegal file sharing).
- Secondary (or indirect) liability - where the intermediary does not directly engage in infringement through their platform to enable such using their platform.

4.2 Safe Harbor (512 DMCA)

Safe Harbor is a provision formulated in the Digital Millennium Copyright Act (DMCA) of 1998, Section 512 that represents a major legal instrument addressing the efforts to conjoin the strength of copyright protection clauses with the hard reality of information distribution as a digital material within the current Internet environment. In response to the prolific scale and dynamism of the user-generated content flows on the internet, Congress encoded these safe harbor provisions within the body of law to establish the conditions under which Online Service Providers (OSPs) including Internet Service Providers (ISPs), Web hosting sites, and cloud-based storage systems may restrict or altogether evade responsibility in the case of infringement in content sent up by third party users online.

4.2.1 Conditional Non-liability as the Means of Legal Immunity

But basically, Section 512 does not leave OSPs unaccountable altogether. Rather, it creates an "immunity on condition" regime in which service providers have to adhere to a series of strict procedural and substantive requirements in order be in a position to enjoy safe harbor immunity. Such responsibilities are, among others:

1. Complying Forced Resignation (512(c)(1)(C))

Once a takedown notice is valid and legally compliant, in the sense of Section 512(c)(3), the service provider has to act with the requisite diligence (pretentiously expeditiously) in order to remove or block access to the infringing material. Otherwise of timely failure, there are chances that the provider would lose immunity and would be held towards contributory or vicarious liability.

2. Designation of A DMCA Agent(512(c)(2))

The provider has to identify one or more registered DMCA agents to be publicly announced and serve infringement on ment claims. This piece of information must be visible on the platform and be registered with U.S. Copyright Office. This is so as to provide a direct and traceable point of contact between the right holders, and this requirement is carried out through the procedure aspect.

3. Lack of actual or red flag knowledge (512(c)(1)(A))

Such safe harbor may be used if the OSP does not have actual knowledge of the infringing material or is not willingly blind to their presence. The statute also muses on what it calls red flag knowledge i.e. the infringing nature of the content is obvious enough that the provider should know it. Regardless, the provider should move swiftly immediately they receive such information to stay out of danger.

4. No Financial Gain by Infringement (512(c)(1)(B))

When the service provider can control directly the infringing activity and has the right and capabilities to do so, the former should not have a direct financial gain that is related to the offending work. Such a provision is used to ensure that platforms do not look the other way in the pursuit of economic incentive with respect to infringement.

4.2.2 Modern Platform Operation

Modern digital services, including Google Drive, Dropbox, and YouTube, have integrated the DMCA compliance mechanism into their logistics in detail. These consist of automation of takedown processes, human audit systems and transparency reporting dashboards. Another example is that such platforms do not pre-screen the content but operate on the reactively mode by seeking to remove the infringing material after a notification is received, thereby maintaining the neutral-host status as required under the U.S. law. They also record detailed takedown requests, counter-notice and reinstatement procedures to counter any claim against them whether legal or otherwise that they are not worthy of safe harbor on their activities.

In addition, these platforms clearly affirm that they do not exercise any editorial control or content curation at all that is pivotal in asserting the shield of Section 512. The blueprint behind this law theory is entrenched based on a so-called passive conduit versus active participant doctrine which is perpetually being perfected by the courts in copyright cases.

4.2.3 Greater Jurisprudential and Policy Impact

The Safe Harbor as postulated in Section 512 has been famously felt all over the world where its effects have been felt by the legal system of many countries such as the EU eCommerce Directive (2000) or in India via the Information Technology (Intermediaries Guidelines) Rules. Nevertheless, it has persistently been scrutinized by the legal and legislative community, especially at times when discussions arise involving copyright protection in the era of artificial intelligence, algorithmic recommendations, and platform responsibility (Hou et al., 2025).

See Figure 4, a typical DMCA Safe Harbor workflow followed by major platforms is shown.

Figure 4. Safe harbor workflow for DMCA §512.

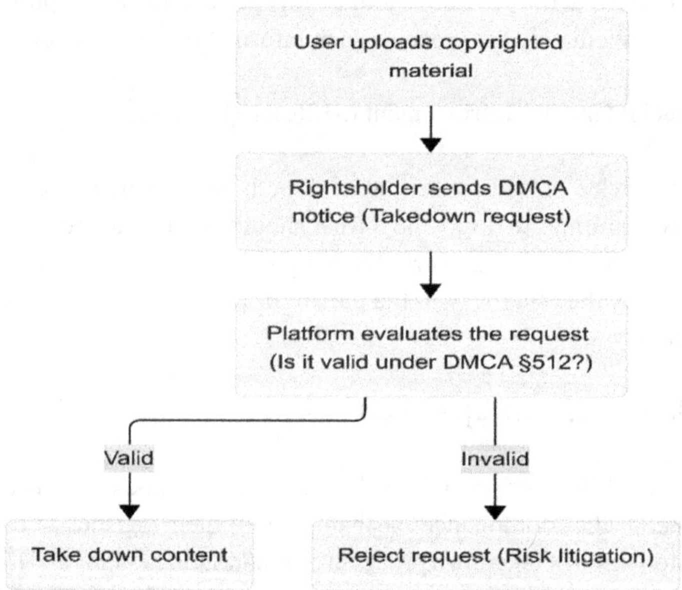

4.3 Limitations of Safe Harbor in the Cloud Era

While safe harbor laws were drafted to protect innovation and free speech, several challenges in cloud environments limit their effectiveness:

A. Cross-border Data Access

- Different countries have varying definitions of copyright and intermediary obligations
- A takedown order in one country may not be enforceable in another.
- Cloud servers are often distributed across regions, complicating jurisdiction.

B. Encrypted Cloud Services

- Platforms offering end-to-end encryption (e.g., Mega.nz) may not have visibility into content.
- This makes proactive monitoring impossible, yet users still share pirated material.
- Legal frameworks are not clear on whether such platforms should still be held liable.

See Figure 5, it shows the cross-jurisdictional and encryption-based issues.

Figure 5. Challenges of cross-border cloud takedown

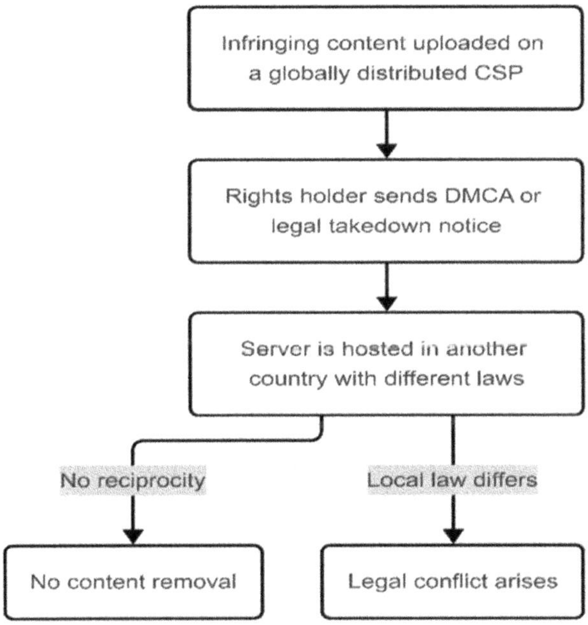

Some notable legal cases highlighting intermediary liability are summarized in Table 4.

Table 4. Famous copyright lawsuits involving intermediaries

Case	Platform	Year	Issue	Verdict
Viacom v. YouTube	YouTube	2007	Whether YouTube had actual knowledge of infringing videos	Ruled in favor of YouTube due to lack of specific knowledge (2013)
Capitol Records v. Vimeo	Vimeo	2013	Whether Vimeo was liable for infringing music uploads	Vimeo was granted safe harbor for user-generated content
UMG v. Shelter Capital	Veoh Networks	2011	Can platforms claim safe harbor for hosting infringing videos?	Veoh was protected under DMCA safe harbor
Megaupload Case	Megaupload	2012	Hosting pirated content on a massive scale	Platform taken down by FBI; founder Kim Dotcom prosecuted
TVCatchup v. ITV	TVCatchup (UK)	2013	Unauthorized streaming of TV content	CJEU ruled against TVCatchup; liability enforced

5 ENFORCEMENT CHALLENGES AND CASE STUDIES

The copyright regulation environment has changed fundamentally with the appearance of cloud computing technologies and their fast deployment. In earlier years, the commission of the copyright crime involved such massive physical acts as the illegal copying and selling of materials by DVD production, CD productions, or else printed works. This is however not the case today with whole libraries of copyrighted movies, e-books, software and music being distributed globally across continents in a matter of seconds courtesy of cloud storage facilities. Seamless collaboration and data democratization with the help of the same architecture similarly enable widespread digital piracy.

Cloud-based platforms enable immediate storage and retrieval but can provide security by encryption, anonymity, file obscurement, decentral assess, and cross-territorial location of data, all capabilities that neutralize traditional copyright active measures. As will be discussed in this section in some detail on three dimensions, the technological affordances of the cloud platforms on which copyright infringements occur (technological dimension); the possible extent of enforcement which is currently limited within the framework of current legislation and safe harbor laws (legal dimension); and a series of practical case studies which illustrate how the process of enforcement fails to provide effective and timely response in defending the copyrights (practical dimension).

5.1 Cloud Platforms with Technological and Architectural Affordance that Enables Breach

The marketing of cloud platforms as mostly productivity, collaboration and personal storage devices may have technical affordances that render them highly vulnerable to being used by either individuals or organized groups of people who aim to share copyrighted content, illegally. These design principles that give importance to privacy, scalability, friendliness and decentralization which are inherent in the design make the concerned services hard to police. The main technological and system related characteristics that can enable copyright misuse are:

a) Dynamically Scalable Storage and Wide Bandwidth Accessibility

Cloud platforms today would provide hundreds of terabytes of space for each user, and essentially limitless bandwidth, making them well suited to holding very large digital media libraries. It is even simple to upload a 4K movie, complete album discography, or even commercial software by dragging it into a window of a browser. The assets are subsequently distributed worldwide with the help of content delivery networks (CDNs) so users in all parts of the world may use it in real time.

b) Obfuscated URLs, Link Masking and Sharing

Almost all the mainstream cloud providers have mechanisms of generating links which enable users to share their files by means of a public URL. Pirates usually camouflage these connections with URL shorteners, redirect chains or deceptive anchor text. As an example, a file called lecture_notes_2023.pdf can turn out to be a bootleg copy of a cherry-selling book or a film to bypass bots scanning names.

c) Inability to Program Real-Time or Preemptive Content Monitoring

Most cloud providers do not actively sniff or actively inspect the deep content, whether because of technical or privacy related constraints. Most cloud storage platforms follow the passive host mode of operation, and most do nothing about copyrighted music and videos until they can receive case-valid legal notices of the takedown requests. Unlike platforms such as YouTube where Content ID systems are in place and are able to automatically track the use of copyrighted music and videos, most other cloud storage sites follow the passive host policy.

d) End-user Privacy and Encryption

Social media like Mega.nz use end-to-end encryption procedures whereby the service provider is also not able to communicate the information being uploaded or shared. The files are each encrypted on the client machine prior to uploading and the key to decryption is given only to users with a decryption key (frequently part of the shared URL). This architecture does not only guarantee privacy but also blinds the provider in the event of copyright contravention.

e) Low User Verification and Non-Identifiability Access

The cloud usually admits users to create accounts with little or no verification of identity. Throw away or disposable email accounts may be used to create anonymous accounts, utilized to post infringing works. Even when content is removed, users can open new accounts in a few minutes, and repost the same content, a case that keeps the enforcement systems overwhelmed in a loop.

5.2 The Legal Restrictions of Enforcement Options in the Cloud Age

The legal system which largely regulates and determines the issues of copyright infringement has had difficulty adapting to the reality of cloud computing. At the core of this inefficiency is the international area of focus because legal systems are jurisdictionally based, and the decentralized, unexcelled nature of cloud services.

a) Safe Harbor Provisions and Burdens of Notifications

In jurisdictions around the world that are governed by such legal instruments as Section 512 of the DMCA (U.S.) and Article 14 of the EU E-Commerce Directive, service providers are generally immune to liability in infringing content published on their sites as long as they reasonably and swiftly act to take down posted infringing content following proper notice to them (Senftleben, 2023).

This safe harbor principle was originally meant to shelter the intermediaries such as ISP and web hosts, but they now safely harbor multi-functional cloud platforms who can be seen as both passive carriers of piracy and active agents of the same.

In this way, enforcement is a game of me-mources. Copyright owners have a consistent task of watching the internet, finding infringing files, serving take downs, and hoping that they are taking actions. Detection and legal articulation of the violation is placed into the hands of the holder of the rights- establishing an intricate system where enforcement functions through laborious measures and procedures.

b) Jurisdiction Clashes and International Hosting of Data

Data on the cloud is usually distributed between data centers that are in different geographical locations. One illegitimate file may be split into segments located on several continents being difficult to find out which of the laws should be applicable and which could take the legal right to do anything. A takedown order issued by one jurisdiction can be legally fought against by the platform even though the file itself may be hosted by a country with other copyright limits or with relaxed systems of enforcement.

c) Privacy-Protective Architectures and Legal and Ethical Dilemmas

Privacy-focused cloud providers like Mega.nz or Proton Drive use the laws on protecting data and personal data to ensure their non-interference policy is sound. Although these privacy-driven systems defend the rights of the users, they also enable criminals to move in the shadows of the digital world. Issues involving the reaching of a balance between the right of privacy and the necessity of effective enforcement of the rights of copyright are more and more frequently faced by the courts, where the legislation may be unclear.

5.3 Case Studies: Dropbox, Google Drive and Mega. nz in the Piracy Ecosystem

1. Dropbox: Gateway to Random Breaking of the Laws

Syncing folder and link sharing are user-friendly features that make Dropbox a popular item to use in personal and academic sharing. The unfortunate consequence of its simplicity is that it also makes casual piracy possible. Online movies, educational textbooks, copies of software, and collection of comic books are regularly found through publicly available dropbox links. In certain cases, files will be encrypted or even fragmented, and the download keys are shared in forums, Discords, or Telegram groups. Though Dropbox does respond to DMCA take down notices and deactivates offending links, because of copyright infringement, it does not actively scan user directories, as it pursues privacy-first policies.

2. Google Drive: Digital Piracy at Scale

Google Drive represents digital piracy at scale, well organized. The massive penetration of Google Drive within the Google ecosystem has brought about the overtaking co-option of Google drive into more organized and professional piracy. Specialized indexing sites extract and organize publicly posted links of pirated movies, programs, and software in the Drive. Google's reaction is to shut down commodity links which are flagged and its enforcement against removal is recorded publicly through the Lumen Database. Yet, it does not have an automatic system, such as YouTube has a Content ID, to identify copyright infringing material, and re-uploading of pirated material with different names is still in process. One also uses it in academic circles to share complete courseware pirated off subscription-based learning sites.

3. Mega.nz: The Heaven of Encryption-Based Piracy

Mega.nz advertises as a privacy-first service, providing client-side encryption and large free storage amount. Its abuse by the piracy communities is due to its strong encryption, low level verification of users and hiding of file names. The copyright owners follow a dilemma: they cannot recognize or verify the content that is copyright infringed without breaking into an encryption and breaching the right of privacy of the user. As Mega argues, it cannot be accountable when it does not see the content that it might be exposed. This argument is valid in most of the legal systems today (Wu et al., 2022). This has resulted in a thriving trade in Mega-hosted piracy databases in third-party indexing websites that publicly share everything including anime boxsets, corporate software packs and more.

Table 5 describes the main cloud platforms, their usage tendencies, encryption levels, and enforcement actions taken against them.

Table 5. Cloud platforms and enforcement response

Platform	Type of Abuse	Encryption Used	Anonymity Level	Enforcement Response
Dropbox	Sharing of books, films, cracked software	No (optional)	Medium	Takedown after DMCA notice; no proactive scanning
Google Drive	Hosting pirated media, indexed through external sites	No (but obscured)	Medium–Low	Links disabled post-takedown; no content fingerprinting or DRM enforcement
Mega.nz	Encrypted sharing of pirated games, media, software	End-to-end encryption	High	Relies solely on reported links; claims lack of visibility shields liability
Megaupload	Hosted and profited from copyrighted content	No	High	Seized by FBI; key executives arrested; set legal precedent for platform liability
Zippyshare	Anonymous, short-term hosting of illegal content	No	High	Blocked in several countries; no internal enforcement measures

6 TECHNICAL SOLUTIONS AND POLICY RECOMMENDATIONS

The issue of copyright breach under cloud computing is deep and fast-changing. It is no longer effective to implement intellectual property rights using regular channels of the law with the outpourings of data in the thousands of terabytes per second, and with every user spread worldwide. Although the implementation of the cloud infrastructure did democratize access to the storage and distribution infrastructures, it has also unintentionally equipped pirates with powerful tools. Hence, it will require a two-pronged solution to this problem; through harnessing the power of technology innovation and fortifying an effective policy reform to establish a lean and futuristic enforcement ecosystem.

This part will take an in-depth look at some of the major technological solutions as well as policy suggestions that can be adopted to drastically change the current copyright happenings without necessarily curbing the freedom of the user, innovation or privacy.

6.1 Solution Using Technology

1. Digital Rights Management on the Cloud Age

Digital Rights Management (DRM) has remained the first line of attack against unauthorized usage and dissemination of copyrighted works. First used to ensure restrictions on access to physical media and the downloaded content, DRM has been extended into cloud-driven architecture to create limitations of what a viewer can do with an item: even without downloading any media, the streaming process can be limited. DRM systems work at platform level in a cloud environment to prevent unauthorized use dynamically. This features the option to turn off the screen recorder, the download blocking, and depriving the access after the expiration of subscriptions. As an example, Netflix, Disney+, and Amazon Prime provide users with very sophisticated DRM technology in large layers (like Widevine and FairPlay) without providing them with the opportunity to read the raw content files, even the most knowledgeable user (Amankwah-Amoah et al., 2024).

There are, however, limits of the DRM. It has received criticism in its perceived inflexibility, and to its effect on fair use and its lack of success in specific cases that involve circumvention tools. Pirates always find loopholes like recording the content through external recording devices or screen recorders. Thus, although DRM must be used as a layer of protection, it cannot even remotely be defined as a way out.

2. Automated Content Recognition Technologies and Filters

With user-generated content going out-of-control on the net, particularly on those sites that have storage and sharing facilities, automated content recognition tools have become indispensable. The manner in which these technologies are implemented is by the use of algorithms that identify copyrighted material in files that are uploaded and act on them before they reach the mainstream. Indeed, the detailed Content ID system of YouTube scans all uploaded videos across an enormous repository of video and audio fingerprints. When a match is detected, the system demonetizes, restricts, or deletes the video, as preferences by the rights-holder. Such real-time filtering system has been attributed to the significant decrease of the unauthorized circulation of content on YouTube.

Regarding cloud storage such as Dropbox or Google Drive, the inclusion of such automated search tools would be helpful in detecting pirated files- even when they have been renamed or altered slightly. As an example, a high-fidelity copy of a film soundtrack, a unique hash of a pirated software installer, may automatically activate an alert or an automatic removal procedure. Privacy laws however have meant that many platforms cannot scan the files of the user unless it is publicly shared, meaning that pirates will keep file sharing restricted to encrypted or invite-only sharing as a loophole.

3. Copyright Proof and Distribution Integrity using Blockchain

The blockchain technology will be a revolutionary disruption since the imparts a decentralized, unchangeable way of managing and preserving copyrights. Registering digital content in a blockchain ledger allows creators to create uncontestable evidence of ownership with timestamps, licensing conditions and transaction history. Every digital asset, whether it is music, video, software, or literature can be provided with a unique cryptographic hash and incorporated into a smart contract. Such smart contracts govern licensing terms automatically, and in such a way that the right to use is only given on certain conditions that can be proved. Such solutions are being piloted by platforms such as Ascribe and Po.et, applied to visual art, journalism and literature.

The real power of the blockchain is that it is open and cannot be altered. After ownership is registered on-chain, it is only possible to change it later; therefore, the ownership of a creative work becomes much more trackable. Nevertheless, mass adoption is not widespread because of the problem of scalability, the absence of standardization, and relatively high technical barrier of entry common users face.

6.2 Policies

Even hi-tech systems have to have a policy background that can help them to be adopted, gives them incentives to act morally and safeguard the rights of all the parties. Technical solutions will not be enough or breach on basic digital rights unless they are planned out. In this way, the implementation of the copyright should be supported by flexible laws, education, and action programs.

1. Revisions to the Intermediary Liability and Safe Harbors Legislation

Poor accountability on cloud service providers (CSPs) is one of the greatest problems of enforcement. The majority of them work on safe harbor laws, which include those in the U.S. Digital Millennium Copyright Act (DMCA) that exempts them when they act on takedown requests. This model, however, was developed way before the end-to-end encryption and large distribution of files globally and does not represent the reality in the operations of the current cloud systems. To make this more modern, regulations should be able to create a thinner line between intermediary services that are passive and those that are active in propelling piracy.

Being able to monetize file-sharing, promoting popular content over its legality, and simply avoiding even basic content protection options should not grant the full immunity to those platforms. Companies might be required to provide a set minimal degree of due diligence, e. g. by providing content filtering APIs, keeping lists of repeat offenders, enforcing the verification of high-volume sharers.

One such case is the Article 17 of the Copyright Directive of the European Union, where platforms now have the obligation to either license or take down infringing material on its own accord. Although it is controversial, it is leading to a shift in the direction of greater platform accountability that might be emulated by other jurisdictions.

2. Advancing Transparency, and Procedural Fairs

Unless the takedown process is transparent and accountable, it may result in either abuse, censorship or unjust penalties. They should have transparency reports of the number of takedown requests they receive and eliminate the people who made the requests, and the reasons on a regular basis. This transparency does not only generate trust, but it also discourages copyright abuse by companies or anyone trying to use it against freedom of expression. Moreover, clear and open means of contesting claims, to users who have their contents removed, should be availed. Such processes should be harmonized across borders perhaps by the WIPO or WTO so that it could be easier to enforce against an international platform and so that users have more cross-border certainty in their digital rights.

Standardized, large scale public repositories, such as the Lumen Database, which already holds the requests made to major sites to have content removed, needs to be expanded to include metadata, such as response time, appeal result, and pattern. Such data can be used in the formulation of policies in the future and assist watchdog organizations in bringing platforms to account.

3. Committing Resources to Digital Literacy and Ethical Consciousness

After all, technology and law cannot exist in vacuum. A good percentage of piracy of online materials is done not by insidious minds but through innocence. A vast number of users and particularly the students, young professionals, or the people living in areas where content isn t legally accessible in large numbers tend to have little knowledge of the legal kind of actions undergo or damage that is inflicted on content creators (Wang et al., 2025).To address this gap, learning education can be incorporated into cloud platforms, in particular those users who are new and upload or post files. Users might be presented with engaging questions that define copyright violation, possible dangers of sharing pirated material, and any alternative means that users can access before activating sharing features. Licensing their own content under Creative Commons could have default templates, which are provided in platforms as well, thus developing more responsible sharing (see Figure 6).

In addition, governments and learning institutions can take the initiative of incorporating the education about copyrights into digital literacy programs. Behavioral programs and partnerships with universities and certifications may help develop a generation of users with the knowledge of how to consume digital media, in a way that is ethical and legal.

Figure 6. DRM-Based copyright enforcement process in the cloud

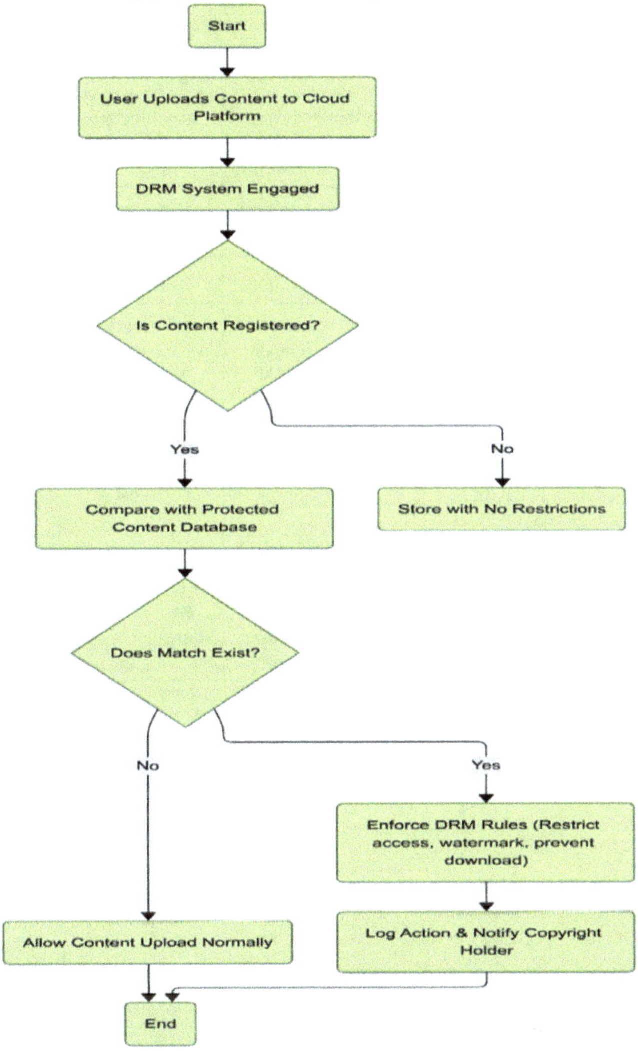

See Figure 6, it depicts the DRM-based enforcement workflow, showing how digital rights are managed and protected in cloud environments.

Table 6. Comparison of technical solutions for copyright protection in cloud environments.

Technology	Function	Benefits	Limitations	Examples
Digital Rights Management (DRM)	Restricts access, copying, and distribution of content	Prevents unauthorized usage; controls content post-distribution	Can be bypassed; may hinder user experience	Netflix, Amazon Prime, Adobe eBooks
Content Recognition Technology (CRT)	Identifies copyrighted material by comparing digital fingerprints	Real-time detection; automation of takedown or monetization	Requires large reference database; false positives possible	YouTube's Content ID, Facebook Rights Manager
Blockchain	Creates immutable records of content ownership and licensing	Transparent tracking; tamper-proof; enables smart contracts	Slow adoption; not yet standardized in legal systems	Ascribe, Po.et, MediaChain
AI-Based Monitoring Tools	Scans metadata, patterns, or user behavior to detect potential infringement	Scalable detection; can adapt to new piracy patterns	Privacy concerns; high development cost	Google AI content scanners, Microsoft Azure AI
Metadata Watermarking	Embeds invisible ownership information in content	Helps trace leaks; doesn't interfere with user experience	Can be removed with advanced tools; not effective alone	Watermarking in documents, videos, and images

Table 6 analyses technical tools such as DRM, blockchain, and AI for improving copyright protection in cloud environments.

7 THE FUTURE OF COPYRIGHT IN CLOUD ENVIRONMENTS

With the displacement of the conventional models of copyright law with the infusion of newer digital technologies in the creation, storage, and sharing of creative contents, there has been great pressure on the traditional paradigms of copyright law. By being decentralized, scalable and enabling anonymity, the cloud computing ecosystem is not only a blessing in terms of the opportunities it provides, but also a nightmare to copyright industries. In the future, the international community will have to reinvent the legal and moral environment of digital rights. It is a future that will be written about transnational collaboration, smart enforcement mechanisms, moral arguments about user right to self-determination, and ownership that is being ushered in to radically challenge copyright itself.

7.1 International standardization of Copyright laws

In a world where infringement of content flows easily across state borders via cloud-based systems, the lack of an integrated international copy right system has become a major hindrance to successful prosecution. The existing copyright regimes are still pretty territorial in their application, where the same action that is an infringement in one country is fair use, educational exemption or statutory license in the other. The result of this fragmentation on the law is the emergence of grey areas in which infringers take advantage of jurisdiction gaps, notably, via international cloud services.

With this in mind, what is required to solve this is an immediate need that is global in introducing uniformity in copyright law- a form of Intellectual Property Digital Geneva Convention. Such a structure, preferably led by global authorities such as the United Nations, the World Intellectual Property Organization (WIPO) or the World Trade Organization (WTO) should seek to develop minimum protection, enforcement, and remedy systems within cloud-based content distribution. WIPO Copyright Treaty, ACTA, and other points of the Digital Services Act within the European Union can also be used as a stepping point in discussion. Moreover, as the General Data Protection Regulation (GDPR) introduced a single legal standard of privacy in Europe, such a binding and certainly exhaustive copyright contract in cyberspace and clouded world could simplify copyright enforcement, mitigate the uncertainties, and safeguard both the right holders and the users on the international level as well.

7.2 Smart Enforcement Powered with AI

Artificial Intelligence (AI) will change copyright enforcement in cloud ecosystems, with innovations that are scalable, predictive and adaptive as compared to the ability of a human being. The takedown and manual review procedures through the traditional system is by its nature reactive and man intensive, making it unsuitable in dealing with the extent of file-sharing activities and daily uploads. Compared to AI, the possibility of proactive enforcement is based on constant monitoring, recognition of patterns, and analytics of behavior. One element that future copyright enforcement mechanisms could potentially be based on are machine learning algorithms that are trained not just to identify exact matches, but also derivative works, small changes such as edits or other ways of modifying copyrighted works. High-risk actions might be anticipated with these systems using metadata, audiovisual signals, user sharing rate, and historical infringement patterns in real time. As an example, a cloud storage system might mark and temporarily put in quarantine files with attributes likely to be found in pirated content, e.g. obfuscated file names, odd file compression schemes, or behavioral access patterns, until a human operator can review it.

Besides, the implementation of AI might be decisive in specific interpretation, secretly separating prohibitive use and lawful conduct, which can be characterized as parody, critique, or pedagogical fare-use. Although such contextual intuition has become a primary technical issue currently, with the development of Natural Language Processing (NLP) models and image recognition frameworks, decision-making based on context shows that it is not too far away. Along with increased efficiency, introduction of AI in the process of copyright enforcement can also decrease false positives and increase user trust, although only on a condition that such algorithms are transparent, auditable, and meet the standards of human rights.

7.3 Ethics vs. Control: Finding the Balance

As technology is being able to enforce copyright to a larger scale, another equally important issue is how to make sure enforcement is not performed at the cost of civil liberties, creativity and digital inclusion. That is why the future of copyright in cloud context should be formed both by means of control and ethical approaches, the key aspect of which lies in rights of users and preservation of democratic principles in regulatory framework.

This is one of the priorities, which is fair use and other legal exceptions, including commentary, satire, instruction, and research. Targeted by overzealous enforcement mechanisms, especially automated takedown systems, such mechanisms tend to prioritize context, and instead have draconian consequences such as the punishment of legitimate uses, smothers free expression and intern novation, which is the requirement to enforce the license. Platforms and regulators should respond by putting the rights of the user first, which means digital rights management has to be struck in a balance between copyright protection, freedom of expression, and access to knowledge.

Also, the increased and normalized use of open licensing systems such as Creative Commons (CC) can serve as a sort of copyright alibi and this is the right way. With these licenses, makers can distribute their works with customized permission thus promoting joint creativity and minimizing the use of strict legal frameworks. Such models can be encouraged by government, institutions and platforms with incentives, education and defaults to share content.

In addition to that, the people should guard the public domain and treat it as a common cultural asset. Good information common in the cloud age needs to make sure that expired copyrights, government work and historical media are freely available. Therefore, the ethical debate over copyrighting should move out of being punitive to being inclusive and participatory where the agency of the user and benefit to society are respected.

7.4 New Forms of Ownership: NFTs and Decentralized Systems

Not only did the emergence of decentralized technologies like blockchain succeed in bringing new enforcement measures, it has re-conceptualized more primary terms of ownership and copyright. Leading this transition is Non-Fungible Tokens (NFTs), a cryptographically secure method of defining ownership of digital assets in form of art, music, software code, video or multimedia pieces. The use of NFTs also disrupts existing models of control over copyright that has seen local control resting in the hands of centralized publishers or distributors and shifts it to a decentralized mode of control wherein individual creators or collectors get control of the copyright. NFTs also incorporate ownership information (and licensing terms) directly into the metadata carried by a token, enabling peer-to-peer transfer of tokens and automatic payments of royalties on transfer, as well as the ability to track the origin of content (provenance). As such, their properties align with the decentralization in the context of clouds. The platform such as OpenSea, Rarible, and Foundation has already established marketplaces to sell, buy, or rent digital rights without the mediation of third parties.

But NFTs come with complications, as well. The possession of one token does not necessarily mean the possession of copyright, which causes misunderstanding between the buyers and litigation about what rights were really sold. Moreover, once written into the blockchain, it is hard to delete or change licensing conditions afterward, which may contradict the changing terms of user agreements or the legal copyright term limit.

And in the long term, it is going to be necessary to align these new models with current legal frameworks. The usage of hybrid systems could be a possibility, where the intellectual property laws of customs on moral and economic rights will be secured by normal copyrights, with the technical aspects of the enforcement and transaction logging to be managed by blockchain technologies. Regulatory frameworks should evolve to shed greater light on the nexus between digital tokens and intellectual property, and that decentralized ownership of intellectual property should add value to the benefit of creators and not to their detriments.

7.5 User-Centered Copyright Enforcement via Participatory Governance

With greater integration of digital platforms in content creation, distribution, and control, the argument of having the participatory form of governance, where end-users have a significant input into the creation of the meaning of copyright, its enforcement, and balancing of loss and benefits in a cloud-based sphere, is even gaining grounds. Instead of either exclusively relying on the top-down regulation format or closed automated practices, the copyright system of the future will have to advance with the ensemble of community governance and shared decision making. It is a vision of participatory enforcement that acknowledges that creators are not just passive consumers and possible infringers, but also educators, and cultural actors. An example of such implementation might be found in decentralized systems of moderation or a copyright council, a multi-stakeholder panel, by whom takedowns in question of dispute, fair use, and licensing will be reviewed. This model brings about openness and fair process into a one-sided and automated takedown process.

Furthermore, systems that allow a level of community moderation based on community reputation could be implemented where a user with experience and the appropriate history of responsible behaviour has a greater say in the identification or yes/no vote on identifying a possible copyright violation. To continue with the above examples, education institutions or credible makers could have the ability to make a contribution to the determination of the fair use scenarios, particularly concerning academic or documentary works.

Also, participatory governance applies to policy design and architecture of the platform. Users must have avenues, i.e., avenues may come in the form of government consultations, stakeholders' forums, or even in the form of online references where they get to present feedback on copyright regulations, platform policies, and enforcement mechanisms via algorithms. Such processes do not only enhance the responsiveness of policies but also create a spirit of digital citizenship and common responsibility. Moreover, algorithm development must become open-source and transparent. In cases where the AI tools used to detect or take some action on the copyrighted material in the cloud, users should be able to access clear explanations of the reasoning that leads to such a decision, what data is accessed, and how to appeal a mistake. Demystifying automated processes can lower the distrust and increase action accuracy by platforms.

The involvement of users in the process of governing copyright is not an unproblematic process that consists of balancing expertise and accountability and inclusiveness issues. Yet, as cloud spaces grow more participatory in nature, encouraging the user to collaborate on the fabric of the rules of digital engagement, it is not only a logical but a democratic process. It takes copyright farther, out of the compliance realm and into the realm of equity, enlightenment and cultural responsiveness.

7.6 Digital Twins, Virtual Worlds, and Copyright Complicatedness

The dawn of the era of immersive technologies is accompanied by the emergence of digital twins, metaverse platforms, and persistent virtual worlds that pose unprecedented copyright complexity and challenges that obscure physical and digital spaces. The Esco described settings that occur in virtual campuses and marketplaces up to fully simulated smart cities are not only hosted with the existence of digital objects but also hosting interactive media, real-time services, and algorithmically created material, all of which are extremely challenging to copyright.

Digital twin is a computer representation of a physical object, system or environment. These models are important in simulation, training, and innovation in other fields such as manufacturing, medicine and education. When these twins use infringed copyrighted architecture design, software interface or media contents (musical tracks, 3D models or real-life trademarks), ownership and rights of their respective digital siblings turn even more tricky. An example is who has the copyright to the digital copy of a copyrighted sculpture in one of the virtual museums? Is simulating a copyrighted object in a new context, an infringement or a fair use?

Those dilemmas increase when it comes to the metaverse, a decentralized network of immersive and persistent 3D spaces. The users enter in interaction, construct, and commerce using virtual objects, most of which are directly or indirectly paraphrased using copyright content. There are branded clothing in avatars, virtual concerts which perform and replay copyrighted music, and digital art installations that draw on prior models- all of these features are present in the user-created worlds that have lax control over property rights finding themselves in a poorly defined ownership right community. Besides, these platforms have various, sometimes obscure, terms of service that can be contrary to national copyright laws or international agreements.

To complicate the matter, there is an emergence of AI-created content in the virtual space. Music, dialogues, imagery and entire narratives can now be generated through machines, finding successful uses in metaverse experiences, but the copyright law that covers most jurisdictions has not yet captured all aspects of whether such works can be possessed or licensed by whom. It begs the question whether a complete automatic virtual performance can be in violation of pre-existing copyright, notwithstanding that no human consciously wrote the infringing materials. Legal systems must be swift. The future copyright law should solve the issues of the mixing of physical and digital IP, the ownership of simulations, and the cross-border practice of transactions of virtual assets. Notably, platform-level governance (upmost in metaverse platforms such as Decentraland, Roblox, and Meta Horizon Worlds), will have to provide advanced right management solutions capable of identifying unauthorized access to the protected content within user-generated worlds.

8 CONCLUSION

The widespread adoption of the cloud computing has fundamentally transformed the dynamics of digital content generation, distribution & consumption. While technology provides extraordinary scale, efficiency and accessibility it also challenges copyright enforcement in hitherto unanticipated ways. As discussed in this chapter, traditional copyright rules fail to keep up with the borderless and decentralized nature of cloud services. The issues of intermediary responsibility, ambiguous jurisdiction, encrypted storage and user anonymity have revealed key weaknesses in existing legal frameworks like DMCA's Safe Harbor clauses. To close these gaps advanced technology solutions (say) the Digital Rights Management (DRM), content identification systems like YouTube's Content ID and the blockchain based copyright tracking have showed great promise. However, technology alone cannot guarantee the long-term viability without concomitant policy innovation. Strengthening international law harmonization, boosting openness in takedown operations, and promoting user education are all essential components of a comprehensive enforcement approach (see Table 7).

Furthermore, as cloud ecosystems grow and intersect with artificial intelligence, decentralized technologies, and global data flows, stakeholders such as politicians, cloud service providers, producers and users must maintain open lines of communication. The goal must be to achieve a careful balance between innovation and security, transparency and control, privacy and accountability. Only via such collaborative and adaptive measures can we hope to create a future-ready copyright ecosystem that protects intellectual property while also respecting the digital freedoms necessary for innovation and progress.

Table 7 identifies important copyright enforcement difficulties in cloud systems and suggests legal and technological solutions.

Table 7. Challenges vs. strategic responses

Challenge	Problem	Proposed Solution	Technological Solution
Intermediary Liability	Unclear responsibility of CSPs	Revise DMCA safe harbor with stricter compliance standards	Automated content filters before file upload
Cross-border Enforcement	Jurisdictional confusion	International copyright treaties	Blockchain timestamping and licensing systems
Encrypted/Anonymous Sharing	Difficult to trace and remove pirated content	Platform accountability regulations for encryption abuse	AI-driven behavior analysis and metadata scanning

continued on following page

Table 7. Continued

Challenge	Problem	Proposed Solution	Technological Solution
Content Duplication on Mirrors	Replication of takedown content on other clouds	Shared industry watchlists and takedown databases	Hash-based file recognition across platforms
Delayed Takedown Mechanisms	Inefficiency in responding to infringement reports	Mandatory response timeframes and transparency reports	Real-time Content ID-style monitoring
User Ignorance on Copyright	Lack of awareness	Mandatory copyright awareness prompts during uploads	Educational banners and guided license selections in UIs

REFERENCES

Adeusi, O. C., Adebayo, Y. O., Ayodele, P. A., Onikoyi, T. T., Adebayo, K. B., & Adenekan, I. O.Oluwafemi Clement AdeusiYusuf Olalekan AdebayoPraise Ayomide AyodeleTajudeen Tunde OnikoyiKayode Blessing AdebayoIbrahim Oyeyemi Adenekan. (2024). IT standardization in cloud computing: Security challenges, benefits, and future directions. *World Journal of Advanced Research and Reviews*, *22*(3), 2050–2057. DOI: 10.30574/wjarr.2024.22.3.1982

Amankwah-Amoah, J., Abdalla, S., Mogaji, E., Elbanna, A., & Dwivedi, Y. K. (2024). The impending disruption of creative industries by generative AI: Opportunities, challenges, and research agenda. *International Journal of Information Management*, *79*, 102759. DOI: 10.1016/j.ijinfomgt.2024.102759

Arora, R., Gera, S., & Saxena, M. (2021, March). Mitigating security risks on privacy of sensitive data used in cloud-based ERP applications. In *2021 8th International Conference on Computing for Sustainable Global Development (INDIACom)* (pp. 458-463). IEEE.

Banerjee, P., Snehal, S., Kumari, S., Kumar, B., Thakur, K., & Patnaik, M. (2024, September). A comparative analysis of different cloud computing method for scheduling healthcare tasks. In *2024 International Conference on Signal Processing and Advance Research in Computing (SPARC)* (Vol. 1, pp. 1–5). IEEE. DOI: 10.1109/SPARC61891.2024.10829361

Binns, R., Veale, M., Van Kleek, M., & Shadbolt, N. (2022). 'It's reducing a human being to a percentage': Perceptions of justice in algorithmic decisions. In *Proceedings of the 2022 ACM Conference on Fairness, Accountability, and Transparency* (pp. 165–176).

Bridy, A. (2022). Algorithms and copyright: Content ID and the automation of IP enforcement. *The Notre Dame Law Review*, *97*(2), 623–670.

Chekka, R. B., & Babu, B. R. (2025). Secure digital data visual sharing schemes in multi-owner public cloud environment applications. Scalable Computing. *Practice and Experience*, *26*(1), 84–95.

Dash, B. (2024). Zero-trust architecture (ZTA): Designing an AI-powered cloud security framework for LLMs' black box problems. *SSRN*. https://ssrn.com/abstract=4726625

De Filippi, P., & Hassan, S. (2022). Blockchain technology as a regulatory technology: From code is law to law is code. *First Monday*, *27*(3). DOI: 10.5210/fm.v27i3.11611

Elkin-Koren, N. (2020). Copyright in the cloud: Who owns what? *Journal of Intellectual Property Law & Practice, 15*(6), 457–466.

Fan, J., Lian, H., & Liu, W. (2024). Privacy-preserving AI analytics in cloud computing: A federated learning approach for cross-organizational data collaboration. *Spectrum of Research, 4*(2).

Hou, Z., Yan, H., Zhang, L., Ma, R., Yan, Q., & Yang, B. (2025). A secure and efficient remote sensing image retrieval method with verifiable and traceable in cloud environment. *IEEE Transactions on Geoscience and Remote Sensing, 63*, 1–16. DOI: 10.1109/TGRS.2025.3539846

Inaganti, A. C., Ravichandran, N., Nersu, S. R. K., & Muppalaneni, R. (2021). Cloud Security Posture Management (CSPM) with AI: Automating Compliance and Threat Detection. *Artificial Intelligence and Machine Learning Review, 2*(4), 8–18.

Kaminski, M. E. (2021). The dangers of user-generated takedowns. *North Carolina Law Review, 99*(5), 1301–1352.

Kashyap, P. K. COPYRIGHT PROTECTION IN DIGITAL ENVIRONMENT: CHALLENGES AND SOLUTIONS. *INTELLECTUAL PROPERTY RIGHTS*, 27.

Liu, Y., Wang, X., & Zhou, Y. (2024). Legal challenges of cloud-based content sharing platforms: A comparative study of DMCA and GDPR implications. *Computer Law & Security Review, 52*, 105755.

Margoni, T., & Kretschmer, M. (2023). Artificial intelligence and copyright: The state of play. *European Intellectual Property Review, 45*(1), 20–30.

Mavani, C., Mistry, H. K., Patel, R., & Goswami, A. (2024). The role of cybersecurity in protecting intellectual property. *International Journal on Recent and Innovation Trends in Computing and Communication, 12*(2), 529–538.

Mogol, N., & Crudu, R. (2022). Challenges and strategies for copyright protection in the digital era. *Journal of Social Sciences, 5*(4), 6–19. DOI: 10.52326/jss.utm.2022.5(4).01

Pendyala, S. K. (2025). Strengthening healthcare cybersecurity: Leveraging multi-cloud and AI solutions. *Journal of Computer Science Applications and Information Technology, 10*(1), 1–8. DOI: 10.15226/2474-9257/10/1/00163

Reese, R. A. (2021). The DMCA's safe harbors, twenty years later. *Columbia Journal of Law & the Arts, 44*(3), 305–340.

Senftleben, M. (2023). The perfect match? Enhancing DRM through AI-based content recognition. *International Review of Intellectual Property and Competition Law, 54*(2), 143–168.

Shabbir, A., Anwar, A. S., Taslima, N., Sayem, M. A., Sikder, A. R., & Sidhu, G. S. (2024). Analyzing enterprise data protection and safety risks in cloud computing using ensemble learning. *International Journal on Recent and Innovation Trends in Computing and Communication, 12*(2), 499–507.

Sinha, A., Banerjee, P., Roy, S., Rathore, N., Singh, N. P., Uddin, M., Abdelhaq, M., & Alsaqour, R. (2024). Improved dynamic Johnson sequencing algorithm (DJS) in cloud computing environment for efficient resource scheduling for distributed overloading. *Journal of Systems Science and Systems Engineering, 33*(4), 391–424. DOI: 10.1007/s11518-024-5606-z

Ukwandu, E., Ben-Farah, M. A., Hindy, H., Bures, M., Atkinson, R., Tachtatzis, C., Andonovic, I., & Bellekens, X. (2022). Cyber-security challenges in aviation industry: A review of current and future trends. *Information (Basel), 13*(3), 146. DOI: 10.3390/info13030146

Urban, J. M., Karaganis, J., & Schofield, B. (2020). Notice and takedown in everyday practice. UC Berkeley Public Law Research Paper No. 2766526.

Wang, H., Tang, N., Zhu, C., Ren, N., & Wang, C. (2025). A blockchain copyright protection model based on vector map unique identification. *ISPRS International Journal of Geo-Information, 14*(2), 53. DOI: 10.3390/ijgi14020053

Wu, X., Duan, R., & Ni, J. (2024). Unveiling security, privacy, and ethical concerns of ChatGPT. *Journal of information and intelligence, 2*(2), 102-115.

Wu, X., Ma, P., Jin, Z., Wu, Y., Han, W., & Ou, W. (2022). A novel zero-watermarking scheme based on NSCT-SVD and blockchain for video copyright. *EURASIP Journal on Wireless Communications and Networking, 2022*(1), 20. DOI: 10.1186/s13638-022-02090-x

Yu, P. K. (2023). Cloud computing and cross-border copyright enforcement. Fordham Intellectual Property. *Media & Entertainment Law Journal, 33*(4), 1153–1205.

Compilation of References

Abdelhakim, A., Saleh, H. I., & Abdelhakim, M. (2019). Fragile Watermarking for Image Tamper Detection and Localization with Effective Recovery Capability Using K-Means Clustering. *Multimedia Tools and Applications*, *78*(22), 32523–32563. DOI: 10.1007/s11042-019-07986-3

Abdulbaqi, H. A., Ghandour, A. M., & Jawad, T. A. (2024). Develop Secure Software specifications for Android App concealing the Information and Safeguarding Data. *Iraqi Journal for Computer Science and Mathematics*, *5*(4), 20. DOI: 10.52866/2788-7421.1215

Aberna, P., & Agilandeeswari, L. (2024). Digital image and video watermarking: Methodologies, attacks, applications, and future directions. *Multimedia Tools and Applications*, *83*(2), 5531–5591. DOI: 10.1007/s11042-023-15806-y

Abuhashish, F., & Sunar, M. S. (2025). Augmented Reality in Cybersecurity: Enhancing Threat Intelligence and Protecting Critical Infrastructure. In Complexities and Challenges for Securing Digital Assets and Infrastructure (pp. 291-322). IGI Global Scientific Publishing.

Abujaber, A. A., & Nashwan, A. J. (2024). Ethical framework for artificial intelligence in healthcare research: A path to integrity. *World Journal of Methodology*, *14*(3). DOI: 10.5662/wjm.v14.i3.94071 PMID: 39310239

Achaal, B., Adda, M., Berger, M., Ibrahim, H., & Awde, A. (2024). Study of smart grid cyber-security, examining architectures, communication networks, cyber-attacks, countermeasure techniques, and challenges. *Cybersecurity*, *7*(1), 10. DOI: 10.1186/s42400-023-00200-w PMID: 38707764

Ackley, D. H., Hinton, G. E., & Sejnowski, T. J. (1985). A learning algorithm for Boltzmann machines. *Cognitive Science*, *9*(1), 147–169.

Adeusi, O. C., Adebayo, Y. O., Ayodele, P. A., Onikoyi, T. T., Adebayo, K. B., & Adenekan, I. O.Oluwafemi Clement AdeusiYusuf Olalekan AdebayoPraise Ayomide AyodeleTajudeen Tunde OnikoyiKayode Blessing AdebayoIbrahim Oyeyemi Adenekan. (2024). IT standardization in cloud computing: Security challenges, benefits, and future directions. *World Journal of Advanced Research and Reviews*, *22*(3), 2050–2057. DOI: 10.30574/wjarr.2024.22.3.1982

Adi, Y., Baum, C., Cisse, M., Pinkas, B., & Keshet, J. 2018. "Turning Your Weakness into a Strength: Watermarking Deep Neural Networks by Backdooring." Pp. 1615–31 in *27th USENIX security symposium (USENIX Security 18)*.

Ahmad, F., & Cheng, L.-M. (2018). Authenticity and copyright verification of printed images. *Signal Processing*, *148*, 322–335. DOI: 10.1016/j.sigpro.2018.02.029

Ahmad, T., Xue, J. L., Seet, B.-C., & Cano, J.-C. (2020). Social Network Analysis Based Localization Technique with Clustered Closeness Centrality for 3D Wireless Sensor Networks. *Electronics (Basel)*, *9*(5), 738. DOI: 10.3390/electronics9050738

Ahsan, M. S., & Pathan, A. S. K. (2025). A Comprehensive Survey on the Requirements, Applications, and Future Challenges for Access Control Models in IoT: The State of the Art. *IoT*, *6*(1), 9. DOI: 10.3390/iot6010009

Aishwarya, R., & Mathivanan, G. Fusion of Edge Computing in AI-Enabled Embedded Technologies. In *Embedded Artificial Intelligence* (pp. 15–31). Chapman and Hall/CRC. DOI: 10.1201/9781003481089-3

Alayrac, J. B., Donahue, J., Luc, P., Miech, A., Barr, I., Hasson, Y., & Simonyan, K. (2022). Flamingo: A visual language model for few-shot learning. *Advances in Neural Information Processing Systems*, *35*, 23716–23736.

Al, B. (2024). System for Certificate Generation and QR Code Integration. *J. Electrical Systems*, *20*(10s), 1915–1923.

Alhakami, H. (2024). Enhancing IoT security: Quantum-level resilience against threats. *Computers, Materials & Continua*, *78*(1), 329–356. DOI: 10.32604/cmc.2023.043439

Ali, A., Mohamed, W., & Sayed, M. (2022). A Survey Paper of Information Hiding by Using Steganography Techniques. *Kafrelsheikh Journal of Information Sciences*, *3*(2), 1–23. DOI: 10.21608/kjis.2022.280155

Ali, M., Khan, S. U., & Vasilakos, A. V. (2015). Security in cloud computing: Opportunities and challenges. *Information Sciences*, *305*, 357–383. DOI: 10.1016/j.ins.2015.01.025

Aljameel, S. S., & Rahman, A. U. (2023). Enhancing Multi-User Detection in Multicarrier 5G and Beyond: A Space-Time Spreading Approach with Parallel Interference Cancellation. Mathematical Modelling of Engineering Problems, 10(4).

Alouffi, B., (2021). Evaluating advanced cybersecurity technologies for cloud environments. *Preprints.org*.

Alquwayzani, A., Aldossari, R., & Frikha, M. (2024). Prominent security vulnerabilities in cloud computing. *International Journal of Advanced Computer Science and Applications*, *15*(2). Advance online publication. https://www.researchgate.net/publication/378721981_Prominent_Security_Vulnerabilities_in_Cloud_Computing. DOI: 10.14569/IJACSA.2024.0150281

Alshathri, S., & Hemdan, E. E.-D. (2023). An efficient audio watermarking scheme with scrambled medical images for secure medical internet of things systems. *Multimedia Tools and Applications*, *82*(13), 20177–20195. DOI: 10.1007/s11042-023-14357-6 PMID: 36685016

Alshoura, W. H., & Alawida, M. (2025). Secure and flexible image watermarking using IWT, SVD, and chaos models for robustness and imperceptibility. *Scientific Reports*, *15*(1), 7231. DOI: 10.1038/s41598-025-91876-2 PMID: 40021900

Alshuraify, N. A., Yassin, A. A., Abduljabbar, Z. A., & Nyangaresi, V. O.Ali A. YassinZaid Ameen AbduljabbarVincent Omollo Nyangaresi. (2024). Monitoring and surveillance systems based IoTs with Blockchain: Literature Review. *Journal of Basrah Researches (Sciences)*, *50*(2), 42–63. DOI: 10.56714/bjrs.50.2.5

Alupotha, J. (2023). Zero-history blockchains and zero-knowledge contracts for the post quantum era (Doctoral dissertation, Queensland University of Technology).

Amankwah-Amoah, J., Abdalla, S., Mogaji, E., Elbanna, A., & Dwivedi, Y. K. (2024). The impending disruption of creative industries by generative AI: Opportunities, challenges, and research agenda. *International Journal of Information Management*, *79*, 102759. DOI: 10.1016/j.ijinfomgt.2024.102759

Amrit, P., & Singh, A. K. (2022). Survey on watermarking methods in the artificial intelligence domain and beyond. *Computer Communications*, *188*, 52–65. DOI: 10.1016/j.comcom.2022.02.023

Araghi, T. K., Megías, D., & Rosales, A. (2023, March). Evaluation and analysis of reversible watermarking techniques in wsn for secure, lightweight design of iot applications: A survey. In Future of Information and Communication Conference (pp. 695-708). Cham: Springer Nature Switzerland. DOI: 10.1007/978-3-031-28073-3_47

Armbrust, M., Fox, A., Griffith, R., Joseph, A. D., Katz, R., Konwinski, A., Lee, G., Patterson, D., Rabkin, A., Stoica, I., & Zaharia, M. (2010). A view of cloud computing. *Communications of the ACM*, *53*(4), 50–58. DOI: 10.1145/1721654.1721672

Arora, P., & Bhardwaj, S. Techniques to Implement Security Solutions and Improve Data Integrity and Security in Distributed Cloud Computing.

Arora, R., Gera, S., & Saxena, M. (2021, March). Mitigating security risks on privacy of sensitive data used in cloud-based ERP applications. In *2021 8th International Conference on Computing for Sustainable Global Development (INDIACom)* (pp. 458-463). IEEE.

Asad, K., & Farooqui, M. F. (2025). A Study of Cyber Threats and Security Frameworks in Cloud Computing. In *Cyberology* (pp. 120–134). Chapman and Hall/CRC. DOI: 10.1201/9781003409571-7

Avram, M. G. (2014). Advantages and challenges of adopting cloud computing from an enterprise perspective. *Procedia Technology*, *12*, 529–534. DOI: 10.1016/j.protcy.2013.12.525

Aydeger, A., Zeydan, E., Yadav, A. K., Hemachandra, K. T., & Liyanage, M. (2024, October). Towards a quantum-resilient future: Strategies for transitioning to post-quantum cryptography. In 2024 15th International Conference on Network of the Future (NoF) (pp. 195-203). IEEE.

Baban, N. S., Saha, S., Jancheska, S., Singh, I., Khapli, S., Khobdabayev, M., Kim, J., Bhattacharjee, S., Song, Y.-A., Chakrabarty, K., & Karri, R. (2023). Material-level countermeasures for securing microfluidic biochips. *Lab on a Chip*, *23*(19), 4213–4231. DOI: 10.1039/D3LC00335C PMID: 37605818

Baiocchi, A., Spinelli, I., Nicolosi, A., & Scardapane, S. (2025). Adaptive token selection for scalable point cloud transformers. *Neural Networks*, *188*, 107477. DOI: 10.1016/j.neunet.2025.107477 PMID: 40273540

Banerjee, P., Snehal, S., Kumari, S., Kumar, B., Thakur, K., & Patnaik, M. (2024, September). A comparative analysis of different cloud computing method for scheduling healthcare tasks. In *2024 International Conference on Signal Processing and Advance Research in Computing (SPARC)* (Vol. 1, pp. 1–5). IEEE. DOI: 10.1109/SPARC61891.2024.10829361

Barni, M., Bartolini, F., & Piva, A. (2001). Improved Wavelet-Based Watermarking through Pixel-Wise Masking. *IEEE Transactions on Image Processing*, *10*(5), 783–791. DOI: 10.1109/83.918570 PMID: 18249667

Barni, M., Campisi, P., Delp, E. J., Doërr, G., Fridrich, J., Memon, N., Pérez-González, F., Rocha, A., Verdoliva, L., & Wu, M. (2023). Information Forensics and Security: A quarter-century-long journey. *IEEE Signal Processing Magazine*, *40*(5), 67–79. DOI: 10.1109/MSP.2023.3275319

Baseri, Y., Chouhan, V., & Ghorbani, A. (2024). Cybersecurity in the quantum era: Assessing the impact of quantum computing on infrastructure. arXiv preprint arXiv:2404.10659.

Bazydło, G., Kozdrój, K., Wiśniewski, R., & Bhattacharjya, A. (2023). Trusted Third Party Application in Durable Medium e-Service. *Applied Sciences (Basel, Switzerland)*, *14*(1), 191. DOI: 10.3390/app14010191

Belinkov, Y., & Glass, J. (2019). Analysis methods in neural language processing: A survey. *Transactions of the Association for Computational Linguistics*, *7*, 49–72. DOI: 10.1162/tacl_a_00254

Bender, E. M., Gebru, T., McMillan-Major, A., & Shmitchell, S. (2021, March). On the dangers of stochastic parrots: Can language models be too big? In *Proceedings of the 2021 ACM conference on fairness, accountability, and transparency* (pp. 610-623). DOI: 10.1145/3442188.3445922

Bennasar, H., Essaaidi, M., Bendahmane, A., & Ben-Othman, J. (2021). A systematic literature review of cloud computing cybersecurity. Advances in Dynamical Systems and Applications, 16, 1883–1919. https://www.ripublication.com/Volume/adsav16n2.htm

Bhadauria, S., Kumar, P., & Mohanty, T. (2021). Intellectual Property Protection using Blockchain and Digital Watermarking. *International Symposium on Advanced Networks and Telecommunication Systems, ANTS, 2021-December*, 1–6. DOI: 10.1109/ANTS52808.2021.9936909

Bhat, R. (2025). GAN Image Encryption. *Bridging Academia and Industry Through Cloud Integration in Education*, 215.

Bhinder, P., Singh, K., & Jindal, N. (2024). Robust Image-Adaptive Watermarking Using Hybrid Strength Factors. *Wireless Personal Communications*, *135*(1), 201–231. DOI: 10.1007/s11277-024-10922-w

Binns, R., Veale, M., Van Kleek, M., & Shadbolt, N. (2022). 'It's reducing a human being to a percentage': Perceptions of justice in algorithmic decisions. In *Proceedings of the 2022 ACM Conference on Fairness, Accountability, and Transparency* (pp. 165–176).

Bishwas, A. K., & Sen, M. (2024). Strategic Roadmap for Quantum-Resistant Security: A Framework for Preparing Industries for the Quantum Threat. arXiv preprint arXiv:2411.09995.

Blodgett, S. L., Barocas, S., Daumé, H.III, & Wallach, H. (2020). Language (technology) is power: A critical survey of" bias" in NLP. In *Proceedings of the 58th Annual Meeting of the Association for Computational Linguistics* (pp. 5454-5476). DOI: 10.18653/v1/2020.acl-main.485

Boato, G., Conci, N., Conotter, V., De Natale, F. G. B., & Fontanari, C. (2008). Multimedia asymmetric watermarking and encryption. *Electronics Letters*, *44*(9), 601–603. DOI: 10.1049/el:20080492

Boenisch, F. (2021). A systematic review on model watermarking for neural networks. *Frontiers in Big Data*, *4*, 729663. DOI: 10.3389/fdata.2021.729663 PMID: 34913032

Bolukbasi, T., Chang, K. W., Zou, J. Y., Saligrama, V., & Kalai, A. T. (2016). Man is to computer programmer as woman is to homemaker? Debiasing word embeddings. arXiv preprint arXiv:1607.06520. https://arxiv.org/abs/1607.06520

Bommasani, R., Hudson, D. A., Adeli, E., Altman, R., Arora, S., von Arx, S., Liang, P. (2021). On the opportunities and risks of foundation models. arXiv preprint arXiv:2108.07258.

Botta, A., De Donato, W., Persico, V., & Pescapé, A. (2016). Integration of cloud computing and Internet of Things: A survey. *Future Generation Computer Systems*, *56*, 684–700. DOI: 10.1016/j.future.2015.09.021

Bridy, A. (2022). Algorithms and copyright: Content ID and the automation of IP enforcement. *The Notre Dame Law Review*, *97*(2), 623–670.

Brown, T., Mann, B., Ryder, N., Subbiah, M., Kaplan, J. D., Dhariwal, P., & Amodei, D. (2020). Language models are few-shot learners. *Advances in Neural Information Processing Systems*, *33*, 1877–1901.

Brzozowska-Rup, K., Nowakowska, M., & Zdradzisz, M. (2024). Cloud computing in the Polish public administration: Current state and development prospects. *Technological Forecasting and Social Change*, *205*, 123500. DOI: 10.1016/j.techfore.2024.123500

Buyya, R., Yeo, C. S., Venugopal, S., Broberg, J., & Brandic, I. (2009). Cloud computing and emerging IT platforms: Vision, hype, and reality for delivering computing as the 5th utility. *Future Generation Computer Systems*, *25*(6), 599–616. DOI: 10.1016/j.future.2008.12.001

Cao, L. (2025). *A Practical Synthesis of Detecting AI-Generated Textual, Visual, and Audio Content* (Version 1). arXiv. DOI: 10.48550/ARXIV.2504.02898

Cao, P., Wang, Y., Si, Z., Lyu, P., & Zhang, H. (2024, June). Cyber Sentinel: Fortifying Voice Assistant Security with Biometric Template Integration in Neural Networks. In International Conference on Wireless Artificial Intelligent Computing Systems and Applications (pp. 184-195). Cham: Springer Nature Switzerland.

Caviglione, L., Comito, C., Guarascio, M., & Manco, G. (2023). Emerging challenges and perspectives in Deep Learning model security: A brief survey. *Systems and Soft Computing*, *5*, 200050. DOI: 10.1016/j.sasc.2023.200050

Chadha, A., Gangundi, S., Goel, R., Dave, H., & Roja, M. M. (2011). *Audio Watermarking with Error Correction*. https://doi.org/DOI: 10.48550/ARXIV.1110.1209

Chan, P. W., Lyu, M. R., & Chin, R. T. (2005). A Novel Scheme for Hybrid Digital Video Watermarking: Approach, Evaluation and Experimentation. *IEEE Transactions on Circuits and Systems for Video Technology*, *15*(12), 1638–1649. DOI: 10.1109/TCSVT.2005.856932

Charanarur, P., & Gundu, S. R. (2025). A taxonomical review on cloud security and its solutions. In *Securing the Digital World* (pp. 141–155). CRC Press.

Chauhan, A., & Shiaeles, S. (2023). A review of cloud computing security frameworks: Mapping industry practices to emerging trends. *Network (Bristol, England)*, *3*(3), 280–301. DOI: 10.3390/network3030018

Chawla, D., & Mehra, P. S. (2023). A roadmap from classical cryptography to post-quantum resistant cryptography for 5G-enabled IoT: Challenges, opportunities and solutions. *Internet of Things : Engineering Cyber Physical Human Systems*, *24*, 100950. DOI: 10.1016/j.iot.2023.100950

Chekka, R. B., & Babu, B. R. (2025). Secure Digital Data Visual Sharing Schemes in Multi-Owner Public Cloud Environment Applications. Scalable Computing. *Practice and Experience*, *26*(1), 84 ?"95.

Chekka, R. B., & Babu, B. R. (2025). Secure digital data visual sharing schemes in multi-owner public cloud environment applications. Scalable Computing. *Practice and Experience*, *26*(1), 84–95.

Chen, K., Li, Y., Lan, W., Mi, B., & Wang, S. (2024). AIGC-Assisted digital watermark services in low-earth orbit satellite-terrestrial edge networks. arXiv preprint arXiv:2407.01534.

Chen, D., & Zhao, H. (2012). Data security and privacy protection issues in cloud computing. In *2012 International Conference on Computer Science and Electronics Engineering* (pp. 647–651). IEEE. DOI: 10.1109/ICCSEE.2012.193

Cheng, P., Wu, Z., Du, W., Zhao, H., Lu, W., & Liu, G. (2025). Backdoor attacks and countermeasures in natural language processing models: A comprehensive security review. *IEEE Transactions on Neural Networks and Learning Systems*, *36*(8), 13628–13648. DOI: 10.1109/TNNLS.2025.3540303 PMID: 40031656

Chen, T., Tan, Y. A., Li, W., Ci, Z., & Shi, N. (2025). Toward secure program execution in multi-tenant cloud FPGA environments. *The Journal of Supercomputing*, *81*(8), 1–25. DOI: 10.1007/s11227-025-07340-5

Chen, W., Ren, N., Zhu, C., Keskinarkaus, A., Seppänen, T., & Zhou, Q. (2021). Joint Image Encryption and Screen-Cam Robust Two Watermarking Scheme. *Sensors (Basel)*, *21*(3), 701. DOI: 10.3390/s21030701 PMID: 33498582

Chen, Z., Li, L., Peng, H., Liu, Y., & Yang, Y. (2018). A Novel Digital Watermarking Based on General Non-Negative Matrix Factorization. *IEEE Transactions on Multimedia*, *20*(8), 1973–1986. DOI: 10.1109/TMM.2018.2794985

Chippagiri, S. A Study of Cloud Security Frameworks for Safeguarding Multi-Tenant Cloud Architectures. *International Journal of Computer Applications*, *975*, 8887. DOI: 10.5120/ijca2025924369

CloudPassage. (2020, August 26). Shared responsibility model explained. Cloud Security Alliance. https://cloudsecurityalliance.org/blog/2020/08/26/shared-responsibility-model-explained/

Cotfas, L. A., & Rekeraho, J. P. (2023). Security monitoring in cloud environments using SIEM: Implementation and evaluation. *Applied Sciences (Basel, Switzerland)*, *13*(22), 12359. DOI: 10.3390/app132212359

Cox, I. J., Kilian, J., Leighton, F. T., & Shamoon, T. (1997). Secure Spread Spectrum Watermarking for Multimedia. *IEEE Transactions on Image Processing*, *6*(12), 1673–1687. DOI: 10.1109/83.650120 PMID: 18285237

Cox, I., Miller, M., Bloom, J., Fridrich, J., & Kalker, T. (2007). *Digital Watermarking and Steganography*. Morgan kaufmann.

CrowdStrike. (2024). Top 8 cloud vulnerabilities. https://www.crowdstrike.com/en-us/cybersecurity-101/cloud-security/cloud-vulnerabilities

Dadheech, A., & Bhavsar, M. (2025). AirNav: A computation-driven cloud-based solution for the drone path planning utilizing machine learning. *Procedia Computer Science, 258,* 1688–1697. DOI: 10.1016/j.procs.2025.04.421

Dandooh, A., El-Fishawy, A. S., & Hemdan, E. E. D. (2025). Digital watermarking using artificial intelligence: Concept, techniques, and future trends. *Security and Privacy, 8*(1), e502. DOI: 10.1002/spy2.502

Darwich, M., Khalil, K., Ismail, Y., & Bayoumi, M. (2023, October). Blockchain-Enhanced Distributed Storage for Cloud-Based Video Streaming: Enhancing Security and Scalability. In *Proceedings of the Future Technologies Conference* (pp. 426-439). Cham: Springer Nature Switzerland. DOI: 10.1007/978-3-031-47454-5_31

Dash, B. (2024). Zero-trust architecture (ZTA): Designing an AI-powered cloud security framework for LLMs' black box problems. *SSRN.* https://ssrn.com/abstract=4726625

De Filippi, P., & Hassan, S. (2022). Blockchain technology as a regulatory technology: From code is law to law is code. *First Monday, 27*(3). DOI: 10.5210/fm.v27i3.11611

Demertzi, V., Demertzis, S., & Demertzis, K. (2023). An overview of cyber threats, attacks and countermeasures on the primary domains of smart cities. *Applied Sciences (Basel, Switzerland), 13*(2), 790. DOI: 10.3390/app13020790

Devi, K. J., Singh, P., Bilal, M., & Nayyar, A. (2024). Enabling secure image transmission in unmanned aerial vehicle using digital image watermarking with H-Grey optimization. *Expert Systems with Applications, 236,* 121190. DOI: 10.1016/j.eswa.2023.121190

Devlin, J., Chang, M. W., Lee, K., & Toutanova, K. (2019). Bert: Pre-training of deep bidirectional transformers for language understanding. arXiv preprint arXiv:1810.04805.

Dewangan, R. R., Soni, S., & Mishal, A. (2025). An approach of privacy preservation and data security in cloud computing for secured data sharing. *Recent Advances in Electrical & Electronic Engineering, 18*(2), 176–195. DOI: 10.2174/0123520965280683240112085521

Dhabliya, D., Soundararajan, R., Selvarasu, P., Balasubramaniam, M. S., Rajawat, A. S., Goyal, S. B., Raboaca, M. S., Mihaltan, T. C., Verma, C., & Suciu, G. (2022). Energy-Efficient Network Protocols and Resilient Data Transmission Schemes for Wireless Sensor Networks—An Experimental Survey. *Energies, 15*(23), 8883. DOI: 10.3390/en15238883

Digital Guardian. (2023). What is digital watermarking? https://www.digitalguardian.com/blog/digital-watermarking

Dikaiakos, M. D., Katsaros, D., Mehra, P., Pallis, G., & Vakali, A. (2009). Cloud computing: Distributed internet computing for IT and scientific research. *IEEE Internet Computing*, *13*(5), 10–13. DOI: 10.1109/MIC.2009.103

Dodge, J., Sap, M., Marasović, A., Agnew, W., Ilharco, G., Groeneveld, D., Gardner, M. (2021). Documenting large webtext corpora: A case study on the colossal clean crawled corpus. arXiv preprint arXiv:2104.08758. DOI: 10.18653/v1/2021.emnlp-main.98

Dukhi, R. G. (2011). Watermarking: A copyright protection tool. *2011 3rd International Conference on Electronics Computer Technology*, 36–41. DOI: 10.1109/ICECTECH.2011.5941952

Dutta, P. (2024). Contributions to Lattice-based Expressive Encryption Systems (Doctoral dissertation, University of Wollongong).

El Azzaoui, A., Chen, H., Kim, S. H., Pan, Y., & Park, J. H. (2022). Blockchain-based distributed information hiding framework for data privacy preserving in medical supply chain systems. *Sensors (Basel)*, *22*(4), 1371. DOI: 10.3390/s22041371 PMID: 35214273

Elharrouss, O., Damseh, R., Belkacem, A. N., Badidi, E., & Lakas, A. (2025). Transformer-Based Image and Video Inpainting: Current Challenges and Future Directions. *Artificial Intelligence Review*, *58*(4), 124. DOI: 10.1007/s10462-024-11075-9

Elkin-Koren, N. (2020). Copyright in the cloud: Who owns what? *Journal of Intellectual Property Law & Practice*, *15*(6), 457–466.

Excel, D. S.David Shamoo Excel. (2024). Edge Computing: Opportunities and Challenges. *World Journal of Advanced Research and Reviews*, *23*(3), 585–596. DOI: 10.30574/wjarr.2024.23.3.2723

Falola, P. B., Adeniyi, E. A., Awotunde, J. B., Jimoh, R. G., & Imoize, A. L. Security challenges and prospects of 6G network in cloud environments. *Security and Privacy Schemes for Dense 6G Wireless Communication Networks*, 471.

Fan, J., Lian, H., & Liu, W. (2024). Privacy-preserving AI analytics in cloud computing: A federated learning approach for cross-organizational data collaboration. *Spectrum of Research, 4*(2).

Fedus, W., Zoph, B., & Shazeer, N. (2022). Switch transformers: Scaling to trillion parameter models with simple and efficient sparsity. *Journal of Machine Learning Research, 23*(1), 5232–5270.

Feng, X., Liu, Y., & Fang, L. (2015). Digital Watermark of 3D CAD Product Model. *International Journal of Security and Its Applications, 9*(9), 305–320. DOI: 10.14257/ijsia.2015.9.9.27

Frattolillo, F. (2021). Blockchain and Cloud to Overcome the Problems of Buyer and Seller Watermarking Protocols. *Applied Sciences (Basel, Switzerland), 11*(24), 12028. DOI: 10.3390/app112412028

Fund, F., Hosseini, S. A., & Panwar, S. S. (2016). Under a cloud of uncertainty: Legal questions affecting internet storage and transmission of copyright-protected video content. arXiv. https://arxiv.org/abs/1602.01547

Garcez, A. S. D. A., Besold, T. R., De Raedt, L., Földiak, P., Hitzler, P., Icard, T., Silver, D. L. (2015, March). Neural-Symbolic Learning and Reasoning: Contributions and Challenges. In AAAI Spring Symposia (pp. 18-21).

Ge, S., Xia, Z., Fei, J., Sun, X., & Weng, J. (2022). *A Robust Document Image Watermarking Scheme using Deep Neural Network* (Version 1). arXiv. DOI: 10.48550/ARXIV.2202.13067

Giri, K. J., & Bashir, R. (2017). Digital Watermarking: A Potential Solution for Multimedia Authentication. In Dey, N., & Santhi, V. (Eds.), *Intelligent Techniques in Signal Processing for Multimedia Security* (Vol. 660, pp. 93–112). Springer International Publishing., DOI: 10.1007/978-3-319-44790-2_5

Gizachew Yirga, T., Gizachew Yirga, H., & Addisu, E. G. (2025). Cryptographic key generation using deep learning with biometric face and finger vein data. *Frontiers in Artificial Intelligence, 8*, 1545946. DOI: 10.3389/frai.2025.1545946 PMID: 40365578

Goel, P. K., & Saraswat, B. K. (2025). Security and Privacy in IoE Systems: Computer Vision Approaches for Surveillance and Threat Detection. In Computer Vision and Internet of Everything (IoE) for Societal Needs (pp. 301-318). IGI Global Scientific Publishing.

Gonzalez, N., Miers, C., Redigolo, F., Simplício, M.Jr, Carvalho, T., Näslund, M., & Pourzandi, M. (2012). *A quantitative analysis of current security concerns and solutions for cloud computing*. Journal of Cloud Computing: Advances. *Systems and Applications, 1*(1), 11.

Gorelik, E. (2013). Cloud computing models. *MIT Sloan School of Management Working Paper*, 13-01.

Goud Allam, T., Mehedi Hasan, A. B. M., Maag, A., & Prasad, P. W. C. (2021). Ledger Technology of Blockchain and its Impact on Operational Performance of Banks: A Review. *CITISIA 2021 - IEEE Conference on Innovative Technologies in Intelligent System and Industrial Application, Proceedings*, 1–10. DOI: 10.1109/CITISIA53721.2021.9719886

Goundar, S. (Ed.). (2023). *Edge Computing: Technology, Management and Integration*. BoD–Books on Demand. DOI: 10.5772/intechopen.105637

Guo, H., Sun, J., & Pang, Z. H. (2023). Analysis of replay attacks with countermeasure for state estimation of cyber-physical systems. *IEEE Transactions on Circuits and Systems. II, Express Briefs*, *71*(1), 206–210. DOI: 10.1109/TCSII.2023.3302151

Gupta, R., Saxena, D., & Singh, A. K. (2021). Data security and privacy in cloud computing: Concepts and emerging trends. *arXiv*.

Gupta, S., & Maple, C. (2023). A survey of security mechanisms for edge computing based connected autonomous vehicles. *Authorea Preprints*, 10.

Hamidi, M., Chetouani, A., El Haziti, M., El Hassouni, M., & Cherifi, H. (2019a). A Robust Blind 3-D Mesh Watermarking Technique Based on SCS Quantization and Mesh Saliency for Copyright Protection. In É. Renault, S. Boumerdassi, C. Leghris, & S. Bouzefrane (Eds.), *Mobile, Secure, and Programmable Networking* (Vol. 11557, pp. 211–228). Springer International Publishing. DOI: 10.1007/978-3-030-22885-9_19

Hamidi, M., Chetouani, A., El Haziti, M., El Hassouni, M., & Cherifi, H. (2019b). Blind Robust 3-D Mesh Watermarking Based on Mesh Saliency and QIM Quantization for Copyright Protection. In Morales, A., Fierrez, J., Sánchez, J. S., & Ribeiro, B. (Eds.), *Pattern Recognition and Image Analysis* (Vol. 11867, pp. 170–181). Springer International Publishing., DOI: 10.1007/978-3-030-31332-6_15

Hamidi, M., Haziti, M. E., Cherifi, H., & Aboutajdine, D. (2017). A robust blind 3-D mesh watermarking based on wavelet transform for copyright protection. *2017 International Conference on Advanced Technologies for Signal and Image Processing (ATSIP)*, 1–6. DOI: 10.1109/ATSIP.2017.8075525

Harini, K. K., & Chakkaravarthy, A. P. (2024, December). Deduplication of Image Files to Reduce the Redundancy in Cloud Storage. In 2024 9th International Conference on Communication and Electronics Systems (ICCES) (pp. 1055-1062). IEEE.

Haryanto, C. Y., Vu, M. H., Nguyen, T. D., Lomempow, E., Nurliana, Y., & Taheri, S. (2024). SecGenAI: Enhancing Security of Cloud-based Generative AI Applications within Australian Critical Technologies of National Interest. *arXiv preprint arXiv:2407.01110.*

Hashem, I. A. T., Yaqoob, I., Anuar, N. B., Mokhtar, S., Gani, A., & Khan, S. U. (2015). The rise of "big data" on cloud computing: Review and open research issues. *Information Systems*, *47*, 98–115. DOI: 10.1016/j.is.2014.07.006

Hashim, W., & Hussein, N. A. H. K. (2024). Securing Cloud Computing Environments: An Analysis of Multi-Tenancy Vulnerabilities and Countermeasures. *SHIFRA*, *2024*, 8–16. DOI: 10.70470/SHIFRA/2024/002

Hassan, Y. A., & Rahma, A. M. S. A Comparative Study Between the Fragile and Robust Watermarking Techniques and Proposing New Fragile Watermarking with Embedded Value.

Hassan, M. (2024). Real-Time Risk Assessment in SaaS Payment Infrastructures: Examining Deep Learning Models and Deployment Strategies. *Transactions on Artificial Intelligence, Machine Learning, and Cognitive Systems*, *9*(3), 1–10.

He, Q., Xi, Z., Feng, Z., Teng, Y., Ma, L., Cai, Y., & Yu, K. (2024). Telemedicine Monitoring System Based on Fog/Edge Computing: A Survey. *IEEE Transactions on Services Computing*.

Hisanori, Y. (2025). *Blockchain Integrated Secure Healthcare Output Protocol.* BISHOP. DOI: 10.20944/preprints202504.1895.v1

Holtzman, A., Buys, J., Du, L., Forbes, M., & Choi, Y. (2019). The curious case of neural text degeneration. arXiv preprint arXiv:1904.09751.

Hosam, O., Abousamra, R., Hassouna, M., & Azzawi, R. (2024). Security analysis and planning for enterprise networks: Incorporating modern security design principles. In Industry 4.0 Key Technological Advances and Design Principles in Engineering, Education, Business, and Social Applications (pp. 85-117). CRC Press.

Hosseini, A., & Butcher, L. (2012). Cloud computing: The concept, impacts and the role of government policy. *Journal of Information Technology & Politics*, *9*(3), 289–302.

Hou, G., Ou, B., Peng, F., & Long, M. (2024). A Traitor Tracing and Access Control Method for Encrypted 3D Models Based on CP-ABE and Fair Watermark. *IEEE Signal Processing Letters*.

Hou, X., Zhao, Y., & Wang, H. (2025). The next frontier of llm applications: Open ecosystems and hardware synergy. arXiv preprint arXiv:2503.04596.

Hou, Z., Yan, H., Zhang, L., Ma, R., Yan, Q., & Yang, B. (2025). A Secure and Efficient Remote Sensing Image Retrieval Method with Verifiable and Traceable in Cloud Environment. *IEEE Transactions on Geoscience and Remote Sensing*, *63*, 1 ?"16. DOI: 10.1109/TGRS.2025.3539846

Hsu, L. Y. (2024). AI-assisted deepfake detection using adaptive blind image watermarking. *Journal of Visual Communication and Image Representation*, *100*, 104094. DOI: 10.1016/j.jvcir.2024.104094

Huang, C., Song, R., Gao, S., Guo, Y., & Xiao, B. (2024). *Data Availability and Decentralization: New Techniques for zk-Rollups in Layer 2 Blockchain Networks*. Retrieved from https://arxiv.org/abs/2403.10828

Huaranga-Junco, E., González-Gerpe, S., Castillo-Cara, M., Cimmino, A., & García-Castro, R. (2024). From cloud and fog computing to federated-fog computing: A comparative analysis of computational resources in real-time IoT applications based on semantic interoperability. *Future Generation Computer Systems*, *159*, 134–150. DOI: 10.1016/j.future.2024.05.001

Hu, H., & Pang, J. (2021, December). Stealing machine learning models: Attacks and countermeasures for generative adversarial networks. In *Proceedings of the 37th Annual Computer Security Applications Conference* (pp. 1-16). DOI: 10.1145/3485832.3485838

Inaganti, A. C., Ravichandran, N., Nersu, S. R. K., & Muppalaneni, R. (2021). Cloud Security Posture Management (CSPM) with AI: Automating Compliance and Threat Detection. *Artificial Intelligence and Machine Learning Review*, *2*(4), 8–18.

Intelligence, T. A., Computing, F., & Analytics, D. Sl. No TITLE OF THE PAPAER.

Jain, H., Kumar, M., & Joshi, A. M. (2022). Intelligent energy cyber physical systems (iECPS) for reliable smart grid against energy theft and false data injection. *Electrical Engineering*, *104*(1), 331–346. DOI: 10.1007/s00202-021-01380-9

Jani Anbarasi, L., & Narendra, M. (2017). Robust watermarking scheme using Weber Law for 3D mesh models. *Imaging Science Journal*, *65*(7), 409–417. DOI: 10.1080/13682199.2017.1359992

Jayamalar, T., & Radha, V. (2010). Survey on Digital Video Watermarking Techniques and Attacks on Watermarks. *International Journal of Engineering Science and Technology*, *2*(12), 6963–6967.

Jeyaraman, M., Balaji, S., Jeyaraman, N., & Yadav, S. (2023). Unraveling the Ethical Enigma: Artificial Intelligence in Healthcare. *Cureus*. DOI: 10.7759/cureus.43262 PMID: 37692617

Jia, S. (2021). Research on data security based on cloud computing. *MMIA 2021.*

Jiang, Z., Guo, M., Hu, Y., & Gong, N. Z. (2024). Watermark-based Attribution of AI-Generated Content. arXiv preprint arXiv:2404.04254.

Jiang, Z., Zhang, M., Dong, W., Jiang, C., & Di, F. (2024). Reversible Data Hiding Algorithm in Encrypted Images Based on Adaptive Median Edge Detection and Ciphertext-Policy Attribute-Based Encryption. *Computers, Materials & Continua, 81*(1), 1123 ?"1155. DOI: 10.32604/cmc.2024.055120

Kabir, M. (2021). An efficient low bit rate image watermarking and tamper detection for image authentication. *SN Applied Sciences, 3*(4), 400. DOI: 10.1007/s42452-021-04387-w

Kalan, R., & Dulger, I. (2024). A Survey on QoE Management Schemes for HTTP Adaptive Video Streaming: Challenges, Solutions, and Opportunities. IEEE Access.

Kale, A. B., & Chanvan, M. S. (2025). Insertion of watermark using a novel hybrid algorithm for secure multimedia digital evidence. *Progress in Artificial Intelligence, 14*(1), 61–73. DOI: 10.1007/s13748-024-00350-z

Kaminski, M. E. (2021). The dangers of user-generated takedowns. *North Carolina Law Review, 99*(5), 1301–1352.

Kaplan, J., McCandlish, S., Henighan, T., Brown, T. B., Chess, B., Child, R., Amodei, D. (2020). Scaling laws for neural language models. arXiv preprint arXiv:2001.08361.

Kashyap, P. K. COPYRIGHT PROTECTION IN DIGITAL ENVIRONMENT: CHALLENGES AND SOLUTIONS. *INTELLECTUAL PROPERTY RIGHTS*, 27.

Kasralikar, P., Polu, O. R., Chamarthi, B., Veer Samara Sihman Bharattej Rupavath, R., Patel, S., & Tumati, R. (2025). Blockchain for Securing AI-Driven Healthcare Systems: A Systematic Review and Future Research Perspectives. *Cureus, 17*(4), e83136. DOI: 10.7759/cureus.83136 PMID: 40438823

Kenioua, L., Lejdel, B., Alamri, S., & Ramadan, Q. (2024). A password-based authentication approach for edge computing architectures. *Egyptian Informatics Journal, 28*, 100543. DOI: 10.1016/j.eij.2024.100543

Khajeh-Hosseini, A., Greenwood, D., & Sommerville, I. (2010). The Cloud Adoption Toolkit: Supporting cloud adoption decisions in the enterprise. *Software, Practice & Experience, 42*(4), 447–465. DOI: 10.1002/spe.1072

Kishan, K., & Vijay Kumar, B. (2023). Efficient Large Invisible Color Watermark Embedding Using Conditional Deep Autoencoder Model for Medical Applications. *Measurement. Sensors*, *29*, 100850. DOI: 10.1016/j.measen.2023.100850

Kobayashi, G., Kuribayashi, T., Yokoi, S., & Inui, K. (2020). Attention is not only a weight: Analyzing transformers with vector norms. arXiv preprint arXiv:2004.10102. DOI: 10.18653/v1/2020.emnlp-main.574

Korada, L. International Journal of Communication Networks and Information Security.

Kotsakis, G., Papaioannou, C., Souflas, T., Tsolkas, D., Kakyris, A., Gounas, P., & Stavropoulos, P. (2025). Development and implementation of an architecture for cloud-based monitoring in machining, focusing on high performance applications. *Procedia CIRP*, *133*, 579–584. DOI: 10.1016/j.procir.2025.02.099

Kreps, S., McCain, R. M., & Brundage, M. (2022). All the news that's fit to fabricate: AI-generated text as a tool of media misinformation. *Journal of Experimental Political Science*, *9*(1), 104–117. DOI: 10.1017/XPS.2020.37

Krishnan, R. B., Thandra, P. K., & Baba, M. S. (2017). An overview of text steganography. *2017 Fourth International Conference on Signal Processing, Communication and Networking (ICSCN)*, 1–6. DOI: 10.1109/ICSCN.2017.8085643

Krutz, R. L., & Vines, R. D. (2010). *Cloud security: A comprehensive guide to secure cloud computing*. Wiley Publishing.

Kumar, A. (2018, August). A review on implementation of digital image watermarking techniques using LSB and DWT. In Third International Conference on Information and Communication Technology for Sustainable Development (ICT4SD 2018), Goa, India, August 30–31, 2018.

Kumar, D., Wadhwa, A., & Garg, P. 2025. "Securing Medical Images in the Cloud: A Hybrid Approach Using Adaptive Strength Control and Content-Aware Watermarking." Pp. 1050–55 in *2025 3rd International Conference on Disruptive Technologies (ICDT)*. DOI: 10.1109/ICDT63985.2025.10986507

Kumar, A. (2019). Design of secure image fusion technique using cloud for privacy-preserving and copyright protection. [IJCAC]. *International Journal of Cloud Applications and Computing*, *9*(3), 22–36. DOI: 10.4018/IJCAC.2019070102

Kumar, A., Ghrera, S. P., & Tyagi, V. (2014). Implementation of wavelet-based modified buyer-seller watermarking protocol. *WSEAS Transactions on Signal Processing*, *10*, 212–220.

Kumar, A., Ghrera, S. P., & Tyagi, V. (2015). Modified buyer-seller watermarking protocol based on discrete wavelet transform and principal component analysis. *Indian Journal of Science and Technology*, *8*(35), 1–9.

Kumar, A., Singh, N., Sharma, S., Joshi, P., & Saraswat, B. K. (2024, December). A Novel Optimization Model for Blockchain-Based Secure Realtime Data Processing in Mobile Edge Computing. In *2024 International Conference on Emerging Technologies and Innovation for Sustainability (EmergIN)* (pp. 565-570). DOI: 10.1109/EmergIN63207.2024.10961497

Kumar, A., Yadav, S. P., & Kumar, A. (2025). An improved feature extraction algorithm for robust Swin Transformer model in high-dimensional medical image analysis. *Computers in Biology and Medicine*, *188*, 109822. DOI: 10.1016/j.compbiomed.2025.109822 PMID: 39983364

Kumar, C. (2024). Hybrid optimization for secure and robust digital image watermarking with DWT, DCT and SPIHT. *Multimedia Tools and Applications*, *83*(11), 31911–31932. DOI: 10.1007/s11042-023-16903-8

Kumar, M. R., Devi, B. R., Rangaswamy, K., Sangeetha, M., & Kumar, K. V. R. (2023, April). IoT-edge computing for efficient and effective information process on industrial automation. In *2023 International Conference on Networking and Communications (ICNWC)* (pp. 1-6). IEEE. DOI: 10.1109/ICNWC57852.2023.10127492

Kyzylkhojaeva, A.National Academy of Sciences of the Kyrgyz Republic. (2024). ANALYSIS OF CRIMINAL JUSTICE AND CYBER CRIME IN THE CONTEXT OF ARTIFICIAL INTELLIGENCE THROUGH THE LENSES OF INTERNATIONAL ORGANIZATIONS. *Alatoo Academic Studies*, *24*(2), 349–361. DOI: 10.17015/aas.2024.242.28

Leal Filho, W., & Gbaguidi, G. J. (2024). Using artificial intelligence in support of climate change adaptation Africa: Potentials and risks. *Humanities & Social Sciences Communications*, *11*(1), 1657. DOI: 10.1057/s41599-024-04223-7

Lepikhin, D., Lee, H., Xu, Y., Chen, D., Firat, O., Huang, Y., Chen, Z. (2020). Gshard: Scaling giant models with conditional computation and automatic sharding. arXiv preprint arXiv:2006.16668.

Lewis, P., Perez, E., Piktus, A., Petroni, F., Karpukhin, V., Goyal, N., & Kiela, D. (2020). Retrieval-augmented generation for knowledge-intensive NLP tasks. *Advances in Neural Information Processing Systems*, *33*, 9459–9474.

Li, X. L., Holtzman, A., Fried, D., Liang, P., Eisner, J., Hashimoto, T., Lewis, M. (2022). Contrastive decoding: Open-ended text generation as optimization. arXiv preprint arXiv:2210.15097.

Li, X., Leng, X., & Chen, Y. (2021). Securing serverless computing: Challenges, solutions, and opportunities. *arXiv, May 25*.

Liang, X., Wang, H., Wang, Y., Song, S., Yang, J., Niu, S., Li, Z. (2024). Controllable text generation for large language models: A survey. arXiv preprint arXiv:2408.12599.

Li, L., Bai, R., Zhang, S., & Zhou, Q. (2021). A Robust Watermarking Algorithm for Video Game Artwork Based on Pose Estimation Neural Network. In Sun, X., Zhang, X., Xia, Z., & Bertino, E. (Eds.), *Advances in Artificial Intelligence and Security* (Vol. 1424, pp. 217–229). Springer International Publishing., DOI: 10.1007/978-3-030-78621-2_17

Li, L., Wang, S., Zhang, S., Luo, T., & Chang, C.-C. (2020). Homomorphic Encryption-Based Robust Reversible Watermarking for 3D Model. *Symmetry*, *12*(3), 347. DOI: 10.3390/sym12030347

Lillis, W., Hoffing, M. C., & Burleson, W. (2024). Survey of security issues in memristor-based machine learning accelerators for RF analysis. *Chips*, *3*(2), 196–215. DOI: 10.3390/chips3020009

Lin, S., Hilton, J., & Evans, O. (2021). Truthfulqa: Measuring how models mimic human falsehoods. arXiv preprint arXiv:2109.07958.

Lingayya, S., Jodumutt, S. B., Pawar, S. R., Vylala, A., & Chandrasekaran, S. (2024). Dynamic task offloading for resource allocation and privacy-preserving framework in Kubeedge-based edge computing using machine learning. *Cluster Computing*, *27*(7), 9415 ?"9431. DOI: 10.1007/s10586-024-04420-8

Li, P., Huang, J., Zhang, S., & Qi, C. (2024). SecureEI: Proactive intellectual property protection of AI models for edge intelligence. *Computer Networks*, *255*, 110825. DOI: 10.1016/j.comnet.2024.110825

Li, S., Chen, Y., Chen, L., Liao, J., Kuang, C., Li, K., Liang, W., & Xiong, N. (2023). Post-quantum security: Opportunities and challenges. *Sensors (Basel)*, *23*(21), 8744. DOI: 10.3390/s23218744 PMID: 37960442

Liu, J. (2023). Quantum copy protection and unclonable cryptography (Doctoral dissertation).

Liu, Y., & Bu, Y. (2024). Adaptive text watermark for large language models. arXiv preprint arXiv:2401.13927.

Liu, Y., Ott, M., Goyal, N., Du, J., Joshi, M., Chen, D., Stoyanov, V. (2019). Roberta: A robustly optimized bert pretraining approach. arXiv preprint arXiv:1907.11692.

Liu, C., Zhang, J., Fang, H., Ma, Z., Zhang, W., & Yu, N. (2023, June). Dear: A deep-learning-based audio re-recording resilient watermarking. *Proceedings of the AAAI Conference on Artificial Intelligence*, *37*(11), 13201–13209. DOI: 10.1609/aaai.v37i11.26550

Liu, J., Wang, Y., Li, Y., Liu, R., & Chen, J. (2017). A robust and blind 3D watermarking algorithm using multiresolution adaptive parameterization of surface. *Neurocomputing*, *237*, 304–315. DOI: 10.1016/j.neucom.2016.12.065

Liu, L., Hu, Y., Zhao, Y., Zhang, X., Ma, Y., & Chang, G. (2024, October). A Novel Federated Learning System with Privacy Protection and Blockchain Consensus Incentive Mechanisms in Cloud-Edge Collaboration Scenarios. In *2024 IEEE International Conference on Systems, Man, and Cybernetics (SMC)* (pp. 3111-3118). IEEE. DOI: 10.1109/SMC54092.2024.10831241

Liu, R., & Tan, T. (2002). An SVD-Based Watermarking Scheme for Protecting Rightful Ownership. *IEEE Transactions on Multimedia*, *4*(1), 121–128. DOI: 10.1109/6046.985560

Liu, X., & Nematollahi, M. A. (2024). Artificial Intelligence Approach for Tuning Speech-Adaptive Watermarking using Higher-Order Statistics (HOS). *Circuits, Systems, and Signal Processing*, *43*(5), 3297–3323. DOI: 10.1007/s00034-024-02618-0

Liu, Y. (2024). Build an audit Framework for data privacy Protection in Cloud Environment. *Procedia Computer Science*, *247*, 166–175. DOI: 10.1016/j.procs.2024.10.020

Liu, Y., Wang, X., & Zhou, Y. (2024). Legal challenges of cloud-based content sharing platforms: A comparative study of DMCA and GDPR implications. *Computer Law & Security Review*, *52*, 105755.

Lopez Velásquez, J. M., Martínez Monterrubio, S. M., Sánchez Crespo, L. E., & Garcia Rosado, D. (2023). Systematic review of SIEM technology: SIEM-SC birth. *International Journal of Information Security*, *22*(3), 691–711. DOI: 10.1007/s10207-022-00657-9

Lukas, N., Diaa, A., Fenaux, L., & Kerschbaum, F. (2023). Leveraging optimization for adaptive attacks on image watermarks. arXiv preprint arXiv:2309.16952.

Luo, H., Yu, F.-X., Huang, Z.-L., & Lu, Z.-M. (2011). Blind Image Watermarking Based on Discrete Fractional Random Transform and Subsampling. *Optik (Stuttgart)*, *122*(4), 311–316. DOI: 10.1016/j.ijleo.2009.12.018

Luxner, T. (2023, April 5). Cloud computing stats: Flexera 2023 state of the cloud report. Flexera Blog. https://www.flexera.com/blog/cloud/cloud-computing-trends-flexera-2023-state-of-the-cloud-report/

Madala, R., Monica, R., Malwade, S. S., Budhavale, S. J., & Sathyabalaji, N. (2023, April). A Novel Dynamic Watermarking for Secure Data Protection from Cyber Theft Based on Artificial Intelligence Supervision. In *2023 Eighth International Conference on Science Technology Engineering and Mathematics (ICONSTEM)* (pp. 1-7). IEEE.

Magdy, M., Hosny, K. M., Ghali, N. I., & Ghoniemy, S. (2022). Security of medical images for telemedicine: A systematic review. *Multimedia Tools and Applications*, *81*(18), 25101–25145. DOI: 10.1007/s11042-022-11956-7 PMID: 35342327

Mahapatra, D., Amrit, P., Singh, O. P., Singh, A. K., & Agrawal, A. K. (2022). Autoencoder-Convolutional Neural Network-Based Embedding and Extraction Model for Image Watermarking. *Journal of Electronic Imaging*, *32*(02). DOI: 10.1117/1.JEI.32.2.021604

Makhrib, Z. F., & Karim, A. A. (2021). Digital Watermark Technique: A Review. *Journal of Physics: Conference Series*, *1999*(1), 012118. DOI: 10.1088/1742-6596/1999/1/012118

Malanowska, A., Mazurczyk, W., Araghi, T. K., Megías, D., & Kuribayashi, M. (2024). Digital watermarking—A meta-survey and techniques for fake news detection. *IEEE Access : Practical Innovations, Open Solutions*, *12*, 36311–36345. DOI: 10.1109/ACCESS.2024.3374201

Margoni, T., & Kretschmer, M. (2023). Artificial intelligence and copyright: The state of play. *European Intellectual Property Review*, *45*(1), 20–30.

Marston, S., Li, Z., Bandyopadhyay, S., Zhang, J., & Ghalsasi, A. (2011). Cloud computing—The business perspective. *Decision Support Systems*, *51*(1), 176–189. DOI: 10.1016/j.dss.2010.12.006

Mavani, C., Mistry, H. K., Patel, R., & Goswami, A. (2024). The role of cybersecurity in protecting intellectual property. *International Journal on Recent and Innovation Trends in Computing and Communication*, *12*(2), 529–538.

Mehar, T. (2022). Advanced Cyber Security Measures in Cloud Computing for Video and Media Processing Using Generative AI.

Meister, C., Vieira, T., & Cotterell, R. (2020). If beam search is the answer, what was the question? arXiv preprint arXiv:2010.02650. DOI: 10.18653/v1/2020.emnlp-main.170

Mell, P., & Grance, T. (2011). *The NIST definition of cloud computing* (Special Publication 800-145). National Institute of Standards and Technology.

Mell, P., & Grance, T. (2011). *Effectively and securely using the cloud computing paradigm*. NIST.

Memon, N., & Wong, P. W. (1998). Protecting Digital Media Content. *Communications of the ACM*, *41*(7), 35–43. DOI: 10.1145/278476.278485

Meng, Z., Morizumi, T., Miyata, S., & Kinoshita, H. (2018). Design Scheme of Copyright Management System Based on Digital Watermarking and Blockchain. *Proceedings - International Computer Software and Applications Conference, 2*, 359–364. DOI: 10.1109/COMPSAC.2018.10258

Mennella, C., Maniscalco, U., De Pietro, G., & Esposito, M. (2024). Ethical and regulatory challenges of AI technologies in healthcare: A narrative review. *Heliyon*, *10*(4), e26297. DOI: 10.1016/j.heliyon.2024.e26297 PMID: 38384518

Michel, P., Levy, O., & Neubig, G. (2019). Are sixteen heads really better than one? *Advances in Neural Information Processing Systems*, 32.

Mogol, N., & Crudu, R. (2022). Challenges and strategies for copyright protection in the digital era. *Journal of Social Sciences*, *5*(4), 6–19. DOI: 10.52326/jss.utm.2022.5(4).01

Mohammed, A. A., Jebur, B. A., & Younus, K. M. (2021). Hybrid DCT-SVD Based Digital Watermarking Scheme with Chaotic Encryption for Medical Images. *IOP Conference Series. Materials Science and Engineering*, *1152*(1), 012025. DOI: 10.1088/1757-899X/1152/1/012025

Moina-Rivera, W., Garcia-Pineda, M., Gutiérrez-Aguado, J., & Alcaraz-Calero, J. M. (2024). Cloud media video encoding: Review and challenges. *Multimedia Tools and Applications*, *83*(34), 81231–81278. DOI: 10.1007/s11042-024-18763-2

Molina, J., Ponomaryov, V., Reyes, R., & Cruz, C. 2019. "Watermarking-Based Self-Recovery and Authentication Framework for Colour Images." Pp. 1–6 in *2019 7th international workshop on biometrics and forensics (IWBF)*. IEEE. DOI: 10.1109/IWBF.2019.8739211

Mummadi, A., Yadav, B. M. K., Sadhwika, R., & Shitharth, S. (2021, December). An appraisal of cyber-attacks and countermeasures using machine learning algorithms. In International Conference on Artificial Intelligence and Data Science (pp. 27-40). Cham: Springer Nature Switzerland.

Mun, S.-M., Nam, S.-H., Jang, H.-U., Kim, D., & Lee, H.-K. (2019). A Robust Blind Watermarking Using Convolutional Neural Network. *Neurocomputing*, *337*, 191–202. DOI: 10.1016/j.neucom.2019.01.067

Murala, D., & Thammireddy, K. (2024). An Efficient Multi-user Integrity and Multi-level Attribute Encryption and decryption framework for audio block-chain communication systems. *Frontiers in Health Informatics*, *13*(3).

Murali, J. A., & Brindha, T. (2024). A multi-objective clustered input oriented salp swarm algorithm in cloud computing. *Computers, Materials & Continua*, *81*(3), 4659–4690. DOI: 10.32604/cmc.2024.058115

Nafea, R. A., & Almaiah, M. A. (2021, July 14–15). Cyber security threats in cloud: Literature review. In *Proceedings of the 2021 International Conference on Information Technology (ICIT)* (pp. 779–786). Amman, Jordan. DOI: 10.1109/ICIT52682.2021.9491638

Nayak, A. A., Venugopala, P. S., Sarojadevi, H., Ashwini, B., & Chiplunkar, N. N. (2024). A novel watermarking technique for video on android mobile devices based on JPG quantization value and discrete cosine transform approach. *Multimedia Tools and Applications*, *83*(16), 47889–47917. DOI: 10.1007/s11042-023-17386-3

Nazir, H., Bajwa, I. S., Samiullah, M., Anwar, W., & Moosa, M. (2021). Robust Secure Color Image Watermarking Using 4D Hyperchaotic System, DWT, HbD, and SVD Based on Improved FOA Algorithm. *Security and Communication Networks*, *2021*, 1–17. DOI: 10.1155/2021/6617944

Nelaturu, K., Mavridou, A., Stachtiari, E., Veneris, A., & Laszka, A. (2023). Correct-by-Design Interacting Smart Contracts and a Systematic Approach for Verifying ERC20 and ERC721 Contracts with VeriSolid. *IEEE Transactions on Dependable and Secure Computing*, *20*(4), 3110–3127. DOI: 10.1109/TDSC.2022.3200840

Nematollahi, M. A., Vorakulpipat, C., & Rosales, H. G. (2017). Three-Dimensional (3D) Watermarking. In M. A. Nematollahi, C. Vorakulpipat, & H. G. Rosales, *Digital Watermarking* (Vol. 11, pp. 81–99). Springer Singapore. DOI: 10.1007/978-981-10-2095-7_6

Nie, H., & Lu, S. (2024). Securing IP in edge AI: Neural network watermarking for multimodal models. *Applied Intelligence*, *54*(21), 10455–10472. DOI: 10.1007/s10489-024-05746-x

NIST. (2011). The NIST definition of cloud computing. *Special Publication 800-145*. DOI: 10.6028/NIST.SP.800-145

Nithyashree, R., & Pawankumar, B. (2025). Steganography in Cloud Computing Environments: Leveraging Data Security for Environmental Pollution Monitoring. In *Enhancing Steganography Through Deep Learning Approaches* (pp. 219-244). IGI Global.

Noteboom, S. H., Kho, E., Galanty, M., Sánchez, C. I., ten Bookum, F. C. P., Veelo, D. P., Vlaar, A. P. J., & van der Ster, B. J. P. (2025). From intensive care monitors to cloud environments: A structured data pipeline for advanced clinical decision support. *EBioMedicine, 111*, 105529. DOI: 10.1016/j.ebiom.2024.105529 PMID: 39731854

Odeh, A. (2025). Healthcare data management using blockchain-enabled sensor networks. In *Sensor Networks for Smart Hospitals* (pp. 139–154). Elsevier. DOI: 10.1016/B978-0-443-36370-2.00009-8

Okonji, O. R., Yunusov, K., & Gordon, B. (2024). *Applications of Generative AI in Healthcare: Algorithmic, ethical, legal and societal considerations. Preprints.* DOI: 10.36227/techrxiv.171527587.75649430/v1

Olusegun, R., & Yang, B. (2023). Enhancing Blockchain Network Scalability Through Parallelization and Aggregation Techniques: A Survey. *Proceedings - 2023 International Conference on Computational Science and Computational Intelligence, CSCI 2023*, 1098–1105. DOI: 10.1109/CSCI62032.2023.00181

Ometov, A., Molua, O. L., Komarov, M., & Nurmi, J. (2022). A survey of security in cloud, edge, and fog computing. *Sensors (Basel), 22*(3), 927. DOI: 10.3390/s22030927 PMID: 35161675

Ouyang, L., Wu, J., Jiang, X., Almeida, D., Wainwright, C., Mishkin, P., & Lowe, R. (2022). Training language models to follow instructions with human feedback. *Advances in Neural Information Processing Systems, 35*, 27730–27744.

Padhi, S. K., Tiwari, A., & Ali, S. S. (2025). Deep learning-based dual watermarking for image copyright protection and authentication. arXiv. https://arxiv.org/abs/2502.18501

Paramkusam, D. A. V., Geetha, M., Sailakshmi, K., Mohansai, M., & Sowmya, L.Department of ECE. (2020). Development of a New Blind Watermarking for Medical Images. *International Journal of Innovative Technology and Exploring Engineering, 9*(9), 50–56. DOI: 10.35940/ijitee.I6845.079920

Parihar, B., Rawat, A. S., & Deshmukh, M. (2024). A survey on counting-based secret sharing schemes for resource-constrained environments: Techniques, security, challenges, and future directions. *The Journal of Supercomputing*, *80*(12), 17633 ?"17687. DOI: 10.1007/s11227-024-06130-9

Patil, A., & Shelke, R. (2022). Digital Audio Watermarking: Techniques, Applications, and Challenges. In Nagar, A. K., Jat, D. S., Marín-Raventós, G., & Mishra, D. K. (Eds.), *Intelligent Sustainable Systems* (Vol. 334, pp. 679–689). Springer Nature Singapore., DOI: 10.1007/978-981-16-6369-7_62

Patterson, D., Gonzalez, J., Le, Q., Liang, C., Munguia, L. M., Rothchild, D., Dean, J. (2021). Carbon emissions and large neural network training. arXiv preprint arXiv:2104.10350.

Pendyala, S. K. (2025). Strengthening healthcare cybersecurity: Leveraging multicloud and AI solutions. *Journal of Computer Science Applications and Information Technology*, *10*(1), 1–8. DOI: 10.15226/2474-9257/10/1/00163

Pereira, F., Crocker, P., & Leithardt, V. R. (2022). PADRES: Tool for privacy, data regulation and security. *SoftwareX*, *17*, 100895. DOI: 10.1016/j.softx.2021.100895

Petitcolas, F. A. P., Anderson, R. J., & Kuhn, M. G. (1999). Information Hiding-a Survey. *Proceedings of the IEEE*, *87*(7), 1062–1078. DOI: 10.1109/5.771065

Polemi, N., Praça, I., Kioskli, K., & Bécue, A. (2024). Challenges and efforts in managing AI trustworthiness risks: A state of knowledge. *Frontiers in Big Data*, *7*, 1381163. DOI: 10.3389/fdata.2024.1381163 PMID: 38798307

Qasim, A. F., Meziane, F., & Aspin, R. (2018). Digital watermarking: Applicability for developing trust in medical imaging workflows state of the art review. *Computer Science Review*, *27*, 45–60. DOI: 10.1016/j.cosrev.2017.11.003

qbal, S., Ahmad, Z., Naeem, W., Ullah, M. O., & Azam, M. (2024). SECURITY THREATS AND COUNTERMEASURES IN CLOUD. *Kashf Journal of Multidisciplinary Research*, *1*(12), 280–300. DOI: 10.71146/kjmr174

Radford, A., Wu, J., Child, R., Luan, D., Amodei, D., & Sutskever, I. (2019). Language models are unsupervised multitask learners. OpenAI blog, 1(8), 9.

Raghu, N., Bhat, R., Nambiar, P. R., Shetty, G. S., & DB, A. K. (2025). Blockchain-Enhanced GAN Image Encryption Scheme for Cloud Computing. In *Intelligent Systems and IoT Applications in Clinical Health* (pp. 367-392). IGI Global.

Rahdari, A., Keshavarz, E., Nowroozi, E., Taheri, R., Hajizadeh, M., Mohammadi, M., Sinaei, S., & Bauschert, T. (2025). A survey on privacy and security in distributed cloud computing: Exploring federated learning and beyond. *IEEE Open Journal of the Communications Society*, *6*, 3710–3744. DOI: 10.1109/OJCOMS.2025.3560034

Raj, D., & Sharma, D. (2024). Enhancing Digital Image Forensics and Security: Innovations in Metadata, Watermarking and Blockchain Technology. *2024 OPJU International Technology Conference on Smart Computing for Innovation and Advancement in Industry 4.0, OTCON 2024*, 1–6. DOI: 10.1109/OTCON60325.2024.10688307

Rani, S., & Halder, R. (2022). Comparative Analysis of Relational Database Watermarking Techniques: An Empirical Study. *IEEE Access : Practical Innovations, Open Solutions*, *10*, 27970–27989. DOI: 10.1109/ACCESS.2022.3157866

Ranjan, A., & Ravinder, M. (2024). Image security using quantum hash functions. In *Digital Image Security* (pp. 20–42). CRC Press. DOI: 10.1201/9781003468974-2

Ratha, N. K., Connell, J. H., & Bolle, R. M. (2001). Enhancing Security and Privacy in Biometrics-Based Authentication Systems. *IBM Systems Journal*, *40*(3), 614–634. DOI: 10.1147/sj.403.0614

Recharla, M. (2025). Revolutionizing Healthcare with Generative AI: Enhancing Patient Care, Disease Research, and Early Intervention Strategies. *American Journal of Psychiatric Rehabilitation*, 98–111. DOI: 10.69980/ajpr.v28i1.70

Reese, R. A. (2021). The DMCA's safe harbors, twenty years later. *Columbia Journal of Law & the Arts*, *44*(3), 305–340.

Regazzoni, F., Palmieri, P., Smailbegovic, F., Cammarota, R., & Polian, I. (2021). Protecting artificial intelligence IPs: A survey of watermarking and fingerprinting for machine learning. *CAAI Transactions on Intelligence Technology*, *6*(2), 180–191. DOI: 10.1049/cit2.12029

Reis, A., Fraga, C., & Gouveia, A. J. (2025). Cloud computing adoption as IT strategy in organizations: A short systematic review. *Procedia Computer Science*, *256*, 122–129. DOI: 10.1016/j.procs.2025.02.104

Ren, X., Xu, M., Niyato, D., Kang, J., Xiong, Z., Qiu, C., & Wang, X. (2025). Building Resilient Web 3.0 Infrastructure With Quantum Information Technologies and Blockchain: An Ambilateral View. *Proceedings of the IEEE.*

Reza, S., Hosen, M. A., Rahman, A., & Galib, S. M. (2025). A Hybrid Approach to Digital Image Watermarking Integrating DWT, DFT, and Genetic Algorithm. In *International Conference on Artificial Intelligence and Smart Energy* (pp. 484-496). Springer, Cham. DOI: 10.1007/978-3-031-90482-0_39

Rittinghouse, J. W., & Ransome, J. F. (2016). *Cloud computing: Implementation, management, and security*. CRC Press.

Rogers, A., Kovaleva, O., & Rumshisky, A. (2020). A primer in BERTology: What we know about how BERT works. *Transactions of the Association for Computational Linguistics*, *8*, 842–866. DOI: 10.1162/tacl_a_00349

Sachdeva, S., Bhatia, S., Anwer, M. K., Philip, A. K., Al Harrasi, A., Shah, Y. A., Shah, S. F. A., Halim, S. A., & Khan, A. (2024). Unraveling the role of cloud computing in health care system and biomedical sciences. *Heliyon*, *10*(7), e29044. DOI: 10.1016/j.heliyon.2024.e29044 PMID: 38601602

Sahoo, A. AK, I. K., & Rajagopal, S. M. (2024, November). Comparative Study of Cryptographic Algorithms in Post Quantum Computing Landscape. In 2024 5th International Conference on Data Intelligence and Cognitive Informatics (ICDICI) (pp. 36-40). IEEE.

Sahu, A. K., Umachandran, K., Biradar, V. D., Comfort, O., Sri Vigna Hema, V., Odimegwu, F., & Saifullah, M. A.Saifullah M. A. (2023). A study on content tampering in multimedia watermarking. *SN Computer Science*, *4*(3), 222. DOI: 10.1007/s42979-022-01657-1

Samha, A. K. (2024). Strategies for efficient resource management in federated cloud environments supporting Infrastructure as a Service (IaaS). *Journal of Engineering Research*, *12*(2), 101–114. DOI: 10.1016/j.jer.2023.10.031

Sanh, V., Debut, L., Chaumond, J., & Wolf, T. (2019). DistilBERT, a distilled version of BERT: smaller, faster, cheaper and lighter. arXiv preprint arXiv:1910.01108.

Saraswat, B. K., Bansal, A., Singhal, A., & Kumar, P. (2024, November). Enhancing Realtime Data Integrity in Healthcare Systems using Blockchain and Optimized Data Encryption. In 2024 4th International Conference on Advancement in Electronics & Communication Engineering (AECE) (pp. 1122-1127). IEEE. DOI: 10.1109/AECE62803.2024.10911610

Satish, K. S. Database Security Issues and Challenges in Cloud Computing.

Sayeh, M. NAIMI, A., & BADAOUI, R. *Watermarking security in IWT transform domain* (Doctoral dissertation, UNIVERSITY OF KASDI MERBAH OUARGLA).

ScienceGate. (2021). *Cloud computing security: A survey of service-based models & trust model analysis*. ScienceGate.

Senftleben, M. (2023). The perfect match? Enhancing DRM through AI-based content recognition. *International Review of Intellectual Property and Competition Law, 54*(2), 143–168.

Senkyire, I. B., & Kester, Q. A. (2019). Validation of Forensic Crime Scene Images Using Watermarking and Cryptographic Blockchain. *2019 ICDSA International Conference on Computer, Data Science and Applications, ICDSA 2019*, 2–5. DOI: 10.1109/ICDSA46371.2019.9404235

Shabbir, A., Anwar, A. S., Taslima, N., Sayem, M. A., Sikder, A. R., & Sidhu, G. S. (2024). Analyzing enterprise data protection and safety risks in cloud computing using ensemble learning. *International Journal on Recent and Innovation Trends in Computing and Communication, 12*(2), 499–507.

Shackleford, D. (2022). SANS 2022 cloud security survey. SANS Institute. https://www.sans.org/white-papers/sans-2022-cloud-security-survey/

Sharifara, A., Rahim, M. S. M., & Bashardoost, M. (2013). A Novel Approach to Enhance Robustness in Digital Image Watermarking Using Multiple Bit-Planes of Intermediate Significant Bits. *2013 International Conference on Informatics and Creative Multimedia*, 22–27. DOI: 10.1109/ICICM.2013.13

Sharma, A., Rana, S., Sharma, A., Singh, A., Datwani, K., Tiwari, D., & Matta, R. 2025. "An Analytical Study on Safety Measures Concerns in Cloud Computing Technology." in *AIP Conference Proceedings*. Vol. 3224. AIP Publishing. DOI: 10.1063/5.0247117

Sharma, R. K. (2025). Multi-Tenant Architectures in Modern Cloud Computing: A Technical Deep Dive.

Sharma, A., Kejriwal, D., & Pakina, A. K. (2023). Generative AI in the deep internet: Treat and counter measures for the next generation resilience. *International Journal of Artificial Intelligence and Data Research, 14*(1).

Sharma, B. M., & Malik, A. (2025). Automated threat attack categorisation into cloud service models. *Procedia Computer Science, 259*, 1883–1892. DOI: 10.1016/j.procs.2025.04.144

Sharma, K. U., Talan, P. P., Nawade, P. P., Ali, M. S., & Sharma, A. U. (2019). Digital Watermarking—An Overview and a Possible Solution. In Satapathy, S. C., & Joshi, A. (Eds.), *Information and Communication Technology for Intelligent Systems* (Vol. 107, pp. 447–455). Springer Singapore., DOI: 10.1007/978-981-13-1747-7_43

Shaw, P., Uszkoreit, J., & Vaswani, A. (2018). Self-attention with relative position representations. arXiv preprint arXiv:1803.02155. DOI: 10.18653/v1/N18-2074

Shukla, D., & Tiwari, N. (2015). Survey on Digital Watermarking Techniques. *International Journal of Signal Processing. Image Processing and Pattern Recognition*, *8*(9), 121–126. DOI: 10.14257/ijsip.2015.8.9.12

Singamaneni, K. K., Muhammad, G., & Ali, Z. (2023). A novel multi-qubit quantum key distribution ciphertext-policy attribute-based encryption model to improve cloud security for consumers. *IEEE Transactions on Consumer Electronics*, *70*(1), 1092 ?"1101. DOI: 10.1109/TCE.2023.3331306

Singh, A. K., Thakur, S., Jolfaei, A., Srivastava, G., Elhoseny, M., & Mohan, A. (2021). Joint Encryption and Compression-Based Watermarking Technique for Security of Digital Documents. *ACM Transactions on Internet Technology*, *21*(1), 1–20. DOI: 10.1145/3414474

Singh, A., Dwivedi, R. K., & Kumar, R. (2021). A Survey of Lung Cancer Detection Using Machine Learning Techniques for Improving Classification Performance. *World J Eng Res Technol*, *7*(4), 149–161.

Singh, K. U., Bhatia, S., Kumar, A., Kautish, S., Kumar, A., Basheer, S., & Hameed, A. A. (2022). A Robust NIfTI Image Authentication Framework Based on DST and Multi-Scale Otsu Thresholding. *IEEE Access : Practical Innovations, Open Solutions*, *10*, 132608–132620. DOI: 10.1109/ACCESS.2022.3225908

Singh, N., Jain, M., & Sharma, S. (2013). A Survey of Digital Watermarking Techniques. *International Journal of Modern Communication Technologies and Research*, *1*(6), 265852.

Sinha, A., Banerjee, P., Roy, S., Rathore, N., Singh, N. P., Uddin, M., Abdelhaq, M., & Alsaqour, R. (2024). Improved dynamic Johnson sequencing algorithm (DJS) in cloud computing environment for efficient resource scheduling for distributed overloading. *Journal of Systems Science and Systems Engineering*, *33*(4), 391–424. DOI: 10.1007/s11518-024-5606-z

Sinhal, R., & Ansari, I. A. (2023). Machine learning based multipurpose medical image watermarking. *Neural Computing & Applications*, *35*(31), 23041–23062. DOI: 10.1007/s00521-023-08457-5 PMID: 37362569

Slocum, C., Zhang, Y., Shayegani, E., Zaree, P., Abu-Ghazaleh, N., & Chen, J. (2024). That Doesn't Go There: Attacks on Shared State in {Multi-User} Augmented Reality Applications. In 33rd USENIX Security Symposium (USENIX Security 24) (pp. 2761-2778).

Smirnov, O. M., Makhathini, S., Kenyon, J. S., Bester, H. L., Perkins, S. J., Ramaila, A. J. T., & Hugo, B. V. (2025). Africanus IV. The Stimela2 framework: Scalable and repeatable workflows, from local to cloud compute. *Astronomy and Computing*, *52*, 100959. DOI: 10.1016/j.ascom.2025.100959

Sober, M., Scaffino, G., & Schulte, S. (2024). Cross-Blockchain Communication Using Oracles With an Off-Chain Aggregation Mechanism Based on zk-SNARKs. *Distributed Ledger Technologies: Research and Practice*. DOI: 10.1145/3678187

Software Engineering Institute. (2019). Overview of risks, threats, and vulnerabilities faced in moving to the cloud. Carnegie Mellon University. https://insights.sei.cmu.edu/library/overview-of-risks-threats-and-vulnerabilities-faced-in-moving-to-the-cloud/

Stiennon, N., Ouyang, L., Wu, J., Ziegler, D., Lowe, R., Voss, C., & Christiano, P. F. (2020). Learning to summarize with human feedback. *Advances in Neural Information Processing Systems*, *33*, 3008–3021.

Stipsits, M. (n.d.). *Scalable Integration of Ethereum in a Microservice based Application through Layer 2 Rollups*. Retrieved from https://www.signature-verification.gv.at

Strubell, E., Ganesh, A., & McCallum, A. (2019). Energy and policy considerations for deep learning in NLP. arXiv preprint arXiv:1906.02243. /arXiv.1906.02243DOI: 10.18653/v1/P19-1355

Subashini, S., & Kavitha, V. (2011). A survey on security issues in service delivery models of cloud computing. *Journal of Network and Computer Applications*, *34*(1), 1–11. DOI: 10.1016/j.jnca.2010.07.006

Sujatha, C. N., & Satyanarayana, P. (2016). Analysis of robust watermarking techniques: A retrospective. *2016 International Conference on Communication and Signal Processing (ICCSP)*, 0336–0341. DOI: 10.1109/ICCSP.2016.7754151

Sultan, N. (2014). Making use of cloud computing for healthcare provision: Opportunities and challenges. *International Journal of Information Management*, *34*(2), 177–184. DOI: 10.1016/j.ijinfomgt.2013.12.011

Supiyandi, S., Lamudur Arta Sihombing, G., Kristian Siburian, H., Purnomo, A., Anam, F., Putut Laksminto Emanuel, E., Siregar, D., Halim Putra, A., E. Laumal, F., Brillian Kharis, O., Akhiruddin, A., Rosnatang, R., Marpaung, P., Ramadani, R., Andry Wikra Wardhana Mamonto, M., Monika Kulsum, N., Salle, S., Nurhayadi, N., & Rahim, R. (2018). Application of Invisible Image Watermarking. *International Journal of Engineering & Technology*, *7*(3.2), 760. DOI: 10.14419/ijet.v7i3.2.18749

Suryawanshi, S., Mhaskar, Y., Meghana, K. L. P., Disa, R., & Gutte, V. S. (2023, November). Enhancing Secure Video Transmission and Cloud-Based Storage through Advanced Encryption, Hashing, and Distributed Processing. In *2023 International Conference on Computing, Communication, and Intelligent Systems (ICCCIS)* (pp. 953-959). IEEE. DOI: 10.1109/ICCCIS60361.2023.10425656

Symmetry Editorial Team. (2023). Special issue: Symmetry in cloud security and cryptographic systems. *Symmetry*, *15*(11), 1981. DOI: 10.3390/sym15111981

Sy, N. C., Kha, H. H., & Hoang, N. M. (2020). An Efficient Robust Blind Watermarking Method Based on Convolution Neural Networks in Wavelet Transform Domain. *International Journal of Machine Learning and Computing*, *10*(5), 675–684. DOI: 10.18178/ijmlc.2020.10.5.990

Tan, C. W., Wong, Y. L., Loh, J. C., & Li, C. Z. Deep Learning & Hybrid Model–The Future Of Medical Image Watermarking.

Tang, Q., Li, Y., Wang, Q., He, W., & Peng, X. (2023). A Dual Blind Watermarking Method for 3D Models Based on Normal Features. *Entropy (Basel, Switzerland)*, *25*(10), 1369. DOI: 10.3390/e25101369 PMID: 37895491

Tauhid, A., Xu, L., Rahman, M., & Tomai, E. (2023). A survey on security analysis of machine learning-oriented hardware and software intellectual property. *High-Confidence Computing*, *3*(2), 100114. DOI: 10.1016/j.hcc.2023.100114

Tay, Y., Dehghani, M., Bahri, D., & Metzler, D. (2023). Efficient transformers: A survey. ACM Computing Surveys, 55(6). *ACM Computing Surveys*, *109*(6), 1–28. DOI: 10.1145/3530811

Tiwari, A., Awasthi, D., & Srivastava, V. K. (2025). RFPPFMark: Robust and false positive problem free image watermarking scheme with its performance comparison by PSO and MRFO in Schur domain. *Signal, Image and Video Processing*, *19*(3), 199. DOI: 10.1007/s11760-024-03704-1

Tiwari, P., Nagra, G. K., Sharma, R., Rakesh, N., & Saraswat, B. K. (2025, February). A Triage System Based Approach With AI-Driven Management In Bugs Resolving Application. In *2025 International Conference on Pervasive Computational Technologies (ICPCT)* (pp. 538-542). DOI: 10.1109/ICPCT64145.2025.10939178

Tu, S., Waqas, M., Meng, Y., Rehman, S. U., Ahmad, I., Koubaa, A., Halim, Z., Hanif, M., Chang, C. C., & Shi, C. (2020). Mobile fog computing security: A user-oriented smart attack defense strategy based on DQL. *Computer Communications*, *160*, 790–798. DOI: 10.1016/j.comcom.2020.06.019

Tu, S., Waqas, M., Rehman, S. U., Mir, T., Abbas, G., Abbas, Z. H., Halim, Z., & Ahmad, I. (2021). Reinforcement learning assisted impersonation attack detection in device-to-device communications. *IEEE Transactions on Vehicular Technology, 70*(2), 1474–1479. DOI: 10.1109/TVT.2021.3053015

Ukwandu, E., Ben-Farah, M. A., Hindy, H., Bures, M., Atkinson, R., Tachtatzis, C., Andonovic, I., & Bellekens, X. (2022). Cyber-security challenges in aviation industry: A review of current and future trends. *Information (Basel), 13*(3), 146. DOI: 10.3390/info13030146

Umamahesh, G., & Rajkumar, G. V. S. (2023). Survey on various security issues associated with cloud authentication techniques. *ICISSC 2022.*

Urban, J. M., Karaganis, J., & Schofield, B. (2020). Notice and takedown in everyday practice. UC Berkeley Public Law Research Paper No. 2766526.

Vanmathi, C., Farouk, A., Alhammad, S. M., Bhattacharya, S., & Kasyapa, M. S. (2024). The role of blockchain in transforming industries beyond finance. *IEEE Access : Practical Innovations, Open Solutions, 12*, 148845–148867. DOI: 10.1109/ACCESS.2024.3468611

Vasconcelos Soares dos Santos, N. (2024). Data Security and User Authentication in Public Cloud Computing Environments.

Vashistha, D., Mehta, D., Kumhar, M., Bhatia, J., & Alkhayyat, A. (2025). Deep learning based load balancing in cloud computing: A survey. *Procedia Computer Science, 259*, 1963–1972. DOI: 10.1016/j.procs.2025.04.152

Vassaux, B., Nguyen, P., Baudry, S., Bas, P., & Chassery, J. M. 2002. "Scrambling Technique for Video Object Watermarking Resisting to Mpeg-4." Pp. 239–44 in *International Symposium on VIPromCom Video/Image Processing and Multimedia Communications*. IEEE. DOI: 10.1109/VIPROM.2002.1026662

Vaswani, A., Shazeer, N., Parmar, N., Uszkoreit, J., Jones, L., Gomez, A. N., & Polosukhin, I. (2017). Attention is all you need. *Advances in Neural Information Processing Systems*, 30.

Vaziry, A., Garzon, S. R., Herbke, P., Segat, C., & Kupper, A. (2025). SoK: A Taxonomy for Distributed-Ledger-Based Identity Management. *arXiv preprint arXiv:2505.05100*. DOI: 10.1109/CVC65719.2025.00015

Verma, H., & Shrivastava, V. (2025). VBDPA multi-criteria task scheduling algorithm in container-based cloud computing environment. *Procedia Computer Science, 252*, 603–612. DOI: 10.1016/j.procs.2025.01.020

Voorsluys, W., Broberg, J., & Buyya, R. (2011). Introduction to cloud computing. In *Cloud computing: Principles and paradigms* (pp. 1–44). Wiley. DOI: 10.1002/9780470940105.ch1

Wadhera, S., Kamra, D., Rajpal, A., Jain, A., & Jain, V. (2022). A comprehensive review on digital image watermarking. arXiv preprint arXiv:2207.06909.

Wang, Y., & Yang, X. (2025). Research on enhancing cloud computing network security using artificial intelligence algorithms. *arXiv, Feb 25*.

Wang, B., Wu, Y., & Wang, G. (2023). Adaptor: Improving the robustness and imperceptibility of watermarking by the adaptive strength factor. *IEEE Transactions on Circuits and Systems for Video Technology*, *33*(11), 6260–6272. DOI: 10.1109/TCSVT.2023.3265970

Wang, C., Wang, Q., Ren, K., Lou, W., & Li, J. (2012). Toward secure and dependable storage services in cloud computing. *IEEE Transactions on Services Computing*, *5*(2), 220–232. DOI: 10.1109/TSC.2011.24

Wang, H., Tang, N., Zhu, C., Ren, N., & Wang, C. (2025). A blockchain copyright protection model based on vector map unique identification. *ISPRS International Journal of Geo-Information*, *14*(2), 53. DOI: 10.3390/ijgi14020053

Wang, L., Ranjan, R., Kolodziej, J., Zomaya, A. Y., & Alem, L. (2015). Software tools and techniques for big data computing in the cloud. *Software, Practice & Experience*, *45*(12), 1607–1614.

Wang, S., Yin, M., Liu, Y., & He, G. (2024). Generative adversarial networks-based security and applications in cloud computing: A survey. *Telecommunication Systems*, *86*(2), 305–331. DOI: 10.1007/s11235-024-01166-x

Wang, X., & Wang, H. (2025). Research on the Identification and Supervision Mechanism of AIGC Based on Blockchain and Digital Watermark. *2025 IEEE International Conference on Electronics, Energy Systems and Power Engineering (EESPE)*, 638–641. DOI: 10.1109/EESPE63401.2025.10986886

Wang, Y., Chen, L., Yu, K., & Fang, H. (2024). Multi-key spatio-temporal chaotic image encryption and retrieval scheme. *Nonlinear Dynamics*, *112*(4), 3003 ?"3025. DOI: 10.1007/s11071-023-09170-7

Wan, W., Wang, J., Zhang, Y., Li, J., Yu, H., & Sun, J. (2022). A Comprehensive Survey on Robust Image Watermarking. *Neurocomputing*, *488*, 226–247. DOI: 10.1016/j.neucom.2022.02.083

Waqas, M., Niu, Y., Li, Y., Ahmed, M., Jin, D., Chen, S., & Han, Z. (2020). A comprehensive survey on mobility-aware D2D communications: Principles, practice and challenges. *IEEE Communications Surveys and Tutorials*, *22*(3), 1863–1886. DOI: 10.1109/COMST.2019.2923708

Wei, J., Tay, Y., Bommasani, R., Raffel, C., Zoph, B., Borgeaud, S., Fedus, W. (2022). Emergent abilities of large language models. arXiv preprint arXiv:2206.07682.

Wei, D., & Deng, Y. (2024). An Optimized IWT–DCT Watermarking Scheme Based on Multiple Matrix Decomposition and MOWOA2. *Circuits, Systems, and Signal Processing*, *43*(8), 5262–5287. DOI: 10.1007/s00034-024-02707-0

Weinhardt, C., Anandasivam, A., Blau, B., & Stößer, J. (2009). Cloud computing – A classification, business models, and research directions. *Business & Information Systems Engineering*, *1*(5), 391–399. DOI: 10.1007/s12599-009-0071-2

Welleck, S., Kulikov, I., Roller, S., Dinan, E., Cho, K., & Weston, J. (2019). Neural text generation with unlikelihood training. arXiv preprint arXiv:1908.04319.

Wikipedia contributors. (2024). Capitol Records, Inc. v. MP3Tunes, LLC. Wikipedia. https://en.wikipedia.org/wiki/Capitol_Records,_Inc._v._MP3Tunes,_LLC

Wikipedia contributors. (2024). Digital Millennium Copyright Act. Wikipedia. https://en.wikipedia.org/wiki/Digital_Millennium_Copyright_Act

Wikipedia contributors. (2024). Digital rights management. Wikipedia. https://en.wikipedia.org/wiki/Digital_rights_management

Wikipedia contributors. (2024). Digital watermarking. Wikipedia. https://en.wikipedia.org/wiki/Digital_watermarking

Wikipedia. (2025, June). *Confidential computing.*

Wikipedia. (2025, June). *Zero Trust Architecture & Secure Access Service Edge (SASE).*

Wikipedia. (2025, March). *EU Cloud Code of Conduct.*

Williamson, S. M., & Prybutok, V. (2024). The Era of Artificial Intelligence Deception: Unraveling the Complexities of False Realities and Emerging Threats of Misinformation. *Information (Basel)*, *15*(6), 299. DOI: 10.3390/info15060299

Wu, X., Duan, R., & Ni, J. (2024). Unveiling security, privacy, and ethical concerns of ChatGPT. *Journal of information and intelligence, 2*(2), 102-115.

Wu, W., Dai, J., Huang, H., Zhao, Q., Zeng, G., & Li, R. (2023). A digital watermark method for in-vehicle network security enhancement. *IEEE Transactions on Vehicular Technology*, *72*(7), 8398–8408. DOI: 10.1109/TVT.2023.3247180

Wu, X., Ma, P., Jin, Z., Wu, Y., Han, W., & Ou, W. (2022). A novel zero-watermarking scheme based on NSCT-SVD and blockchain for video copyright. *EURASIP Journal on Wireless Communications and Networking*, *2022*(1), 20. DOI: 10.1186/s13638-022-02090-x

Wu, Y., Weng, J., Wang, Z., Wei, K., Wen, J., Lai, J., & Li, X. (2022). Attacks and countermeasures on privacy-preserving biometric authentication schemes. *IEEE Transactions on Dependable and Secure Computing*, *20*(2), 1744–1755. DOI: 10.1109/TDSC.2022.3162623

Xiao, X., Zhang, Y., Zhang, L. Y., Hua, Z., Liu, Z., & Huang, J. (2021). FairCMS: Cloud media sharing with fair copyright protection. arXiv. https://arxiv.org/abs/2105.08899

Xiong, R., Yang, Y., He, D., Zheng, K., Zheng, S., Xing, C., & Wang, L. (2020). On layer normalization in the transformer architecture. In *International Conference on Machine Learning* (pp. 10524-10533). PMLR.

Xu, H. B., Wang, R., Wei, J., & Lu, S. P. (2021). A compact neural network-based algorithm for robust image watermarking. *arXiv preprint arXiv:2112.13491*.

Xue, X., Shang, G., Ma, Z., Xu, M., Guo, H., Li, K., & Cheng, X. (2024). DataSafe: Copyright protection with PUF watermarking and blockchain tracking. arXiv. https://arxiv.org/abs/2405.19099

Xu, J., Zhang, J., & Wang, J. (2025). Digital Image Copyright Protection and Management Approach—Based on Artificial Intelligence and Blockchain Technology. *Journal of Theoretical and Applied Electronic Commerce Research*, *20*(2), 76. DOI: 10.3390/jtaer20020076

Yadav, N., Rajpoot, D., & Dhakad, S. K. (2020). Optimization of Watermarking in Image by Using Particle Swarm Optimization Algorithm. *2020 6th International Conference on Signal Processing and Communication (ICSC)*, 85–90. DOI: 10.1109/ICSC48311.2020.9182716

Yadav, S. P. (2025). An improved image compression framework in modern multimedia applications using tetrolet transformation. *Multimedia Tools and Applications*, *84*(6), 3305 ?"3338. DOI: 10.1007/s11042-024-20578-0

Yang, H., & Tate, M. (2012). A descriptive literature review and classification of cloud computing research. *Communications of the Association for Information Systems*, *31*(1), 35–60. DOI: 10.17705/1CAIS.03102

Yang, T., Li, Y., He, J., Liu, Z., Ren, F., Wang, T., & Hou, G. (2024). Secure and traceable multikey image retrieval in cloud-assisted internet of things. *IEEE Internet of Things Journal*, *11*(24), 40875 ?"40887. DOI: 10.1109/JIOT.2024.3457017

Yang, Y. (2020). Medical Multimedia Big Data Analysis Modeling Based on DBN Algorithm. *IEEE Access : Practical Innovations, Open Solutions*, *8*, 16350–16361. DOI: 10.1109/ACCESS.2020.2967075

Ye, P., Li, Z., Yang, Z., Chen, P., Zhang, Z., Li, N., & Zheng, J. (2025). Periodic watermarking for copyright protection of large language models in cloud computing security. *Computer Standards & Interfaces*, *94*, 103983. DOI: 10.1016/j.csi.2025.103983

Yi, Y. (2024). *The Investigation of Layer 2 Blockchain Technologies for Decentralized Applications*. 326–333. DOI: 10.5220/0012837400004547

Youssef, A. E. (2012). Exploring cloud computing services and applications. *Journal of Emerging Trends in Computing and Information Sciences*, *3*(6), 838–847.

Yuan, Z., Zhang, X., Wang, Z., & Yin, Z. 2024. "Semi-Fragile Neural Network Watermarking Based on Adversarial Examples." *IEEE Transactions on Emerging Topics in Computational Intelligence*. https://ieeexplore.ieee.org/abstract/document/10474363/

Yu, L., Xu, H., Zeng, Y., & Deng, J. (2024). Delay-aware resource allocation for partial computation offloading in mobile edge cloud computing. *Pervasive and Mobile Computing*, *105*, 101996. DOI: 10.1016/j.pmcj.2024.101996

Yu, P. K. (2023). Cloud computing and cross-border copyright enforcement. Fordham Intellectual Property. *Media & Entertainment Law Journal*, *33*(4), 1153–1205.

Yu, X., Wang, C., & Zhou, X. (2018). A Survey on Robust Video Watermarking Algorithms for Copyright Protection. *Applied Sciences (Basel, Switzerland)*, *8*(10), 1891. DOI: 10.3390/app8101891

Zaheer, M., Guruganesh, G., Dubey, K. A., Ainslie, J., Alberti, C., Ontanon, S., Pham, P., Ravula, A., Wang, Q., Yang, L., & Ahmed, A. (2020). Big bird: Transformers for longer sequences. arXiv preprint arXiv:2007.14062. https://arxiv.org/abs/2007.14062

Zainal, N., Hoshi, A. R., Ismail, M., Rahem, A. A. R. T., & Wadi, S. M. (2024). A hybrid steganography and watermark algorithm for copyright protection by using multiple embedding approaches. *Bulletin of Electrical Engineering and Informatics*, *13*(3), 1877–1896. DOI: 10.11591/eei.v13i3.6337

Zhang, J., Qiao, D., Yang, M., & Wei, Q. (2024). Regurgitative training: The value of real data in training large language models. arXiv preprint arXiv:2407.12835.

Zhang, G. D., Zhang, Z. X., Li, J. Y., Guo, Y., Ding, H., Xi, X. T., & Han, Y. C. (2025). Robust Image Watermarking in Wavelet Domain using RDWT-HD-SVD and Whale Optimization Algorithm. *Circuits, Systems, and Signal Processing*, *44*(4), 2681–2705. DOI: 10.1007/s00034-024-02930-9

Zhang, P., Li, J., Aslam Bhatti, U., Liu, J., Chen, Y., Li, D., & Cao, L. (2023). Robust Watermarking Algorithm for Medical Volume Data Based on Polar Cosine Transform and 3D-DCT. *Computers, Materials & Continua*, *75*(3), 5853–5870. DOI: 10.32604/cmc.2023.036462

Zhang, Q., Cheng, L., & Boutaba, R. (2013). Cloud computing: State-of-the-art and research challenges. *Journal of Internet Services and Applications*, *1*(1), 7–18. DOI: 10.1007/s13174-010-0007-6

Zhang, Y., Li, Y., Cui, L., Cai, D., Liu, L., Fu, T., Huang, X., Zhao, E., Zhang, Y., Chen, Y., Wang, L., Luu, A. T., Bi, W., Shi, F., & Shi, S. (2025). Siren's song in the ai ocean: A survey on hallucination in large language models. *Computational Linguistics*, 1–45. DOI: 10.1162/coli.a.16

Zhao, X., Ananth, P., Li, L., & Wang, Y. X. (2023). Provable robust watermarking for ai-generated text. arXiv preprint arXiv:2306.17439.

Zhao, X., Gunn, S., Christ, M., Fairoze, J., Fabrega, A., Carlini, N., Garg, S., Hong, S., Nasr, M., Tramer, F., Jha, S., Li, L., Wang, Y.-X., & Song, D. (2024). *SoK: Watermarking for AI-Generated Content* (Version 2). arXiv. DOI: 10.48550/ARXIV.2411.18479

Zhao, B., Zhong, Y., Xia, G.-S., & Zhang, L. (2016). Dirichlet-Derived Multiple Topic Scene Classification Model for High Spatial Resolution Remote Sensing Imagery. *IEEE Transactions on Geoscience and Remote Sensing*, *54*(4), 2108–2123. DOI: 10.1109/TGRS.2015.2496185

Zheng, J., Teng, S., Li, P., Ou, W., Zhou, D., & Ye, J. (2021). A Novel Video Copyright Protection Scheme Based on Blockchain and Double Watermarking. *Security and Communication Networks*, *2021*, 1–16. DOI: 10.1155/2021/6493306

Zhong, X., Das, A., Alrasheedi, F., & Tanvir, A. (2023). *A Brief Yet In-Depth Survey of Deep Learning-Based Image Watermarking* (Version 3). arXiv. DOI: 10.48550/ARXIV.2308.04603

Zhu, H., Liang, S., Hu, W., Fangqi, L., Jia, J., & Wang, S. L. (2024, October). Reliable model watermarking: Defending against theft without compromising on evasion. In *Proceedings of the 32nd ACM International Conference on Multimedia* (pp. 10124-10133). DOI: 10.1145/3664647.3681610

Zhu, J., Kaplan, R., Johnson, J., & Li, F.-F. 2018. "Hidden: Hiding Data with Deep Networks." Pp. 657–72 in *Proceedings of the European conference on computer vision (ECCV).*

Zhukabayeva, T., Zholshiyeva, L., Karabayev, N., Khan, S., & Alnazzawi, N. (2025). Cybersecurity Solutions for Industrial Internet of Things–Edge Computing Integration: Challenges, Threats, and Future Directions. *Sensors (Basel)*, *25*(1), 213. DOI: 10.3390/s25010213 PMID: 39797003

Zu, L., Li, H., Zhang, L., Lu, Z., Ye, J., Zhao, X., & Hu, S. (2023). E-SAWM: A Semantic Analysis-Based ODF Watermarking Algorithm for Edge Cloud Scenarios. *Future Internet*, *15*(9), 283. DOI: 10.3390/fi15090283

Zu, L., Qi, W., Li, H., Men, X., Lu, Z., Ye, J., & Zhang, L. (2024). UP-SDCG: A Method of Sensitive Data Classification for Collaborative Edge Computing in Financial Cloud Environment. *Future Internet*, *16*(3), 102. DOI: 10.3390/fi16030102

Zurqani, H. A. (2024). The first generation of a regional-scale 1-m forest canopy cover dataset using machine learning and Google Earth Engine cloud computing platform: A case study of Arkansas, USA. *Data in Brief*, *52*, 109986. DOI: 10.1016/j.dib.2023.109986 PMID: 38293581

About the Contributors

Ashwani Kumar is an Associate Professor in School of Computer Science Engineering and Technology, Bennett University, Greater Noida, India. He received his doctorate of philosophy (Ph.D) in Computer Science and Engineering, from Jaypee University of Information Technology, H.P in 2017. He received his M.Tech (CSE) from Jaypee University of Information Technology, H.P in 2011. He has done B.Tech from Uttar Pradesh Technical University (U.P.T.U) Lucknow, U.P in 2009. He has more than 12 years of teaching and research experience. He published more than 75 research papers in international reputed journals indexed in SCI/SCIE Web of Science & SCOPUS and top rank conferences as authored or co-authored. His research findings are published in Wiley, Springer Journal, Procedia Computer Science Elsevier, JST Universiti Putra Malaysia, IJCAC IGI Global USA, IEEE Xplore. He is serving as the reviewer of many SCI Journals- IET Information IET Digital Library, Multimedia Tools and Application (MTAP) Springer, National Academy Science Letters Springer, Journal of Intelligent and Fuzzy Systems (JIFS) IOS Press. Currently, he is editorial board member of many reputed Journals-IJDCF, IJISP, IJEUCD, IGI Global Journal USA indexed in WOS/SCOPUS. He has been guest editor for International Journal Recent Patent of Engineering, Bentham Publication indexed in SCOPUS. He is the Editor of Book Series: Advancements in Security and Privacy Initiatives for Multimedia Images, IGI Global Journal USA. He is awarded as Bentham Brand Ambassador Award for the year 2019-2020. He served as session chair in several international conferences-ICIIP-2019, MISS-2020, IC4S-2020, PGDC-2020. He has filing an Australian patent in the year 2020. His research area includes Image Security, Watermarking Techniques, Multimedia Application, Security & Privacy, Cryptography and Network Security. He is also a lifetime member of professional societies like IEEE, ISTE, IACSIT, IAENG and SDIWC.

Auzuir Ripardo de Alexandria is a computer scientist, electrical engineer, researcher, and full professor at IFCE, holding a master's and a PhD in Teleinformatics Engineering (from UFC, 2005 and 2011). He currently serves as a permanent faculty member in the Graduate Program in Telecommunications Engineering (PPGET), the Graduate Program in Renewable Energies (PPGER), and the Northeast Teaching Network (Doctorate), as well as in the Mechatronics Engineering and Industrial Mechatronics Technology programs. Furthermore, he enjoys working in teams and in an interdisciplinary manner, having been involved in the conception, coordination, and execution of interdisciplinary projects in recent years. His project history spans areas such as Biomedical Engineering, Health Informatics, Robotics, Computer Vision, Artificial Intelligence, among others. His key competencies include: Computer Vision, Robotics, Cloud Computing, C++, and Artificial Intelligence. He is a CNPq productivity fellow in Technological Development, focusing on health technologies.

Satya Prakash Yadav (FIETE & SMIEEE) is currently the Associate Professor of the Department of Computer Science and Engineering, Madan Mohan Malaviya University of Technology, Gorakhpur, U.P., India and has completed his Postdoctoral Research Fellow from Federal Institute of Education, Science and Technology of Ceará, Brazil. He has awarded his PhD degree from Dr. A.P.J. Abdul Kalam Technical University (AKTU) (formerly UPTU). Currently, 4 students are working for Ph.D. under his guidance. A seasoned academician having more than 18 years of experience, he has published four books (Programming in C, Programming in C++ and Blockchain and Cryptocurrency) under I.K. International Publishing House Pvt. Ltd. Including Distributed Artificial Intelligence: A Modern Approach, Published December 18, 2020 by CRC Press. He has undergone industrial training programs during which he was involved in live projects with companies in the areas of SAP, Railway Traffic Management Systems, and Visual Vehicles Counter and Classification (used in the Metro rail network design). He is an alumnus of Netaji Subhas Institute of Technology (NSIT), Delhi University. A prolific writer, Dr. Satya Prakash Yadav has published six patents and authored many research papers in web of science indexed journals. Additionally, His area of specialisation is in the areas of Image Processing, Information retrieval and Features extraction. Also, he is a Editor in Chief in Journal of Cyber Security in Computer System & Journal of Soft Computing and Computational Intelligence (MAT journals), Series Editor in DeGruyter International Publisher, Bentham Science and CRC Press, Taylor and Francis Group Publisher (U.S.A), Lead Editor in Tech Science Press (Computer Systems Science and Engineering), International Journal of Experimental Research and Review, Measurement: Sensors (Elsevier Publisher), International Journal of Advanced Technology and Engineering Exploration (IJATEE) Journal of Electrical

Systems (JES), Journal of Advances in Information Technology (JAIT) and Informing Science Journal.

Antonino Galletta is an assistant professor in Computer Science (INF/01) at the University of Messina. In 2020 he received a PhD from the inter-university consortium composed of the University of Reggio Calabria (Italy) and the University of Messina (Italy). He received his B.Sc. and M.Sc. (with honours) in Computer Engineering from the University of Messina. Before starting the PhD, he worked as a senior software developer and a team leader at the University of Messina from 2013 to 2016. In 2019 he was the PI of NAME (Helsinki Noise and Air quality Monitoring systEm) a project funded by the European Pre -Commercial Procurement Project "Select for Cities" (Grant Agreement No 688196). His main research activities focus on Cloud/Edge/IoT technologies for Smart cities and eHealth including Big Data management and Blockchain. He has several international collaborations with worldwide research centers such as the University of Karlstad and of Mälardalen (Sweden), Cardiff University (UK), the Technische Universität of Wien (Austria) and the Federal University of Juiz de Fora (Brasil). Due to his contribution to the research, he has been selected among 200 top young researchers in Mathematics and Computer Science to participate at the prestigious "Heidelberg Laureate Forum" held in Heidelberg in September 2019. He has been the winner of two editions of the precious "Leonardo Innovation Award" in 2018 (First Placed) and in 2017 (Second Placed). In 2019 he was one of the winners of the FIWARE Genoa Hackathon. In 2018, in December he won the Vienna FIWARE challenge and in April, during the "International Conference on Geoinformatics and Data Analysis" (ICGDA, Prague 20-22 April), he won the "Best Presentation Award". He is a reviewer of more than 15 respected Journals, Chair of several International Conferences and co-author of more than 50 manuscripts.

***

Pallab Banerjee was born in Ranchi, Jharkhand, India, in 1984. He received the B.Tech. degree in computer science and engineering and the M.Tech. degree in CSE from the Biju Patnaik University of Technology (BPUT), in 2008,and 2015, respectively. He has completed his Ph.D from Usha Martin University,Ranchi in year 2023. In 2008, he started his professional career as a Lecturer with the CSE Department, CIT, Ranchi. He is an Assistant Professor with the Department of Computer Science and Engineering, Amity University, Ranchi. More specifically, his work examines in the field of operating systems, real time operating systems, and cloud computing. He is currently an Associate Professor with the Computer Science and Engineering Department, Amity University. He excelled in teaching field since last 16 years. His current research interests include task scheduling in cloud computing, RTOS, and algorithm design. He is a Life Member of the Computer Society of India.

Pashupati Baniya is an Assistant Professor in the Department of Computer Science and Engineering (CSE) at the School of Engineering and Technology, ITS Engineering College in Greater Noida, India. He obtained his Bachelor's degree (B.Sc) in Computer Science and Information Technology in 2015 from Tribhuvan University and later pursued a Master's degree (M-Tech) specializing in Networking and Cybersecurity from Sharda University, Knowledge Park-3, Greater Noida, India. He has shown a strong commitment to advancing his expertise through professional training and self-study, earning several international certifications, including CCNA, RHCSA, Ethical Hacker, Google IT Support Professional Certificate, and Cybersecurity Essentials. In addition to his academic pursuits, Mr. Baniya has contributed significantly to research and publication. He has authored over 8 research papers presented at various renowned International Conferences and contributed more than 2 book chapters to publications by IGI Global and CRC Press. Prior to his current role, Mr. Baniya gained substantial experience as a Hardware and Network Maintenance Technician at different institute of Nepal.

Ahimsa Bhardwaj has more than 19 years of teaching and research experience,her areas of interests are Data mining,DataBase, Artificial Intelligence. She has published various papers in repute Journals.

Srinivas Chippagiri is a highly skilled software engineering leader with over a decade of experience in cloud computing, distributed systems, virtualization, and AI/ML-applications across multiple industries, including telecommunications, healthcare, energy, and CRM software. Srinivas has a proven track record of success, demonstrated by multiple awards recognizing his commitment to excellence and innovation. With a strong background in systems and cloud engineering at GE Healthcare, Siemens, and RackWare Inc, Srinivas also possesses expertise in designing and developing complex software systems in regulated environments. He holds an Master's degree from the University of Utah, where he was honored for his academic achievements and leadership contributions.

Kavya Goswami is an enthusiastic academic professional with over 1.2 years of teaching experience and 1 year of industry exposure. She has taught subjects like Data Analytics, DBMS, and Core Java, and is passionate about emerging technologies and student-centered learning. With a strong foundation in computer science, she is committed to contributing to research and academic excellence.

Mohammad Hashim is a Bachelor of Technology (B.Tech) scholar in Computer Science and Engineering at Amity University Jharkhand, India, expected to graduate in 2027. He has undertaken multiple academic and independent projects in artificial intelligence, machine learning, and cybersecurity, with a focus on developing innovative and secure technological solutions. His research interests span AI-driven automation, ethical hacking, network security, and emerging digital technologies. Passionate about bridging theoretical knowledge with practical applications, he actively explores new advancements to contribute to the evolving landscape of technology.

Mohit Kumar received his Ph.D. degree from Jaipur National University. He has published papers in reputed top-cited journals like IEEE Transaction in Industrial Informatics, IEEE Transaction on Network Science and Engineering, HCIS Springer, Journal of Information Science & Engineering, MDPI Sensors, Symmetry, and many more. He is the reviewer of top-cited journals. He also has been granted two patents. He is currently guiding four Ph.D. students. Dr. Kumar has also worked as a consultant in Govt. funded projects. His research area includes WSN, IoT, Optimization, ML, AI, DL. Data Science.

Chakridhar Reddy is a B.Tech student in Blockchain Technology at Sharda University, India. He is passionate about blockchain and how it can be used to solve real-world problems. His main interests are in blockchain applications for secure voting, digital rights, and transparent finance systems. He has worked on several blockchain-based projects like a decentralized freelance marketplace, an e-voting system, and a platform for tracking electoral bond funding. Chakridhar reddy enjoys learning about new blockchain tools and technologies and aims to create secure and transparent digital systems using blockchain.

Anand Muni Mishra received the B.E degree in computer science and engineering from Pd. Ravi Shanker Shukla University, Raipur, Chhattisgarh, 2010, and the M.Tech. degree from SRM University Chennai. He is currently working as an associate professor in the Dept. of IT at GLBITM. He is also a research student, and with the Weed impact on agriculture using Deep Learning, Department of Computer science and engineering at Chitkara University of Punjab. His research interests include His research interests include deep learning, artificial intelligence, machine learning, remote sensing, deep learning, ICT applications in agriculture, and identification and detection of disease and impact on target crop using deep learning.

Renu Mishra is presently working as an Associate Professor at Sharda University, Greater Noida, U.P. She obtained Ph.D. from the School of IT, Rajiv Gandhi Proudyogiki Vishwavidyalaya (RGPV), Bhopal, India. She holds an M-Tech

(Honors) from RGPV, Bhopal (M.P.), and a B-Tech from Uttar Pradesh Technical University (UPTU), Lucknow, U.P. With 18 years of teaching experience, Dr. Renu's research interests include Blockchain Technology, Mobile Ad-hoc Networks, Computer Networks, Wireless Sensor Networks, Cryptography, and Network Security. She has also made significant contributions to the academic community by publishing various books and book chapters.

Dipra Mitra has completed Ph.D. from Chandigarh University, Chandigarh, India, in the Computer Science and Engineering department. He received his MTech. in Computer Engineering from Birla Institute of Technology, Ranchi, India, in 2017, His areas of interest include routing protocol, security, data structure and algorithms, machine learning, and deep learning image processing . Dipra Mitra has more than 13 years of teaching and research experience. He has published around 40 research papers in reputed international journals and conferences, such as Scopus and WoS.

Ashima Narang is a distinguished Academician working as an Assistant Professor, with extensive experience of more than 13 years in the field of Computer Science and Engineering. She has contributed significantly to the research Field in the various Areas including Cloud Computing, Virtualization, Artificial Intelligence. With a strong background in Academics in Computer Sciences, she has various research papers, conference papers and book chapters to her account and has been an active participant in various international conferences and a member of different professional bodies. Her ability to quickly adapt to new technologies, coupled with a creative approach to problem-solving, makes her an effective educator and mentor.

Preeti Rani is an Assistant Professor of College of Computing Sciences & IT (CCSIT) at Teerthanker Mahaveer University Moradabad. She did Ph. D in the Wireless Communication System from SRM Institute of Science and Technology, Delhi-NCR Campus, Modinagar Ghaziabad, India. She did her M. Tech in Remote Sensing from Banasthali Vidyapeeth, Rajasthan. She received her bachelor's degree in Electronics & Communication Engineering from the Raj Kumar Goel Institute of Technology for Women, Ghaziabad. She has 10 years of Experience in Teaching/ Research/Industry. She obtained her one-year research from CSIR-NIO, Dona Paula Goa, in the area of Satellite Communication. She is served as reviewer various international journals and conferences. Her interested areas of research are Image Processing, Wireless Sensor Network, Wireless Communication, Mobile Ad-hoc Network, Vehicular Ad-hoc Network, Internet of Vehicles, Communication Network Protocols, Network Security, Artificial Intelligence Applications and Algorithms, Modelling and Simulation Applications, Optimization Applications, and Machine

Learning. In addition, she has also published more than 20 research papers in various journals.

Daksh Rawat is a recent graduate in Computer Science and Engineering from Graphic Era Hill University (GEHU), Dehradun. He is actively involved in the domains of Artificial Intelligence and Machine Learning, with a strong focus on research and innovation. He has authored multiple research articles presented at IEEE international conferences, addressing secure AI applications and intelligent systems. In recognition of his contributions, he has been honored with the Young Scientist Award by his university. Daksh continues to pursue impactful work at the intersection of AI research and real-world applications.

Smriti Sachan worked as a assistant professor in Poornima College of Engineering, Jaipur from 2011 to 2016, Currently working as a assistant professor in G.LBAJAJ Institute of Technology and Management. Coordinator for various mass events, organizes and attended various conferences, workshops, seminars........ published papers in international journals.........An Effective Communicator with Excellent Interpersonal Skills. Strong ability to master a situation and proficient enough in organizing and directing turnaround situations. Adept at handling day-to day activities in coordination with internal and external departments. Excellent Technical Skill.

Avinash Kumar Sharma currently working as Associate Professor, Department of Computer Science & Engineering, Sharda School of Engineering & Technology (SSET), Sharda University, Greater Noida. Dr. Avinash Kumar Sharma has completed Ph.D from Uttarakhand Technical University, Dehradun (A State Govt. University) in Cloud Computing. His research areas are Cloud Computing, Machine Learning, Smart Agriculture, Artificial Intelligence. He has more than 17 years of teaching experience. He has published about 30 research articles in national / international conferences, journals, and book chapters. Dr. Avinash Kumar Sharma edited 04 books with IGI Global. He has also published 03 patents including 01 design patent.

Devashish Sharma, being a graduate student, has done his Bachelor's - specialized in Computer Science and Engineering. During his course, he completed multiple projects in the domains of Full-stack Web Development and Deep Learning, and has integrated to them - advancements such as web sockets and simulated environments respectively. He has shown observable enthusiasm for applying research-based knowledge and developing his own methods to achieve definite objectives. Being a self-motivated achiever, he has authored multiple conference papers and book chapters.

Vikrant Sharma is an Assistant Professor with over a decade of academic and research experience in the field of Computer Science and Engineering. Holding a Ph.D. in Computer Science and Engineering from Uttarakhand Technical University, Dehradun, he has dedicated his expertise to Wireless Sensor Networks, IoT, Machine Learning, and Signal Processing. Dr. Sharma's educational journey includes a BTech in Information Technology from Himachal Pradesh University, an MTech from Maharishi Markandeshwar University, and a Diploma in Information Technology from Govt. Polytechnic College. His commitment to excellence is evident in his academic achievements, including securing the second position in his MTech program and being recognized as the board topper during his Diploma. With a substantial record of research contributions, Dr. Sharma has published extensively in reputable journals including (SCI, SCIE, and Scopus indexed) and conferences. His research efforts are focused on optimizing deployment strategies in wireless sensor networks, achieving blanket coverage, and advancing the applications of IoT and machine learning. Notably, Dr. Sharma's expertise has been acknowledged through patents granted and published, demonstrating his innovative approach to problem-solving. He has also organized and chaired sessions at prestigious conferences, such as the International Conference on Automation and Computation (AutoCom-22). His commitment to the academic community extends to his role as a reviewer for several conferences and Journals from publishers including Springer, IEEE, Elsevier, etc. Currently he is working on development of machine learning and deep learning-based algorithms for, signal processing, image processing, Sensor Networks, IOT, etc.

Mayank Singh is currently working as a Professor and Dean (Research) at G. L. Bajaj Institute of Technology and Management, Greater Noida, India. Previously, I worked as a Professor at JSS Academy of Technical Education, Noida, and as the Director at Consilio Research Lab, Tallinn, Estonia. He also worked as a Postdoctoral Fellow at the University of KwaZulu-Natal Durban, South Africa, and as Professor & Head of the Department of Computer Science and Engineering at Krishna Engineering College, Ghaziabad, from January 2013 to September 2017. He has over 19 years of extensive experience in the IT industry, as well as Academics and Research in India and abroad.

Nidhi Singh is a Assistant Professor at Teerthankar Mahaveer University in Computer Science and Engineering Department, Moradabad. She did Master's from National Institute of Technology Hamirpur specialised in Artificial intelligence. She received her Bachelor's degree from Institute of Technology and Management GIDA, Gorakhpur specialised in Computer Science and Engineering. Her Interested areas are Artificial Intelligence, Machine Learning, Deep Learning and Cloud Computing.

Vipin Tyagi is a distinguished academician, researcher and author, currently serving as Dean (Academic and Research) at Jaypee University of Engineering and Technology in Guna, Madhya Pradesh. Prof. Tyagi joined JUET, Guna, in July 2005. His expertise spans image processing, Cyber Forensics, and Speech Recognition. He is also the Director – IQAC of JUET Guna and the UGC University coordinator for NEP 2020. Starting his teaching career as a lecturer in July 1993, Prof. Tyagi joined the Mody Institute of Technology and Science in Lakshmangarh, Sikar, Rajasthan, in 1999. His tenure at Mody Institute saw him become a member of the Senate and the Board of Studies. Prof. Tyagi has had a notable academic journey, completing his post-graduation in 1989 and his doctorate in 1999 under the guidance of Prof. V. K. Agarwal, Principal, D. N. College, Meerut. He has also worked on a project on Speech Recognition under the mentorship of Dr S. S. Agarwal, Scientist G and Ex-Head of CEER-Delhi Center at CEERI, Delhi.

Satvik Vats (SMIEEE) is an Assistant Professor in department of Computer Science and Engineering, Madan Mohan Malaviya University of Technology (MMMUT), Gorakhpur. He has done his PhD from Birla Institute of Technology, Mesra-Ranchi (Deemed University), Jharkhand, India. He holds a master's degree, MTech (with a specialization in Software Engineering), from the School of Engineering and Technology at Sharda University, Greater Noida, Uttar Pradesh, India. Dr. Vats is actively engaged in the fields of Big Data Analytics and Machine Learning/ Deep Learning. He has authored 15 research papers in a journal of international repute (SCI/SCIE/ESCI/SCOPUS/WEB of SCIENCE) and holds two Indian, one Australian and one German-granted patents. He has written three books and five book chapters published by international publishers. He is the reviewer of several international Journals i.e. Elsevier, MDPI, Springer & IEEE Transactions.

Neha Yadav, Ph.D. (Submitted), is currently serving as an Assistant Professor of Engineering in the Department of Computer Science (AIML) at G. L. Bajaj Institute of Technology and Management, Greater Noida, India. She is pursuing her PhD and has earned an M.Tech in Computer Science and Engineering from Jaypee Institute of Information Technology Technology (JIIT), Noida, as well as a B.Tech. in Computer Science from Bundelkhand University, India. She is in the final stage of her doctoral studies (PhD submitted) at JIIT, Noida. She has over 10 publications in reputable journals and conferences. She serves as a reviewer in various reputable journals, including Informatica and IEEE Access.

R.K. Yadav is a Professor and Head of the Electronics and Communication Engineering Department at RKGIT, Ghaziabad. He has more than 29 years of experience in teaching and research. His main areas of expertise include Microwave

Engineering, Electromagnetic (EM) Waves, and Image Processing. He has published over 120 research papers in reputed national and international journals and conferences. He is also the author of a book on Microwave Engineering. Dr. Yadav is an active member of IEEE (a global professional body for engineers). He has successfully organized several international conferences in collaboration with IEEE and Elsevier. He also serves as an editor for a Springer journal and has worked as an editor for several books published by IGI Global, Nova Science Publishers, CRC Press, and others. At present, he is guiding eight Ph.D. scholars who are working in different research areas such as Microwave Engineering, Image Processing, and Integrated Circuits.

Index

A

B

C

D

F

G

H

S

T

U

V

W

www.ingramcontent.com/pod-product-compliance
Lightning Source LLC
LaVergne TN
LVHW062329300926
849161LV00007B/1623

* 9 7 9 8 3 3 7 3 3 7 8 5 2 *